S0-AEE-753

THE CUBAN MISSILE CRISIS

E
841
.C84
1988

THE CUBAN MISSILE CRISIS

Second Edition

Edited with commentary
by Robert A. Divine

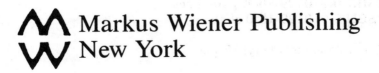

Markus Wiener Publishing
New York

GOSHEN COLLEGE LIBRARY
GOSHEN, INDIANA

© 1988 by Robert A. Divine

All rights reserved. No part of this book may be reproduced in any form without prior written permission from the copyright holder.

Second edition published in 1988 by
Markus Weiner Publishing.

2901 Broadway, New York, NY 10025

Library of Congress Cataloging-in-Publication Data

The Cuban missile crisis.

Bibliography: p.
1. Cuban Missile Crisis, Oct. 1962. I. Divine, Robert A.
E841.C84 1988 327.73047 88-9
ISBN 0-910129-86-X paperback
ISBN 0-910129-15-0 cloth

Cover design by Cheryl Mirkin

Printed in the United States of America

CONTENTS

	Introduction		3
I.	**THE CRISIS**		9
II.	**INITIAL REACTIONS TO THE CRISIS**		60
	Stewart Alsop and Charles Bartlett	Eyeball to Eyeball	61
	Roger Hagan	Righteous Realpolitic	74
	David Lowenthal	The Lost Opportunity	92
III.	**THE PROBLEM OF SOVIET MOTIVATION**		101
	Nikita Khrushchev	In Defense of Cuba	102
	John F. Kennedy	The Nuclear Balance of Power	108
	Roger Hilsman	The Missile Gap	111
	Arnold Horelick	The Soviet Gamble	117
	Adam Ulam	Khrushchev's Grand Design	135

2-19-91 HLS/TS

IV. THE CONTINUING DEBATE		149
I. F. Stone	What Price Prestige?	151
Leslie Dewart	The Kennedy Trap	160
Dean Acheson	Homage to Plain Dumb Luck	186
Theodore Sorenson	Kennedy Vindicated	197
Ronald Steel	Lessons of the Missile Crisis	202
Roger Hilsman and Ronald Steel	An Exchange of Views	224
V. SCHOLARLY REASSESSMENT		236
Barton J. Bernstein	A Jupiter Swap?	239
Thomas G. Paterson and William J. Brophy	The Political Dimension	278
James A. Nathan	Cold War Model	326
Bibliography		

Introduction

THE CUBAN misile crisis marks the closest the world has yet come to nuclear destruction. For six harrowing days in 1962, from the time President John F. Kennedy informed the nation of the Soviet missile buildup in Cuba until Nikita Khrushchev agreed to pull back, the American people lived under the threat of disaster. The armed forces went from Defense Condition Five (peacetime alert) to Defcon 3 (war alert), and the Strategic Air Command was ordered to Defcon 2 (full war footing), only one step away from actual hostilities. Five of the eight divisions of the Army Strategic Reserve were placed on alert; the First Armored Division moved from Texas to Fort Stewart, Georgia; and in Florida, Lieutenant General Hamilton Howze set up a command post for the invasion of Cuba. Polaris-armed nuclear submarines left their base in Holy Loch, Scotland, to take up stations at sea within range of the Soviet Union; SAC scattered its B-47 bombers to civilian airfields around the United States and kept a major portion of its long-range B-52 bombers, loaded with nuclear weapons, in the air. These planes, together with 105 short-range missiles in Europe and 156 intercontinental missiles in the United States, were ready to deliver the nuclear equivalent of thirty billion tons of TNT upon the Soviet Union at the command of the President.

The command never came. At the last minute, Khrushchev accepted the graceful way out that Kennedy had left him, withdrawing the missiles in return for an American pledge not to invade Cuba. With the Russian retreat there came a heady sense of triumph. President Kennedy's popularity, down sharply in the summer, rose dramatically as journalists hailed him as the architect of a great diplomatic victory. His courage, his coolness, above all his carefully calculated combination of firmness and restraint won him the plaudits of the American press. And the people responded by returning a Democratic Congress in the mid-term elections, held only nine days after the crisis had broken. Though a few dissident voices questioned the nature of Kennedy's triumph, the vast majority of Americans accepted the Cuban missile crisis as JFK's finest hour.

The tragic assassination in Dallas little more than a year later elevated the prevailing view of Kennedy's handling of the Cuban crisis into a legend. From the depths of the Bay of Pigs fiasco, Kennedy had risen to the heights of world statesmanship in accepting Khrushchev's challenge in Cuba; without flinching from the prospect of thermonuclear war, he forced the reckless Russian leader to back down. Though Kennedy himself had tried to prevent members of his administration from gloating over Khrushchev's humiliation, his death undercut this wise counsel. Thus Arthur Schlesinger, Jr., would write in 1965 that Kenndy's actions in the crisis "dazzled the world" and "displayed the ripening of an American leadership unsurpassed in the responsible management of power."[1] Even Richard M. Nixon, his bitter antagonist in 1960, tried to associate himself

[1] Arthur M. Schlesinger, Jr., *A Thousand Days: John F. Kennedy in the White House* (Boston, 1965), pp. 840, 841.

with Kennedy's Cuban triumph when he delivered his fateful address to the nation on the eve of the invasion of Cambodia on April 30, 1970, noting that he spoke to the nation from the same room where "John F. Kennedy in his finest hour made the great decision which removed Soviet nuclear missiles from Cuba and the western hemisphere."[2]

With the passage of time, and especially with the growing disillusionment over the war in Vietnam, observers began to take a more critical look at the missile crisis. Right-wingers, who saw in Castro's dominance of Cuba a continuing threat to American security, attacked Kennedy for his promise not to invade the island. They felt that Kennedy had missed an opportunity to remove a dangerous communist regime from the sensitive Caribbean region and thus had turned a victory into a stalemate. Liberal writers began to question Kennedy's decision to forego traditional diplomacy, particularly his refusal to pursue the idea of a swap of obsolete American missile bases in Turkey for the Russian sites in Cuba. And the radical New Left charged that perhaps Kennedy's great victory was no accident but the result of Khrushchev's falling into a neatly laid, deviously sprung trap. The luster of Kennedy's triumph dimmed as the controversy developed among scholars who gradually freed themselves from the spell of his charm.

In the course of the 1960s and 1970s, historians and political scientists began to probe into the unresolved questions raised by the crisis. Why did Khrushchev place the missiles in Cuba and thus run the risk of nuclear war? Did he act defensively, to protect the Castro regime or to redress an unfavorable strategic balance? Or did he plan to use the missiles as part of a diplomatic offensive over Berlin or other outstanding issues, or did he even contemplate a first strike once the weapons were operational? And there is the equally important question of whether or not the Soviet missiles in fact threatened the security of the United States. If they did, then why did Kennedy stop short of invading Cuba in order to end this deadly peril for all time? If not, then why didn't the President let Khrushchev

[2] *New York Times*, May 1, 1970, p. 2.

know that he was aware of the missiles and offer to negotiate a deal for their removal, such as trading off obsolete American Jupiter intermediate-range ballistic missiles (IRBMs) in Turkey for those in Cuba? What role did politics play in Kennedy's decisions to stage a nuclear confrontation with the Soviet Union? Was the President most concerned with the perception of American power in international politics, or was he thinking primarily of the upcoming Congressional elections at home?

Despite the gradual release of documents and new information by participants, scholars have yet to find satisfactory answers to all these questions. Kennedy's premature death removed one vital source. Despite all the accounts by those close to JFK, most notably his brother Bobby's memoir, *Thirteen Days,* we cannot be sure exactly how the President saw the issues in 1962. And on the Soviet side, the secrecy of a closed society has led to wide-ranging speculation on Khrushchev's motives based on a paucity of hard evidence.

The most intriguing effort to reassess the Cuban crisis came in March, 1987 when a group of Kennedy aides, along with a dozen scholars, held a conference on Hawk's Cay in the Florida Keys. The site was aptly chosen, since the popular use of the words "hawks" and "doves" to describe those taking a hard and a soft line toward the Soviet Union dates from the days of the Kennedy administration. The general tone of the reminiscences was defensive, playing down the aggressiveness of Kennedy's response and generally minimizing the seriousness of the crisis itself. The discussion revealed that at the time American leaders were not sure whether or not the Soviets had actually placed nuclear warheads on the missiles in Cuba, but despite this uncertainty, they felt they had to assume the weapons were armed. Most felt that Kennedy was determined to ensure a peaceful outcome, but several admitted that they were not at all certain that the world would be spared its first nuclear conflict. And one former State Department expert on the Soviet Union, Raymond L. Garthoff, surprised even Robert McNamara, Kennedy's Secretary of Defense, by telling the group that General Thomas Power, the SAC commander, had sent out the full alert to American bombers and missiles in the clear, rather than in code as the Joint Chiefs of Staff had intended, to make sure that the Kremlin understood the American determination to remove the missiles from Cuba.[3]

The most startling revelation came in a letter from former Secretary of State Dean Rusk, whose health prevented him from attending the Hawk's Cay reunion. Rusk reinforced the image of Kennedy's desire for a peaceful solution by writing, "It was clear to me that President Kennedy would not let the Jupiters in Turkey become an obstacle to the removal of the missile sites in Cuba." For the first time, Rusk disclosed that the President had instructed him to approach U Thant, the Secretary General of the United Nations, through an intermediary and propose "the removal of both the Jupiters and the missiles in Cuba." But before Rusk could act, Khrushchev, to Kennedy's surprise, agreed to take the missiles out of Cuba without insisting on a firm American commitment regarding the Jupiters in Turkey.[4]

Rusk's letter does suggest that Kennedy was prepared to engage in further diplomatic negotiations rather than risk nuclear war at the height of the crisis. But as one of the scholars at Hawk's Cay noted, even the peaceful resolution of the Cuban missile crisis left an unfortunate legacy. The Soviet Union, forced to back down because the nuclear balance was heavily in America's favor, responded with a massive buildup of ICBM's throughout the 1960s, eventually overcoming the American strategic superiority and thus intensifying the arms race in the 1970s.

Despite the passage of time, the Cuban missile crisis is as relevant today as it was in the 1960s. It remains the one time the two superpowers went to the brink of nuclear war. The central question must always be the wisdom of John F. Kennedy's decision to elevate the issue of Soviet missiles in Cuba into an all-out military confrontation. For many Americans, his actions in 1962 set an example that may well be followed in the inevitable crises that lie ahead between the United States and the

[3] Raymond L. Garthoff, *Reflections on the Cuban Missile Crisis* (Washington, 1987), pp. 37–38.

[4] J. Anthony Lukas, "Class Reunion: Kennedy's Men Relive the Cuban Missile Crisis," *New York Times Magazine,* Aug. 30, 1987, p. 58.

Soviet Union. For others, the Kennedy policy of nuclear brinkmanship provides a model of how *not* to behave in a world where one small misstep can lead to total destruction.

I

The Crisis

In late July 1962, shortly after a visit to Moscow by Raúl Castro, Cuba's defense minister and brother of Fidel, the Soviet Union began sending weapons and military personnel to Cuba. A little more than a year before, an American-equipped and -sponsored force of Cuban exiles had met a disastrous defeat at the Bay of Pigs. The Russians, citing the abortive invasion, explained that the arms they were shipping to Cuba would enable Fidel Castro to defend his regime against future American attacks. Republican politicians, however, became alarmed at the size of the Soviet buildup so close to the United States, and began demanding that the Kennedy administration take action to stop it. On August 31, Senator Kenneth B. Keating of New York rose in the Senate chamber to charge that he had evidence that there were twelve hundred Russian troops in Cuba as well as "concave metal structures supported by tubing" that appeared destined for "a rocket installation." Warning that the Russians might be constructing a missile base, Keating called on the President to ask the Organization of American States to send an investigating team to Cuba.

Two days before Keating spoke, an American U-2 plane had taken photographs of Cuba that revealed the construction of a surface-to-air missile (SAM) site. Most of the President's advisers interpreted this as a defensive move by the Soviets, but CIA Director John McCone wondered if the SAMs were a prelude to the introduction of surface-to-surface missiles, which would have offensive capabilities. McCone's speculation received little attention; Kennedy and his associates were more concerned with the impact of Keating's charges on the upcoming congressional elections. On September 4, Anatoly F. Dobrynin, the Soviet ambassador, called on Attorney General Robert F. Kennedy and asked him to pass on a secret message from Nikita Khrushchev to the President to the effect that the Russians would refrain from making any aggressive moves before the November elections. When Robert Kennedy referred specifically to military aid to Cuba, Dobrynin replied that he was instructed to state that no offensive weapons would be placed in Cuba. The Attorney General reported this conversation to President Kennedy and then suggested that the President make the administration's position on Cuba absolutely clear both to the Russians and to domestic critics. Later that day, September 4, Press Secretary Pierre Salinger released the following White House statement of policy: [1]

All Americans, as well as all our friends in this Hemisphere, have been concerned over the recent moves of the Soviet Union to bolster the military power of the Castro regime in Cuba. Information has reached this Government in the last four days from a variety of sources which establishes without doubt that the Soviets have provided the Cuban Government with a number of anti-aircraft defense missiles with a slant range of twenty-five miles which are similar to early models of our Nike. Along with these missiles, the Soviets are apparently providing the extensive radar and other electronic equipment which is required for their operation. We can also con-

[1] U.S. Department of State, *Bulletin,* XLVII (September 24, 1962), 450

firm the presence of several Soviet-made motor torpedo boats carrying ship-to-ship guided missiles having a range of fifteen miles. The number of Soviet military technicians now known to be in Cuba or en route—approximately 3,500—is consistent with assistance in setting up and learning to use this equipment. As I stated last week, we shall continue to make information available as fast as it is obtained and properly verified.

There is no evidence of any organized combat force in Cuba from any Soviet bloc country; of military bases provided to Russia; of a violation of the 1934 treaty relating to Guantánamo; of the presence of offensive ground-to-ground missiles; or of other significant offensive capability either in Cuban hands or under Soviet direction and guidance. Were it to be otherwise, the gravest issues would arise.

The Cuban question must be considered as a part of the worldwide challenge posed by Communist threats to the peace. It must be dealt with as a part of that larger issue as well as in the context of the special relationships which have long characterized the inter-American system.

It continues to be the policy of the United States that the Castro regime will not be allowed to export its aggressive purposes by force or the threat of force. It will be prevented by whatever means may be necessary from taking action against any part of the Western Hemisphere. The United States, in conjunction with other Hemisphere countries, will make sure that while increased Cuban armaments will be a heavy burden to the unhappy people of Cuba themselves, they will be nothing more.

Republican politicians continued to hammer away at the Cuban issue despite the President's statement. Keating, relying on information leaked to him by the intelligence services and on reports from anti-Castro refugees, warned that the situation endangered American security. His colleague, Indiana Senator Homer E. Capehart, went further, calling for an American invasion of Cuba to end the menace. The Soviets, however, responded to Kennedy's statement with new assurances of their defensive intentions. In a long release on September 11, the official Soviet news agency TASS stated: [2]

. . . The Soviet Union could not fail to take account of the situation in which Cuba had found itself as a result of imperialist provocations and threats, and it went fraternally to the Cuban people's

[2] *New York Times,* September 12, 1962, p. 16. Copyright © 1962 by The New York Times Company. Reprinted by permission.

assistance. This is being done by the other Socialist countries, too, and also by other peace-loving states which maintain trade relations with Cuba. Soviet ships carry to Cuba the goods she needs and return with commodities she has in abundance, particularly sugar, which the United States—previously the main importer—has refused to buy in the hope of undermining the economy of the Cuban Republic. This is why the Soviet Union and other Socialist countries are buying this sugar—to support the economy of the Cuban state.

If one is honest and proceeds from the understanding of the need of living in peace, declared by the United States President himself, i.e., to safeguard peaceful coexistence between states irrespective of their socio-political order, what could have alarmed the American leaders, what is the reason for this devil's Sabbath raised in Congress and in the American press around Cuba?

To this one can say: Gentlemen, you are evidently so frightened that you are afraid of your own shadow and you do not believe in the strength of your ideas and your capitalist order. You have been so much frightened by the October Socialist Revolution and the success of the Soviet Union, achieved and developed on the basis of this revolution, that it seems to you some hordes are supposedly moving to Cuba when potatoes or oil, tractors, harvesters, combines and other farming and industrial machinery are carried to Cuba to maintain the Cuban economy.

We can say to these people that these are our ships, and that what we carry in them is no business of theirs. It is the internal affair of the sides engaged in this commercial transaction. We can say, quoting the popular saying: "Don't butt your noses where you oughtn't."

But we do not hide from the world public that we really are supplying Cuba with industrial equipment and goods which are helping to strengthen her economy and raise the well-being of the Cuban people.

At the request of the Cuban Government, we also send Soviet agronomists, machine-operators, tractor-drivers and livestock experts to Cuba to share their experience and knowledge with their Cuban friends in order to help them raise the country's economy. We also send rank-and-file state and collective farm workers to Cuba, and accept thousands of Cubans to the Soviet Union to exchange experience and teach them the more progressive methods of agriculture, to help them master the Soviet farm machinery which is being supplied to Cuba.

It will be recalled that a certain amount of armaments is also being shipped from the Soviet Union to Cuba at the request of the Cuban Government in connection with the threats by aggressive imperialist circles. The Cuban statesmen also requested the Soviet

Government to send to Cuba Soviet military specialists, technicians who would train the Cubans in handling up-to-date weapons, because up-to-date weapons now call for high skill and much knowledge. It is but natural that Cuba does not yet have such specialists. That is why we considered this request. It must, however, be said that the number of Soviet military specialists sent to Cuba can in no way be compared to the number of workers in agriculture and industry sent there. The armaments and military equipment sent to Cuba are designed exclusively for defensive purposes and the President of the United States and the American military just as the military of any country know what means of defense are. How can these means threaten the United States?

No, gentlemen, it is not this that alarms you. You yourselves realize all the absurdity of your claims that there is some threat to the United States emerging on the part of Cuba. You have invented this threat yourselves, and you now want to persuade others of its existence. It is the revolutionary spirit that you fear, and not the military equipment received by the Cubans for their own defense. And why should this alarm you if the statement by the President of the United States that the U[nited] S[tates] is not preparing an aggression against Cuba, is not contemplating an attack against her, accords with the real intentions of the American Government? If this is an honest statement, and the Government of the United States abides by it in its policy, then the means of defense which Cuba is getting will not be used because the need to use them will arise only in the event of aggression against Cuba.

The Government of the Soviet Union also authorized *Tass* to state that there is no need for the Soviet Union to shift its weapons for the repulsion of aggression, for a retaliatory blow, to any other country, for instance Cuba. Our nuclear weapons are so powerful in their explosive force and the Soviet Union has so powerful rockets to carry these nuclear warheads, that there is no need to search for sites for them beyond the boundaries of the Soviet Union. We have said and we do repeat that if war is unleashed, if the aggressor makes an attack on one state or another and this state asks for assistance, the Soviet Union has the possibility from its own territory to render assistance to any peace-loving state and not only to Cuba. And let no one doubt that the Soviet Union will render such assistance just as it was ready in 1956 to render military assistance to Egypt at the time of the Anglo-French-Israeli aggression in the Suez Canal region.

We do not say this to frighten someone. Intimidation is alien to the foreign policy of the Soviet State. Threats and blackmail are an integral part of the imperialist states. The Soviet Union stands for peace and wants no war. . . .

President Kennedy responded to the Soviet statement on September 13 when he opened his press conference with a second and more precise declaration of policy on the Russian arms buildup in Cuba.[3]

The President. I have a preliminary statement.

There has been a great deal of talk on the situation in Cuba in recent days both in the Communist camp and in our own, and I would like to take this opportunity to set the matter in perspective.

In the first place, it is Mr. Castro and his supporters who are in trouble. In the last year his regime has been increasingly isolated from this hemisphere. His name no longer inspires the same fear or following in other Latin American countries. He has been condemned by the OAS, excluded from the Inter-American Defense Board, and kept out of the Free Trade Association. By his own monumental economic mismanagement, supplemented by our refusal to trade with him, his economy has crumbled, and his pledges for economic progress have been discarded, along with his pledges for political freedom. His industries are stagnating, his harvests are declining, his own followers are beginning to see that their revolution has been betrayed.

So it is not surprising that in a frantic effort to bolster his regime he should try to arouse the Cuban people by charges of an imminent American invasion, and commit himself still further to a Soviet takeover in the hope of preventing his own collapse.

Ever since communism moved into Cuba in 1958, Soviet technical and military personnel have moved steadily onto the island in increasing numbers at the invitation of the Cuban Government.

Now that movement has been increased. It is under our most careful surveillance. But I will repeat the conclusion that I reported last week: that these new shipments do not constitute a serious threat to any other part of this hemisphere.

If the United States ever should find it necessary to take military action against communism in Cuba, all of Castro's Communist-supplied weapons and technicians would not change the result or significantly extend the time required to achieve that result.

However, unilateral military intervention on the part of the United States cannot currently be either required or justified, and it is regrettable that loose talk about such action in this country might serve to give a thin color of legitimacy to the Communist pretense that such a threat exists. But let me make this clear once again: If at any time the Communist buildup in Cuba were to endanger or

[3] *Public Papers of the Presidents: Kennedy, 1962* (Washington, D.C., 1963), pp. 674–675.

interfere with our security in any way, including our base at Guantánamo, our passage to the Panama Canal, our missile and space activities at Cape Canaveral, or the lives of American citizens in this country, or if Cuba should ever attempt to export its aggressive purposes by force or the threat of force against any nation in this hemisphere, or became an offensive military base of significant capacity for the Soviet Union, then this country will do whatever must be done to protect its own security and that of its allies.

We shall be alert, too, and fully capable of dealing swiftly with any such development. As President and Commander in Chief I have full authority now to take such action, and I have asked the Congress to authorize me to call up reserve forces should this or any other crisis make it necessary.

In the meantime, we intend to do everything within our power to prevent such a threat from coming into existence.

Our friends in Latin America must realize the consequences such developments hold out for their own peace and freedom, and we shall be making further proposals to them. Our friends in NATO must realize the implications of their ships engaging in the Cuban trade.

We shall continue to work with Cuban refugee leaders who are dedicated as we are to that nation's future return to freedom. We shall continue to keep the American people and the Congress fully informed. We shall increase our surveillance of the whole Caribbean area. We shall neither initiate nor permit aggression in this hemisphere.

With this in mind, while I recognize that rash talk is cheap, particularly on the part of those who do not have the responsibility, I would hope that the future record will show that the only people talking about a war or an invasion at this time are the Communist spokesmen in Moscow and Havana, and that the American people defending as we do so much of the free world, will in this nuclear age, as they have in the past, keep both their nerve and their head.

Q. Mr. President, coupling this statement with the one of last week, at what point do you determine that the buildup in Cuba has lost its defensive character and become offensive? Would it take an overt act?

The President. I think if you read last week's statement and the statement today, I made it quite clear, particularly in last week's statement, when we talked about the presence of offensive military missile capacity or development of military bases and other indications which I gave last week, all these would, of course, indicate a change in the nature of the threat.

Q. Well, Mr. President, in this same line, have you set for yourself any rule or set of conditions at which you will determine the existence of an offensive rather than a defensive force in Cuba, and, in that same connection, in your reading of the Monroe Doctrine, how do you define "intervention"? Will it require force to contravene the Monroe Doctrine or does the presence of a foreign power in any force, but not using that force in this hemisphere, amount to contravention of the Doctrine?

The President. Well, I have indicated that if Cuba should possess a capacity to carry out offensive actions against the United States, that the United States would act. I've also indicated that the United States would not permit Cuba to export its power by force in the hemisphere. The United States will make appropriate military judgments after consultation with the Joint Chiefs of Staff and others, after carefully analyzing whatever new information comes in, as to whether that point has been reached where an offensive threat does exist. And at that time the country and the Congress will be so notified. . . .

Kennedy's statement failed to quiet his Republican critics. Motivated both by concern over the situation in Cuba and the administration's vulnerability as a result of the Bay of Pigs, such GOP spokesmen as Senator Barry Goldwater of Arizona and Richard Nixon, candidate for governor of California, accused Kennedy of appeasing both Castro and Khrushchev and proposed a blockade of Cuba to halt the arms shipments. With Congress preparing to adjourn until after the elections, Senator Keating delivered a long speech on October 9 repeating his warnings about the nature and extent of the Soviet presence in Cuba. The next day he rose to report a new and far more ominous development to his fellow Senators.[4]

Mr. President, yesterday I spoke on the subject of Cuba. At that time I did not have fully confirmed the matter to which I shall address myself now. I now have it fully confirmed. As a result, I call upon the appropriate Government officials to confirm or to deny reports of intermediate range missile bases in Cuba.

Construction has begun on at least a half dozen launching sites for intermediate-range tactical missiles. Intelligence authorities must have advised the President and top Government officials of this fact, and they must now have been told that ground-to-ground missiles can be operational from the island of Cuba within six months.

[4] *Congressional Record,* October 10, 1962, p. 22957.

My own sources on the Cuban situation, which have been 100 percent reliable, have substantiated this report completely.

When are the American people going to be given all of the facts about the military buildup in Cuba?

Yesterday I pointed out, for either the nineteenth or twentieth time, that we are not getting the whole story on Cuba. I referred to the recent testimony by Under Secretary of State George Ball before the House Select Committee on Export Control. Presumably the report was supposed to be in line with the President's commitment of September 4 that, "We shall continue to make information available as fast as it is obtained and properly verified."

I stated that Mr. Ball had confirmed facts which some of us had previously reported; that he had identified three, possibly four, short-range missile sites in Cuba. I commented, however, that the significant sentence in his testimony, which was buried away, perhaps in the hope that no one would notice it, was this: "Quite likely several more such sites will be installed."

The fact of the matter is, according to my reliable sources, that six launching sites are under construction—pads which will have the power to hurl rockets into the American heartland and as far as the Panama Canal Zone.

Why would Under Secretary Ball give the committee the impression that new missile sites were a possibility rather than a fact? Even as possibilities, he indicated they would be short range rather than intermediate range missile sites. Why has such a veil been thrown around Cuba, keeping this new information from the American people? Are they still trying to perpetuate the myth that the buildup is defensive? Is it possible anyone in Government is childish enough to believe that?

According to Mr. Walter Lippmann's column of yesterday, the United States has "an elaborate system of surveillance by sea, by air, and by land, and there is every reason to think that its accuracy is very high. Little of military interest can happen without our knowing it. We do not have to guess. We know."

If this is true, our Government is well aware of the fact that within a matter of months, Cuba may have the capability of launching intermediate-range missiles, but the American people are being kept in the dark. The Soviets know the fact. The Cubans know this fact. But in the view of the administration our people are not entitled to know it.

Mr. President, let us have all the facts, and have them now.

Senator Keating never disclosed the source for his statement that the Soviets were placing surface-to-surface missiles in Cuba. At the time of his speech, American intelligence apparently had not yet discovered the missile sites. U-2 planes had been overflying Cuba regularly since the Soviet shipments began, and the flights had been intensified after the discovery of the first SAM installation on August 29. Fearful of the ability of a SAM to shoot down a U-2, however, the CIA had concentrated on eastern Cuba in its September flights and thus had avoided the Pinar del Río area west of Havana where the first SAMs had been spotted. When CIA Director John McCone returned to Washington from a trip to Europe, he immediately ordered U-2 flights over western Cuba. Heavy cloud cover prevented the prompt execution of McCone's order, but finally on October 14 a pair of U-2s flown by SAC pilots (to avoid another Francis Gary Powers incident in case a plane were downed) took extensive aerial photographs of western Cuba. By Monday evening, October 15, CIA photographic analysts had studied the U-2 pictures and informed McGeorge Bundy, President Kennedy's national security adviser, that the Soviet Union was in the process of building launching sites for both 1,000-mile medium-range missiles (MRBM) and 2,200-mile intermediate-range missiles (IRBM).

The next morning, October 16, Bundy informed the President of this ominous information. Kennedy immediately ordered additional U-2 flights to gain further evidence of the Soviet action and then asked Bundy to assemble, with great secrecy, a select group of advisers and have them in the Cabinet Room of the White House at 11:45. The Executive Committee of the National Security Council, as this group called itself, became the body which the President used to shape and conduct policy throughout the missile crisis. Its members, in addition to Bundy, were Secretary of State Dean Rusk; Secretary of Defense Robert McNamara; Attorney General Robert Kennedy; CIA Director McCone; Secretary of the Treasury Douglas Dillon; Presidential Counsel Theodore Sorensen; Under-Secretary of State George Ball; Deputy Under-Secretary of State U. Alexis Johnson; Chairman of the Joint Chiefs of Staff, General Maxwell Taylor; Assistant Secretary of State for Latin America Edward Martin; former Ambassador to Russia Llewellyn Thompson; Deputy

Secretary of Defense Roswell Gilpatric; and Assistant Secretary of Defense Paul Nitze. In addition, Vice-President Lyndon B. Johnson, Ambassador to the United Nations Adlai Stevenson, and White House Appointments Secretary Kenneth O'Donnell met with the others intermittently. Former Secretary of State Dean Acheson, a private citizen, met with the group during its early sessions, but dropped out once a decision had been reached.

The deliberations that began on Tuesday morning in the Cabinet Room continued all week. At the outset President Kennedy decided to withhold news of the missile sites from the Russians and from the American people until he could decide what action his administration would take. To maintain the pretense that nothing unusual was happening, the President decided to honor a commitment to Abraham Ribicoff to travel to Connecticut on behalf of his campaign for the Senate. In the President's absence, the Executive Committee continued its deliberations on the seventh floor of the State Department building. The meetings had no formal structure, but gradually Robert Kennedy emerged as the moderator, focusing the discussion on the crucial policy issues and taking careful notes of all that was said. Theodore Sorensen, who was present throughout these meetings, describes the nature of the discussion in his book *Kennedy*.[5]

. . . The bulk of our time Tuesday through Friday was spent in George Ball's conference room canvassing all the possible courses as the President had requested, and preparing the back-up material for them: suggested time schedules or scenarios, draft messages, military estimates and predictions of Soviet and Cuban responses. Initially the possibilities seemed to divide into six categories, some of which could be combined:

1. Do nothing.

2. Bring diplomatic pressures and warnings to bear upon the Soviets. Possible forms included an appeal to the UN or OAS for an inspection team, or a direct approach to Khrushchev, possibly at a summit conference. The removal of our missile bases in Turkey

[5] Theodore C. Sorensen, *Kennedy* (New York, 1965), pp. 682–692. Copyright © 1965 by Theodore C. Sorensen. Reprinted by permission of Harper & Row, Inc.

in exchange for the removal of the Cuban missiles was also listed in our later discussions as a possibility which Khrushchev was likely to suggest if we didn't.

3. Undertake a secret approach to Castro, to use this means of splitting him off from the Soviets, to warn him that the alternative was his island's downfall and that the Soviets were selling him out.

4. Initiate indirect military action by means of a blockade, possibly accompanied by increased aerial surveillance and warnings. Many types of blockades were considered.

5. Conduct an air strike—pinpointed against the missiles only or against other military targets, with or without advance warning. (Other military means of directly removing the missiles were raised—bombarding them with pellets that would cause their malfunctioning without fatalities, or suddenly landing paratroopers or guerrillas—but none of these was deemed feasible.)

6. Launch an invasion—or, as one chief advocate of this course put it: "Go in there and take Cuba away from Castro."

Other related moves were considered—such as declaring a national emergency, sending a special envoy to Khrushchev or asking Congress for a declaration of war against Cuba (suggested as a means of building both Allied support and a legal basis for blockade, but deemed not essential to either). But these six choices were the center of our deliberations.

Choice No. 1—doing nothing—and choice No. 2—limiting our response to diplomatic action only—were both seriously considered. As some (but not all) Pentagon advisers pointed out to the President, we had long lived within range of Soviet missiles, we expected Khrushchev to live with our missiles nearby, and by taking this addition calmly we could prevent him from inflating its importance. All the other courses raised so many risks and drawbacks that choice No. 2 had its appeal. All of us came back to it at one discouraged moment or another; and it was advocated to the President as a preferable alternative to blockade by one of the regular members of our group in the key Thursday night meeting discussed below.

But the President had rejected this course from the outset. He was concerned less about the missiles' military implications than with their effect on the global political balance. The Soviet move had been undertaken so swiftly, so secretly, and with so much deliberate deception—it was so sudden a departure from Soviet practice—that it represented a provocative change in the delicate status quo. Missiles on Soviet territory or submarines were very different from missiles in the Western Hemisphere, particularly in their political and psychological effect on Latin America. The history of Soviet intentions toward smaller nations was very different from our own. Such a step, if accepted, would be followed by more; and the President's September pledges of action clearly called this step unacceptable. While he desired to combine diplomatic moves with military action, he was not willing to let the UN debate and Khrushchev equivocate while the missiles became operational.

Various approaches to Castro (choice No. 3)—either instead of or as well as to Khrushchev—were also considered many times during the week. This course was set aside rather than dropped. The President increasingly felt that we should not avoid the fact that this was a confrontation of the great powers—that the missiles had been placed there by the Soviets, were manned and guarded by the Soviets, and would have to be removed by the Soviets in response to direct American action.

The invasion course (choice No. 6) had surprisingly few supporters. One leader outside our group whose views were conveyed to us felt that the missiles could not be tolerated, that the Soviet motivation was baffling, that a limited military action such as a blockade would seem indecisive and irritating to the world, and that an American airborne seizure of Havana and the government was the best bet. But with one possible exception, the conferees shared the President's view that invasion was a last step, not the first; that it should be prepared but held back; that an invasion—more than any other course—risked a world war, a Soviet retaliation at Berlin or elsewhere, a wreckage of our Latin-American policy and the indictment of history for our aggression.

Thus our attention soon centered on two alternatives—an air strike and a blockade—and initially more on the former. The idea of American planes suddenly and swiftly eliminating the missile complex with conventional bombs in a matter of minutes—a so-called "surgical" strike—had appeal to almost everyone first considering the matter, including President Kennedy on Tuesday and Wednesday. It would be over quickly and cleanly, remove the missiles effectively, and serve as a warning to the Communists. It could be accompanied by an explanatory address to the nation and by a blockade or increased aerial surveillance to guard against future installations. The air-strike advocates in our group prepared an elaborate scenario, which provided for a presidential announcement of the missiles' presence Saturday, calling Congress back into emergency session, and then knocking the missiles out early Sunday morning, simultaneously notifying Khrushchev of our action and recommending a summit. Cuba was to be notified at the UN shortly in advance. Leaflet warnings to Russians at the sites were also considered.

But there were grave difficulties to the air-strike alternative, which became clearer each day.

1. The "surgical" strike, like the April 1961 overthrow of Castro by a small exile brigade, was merely a hopeful illusion—and this time it was so recognized. It could not be accomplished by a few sorties in a few minutes, as hoped, nor could it be limited to the missile sites alone. To so limit the strike, declared the Joint Chiefs firmly, would be an unacceptable risk. Castro's planes—and newly arrived Soviet MIGs and IL-28 bombers, if operative—might respond with an attack on our planes, on Guantánamo or even on the Southeastern United States. The SAMs would surely fire at our planes. Cuban batteries opposite Guantánamo might open fire. The nuclear warhead storage sites, if identified, should not remain. All or most of these targets would have to be taken out in a massive bombardment. Even then, admitted the Air Force—and this in particular influenced the President—there could be no assurance that all the missiles would have been removed or that some of them would not fire first, unleashing their nuclear warheads on American soil. The more we looked at the air strike, the clearer it became that the resultant chaos and political collapse would ultimately necessitate a U.S. invasion. Most of the air-strike advocates openly agreed that their route took us back to the invasion course, and they added Cuban military installations and invasion support targets to the list of sites to be bombed. But invasion with all its consequences was still opposed by the President.

2. The problem of advance warning was unsolvable. A sudden air strike at dawn Sunday without warning, said the Attorney General in rather impassioned tones, would be "a Pearl Harbor in reverse, and it would blacken the name of the United States in the pages of history" as a great power who attacked a small neighbor. The Suez fiasco was also cited as comparable. Latin Americans would produce new Castros in their bitterness; the Cuban people would not forgive us for decades; and the Soviets would entertain the very dangerous notion that the United States, as they had feared all these years, was indeed capable of launching a pre-emptive first strike. But to provide advance warning raised as many difficulties as no warning at all. It would enable the Soviets to conceal the missiles and make their elimination less certain. It would invite Khrushchev to commit himself to bombing us if we carried out our attack, give him time to take the propaganda and diplomatic initiative, and stir up a host of UN, Latin-American and Allied objections which we would have to defy or let the missiles stand. Many of those originally attracted to the air-strike course had favored it in the hope that a warning would suffice, and that the Soviets would then withdraw their missiles. But no one could devise any method of warning that would not enable Khrushchev either to tie us into knots or force us into obloquy. I tried my hand, for example, at

an airtight letter to be carried from the President to the Soviet Chairman by a high-level personal envoy. The letter would inform Khrushchev that only if he agreed in his conference with that courier (and such others as he called in) to order the missiles dismantled would U.S. military action be withheld while our surveillance oversaw their removal. But no matter how many references I put in to a summit, to peaceful intentions and to previous warnings and pledges, the letter still constituted the kind of ultimatum which no great power could accept, and a justification for either a pre-emptive strike against this country or our indictment in the court of history. From that point on, I veered away from the air-strike course.

3. The air strike, unlike the blockade, would directly and definitely attack Soviet military might, kill Russians as well as Cubans and thus more likely provoke a Soviet military response. Not to respond at all would be too great a humiliation for Khrushchev to bear, affecting his relations not only at home and with the Chinese but with all the Communist parties in the developing world. Any Cuban missiles operational by the time of our strike might be ordered by Khrushchev to fire their nuclear salvos into the United States before they were wiped out—or, we speculated, the local Soviet commander, under attack, might order the missiles fired on the assumption that war was on. The air-strike advocates did not shrink from the fact that a Soviet military riposte was likely. "What will the Soviets do in response?" one consultant favoring this course was asked. "I know the Soviets pretty well," he replied. "I think they'll knock out our missile bases in Turkey." "What do we do then?" "Under our NATO Treaty, we'd be obligated to knock out a base inside the Soviet Union." "What will they do then?" "Why, then we hope everyone will cool down and want to talk." It seemed rather cool in the conference room as he spoke.

On that same day, Wednesday, October 17, the President—after a brief review of the situation with aides in the morning—had flown to Connecticut to keep a campaign commitment. Cancellation would only have aroused suspicion, and Vice President Johnson also flew west to carry on his campaign tour. A day of meetings in the State Department conference room had made some progress in defining the issues; and when we recessed for dinner until 9 P.M., the Attorney General and I decided to meet the President's plane at eight. It was after nine when he arrived, to find us sitting in his car to avoid attention. I have the most vivid memory of the smiling campaigner alighting from his plane, waving casually to onlookers at the airport, and then instantly casting off that pose and taking up the burdens of crisis as he entered his car and said almost immediately to the driver, "Let's go, Bill." We promptly filled him in as we drove to the White House. I had prepared a four-page memorandum outlining the areas of agreement and disagreement, the full list of possibilities and (longest of all) the unanswered questions. With this to ponder, and for the reasons earlier mentioned, the President decided not to attend our session that night. Dropping him at the White House, the Attorney General and I returned to the State Department.

At that meeting, one of the most influential participants—who had theretofore not indicated which course he favored—read a brief paper he had prepared on his position: On the following Wednesday, after informing Macmillan, de Gaulle, Adenauer and possibly Turkey and a few Latin Americans, a limited air strike wiping out the missiles should be accompanied by a simultaneous Presidential announcement to the world and formal reference to the UN and OAS. We would expect a Soviet attack on Berlin, possibly Korea, or possibly the Turkish missile bases in response; and NATO and our armed forces should be so prepared.

This paper, another adviser pointed out, by-passed the question of warning to the Soviets and Castro. Advance warning, he said, was required if the rest of the world was not to turn against us. Moreover, if Khrushchev defied our warning or in response lied about the existence of offensive weapons, our hand would be strengthened. Others pointed out the objections to advance warning, the dangers of being trapped in a diplomatic wrangle, and the fact that no air strike could be limited and still effective. Still others repeated the objections to no warning. The original proponent, undecided on this key element, began to back away from his plan.

That discussion, and my inability the next day to draft a letter to Khrushchev that could stand the light of logic and history, turned increasing attention upon the blockade route. Most of the career diplomats in our group had initially favored the blockade course, although some had preferred waiting for Khrushchev's response to a letter before deciding which military move to make. As the consensus shifted away from any notion of trying political or diplomatic pressure before resorting to military action, and away from the "surgical" air strike as an impossibility, it shifted on Thursday toward the notion of blockade. It was by no means unanimous—the advocates of a broad air strike were still strong—but the blockade alternative was picking up important backers.

At first there had been very little support of a blockade. It sounded like Senator Capehart trying to starve Cuba out before there were even missiles on the island. It appeared almost irrelevant to the problem of the missiles, neither getting them out nor seeming justifiable to our many maritime allies who were sensitive to freedom of the seas. Blockade was a word so closely associated with Berlin that it almost guaranteed a new Berlin blockade in response. Both our allies and world opinion would then blame the U.S. and impose as a "solution" the lifting of both blockades simultaneously, thus accomplishing nothing.

Moreover, blockade had many of the drawbacks of the airstrike plan. If Soviet ships ignored it, U.S. forces would have to fire the first shot, provoking Soviet action elsewhere—by their submarines against our ships there or in other waters, by a blockade of our overseas bases or by a more serious military move against Berlin, Turkey, Iran or the other trouble spots mentioned. One view held that Khrushchev and the U.S. could both pretend that an air strike on Cuba was no affair of the Soviet Union but a blockade of Soviet ships was a direct challenge from which he could not retreat. And if Castro thought a blockade was effectively cutting him off, he might in desperation—or to involve Soviet help—attack our ships, Guantánamo or Florida.

We could not even be certain that the blockade route was open to us. Without obtaining a two-thirds vote in the OAS—which appeared dubious at best—allies and neutrals as well as adversaries might well regard it as an illegal blockade, in violation of the UN Charter and international law. If so, they might feel free to defy it. One member of the group with a shipping background warned of the complications of maritime insurance and claims in an illegal blockade.

But the greatest single drawback to the blockade, in comparison with the air strike, was time. Instead of presenting Khrushchev and the world with a *fait accompli,* it offered a prolonged and agonizing approach, uncertain in its effect, indefinite in its duration, enabling the missiles to become operational, subjecting us to counterthreats from Khrushchev, giving him a propaganda advantage, stirring fears and protests and pickets all over the world, causing Latin-American governments to fall, permitting Castro to announce that he would execute two Bay of Pigs prisoners for each day it continued, encouraging the UN or the OAS or our allies to bring pressure for talks, and in all these ways making more difficult a subsequent air strike if the missiles remained. Our own people would be frustrated and divided as tensions built. One of the air-strike advocates, a Republican, passed a note to me across the table reading:

> Ted—Have you considered the very real possibility that if we allow Cuba to complete installation and operational readiness of missile bases, the next House of Representatives is

likely to have a Republican majority? This would completely paralyze our ability to react sensibly and coherently to further Soviet advances.

Despite all these disadvantages, the blockade route gained strength on Thursday as other choices faded. It was a more limited, low-key military action than the air strike. It offered Khrushchev the choice of avoiding a direct military clash by keeping his ships away. It could at least be initiated without a shot being fired or a single Soviet or Cuban citizen being killed. Thus it seemed slightly less likely to precipitate an immediate military riposte. Moreover, a naval engagement in the Caribbean, just off our own shores, was the most advantageous military confrontation the United States could have, if one were necessary. Whatever the balance of strategic and ground forces may have been, the superiority of the American Navy was unquestioned; and this superiority was world-wide, should Soviet submarines retaliate elsewhere. To avoid a military defeat, Khrushchev might well turn his ships back, causing U.S. allies to have increased confidence in our credibility and Cuba's Communists to feel they were being abandoned.

Precisely because it was a limited, low-level action, the argument ran, the blockade had the advantage of permitting a more controlled escalation on our part, gradual or rapid as the situation required. It could serve as an unmistakable but not sudden or humiliating warning to Khrushchev of what we expected from him. Its prudence, its avoidance of casualties and its avoidance of attacking Cuban soil would make it more appealing to other nations than an air strike, permitting OAS and Allied support for our initial position, and making that support more likely for whatever air-strike or other action was later necessary.

On Thursday afternoon subcommittees were set up to plot each of the major courses in detail. The blockade subcommittee first had to decide what kind of blockade it recommended. We chose to begin with the lowest level of action—also the level least likely to anger allies engaged in the Cuban trade—a blockade against offensive weapons only. Inasmuch as the President had made clear that defensive weapons were not intolerable, and inasmuch as the exclusion of all food and supplies would affect innocent Cubans most of all, this delineation helped relate the blockade route more closely to the specific problem of missiles and made the punishment more nearly fit the crime. It also avoided the difficulty of stopping submarines and planes (which would have difficulty bringing in missiles and bombers even in sections).

The next question, and one that would recur throughout the next ten days, was whether to include "POL," as the military called it—petroleum, oil and lubricants. A POL blockade, automatically turning back all tankers, would lead directly though not immediately to a collapse of the Cuban economy. Although these commodities could be justifiably related to the offensive war machine, it seemed too drastic a step for the first move, too likely to require a more belligerent response and too obviously aimed more at Castro's survival than at Khrushchev's missiles. We recommended that this be held back as a means of later tightening the blockade should escalation be required.

Our next consideration was the likely Soviet response. The probability of Soviet acquiescence in the blockade itself—turning their ships back or permitting their inspection—was "high, but not certain," in the words of one Kremlinologist; but it was predicted that they might choose to force us to fire at them first. Retaliatory action elsewhere in the world seemed almost certain. The Soviets, we estimated, would blockade Berlin—not merely against offensive weapons, which would mean little, but a general blockade, including the air routes and all civilian access as well, thus precipitating another serious military confrontation for both powers. Other blockades were listed as a possibility, as well as increased Communist threats in Bolivia, Venezuela, Guatemala, Ecuador, Haiti and elsewhere in Latin America. Inside Cuba a long and gradually tighter blockade would in time, it was predicted, produce both military and political action.

We then suggested possible U.S. responses to these Communist responses, advocating that Berlin be treated on the basis of its own previously prepared contingency plans without regard to actions elsewhere. These studies completed, we rejoined the air-strike subcommittee and the others in the conference room to compare notes.

Meanwhile, the President—with whom some of us had met both in the morning and afternoon of that Thursday—was holding a long-scheduled two-hour meeting with Soviet Foreign Minister Gromyko prior to the latter's return to Moscow from the UN. While all of us wondered whether this could possibly be the moment planned by the Soviets to confront Kennedy with their new threat, all agreed that the President should not tell Gromyko what we knew. Not only was our information incomplete after only two days, with new evidence coming in every day, but we were not yet ready to act—and Gromyko's relay of our information to Moscow would bring on all the delays, evasions, threats and other disadvantages of a diplomatic warning. Alternatively, the wily Soviet Foreign Minister might decide to announce the build-up himself from the White House steps; and Kennedy felt strongly that, to retain the initiative and public confidence, it was essential that the facts first be disclosed to the people of the United States by their President along with an announced plan of action. He was anxious as the meeting approached, but managed to smile as he welcomed Gromyko and Dobrynin to his office.

Gromyko, seated on the sofa next to the President's rocker, not only failed to mention the offensive weapons but carried on the deception that there were none. In a sense, Kennedy had hoped for this, believing it would strengthen our case with world opinion. The chief topic of conversation was Berlin, and on this Gromyko was tougher and more insistent than ever. After the U.S. election, he said, if no settlement were in sight, the Soviets would go ahead with their treaty. ("It all seemed to fit a pattern," the President said to me later, "everything coming to a head at once—the completion of the missile bases, Khrushchev coming to New York, a new drive on West Berlin. If that move is coming anyway, I'm not going to feel that a Cuban blockade provoked it.") Then the Soviet Minister turned to Cuba, not with apologies but complaints. He cited the Congressional resolution, the Reservists call-up authority, various statements to the press and other U.S. interference with what he regarded as a small nation that posed no threat. He called our restrictions on Allied shipping a blockade against trade and a violation of international law. All this could only lead to great misfortunes for mankind, he said, for his government could not sit by and observe this situation idly when aggression was planned and a threat of war was looming.

The President made no response, and Gromyko then read from his notes:

> As to Soviet assistance to Cuba, I have been instructed to make it clear, as the Soviet Government has already done, that such assistance pursued solely the purpose of contributing to the defense capabilities of Cuba and to the development of its peaceful economy . . . training by Soviet specialists of Cuban nationals in handling defensive armaments was by no means offensive. If it were otherwise, the Soviet Government would have never become involved in rendering such assistance.

Kennedy remained impassive, neither agreeing nor disagreeing with Gromyko's claim. He gave no sign of tension or anger. But to avoid misleading his adversary, he sent for and read aloud his September warning against offensive missiles in Cuba. Gromyko "must have wondered why I was reading it," he said later. "But he did not respond."

Two days earlier, the President had been informed, on the very day he had learned of the missiles, a similar deception had taken place. Chairman Khrushchev, upon receiving our new Ambassador to Moscow, Foy Kohler, had complained vigorously about reports that a new Russian fishing port in Cuba would become a submarine base. He would have held up the announcement of the port, he said, because he did not want to burden Kennedy during the campaign. He also wanted to state once again that all activity in Cuba was defensive. (The one ominous note in that otherwise genial conversation had been a sharp reference to the U.S. Jupiter bases in Turkey and Italy.)

As Gromyko arrived at 8 P.M. that Thursday evening for a black-tie dinner on the State Department's eighth floor, our group was meeting on the seventh floor (minus Rusk and Thompson, who were with Gromyko). McNamara and McCone, surprised to see a band of reporters as they drove up, replied in the affirmative when asked if they were there for the Gromyko dinner. Obviously they had been too busy to don formal wear.

In our earlier sessions that day the President had requested a 9 P.M. conference at the White House. While we had been meeting for only three days (that seemed like thirty), time was running out. Massive U.S. military movements had thus far been explained by long-planned Naval exercises in the Caribbean and an earlier announced buildup in Castro's air force. But the secret would soon be out, said the President, and the missiles would soon be operational.

The blockade course was now advocated by a majority. We were prepared to present the full range of choices and questions to the President. George Ball had earlier directed that the official cars conspicuously gathered by the front door be dispersed to avoid suspicion. With the exception of Martin, who preferred to walk, we all piled into the Attorney General's limousine, some seated on laps, for the short ride over to the White House. "It will be some story if this car is in an accident," someone quipped.

In the Oval Room on the second floor of the Mansion, the alternatives were discussed. Both the case for the blockade and the case for simply living with this threat were presented. The President had already moved from the air-strike to the blockade camp. He liked the idea of leaving Khrushchev a way out, of beginning at a low level that could then be stepped up; and the other choices had too many insuperable difficulties. Blockade, he indicated, was his tentative decision. . . .

While the Executive Committee deliberated, the construction crews in Cuba moved ahead rapidly on the missile sites. By the end of the week the U-2 photographs revealed that the Russians were building six medium-range and three intermediate-range missile sites. There were four launching pads at each site, which meant the completed bases would be capable of hurling thirty-six nuclear warheads at the United States and, according to Robert Kennedy, killing as many as eighty million Americans. There is no evidence, however, that the Russians had actually introduced any IRBMs into Cuba; the U-2s spotted only the MRBMs, whose one-thousand-mile limit placed most of the American population beyond their reach. Nor was there any direct evidence that the Soviet Union had placed nuclear warheads in Cuba, or, if they had, whether they were under Cuban or Russian control. Nevertheless, the sense of danger intensified in Washington as intelligence sources predicted that the IRBM sites would be operational before the end of October.

On Friday, October 18, the President left Washington for another round of congressional campaigning in the Midwest. On Saturday morning, however, he decided to return to Washington to preside over the final deliberations of the Executive Committee. Press Secretary Pierre Salinger, unaware of the real reason, informed newsmen that the President had a slight cold and was returning to Washington to rest over the weekend. Kennedy arrived back at the White House in the early afternoon.

In his excellent book *The Missile Crisis,* television journalist Elie Abel describes the scene which ensued.[6]

. . . The die was cast when the President met with his Executive Committee in the Oval Room at 2:30 P.M. It was a long and—toward the end—an unexpectedly bitter session. The choices put before Kennedy that afternoon were two: begin with the naval blockade and, if need be, move up the ladder of military responses, rung by rung; or begin with an air strike, then move almost certainly to a full-scale invasion of Cuba. Dean Rusk had prepared a two-page summary in his own handwriting, carefully marked TOP SECRET. He read it to the assembled group, then handed the papers to the President, who handed them back. Rusk kept the document for his files. It recommended that the President choose the blockade track, while warning that this course would be neither safe nor comfortable, carrying with it the risks of rapid escalation. The Rusk document listed seven reasons for choosing blockade

[6] Elie Abel, *The Missile Crisis* (Philadelphia, 1966), pp. 78–81. Copyright © 1966 by Elie Abel. Reprinted by permission of J. B. Lippincott Company.

instead of the air strike he had argued for earlier. Of these, the most cogent was that the air strike would be an irreversible step. The blockade, by contrast, promised to keep other avenues open while providing time and opportunity for the Russians to reconsider carefully the dangers of their chosen course. McNamara also argued for blockade, saying that while either choice was risky, blockade appeared the more likely to achieve the removal of Soviet missiles from Cuba with the least risk.

The President paused gravely before speaking his mind. He said that he preferred to start with limited action. An air attack, he felt, was the wrong way to start. The modern bomber seemed to him hardly a surgical tool, but, rather, a blunt instrument. Before making his final decision he wanted to talk with the tactical bombing specialists. But the blockade, he felt, was the way to begin. He asked the air-strike advocates to understand that their alternative was by no means ruled out for the future. It might become necessary if the blockade failed in its purpose. For the moment, the blockade track had the advantage of preserving his own options and leaving some for Khrushchev. It applied enough pressure to make clear America's determination, but not so much as to force the Russians into desperate actions. Kennedy was still expecting a Soviet move against Berlin, whatever happened in Cuba. He inquired about the state of contingency planning for Berlin, then confessed that he was not happy with either alternative. "The ones whose plans we're not taking are the lucky ones," he said.

Adlai Stevenson, who had returned from New York for the decisive meetings, suggested that—simultaneous with the President's speech, already set for 7 P.M. Monday—the United States should call for an emergency session of the United Nations Security Council. Stevenson stressed the importance of getting in ahead of the Russians with a resolution that was acceptable to the United States. The President agreed. He also endorsed the plans Ed Martin had drafted for going to the Organization of American States. Stevenson had approved the blockade decision, insisting that OAS approval was vital. On Saturday afternoon he started thinking aloud about further diplomatic moves. The President, he urged, should consider offering to withdraw from the Guantánamo naval base as part of a plan to demilitarize, neutralize, and guarantee the territorial integrity of Cuba. Stevenson held that Guantánamo, in any event, was of little value. He also forecast grave difficulties concerning the Jupiter bases in Turkey. People would certainly ask why it was right for the United States to have bases in Turkey, but wrong for the Russians to have bases in Cuba. The President, he said, should consider offering to remove the Jupiters in exchange for the removal of Russian missiles from Cuba. Perhaps UN inspection teams could be set up to inspect all foreign bases, Russian as well as American, to guard against a surprise attack while the dismantling was being carried out.

Kennedy addressed himself directly to Stevenson's proposals, rejecting both. The United States, he said, simply could not at this stage consider giving up Guantánamo. As for the Jupiters, the President had his own doubts about their continued value and was willing to consider removing them in the right circumstances. But this was not the time for concessions that could wreck the Western alliance; seeming to confirm the suspicion Charles de Gaulle had planted that the United States would sacrifice the interests of its allies to protect its own security. Dillon, Lovett and McCone sharply attacked Stevenson, but the UN Ambassador stood his ground. This was the exchange that later led to published charges that "Adlai wanted a Munich." In fairness to Stevenson, Paul Nitze submits that as Ambassador to the United Nations, "Adlai had to be the one who looked at this proposition from the UN standpoint, the standpoint of simple equities and the hazards of war." Dean Rusk's impression is that Stevenson was not in fact advocating an American withdrawal from Guantánamo or from Turkey. He was trying to suggest what kinds of demands might be raised if, as many others also expected, the Russians dragged their feet after agreeing to remove the missiles from Cuba and thus involved the United States in a long, wearying negotiation.

Stevenson's own recollection was that he argued the United States ought to be willing to pay some price for the neutralization of Cuba if that meant getting the Russians out, along with their missiles. The bitter aftertaste of that Saturday afternoon in the Oval Room stayed with him until his death. It was after this encounter that Robert Kennedy decided Stevenson lacked the toughness to deal effectively with the Russians at the UN in liquidating the missile crisis. He suggested to the President that John McCloy or Herman Phleger, the California Republican who had served as chief legal adviser to John Foster Dulles, be asked to help in the UN negotiations. McCloy got the job. . . .

The full National Security Council met for the first time on the Cuban issue on Sunday afternoon, October 21, to ratify the decision reached in the Executive Committee. The plan called for President Kennedy to inform the nation and the world of the existence of the Soviet missiles in a televised address on Monday evening. He would announce plans for a "quarantine" (to avoid the warlike sound of blockade) of Cuba to be imposed by the United States with the approval of the Organization of American States, and he would call upon the Russians to withdraw the missiles already in Cuba. Realizing the importance of informing American allies of this impending step, Kennedy asked Dean Acheson to fly to Paris to brief Charles de Gaulle. Acheson agreed to undertake this delicate assignment, leaving by Air Force jet on Sunday and arriving in Paris early Monday after a stop in England to confer with Ambassador David Bruce, who would inform British Prime Minister Harold Macmillan. Although de Gaulle made clear to Acheson that he realized he was being informed rather than consulted, he approved of the American policy, saying, "I think that under the circumstances President Kennedy had no other choice."

In Washington, experienced reporters began to sense that a major story was breaking. James Reston, Washington bureau chief for the *New York Times,* uncovered the basic facts over the weekend; but after conferring with administration leaders he agreed to remain silent. By Monday, when the President's request for air time had become public, speculation of a grave crisis flourished, though many journalists focused on Berlin rather than Cuba. At five that evening, two hours before his telecast, President Kennedy met with congressional leaders to inform them of the missile crisis. Their reaction surprised and dismayed the President. Senator Richard Russell of Georgia dismissed the blockade as a weak measure and advocated an invasion of Cuba; Arkansas Senator William Fulbright, chairman of the Foreign Relations Committee and critic of the Bay of Pigs, took a similar position. After a brief exchange with these Democratic Senators, Kennedy retired to his study to look over the speech, which had been drafted by Theodore Sorensen and carefully revised and altered by the Executive Committee. At six o'clock Secretary of State Dean Rusk handed Russian Ambassador Dobrynin a copy of the speech and fifteen minutes later Under-Secretary Ball informed the ambassadors of forty-six allied and friendly countries of the American decision. Then, at seven o'clock, President Kennedy began reading to the nation the most important and most somber speech of his career.[7]

[7] *Public Papers of the Presidents: Kennedy, 1962,* pp. 806–809.

Good evening, my fellow citizens: This Government, as promised, has maintained the closest surveillance of the Soviet military buildup on the island of Cuba. Within the past week, unmistakable evidence has established the fact that a series of offensive missile sites is now in preparation on that imprisoned island. The purpose of these bases can be none other than to provide a nuclear strike capability against the Western Hemisphere.

Upon receiving the first preliminary hard information of this nature last Tuesday morning at 9 A.M., I directed that our surveillance be stepped up. And having now confirmed and completed our evaluation of the evidence and our decision on a course of action, this Government feels obliged to report this new crisis to you in fullest detail.

The characteristics of these new missile sites indicate two distinct types of installations. Several of them include medium range ballistic missiles, capable of carrying a nuclear warhead for a distance of more than 1,000 nautical miles. Each of these missiles, in short, is capable of striking Washington, D.C., the Panama Canal, Cape Canaveral, Mexico City, or any other city in the southeastern part of the United States, in Central America, or in the Caribbean area.

Additional sites not yet completed appear to be designed for intermediate range ballistic missiles—capable of traveling more than twice as far—and thus capable of striking most of the major cities in the Western Hemisphere, ranging as far north as Hudson Bay, Canada, and as far south as Lima, Peru. In addition, jet bombers, capable of carrying nuclear weapons, are now being uncrated and assembled in Cuba, while the necessary air bases are being prepared.

This urgent transformation of Cuba into an important strategic base—by the presence of these large, long-range, and clearly offensive weapons of sudden mass destruction—constitutes an explicit threat to the peace and security of all the Americas, in flagrant and deliberate defiance of the Rio Pact of 1947, the traditions of this Nation and hemisphere, the joint resolution of the 87th Congress, the Charter of the United Nations, and my own public warnings to the Soviets on September 4 and 13. This action also contradicts the repeated assurances of Soviet spokesmen, both publicly and privately delivered, that the arms buildup in Cuba would retain its original defensive character, and that the Soviet Union had no need or desire to station strategic missiles on the territory of any other nation.

The size of this undertaking makes clear that it has been planned for some months. Yet only last month, after I had made clear the distinction between any introduction of ground-to-ground missiles and the existence of defensive antiaircraft missiles, the Soviet Government publicly stated on September 11 that, and I quote, "the armaments and military equipment sent to Cuba are designed exclusively for defensive purposes," that, and I quote the Soviet Government, "there is no need for the Soviet Government to shift its weapons . . . for a retaliatory blow to any other country, for instance Cuba," and that, and I quote their government, "the Soviet Union has so powerful rockets to carry these nuclear warheads that there is no need to search for sites for them beyond the boundaries of the Soviet Union." That statement was false.

Only last Thursday, as evidence of this rapid offensive buildup was already in my hand, Soviet Foreign Minister Gromyko told me in my office that he was instructed to make it clear once again, as he said his government had already done, that Soviet assistance to Cuba, and I quote, "pursued solely the purpose of contributing to the defense capabilities of Cuba," that, and I quote him, "training by Soviet specialists of Cuban nationals in handling defensive armaments was by no means offensive, and if it were otherwise," Mr. Gromyko went on, "the Soviet Government would never become involved in rendering such assistance." That statement also was false.

Neither the United States of America nor the world community of nations can tolerate deliberate deception and offensive threats on the part of any nation, large or small. We no longer live in a world where only the actual firing of weapons represents a sufficient challenge to a nation's security to constitute maximum peril. Nuclear weapons are so destructive and ballistic missiles are so swift, that any substantially increased possibility of their use or any sudden change in their deployment may well be regarded as a definite threat to peace.

For many years, both the Soviet Union and the United States, recognizing this fact, have deployed strategic nuclear weapons with great care, never upsetting the precarious status quo which insured that these weapons would not be used in the absence of some vital challenge. Our own strategic missiles have never been transferred to the territory of any other nation under a cloak of secrecy and deception; and our history—unlike that of the Soviets since the end of World War II—demonstrates that we have no desire to dominate or conquer any other nation or impose our system upon its people. Nevertheless, American citizens have become adjusted to living daily on the bull's-eye of Soviet missiles located inside the USSR or in submarines.

In that sense, missiles in Cuba add to an already clear and present danger—although it should be noted the nations of Latin America have never previously been subjected to a potential nuclear threat.

But this secret, swift, and extraordinary buildup of Communist missiles—in an area well known to have a special and historical relationship to the United States and the nations of the Western Hemisphere, in violation of Soviet assurances, and in defiance of American and hemispheric policy—this sudden, clandestine decision to station strategic weapons for the first time outside of Soviet soil—is a deliberately provocative and unjustified change in the status quo which cannot be accepted by this country, if our courage and our commitments are ever to be trusted again by either friend or foe.

The 1930's taught us a clear lesson: aggressive conduct, if allowed to go unchecked and unchallenged, ultimately leads to war. This nation is opposed to war. We are also true to our word. Our unswerving objective, therefore, must be to prevent the use of these missiles against this or any other country, and to secure their withdrawal or elimination from the Western Hemisphere.

Our policy has been one of patience and restraint, as befits a peaceful and powerful nation, which leads a worldwide alliance. We have been determined not to be diverted from our central concerns by mere irritants and fanatics. But now further action is required—and it is under way; and these actions may only be the beginning. We will not prematurely or unnecessarily risk the costs of worldwide nuclear war in which even the fruits of victory would be ashes in our mouth—but neither will we shrink from that risk at any time it must be faced.

Acting, therefore, in the defense of our own security and of the entire Western Hemisphere, and under the authority entrusted to me by the Constitution as endorsed by the resolution of the Congress, I have directed that the following *initial* steps be taken immediately:

First: To halt this offensive buildup, a strict quarantine on all offensive military equipment under shipment to Cuba is being initiated. All ships of any kind bound for Cuba from whatever nation or port will, if found to contain cargoes of offensive weapons, be turned back. This quarantine will be extended, if needed, to other types of cargo and carriers. We are not at this time, however, denying the necessities of life as the Soviets attempted to do in their Berlin blockade of 1948.

Second: I have directed the continued and increased close surveillance of Cuba and its military buildup. The foreign ministers of the OAS, in their communiqué of October 6, rejected secrecy on such matters in this hemisphere. Should these offensive military preparations continue, thus increasing the threat to the hemisphere, further action will be justified. I have directed the Armed Forces to prepare for any eventualities; and I trust that in the interest of both the

Cuban people and the Soviet technicians at the sites, the hazards to all concerned of continuing this threat will be recognized.

Third: It shall be the policy of this Nation to regard any nuclear missile launched from Cuba against any nation in the Western Hemisphere as an attack by the Soviet Union on the United States, requiring a full retaliatory response upon the Soviet Union.

Fourth: As a necessary military precaution, I have reinforced our base at Guantánamo, evacuated today the dependents of our personnel there, and ordered additional military units to be on a standby alert basis.

Fifth: We are calling tonight for an immediate meeting of the Organ of Consultation under the Organization of American States, to consider this threat to hemispheric security and to invoke articles 6 and 8 of the Rio Treaty in support of all necessary action. The United Nations Charter allows for regional security arrangements—and the nations of this hemisphere decided long ago against the military presence of outside powers. Our other allies around the world have also been alerted.

Sixth: Under the Charter of the United Nations, we are asking tonight that an emergency meeting of the Security Council be convoked without delay to take action against this latest Soviet threat to world peace. Our resolution will call for the prompt dismantling and withdrawal of all offensive weapons in Cuba, under the supervision of UN observers, before the quarantine can be lifted.

Seventh and finally: I call upon Chairman Khrushchev to halt and eliminate this clandestine, reckless, and provocative threat to world peace and to stable relations between our two nations. I call upon him further to abandon this course of world domination, and to join in an historic effort to end the perilous arms race and to transform the history of man. He has an opportunity now to move the world back from the abyss of destruction—by returning to his government's own words that it had no need to station missiles outside its own territory, and withdrawing these weapons from Cuba—by refraining from any action which will widen or deepen the present crisis—and then by participating in a search for peaceful and permanent solutions.

This Nation is prepared to present its case against the Soviet threat to peace, and our own proposals for a peaceful world, at any time and in any forum—in the OAS, in the United Nations, or in any other meeting that could be useful—without limiting our freedom of action. We have in the past made strenuous efforts to limit the spread of nuclear weapons. We have proposed the elimination of all arms and military bases in a fair and effective disarmament treaty. We are prepared to discuss new proposals for the removal of tensions on both sides—including the possibilities of a genuinely independent Cuba, free to determine its own destiny. We have no wish to war with the Soviet Union—for we are a peaceful people who desire to live in peace with all other peoples.

But it is difficult to settle or even discuss these problems in an atmosphere of intimidation. That is why this latest Soviet threat—or any other threat which is made either independently or in response to our actions this week—must and will be met with determination. Any hostile move anywhere in the world against the safety and freedom of peoples to whom we are committed—including in particular the brave people of West Berlin—will be met by whatever action is needed.

Finally, I want to say a few words to the captive people of Cuba, to whom this speech is being directly carried by special radio facilities. I speak to you as a friend, as one who knows of your deep attachment to your fatherland, as one who shares your aspirations for liberty and justice for all. And I have watched and the American people have watched with deep sorrow how your nationalist revolution was betrayed—and how your fatherland fell under foreign domination. Now your leaders are no longer Cuban leaders inspired by Cuban ideals. They are puppets and agents of an international conspiracy which has turned Cuba against your friends and neighbors in the Americas—and turned it into the first Latin American country to become a target for nuclear war—the first Latin American country to have these weapons on its soil.

These new weapons are not in your interest. They contribute nothing to your peace and well-being. They can only undermine it. But this country has no wish to cause you to suffer or to impose any system upon you. We know that your lives and land are being used as pawns by those who deny your freedom.

Many times in the past, the Cuban people have risen to throw out tyrants who destroyed their liberty. And I have no doubt that most Cubans today look forward to the time when they will be truly free—free from foreign domination, free to choose their own leaders, free to select their own system, free to own their own land, free to speak and write and worship without fear or degradation. And then shall Cuba be welcomed back to the society of free nations and to the associations of this hemisphere.

My fellow citizens: let no one doubt that this is a difficult and dangerous effort on which we have set out. No one can foresee precisely what course it will take or what cost or casualties will be incurred. Many months of sacrifice and self-discipline lie ahead—months in which both our patience and our will will be tested—months in which many threats and denunciations will keep us aware of our dangers. But the greatest danger of all would be to do nothing.

The path we have chosen for the present is full of hazards, as all paths are—but it is the one most consistent with our character and courage as a nation and our commitments around the world. The cost of freedom is always high—but Americans have always paid it. And one path we shall never choose, and that is the path of surrender or submission.

Our goal is not the victory of might, but the vindication of right—not peace at the expense of freedom, but both peace *and* freedom, here in this hemisphere, and, we hope, around the world. God willing, that goal will be achieved.

Thank you and good night.

The next morning Secretary Rusk presented a resolution to the Council of the Organization of American States calling for a quarantine of Cuba and authorizing members of the OAS to take "all measures, individually and collectively, including the use of armed force," against Cuba. In an impressive display of unity, all the Latin American delegations except the one from Uruguay, which was still waiting for instructions from home, voted for the quarantine. Three countries, Brazil, Mexico, and Bolivia, abstained from the section authorizing the use of force. Later that day, citing the OAS action, President Kennedy declared the quarantine of Cuba on the basis of defending the hemisphere against an external threat. In New York, Ambassador Stevenson delivered an eloquent indictment of the Soviet action, which was quickly rebutted by the Soviet representative, Valerian Zorin, who denied the existence of the missile bases and accused the United States of threatening the world with nuclear war. Although the United States could count on the support of a majority on the Security Council, the certainty of a Soviet veto ruled out any chance of effective action by the United Nations.

On Tuesday, President Kennedy received the first of an almost daily series of communications from Premier Khrushchev. Replying to a note Kennedy had sent the day before, the Russian leader denounced the American blockade as an act of "outright banditry" and accused Kennedy of pushing mankind "to the abyss of a world missile-nuclear war." He ended by declaring that he had ordered Russian ships on the high seas to proceed to Cuba in defiance of the American blockade. The next day Khrushchev made his position public in replying to an appeal for peace from Bertrand Russell, the British pacifist.[8]

I received your telegram and express sincere gratitude for the concern you have displayed in connection with the aggressive actions of the United States in pushing the world to the brink of war.

I understand your worry and anxiety. I should like to assure you that the Soviet Government will not take any reckless decisions, will not permit itself to be provoked by the unwarranted actions of the United States of America and will do everything to eliminate the situation fraught with irreparable consequences which has arisen in connection with the aggressive actions of the United States Government. We shall do everything in our power to prevent war from breaking out. We are fully aware of the fact that if this war is unleashed, from the very first hour it will become a thermonuclear and world war. This is perfectly obvious to us, but clearly is not to the Government of the United States which has caused this crisis.

The American Government is said to have embarked on such a reckless course not only because of hatred for the Cuban people and their Government, but also out of pre-election considerations, in the flurry of interparty pre-election excitement. But this is madness which may lead the world to the catastrophe of a thermonuclear war. The persons who are responsible for the United States policy should ponder the consequences to which their rash actions may lead if a thermonuclear war is unleashed. If the way to the aggressive policy of the American Government is not blocked, the people of the United States and other nations will have to pay with millions of lives for this policy.

I beg you, Mr. Russell, to meet with understanding our position, our actions. Realizing the entire complexity of the situation brought about by the piratic actions of the American Government, we cannot agree with them in any form. If we encourage piracy and banditry in international relations, this will not conduce to consolidation of the norms of international law and, consequently, of legal order on which normal relations are based between states, between nations, between people.

Therefore if the United States Government will crudely trample upon and violate international rights, if it does not follow in its actions the appeals of reason, the situation having tensed up to the

[8] *New York Times,* October 25, 1962. Copyright © 1962 by The New York Times Company. Reprinted by permission.

limit may get out of hand and this may resolve into a world war with all the regretful consequences to the peoples of all countries.

This is why what is needed now is not only the efforts of the Soviet Union, the Socialist countries and Cuba, which has become, as it were the main focus of the world crisis, but also the efforts of all states, all peoples and all segments of society to avert a military catastrophe. Clearly if this catastrophe breaks out, it will bring extremely grave consequences to mankind and will spare neither right nor left, neither those who champion the cause of peace nor those who want to stay aloof.

I want to say once more: we shall do everything possible to prevent this catastrophe. But it must be borne in mind that our efforts may prove insufficient. Indeed, our efforts and possibilities are efforts and possibilities of one side. If the American Government will be carrying the program of piratic actions outlined by it, we shall have to resort to means of defense against an aggressor to defend our rights and international rights which are written down in international agreements and expressed in the United Nations Charter. We have no other way out. It is well known that if one tries to mollify a robber by giving him at first one's purse, then one's coat, etc., the robber will not become more merciful, will not stop robbing. On the contrary, he will become increasingly insolent. Therefore it is necessary to curb the highwayman in order to prevent the jungle law from becoming the law governing relations between civilized people and states.

The Soviet Government considers that the Government of the United States of America must display reserve and stay the execution of its piratical threats which are fraught with most serious consequences.

The question of war and peace is so vital that we should consider useful a top-level meeting in order to discuss all the problems which have arisen, to do everything to remove the danger of unleashing a thermonuclear war. As long as rocket nuclear weapons are not put into play it is still possible to avert war. When aggression is unleashed by the Americans such a meeting will already become impossible and useless.

I thank you once more for your appeal, prompted as it is by concern for the destinies of the world.

The quarantine went into effect on Wednesday morning, October 24. A naval task force of nineteen ships set up a picket line in the Atlantic five hundred miles from Cuba and prepared to intercept any Russian ships that might be carrying missiles to the island. Naval reconnaissance aircraft from the Azores,

Puerto Rico, Bermuda, and Newfoundland had located more than fifty ships in the Atlantic and had photographed each one in detail. As a result the Navy had identified twenty-five Russian vessels steaming toward the American quarantine line around Cuba. In his posthumously published account, Robert Kennedy describes the tension inside the White House on October 24 as the President and his advisers awaited word from the Navy.[9]

The next morning, Wednesday, the quarantine went into effect, and the reports during the early hours told of the Russian ships coming steadily on toward Cuba. I talked with the President for a few moments before we went in to our regular meeting. He said, "It looks really mean, doesn't it? But then, really there was no other choice. If they get this mean on this one in our part of the world, what will they do on the next?" "I just don't think there was any choice," I said, "and not only that, if you hadn't acted, you would have been impeached." The President thought for a moment and said, "That's what I think—I would have been impeached."

The choice was to have gone in and taken steps which were not necessary or to have acted as we did. At least we now had the support of the whole Western Hemisphere and all our allies around the world.

This Wednesday-morning meeting, along with that of the following Saturday, October 27, seemed the most trying, the most difficult, and the most filled with tension. The Russian ships were proceeding, they were nearing the five-hundred-mile barrier, and we either had to intercept them or announce we were withdrawing. I sat across the table from the President. This was the moment we had prepared for, which we hoped would never come. The danger and concern that we all felt hung like a cloud over us all and particularly over the President.

The U-2s and low-flying planes had returned the previous day with their film, and through the evening it was analyzed—by now in such volume that the film alone was more than twenty-five miles long. The results were presented to us at the meeting. The launching pads, the missiles, the concrete boxes, the nuclear storage bunkers, all the components were there, by now clearly defined and obvious. Comparisons with the pictures of a few days earlier made clear that the work on those sites was proceeding and that within

[9] Robert F. Kennedy, *Thirteen Days: A Memoir of the Cuban Missile Crisis* (New York, 1969), pp. 67–72. Reprinted by permission of W. W. Norton & Company, Inc. Copyright © 1969 by W. W. Norton & Company, Inc. Copyright © 1968 by McCall Corporation.

a few days several of the launching pads would be ready for war.

It was now a few minutes after 10:00. Secretary McNamara announced that two Russian ships, the *Gagarin* and the *Komiles,* were within a few miles of our quarantine barrier. The interception of both ships would probably be before noon Washington time. Indeed, the expectation was that at least one of the vessels would be stopped and boarded between 10:30 and 11:00.

Then came the disturbing Navy report that a Russian submarine had moved into position between the two ships.

It had originally been planned to have a cruiser make the first interception, but, because of the increased danger, it was decided in the past few hours to send in an aircraft carrier supported by helicopters, carrying antisubmarine equipment, hovering overhead. The carrier *Essex* was to signal the submarine by sonar to surface and identify itself. If it refused, said Secretary McNamara, depth charges with a small explosive would be used until the submarine surfaced.

I think these few minutes were the time of gravest concern for the President. Was the world on the brink of a holocaust? Was it our error? A mistake? Was there something further that should have been done? Or not done? His hand went up to his face and covered his mouth. He opened and closed his fist. His face seemed drawn, his eyes pained, almost gray. We stared at each other across the table. For a few fleeting seconds, it was almost as though no one else was there and he was no longer the President.

Inexplicably, I thought of when he was ill and almost died; when he lost his child; when we learned that our oldest brother had been killed; of personal times of strain and hurt. The voices droned on, but I didn't seem to hear anything until I heard the President say: "Isn't there some way we can avoid having our first exchange with a Russian submarine—almost anything but that?" "No, there's too much danger to our ships. There is no alternative," said McNamara. "Our commanders have been instructed to avoid hostilities if at all possible, but this is what we must be prepared for, and this is what we must expect."

We had come to the time of final decision. "We must expect that they will close down Berlin—make the final preparations for that," the President said. I felt we were on the edge of a precipice with no way off. This time, the moment was now—not next week—not tomorrow, "so we can have another meeting and decide"; not in eight hours, "so we can send another message to Khrushchev and perhaps he will finally understand." No, none of that was possible. One thousand miles away in the vast expanse of the Atlantic Ocean the final decisions were going to be made in the next few minutes. President Kennedy had initiated the course of events, but he no longer had control over them. He would have to wait—we would have to wait. The minutes in the Cabinet Room ticked slowly by. What could we say now—what could we do?

Then it was 10:25—a messenger brought in a note to John McCone. "Mr. President, we have a preliminary report which seems to indicate that some of the Russian ships have stopped dead in the water."

Stopped dead in the water? Which ships? Are they checking the accuracy of the report? Is it true? I looked at the clock. 10:32. "The report is accurate, Mr. President. Six ships previously on their way to Cuba at the edge of the quarantine line have stopped or have turned back toward the Soviet Union. A representative from the Office of Naval Intelligence is on his way over with the full report." A short time later, the report came that the twenty Russian ships closest to the barrier had stopped and were dead in the water or had turned around.

"So no ships will be stopped or intercepted," said the President. I said we should make sure the Navy knew nothing was to be done, that no ships were to be interfered with. Orders would go out to the Navy immediately. "If the ships have orders to turn around, we want to give them every opportunity to do so. Get in direct touch with the *Essex,* and tell them not to do anything, but give the Russian vessels an opportunity to turn back. We must move quickly because the time is expiring," said the President.

Then we were back to the details. The meeting droned on. But everyone looked like a different person. For a moment the world had stood still, and now it was going around again.

Although the Russian decision not to challenge the quarantine was a hopeful sign, it did not alter the fundamental danger—the missile sites in Cuba where work continued without pause. President Kennedy was determined to maintain the pressure until the Russians dismantled the missile bases. Thus he was dismayed when United Nations Secretary General U Thant sent a note to the United States and Russia asking the two governments to step back from the brink of nuclear war by suspending both the shipments to Cuba and the quarantine for two to three weeks. In that breathing space, U Thant hoped, peaceful negotiations could resolve the other issues. Kennedy politely declined the next day, pointing out that only the removal of missiles from Cuba could end the crisis; but he agreed to instruct Ambassador Stevenson to enter into "preliminary talks to determine whether satisfactory arrangements can be secured."

On Thursday morning pressure for a diplomatic solution to the crisis came from another highly influential source. In his syndicated column, Walter Lippmann raised in public the concern that Stevenson had expressed earlier in the Executive Committee.[10]

> It is Wednesday morning as I am writing this article, and the President's proclamation of a selective blockade has just gone into effect. We are now waiting for the other shoe to drop. There are a number of Soviet and Communist bloc ships on their way to Cuba. One in particular is presumed to be carrying contraband. There has as yet been no contact between these ships and our forces and we do not know what orders Moscow has given to the ship captains.
>
> For the present, all depends upon these orders. As of the present moment we do not know whether the orders are to turn away from Cuba, to proceed and submit to search, or to proceed and to refuse to submit to search.
>
> Until we do know, we can only speculate as to whether the Soviets will engage themselves at sea on the way to Cuba, will submit to the blockade and retaliate elsewhere, or will limit themselves to violent statements without violent action. There are those, for whose judgment I have profound respect, who think that it is now too late for this country to influence the decisions of the Soviet Union and that the President is now irretrievably committed to a course which can end only with a total blockade or an invasion of Cuba.
>
> They may be right. But I have lived through two World Wars, and in both of them, once we were engaged, we made the same tragic mistake. We suspended diplomacy when the guns began to shoot. In both wars as a result we achieved a great victory but we could not make peace. There is a mood in this country today which could easily cause us to make the same mistake again. We must in honor attempt to avoid it.
>
> I see danger of this mistake in the fact that when the President saw Mr. Gromyko on Thursday, and had the evidence of the missile build-up in Cuba, he refrained from confronting Mr. Gromyko with this evidence. This was to suspend diplomacy. If it had not been suspended, the President would have shown Mr. Gromyko the pictures, and told him privately about the policy which in a few days he intended to announce publicly. This would have made it more likely that Moscow would order the ships not to push on to

[10] *Washington Post,* October 25, 1962, p. 25. Reprinted by permission.

GOSHEN COLLEGE LIBRARY
GOSHEN, INDIANA

Cuba. But if such diplomatic action did not change the orders, if Mr. Khrushchev persisted in spite of it, the President's public speech would have been stronger. For it would not have been subject to the criticism that a great power had issued an ultimatum to another great power without first attempting to negotiate the issue. By confronting Mr. Gromyko privately, the President would have given Mr. Khrushchev what all wise statesmen give their adversaries—the chance to save face.

There is, I know, no use crying over spilt milk. But I am making the point because there is still so much milk that can be spilt.

We have, we must note, made two separate demands. One is that no more "offensive weapons" shall be brought into Cuba. On this demand, we shall soon have a showdown. Considering the unanimity of the other American states, considering the strategic weakness of the Soviet Union in this hemisphere, there is reason to hope that the quarantine of Cuba will work, though we must expect retaliation elsewhere.

But the President has laid down a second demand, which is that the missile installations already in Cuba be dismantled and removed. How this is to be done is a very great question, even supposing that there is no shooting conflict at sea. And it is here, I believe, that diplomacy must not abdicate.

There are three ways to get rid of the missiles already in Cuba. One is to invade and occupy Cuba. The second way is to institute a total blockade, particularly of oil shipments, which would in a few months ruin the Cuban economy. The third way is to try, I repeat to try, to negotiate a face-saving agreement.

I hasten to say at once that I am not talking about and do not believe in a "Cuba-Berlin" horse trade. Cuba and Berlin are wholly different cases. Berlin is not an American missile base, it is not a base for any kind of offensive action, as Cuba is by way of becoming.

The only place that is truly comparable with Cuba is Turkey. This is the only place where there are strategic weapons right on the frontier of the Soviet Union. There are none in Norway, there are none in Iran, there are none in Pakistan. There are some in Italy. But Italy is not on the frontier of the Soviet Union.

There is another important similarity between Cuba and Turkey. The Soviet missile base in Cuba, like the U.S.-NATO base in Turkey, is of little military value. The Soviet military base in Cuba is defenseless, and the base in Turkey is all but obsolete. The two bases could be dismantled without altering the world balance of power.

If, as the first concrete step in the disarmament we've talked so much about, there could be an agreement to remove offensive weapons from fringe countries, it would not mean, of course, that Turkey would cease to be under the protection of NATO. Norway does not have strategic weapons on her soil and she is still an allied nation. Great Britain, which is a pillar of NATO, is actually liquidating U.S. missile and bomber bases on her own soil, in accordance with Western strategic doctrine.

For all these reasons I say that an agreement of this sort may be double and that there may exist a way out of the tyranny of automatic and uncontrollable events.

Kennedy ignored Lippmann's advice, just as he had the earlier suggestion by Adlai Stevenson for a possible swap of bases. At the same time he did everything possible to avoid an incident with Russia at sea. On Thursday morning, when the Soviet tanker *Bucharest* approached the quarantine line, the President gave orders to allow it to proceed after a visual inspection confirmed that it was not carrying missiles or missile parts. Later that day Kennedy personally selected the first ship to be stopped, the *Marcula.* She was an American-build ship, flying the Lebanese flag, sailing under a Panamanian registry, chartered by Russia, and manned by a Greek crew. Just after dawn the destroyer *Joseph P. Kennedy,* named for the President's older brother, stopped the *Marcula.* Five officers and men conducted a thorough, two-hour search, and when they found the cargo to pass inspection they permitted the *Marcula* to proceed to Cuba. Thus the United States had enforced the quarantine and yet had carefully refrained from an open challenge to Russian pride or national honor.

The fundamental problem still remained, however. U-2 photos taken on Thursday indicated that the Soviets were speeding work on the missile sites and that Russian technicians were uncrating and assembling IL-28 bombers that were capable of delivering nuclear weapons. The Executive Committee began discussing plans for an aerial strike and a possible invasion of Cuba the next week. Then, in the early evening, a new message from Khrushchev to Kennedy was received over the State Department teletype. In his book *Thirteen Days* Robert Kennedy describes its contents.[11]

[11] Kennedy, *Thirteen Days,* pp. 86–90. Reprinted by permission.

. . . A great deal has been written about this message, including the allegation that at the time Khrushchev wrote it he must have been so unstable or emotional that he had become incoherent. There was no question that the letter had been written by him personally. It was very long and emotional. But it was not incoherent, and the emotion was directed at the death, destruction, and anarchy that nuclear war would bring to his people and all mankind. That, he said again and again and in many different ways, must be avoided.

We must not succumb to "petty passions" or to "transient things," he wrote, but should realize that "if indeed war should break out, then it would not be in our power to stop it, for such is the logic of war. I have participated in two wars and know that war ends when it has rolled through cities and villages, everywhere sowing death and destruction." The United States, he went on to say, should not be concerned about the missiles in Cuba; they would never be used to attack the United States and were there for defensive purposes only. "You can be calm in this regard, that we are of sound mind and understand perfectly well that if we attack you, you will respond the same way. But you too will receive the same that you hurl against us. And I think that you also understand this. . . . This indicates that we are normal people, that we correctly understand and correctly evaluate the situation. Consequently, how can we permit the incorrect actions which you ascribe to us? Only lunatics or suicides, who themselves want to perish and to destroy the whole world before they die, could do this."

But he went on: "We want something quite different . . . not to destroy your country . . . but despite our ideological differences, to compete peacefully, not by military means."

There was no purpose, he said, for us to interfere with any of his ships now bound for Cuba, for they contained no weapons. He then explained why they carried no missiles: all the shipments of weapons were already within Cuba. This was the first time he had acknowledged the presence of missiles in Cuba. He made reference to the landing at the Bay of Pigs and the fact that President Kennedy had told him in Vienna that this was a mistake. He valued such frankness, wrote Khrushchev, and he, too, had similar courage, for he had acknowledged "those mistakes which had been committed during the history of our state and I not only acknowledge but sharply condemned them." (President Kennedy had told him in Vienna that he was quick to acknowledge and condemn the mistakes of Stalin and others, but he never acknowledged any mistakes of his own.)

The reason he had sent these weapons to Cuba was because the U.S. was interested in overthrowing the Cuban government, as the

U.S. had actively attempted to overthrow the Communist government in the Soviet Union after their revolution. Khrushchev and the Soviet people wished to help Cuba protect herself.

But then he went on: "If assurances were given that the President of the United States would not participate in an attack on Cuba and the blockade lifted, then the question of the removal or the destruction of the missile sites in Cuba would then be an entirely different question. Armaments bring only disasters. When one accumulates them, this damages the economy, and if one puts them to use, then they destroy people on both sides. Consequently, only a madman can believe that armaments are the principal means in the life of society. No, they are an enforced loss of human energy, and what is more are for the destruction of man himself. If people do not show wisdom, then in the final analysis they will come to a clash, like blind moles, and then reciprocal extermination will begin."

This is my proposal, he said. No more weapons to Cuba and those within Cuba withdrawn or destroyed, and you reciprocate by withdrawing your blockade and also agree not to invade Cuba. Don't interfere, he said, in a piratical way with Russian ships. "If you have not lost your self-control and sensibly conceive what this might lead to, then, Mr. President, we and you ought not to pull on the ends of the rope in which you have tied the knot of war, because the more the two of us pull, the tighter the knot will be tied. And a moment may come when that knot will be tied so tight that even he who tied it will not have the strength to untie it, and then it will be necessary to cut that knot, and what that would mean is not for me to explain to you, because you yourself understand perfectly of what terrible forces our countries dispose. Consequently, if there is no intention to tighten that knot, and thereby to doom the world to the catastrophe of thermonuclear war, then let us not only relax the forces pulling on the ends of the rope, let us take measures to untie that knot. We are ready for this." . . .

The Executive Committee studied the Khrushchev letter until the early hours of the morning. During the evening, John Scali, a television reporter, brought a fascinating story to the State Department which seemed to confirm the deal the Soviet leader was offering. An official of the Russian embassy had contacted Scali on Friday and had asked him to inform the American government that Russia would withdraw the missiles under UN supervision if the United States would lift the blockade and promise not to invade Cuba. Though a number of Kennedy's advisers expressed skepticism about the proposed deal, the Executive Committee finally agreed to submit the proposal to the State Department for further analysis and then meet again for a decision the next day.

When the group reassembled on Saturday morning, they learned that a *second* letter from Khrushchev had arrived. Written in formal, diplomatic language, it offered a very different kind of settlement.[12]

I understand your concern for the security of the United States, Mr. President, because this is the first duty of the president. However, these questions are also uppermost in our minds. The same duties rest with me as chairman of the USSR Council of Ministers. You have been worried over our assisting Cuba with arms designed to strengthen its defensive potential—precisely defensive potential—because Cuba, no matter what weapons it had, could not compare with you since these are different dimensions, the more so given up-to-date means of extermination.

Our purpose has been and is to help Cuba, and no one can challenge the humanity of our motives aimed at allowing Cuba to live peacefully and develop as its people desire. You want to relieve your country from danger and this is understandable. However, Cuba also wants this. All countries want to relieve themselves from danger. But how can we, the Soviet Union and our government, assess your actions which, in effect, mean that you have surrounded the Soviet Union with military bases, surrounded our allies with military bases, set up military bases literally around our country, and stationed your rocket weapons at them? This is no secret. High-placed American officials demonstratively declare this. Your rockets are stationed in Britain and in Italy and pointed at us. Your rockets are stationed in Turkey.

You are worried over Cuba. You say that it worries you because it lies at a distance of 90 miles across the sea from the shores of the United States. However, Turkey lies next to us. Our sentinels are pacing up and down and watching each other. Do you believe that you have the right to demand security for your country and the removal of such weapons that you qualify as offensive, while not recognizing this right for us?

You have stationed devastating rocket weapons, which you call offensive, in Turkey literally right next to us. How then does recognition of our equal military possibilities tally with such unequal relations between our great states? This does not tally at all.

It is good, Mr. President, that you agreed for our representatives

[12] U.S. Department of State, *Bulletin,* XLVII (November 12, 1962), 741–742.

to meet and begin talks, apparently with the participation of UN Acting Secretary General U Thant. Consequently, to some extent, he assumes the role of intermediary, and we believe that he can cope with the responsible mission if, of course, every side that is drawn into this conflict shows good will.

I think that one could rapidly eliminate the conflict and normalize the situation. Then people would heave a sigh of relief, considering that the statesmen who bear the responsibility have sober minds, an awareness of their responsibility, and an ability to solve complicated problems and not allow matters to slide to the disaster of war.

This is why I make this proposal: We agree to remove those weapons from Cuba which you regard as offensive weapons. We agree to do this and to state this commitment in the United Nations. Your representatives will make a statement to the effect that the United States, on its part, bearing in mind the anxiety and concern of the Soviet state, will evacuate its analogous weapons from Turkey. Let us reach an understanding on what time you and we need to put this into effect.

After this, representatives of the UN Security Council could control on-the-spot the fulfillment of these commitments. Of course, it is necessary that the Governments of Cuba and Turkey would allow these representatives to come and check fulfillment of this commitment, which each side undertakes. Apparently, it would be better if these representatives enjoyed the trust of the Security Council and ours—the United States and the Soviet Union—as well as of Turkey and Cuba. I think that it will not be difficult to find such people who enjoy the trust and respect of all interested sides.

We, having assumed this commitment in order to give satisfaction and hope to the peoples of Cuba and Turkey and to increase their confidence in their security, will make a statement in the Security Council to the effect that the Soviet Government gives a solemn pledge to respect the integrity of the frontiers and the sovereignty of Turkey, not to intervene in its domestic affairs, not to invade Turkey, not to make available its territory as a *place d'armes* for such invasion, and also will restrain those who would think of launching an aggression against Turkey either from Soviet territory or from the territory of other states bordering on Turkey.

The U.S. Government will make the same statement in the Security Council with regard to Cuba. It will declare that the United States will respect the integrity of the frontiers of Cuba, its sovereignty, undertakes not to intervene in its domestic affairs, not to invade and not to make its territory available as *place d'armes* for the invasion of Cuba, and also will restrain those who would think of launching an aggression against Cuba either from U.S.

territory or from the territory of other states bordering on Cuba.

Of course, for this we would have to reach agreement with you and to arrange for some deadline. Let us agree to give some time, but not to delay, two or three weeks, not more than a month.

The weapons on Cuba, that you have mentioned and which, as you say, alarm you, are in the hands of Soviet officers. Therefore any accidental use of them whatsoever to the detriment of the United States of America is excluded. These means are stationed in Cuba at the request of the Cuban Government and only in defensive aims. Therefore, if there is no invasion of Cuba, or an attack on the Soviet Union, or other of our allies then, of course, these means do not threaten anyone and will not threaten. For they do not pursue offensive aims. . . .

President Kennedy realized the seriousness of the new Soviet proposal. Earlier he had rejected the idea of a trade of missile bases when Stevenson had suggested it; now he felt it would be impossible to do so under pressure from the Russians. Yet he knew the Soviet proposal would appear to world opinion as a reasonable one, and that an abrupt American rejection might place the United States in a bad light. Moreover, he realized that the Turkish bases were without military value. Two months before he had ordered the Defense Department to reassess the military value of the Jupiter missiles in Turkey, and he became quite upset when he learned that no further action had been taken toward the removal of these outdated weapons.

At midday the Joint Chiefs of Staff joined the deliberations of the Executive Committee, smugly commenting that just as they had predicted, the soft blockade policy had failed. The military leaders now proposed an aerial strike against the missile bases on Monday to be followed by a full-scale invasion of Cuba. As the Executive Committee discussed this alternative, word came in that a SAM had shot down a U-2 flown by Major Rudolf Anderson, Jr., pilot of the plane that had first uncovered the missile bases. When several individuals suggested the United States retaliate with an air attack to destroy the SAM bases early the next morning, President Kennedy exerted his leadership. "We won't attack tomorrow," his brother reports him as saying. "We shall try again."

The State Department representatives submitted a legalistic

letter rejecting the Soviet demand for a missile base swap. Robert Kennedy and Ted Sorensen objected, and the Attorney General then made the shrewd suggestion that his brother ignore the second letter and respond instead to the first, in which Khrushchev had asked only for a no-invasion pledge in return for withdrawing the missiles. After a long discussion, the Executive Committee approved a draft prepared by Robert Kennedy and Sorensen. Later that evening it went out over the teletype to Moscow.[13]

Dear Mr. Chairman: I have read your letter of October 26th with great care and welcomed the statement of your desire to seek a prompt solution to the problem. The first thing that needs to be done, however, is for work to cease on offensive missile bases in Cuba and for all weapons systems in Cuba capable of offensive use to be rendered inoperable, under effective United Nations arrangements.

Assuming this is done promptly, I have given my representatives in New York instructions that will permit them to work out this weekend—in cooperation with the Acting Secretary General and your representative—an arrangement for a permanent solution to the Cuban problem along the lines suggested in your letter of October 26th. As I read your letter, the key elements of your proposals—which seem generally acceptable as I understand them—are as follows:

1. You would agree to remove these weapons systems from Cuba under appropriate United Nations observation and supervision; and undertake, with suitable safeguards, to halt the further introduction of such weapons systems into Cuba.

2. We, on our part, would agree—upon the establishment of adequate arrangements through the United Nations to ensure the carrying out and continuation of these commitments—(a) to remove promptly the quarantine measures now in effect and (b) to give assurances against an invasion of Cuba. I am confident that other nations of the Western Hemisphere would be prepared to do likewise.

If you will give your representative similar instructions, there is no reason why we should not be able to complete these arrangements and announce them to the world within a couple of days. The effect of such a settlement on easing world tensions would enable us to work toward a more general arrangement regarding "other armaments," as proposed in your second letter which you

[13] *Public Papers of the Presidents: Kennedy, 1962,* pp. 813–814.

made public. I would like to say again that the United States is very much interested in reducing tensions and halting the arms race; and if your letter signifies that you are prepared to discuss a detente affecting NATO and the Warsaw Pact, we are quite prepared to consider with our allies any useful proposals.

But the first ingredient, let me emphasize, is the cessation of work on missile sites in Cuba and measures to render such weapons inoperable, under effective international guarantees. The continuation of this threat, or a prolonging of this discussion concerning Cuba by linking these problems to the broader questions of European and world security, would surely lead to an intensification of the Cuban crisis and a grave risk to the peace of the world. For this reason I hope we can quickly agree along the lines outlined in this letter and your letter of October 26th. John F. Kennedy

While the letter was being sent to Moscow, Robert Kennedy met once again with Anatoly Dobrynin to convey personally the President's determination not to back down.[14]

I telephoned Ambassador Dobrynin about 7:15 P.M. and asked him to come to the Department of Justice. We met in my office at 7:45. I told him first that we knew that work was continuing on the missile bases in Cuba and that in the last few days it had been expedited. I said that in the last few hours we had learned that our reconnaissance planes flying over Cuba had been fired upon and that one of our U-2s had been shot down and the pilot killed. That for us was a most serious turn of events.

President Kennedy did not want a military conflict. He had done everything possible to avoid a military engagement with Cuba and with the Soviet Union, but now they had forced our hand. Because of the deception of the Soviet Union, our photographic reconnaissance planes would have to continue to fly over Cuba, and if the Cubans or Soviets shot at these planes, then we would have to shoot back. This would inevitably lead to further incidents and to escalation of the conflict, the implications of which were very grave indeed.

He said the Cubans resented the fact that we were violating Cuban air space. I replied that if we had not violated Cuban air space, we would still be believing what Khrushchev had said—that there would be no missiles placed in Cuba. In any case, I said, this matter was far more serious than the air space of Cuba—it involved the peoples of both of our countries and, in fact, people all over the globe.

The Soviet Union had secretly established missile bases in Cuba

[14] Kennedy, *Thirteen Days,* pp. 107–109. Reprinted by permission.

while at the same time proclaiming privately and publicly that this would never be done. We had to have a commitment by tomorrow that those bases would be removed. I was not giving them an ultimatum but a statement of fact. He should understand that if they did not remove those bases, we would remove them. President Kennedy had great respect for the Ambassador's country and the courage of its people. Perhaps his country might feel it necessary to take retaliatory action; but before that was over, there would be not only dead Americans but dead Russians as well.

He asked me what offer the United States was making, and I told him of the letter that President Kennedy had just transmitted to Khrushchev. He raised the question of our removing the missiles from Turkey. I said that there could be no quid pro quo or any arrangement made under this kind of threat or pressure, and that in the last analysis this was a decision that would have to be made by NATO. However, I said, President Kennedy had been anxious to remove those missiles from Turkey and Italy for a long period of time. He had ordered their removal some time ago, and it was our judgment that, within a short time after this crisis was over, those missiles would be gone.

I said President Kennedy wished to have peaceful relations between our two countries. He wished to resolve the problems that confronted us in Europe and Southeast Asia. He wished to move forward on the control of nuclear weapons. However, we could make progress on these matters only when the crisis was behind us. Time was running out. We had only a few more hours—we needed an answer immediately from the Soviet Union. I said we must have it the next day.

I returned to the White House. The President was not optimistic, nor was I. He ordered twenty-four troop-carrier squadrons of the Air Force Reserve to active duty. They would be necessary for an invasion. He had not abandoned hope, but what hope there was now rested with Khrushchev's revising his course within the next few hours. It was a hope, not an expectation. The expectation was a military confrontation by Tuesday and possibly tomorrow. . . .

At precisely nine o'clock on Sunday morning, October 28, Moscow Radio began broadcasting Khrushchev's reply to President Kennedy's letter.[15]

Dear Mr. President: I have received your message of 27 October. I express my satisfaction and thank you for the sense of proportion you have displayed and for realization of the responsi-

[15] U.S. Department of State, *Bulletin,* XLVII (November 12, 1962), 743–744.

bility which now devolves on you for the preservation of the peace of the world.

I regard with great understanding your concern and the concern of the United States people in connection with the fact that the weapons you describe as offensive are formidable weapons indeed. Both you and we understand what kind of weapons these are.

In order to eliminate as rapidly as possible the conflict which endangers the cause of peace, to give an assurance to all people who crave peace, and to reassure the American people, who, I am certain, also want peace, as do the people of the Soviet Union, the Soviet Government, in addition to earlier instructions on the discontinuation of further work on weapons constructions sites, has given a new order to dismantle the arms which you described as offensive, and to crate and return them to the Soviet Union.

Mr. President, I should like to repeat what I had already written to you in my earlier messages—that the Soviet Government has given economic assistance to the Republic of Cuba, as well as arms, because Cuba and the Cuban people were constantly under the continuous threat of an invasion of Cuba. . . .

Mr. President, I should like to say clearly once more that we could not remain indifferent to this. The Soviet Government decided to render assistance to Cuba with means of defense against aggression—only with means for defense purposes. We have supplied the defense means which you describe as offensive means. We have supplied them to prevent an attack on Cuba—to prevent rash acts.

I regard with respect and trust the statement you made in your message of 27 October 1962 that there would be no attack, no invasion of Cuba, and not only on the part of the United States, but also on the part of other nations of the Western Hemisphere, as you said in your same message. Then the motives which induced us to render assistance of such a kind to Cuba disappear.

It is for this reason that we instructed our officers—these means as I had already informed you earlier are in the hands of the Soviet officers—to take appropriate measures to discontinue construction of the aforementioned facilities, to dismantle them, and to return them to the Soviet Union. As I had informed you in the letter of 27 October, we are prepared to reach agreement to enable UN representatives to verify the dismantling of these means. Thus in view of the assurances you have given and our instructions on dismantling, there is every condition for eliminating the present conflict. . . .

President Kennedy decided not to wait for the official text of Khrushchev's reply to arrive through State Department channels. At noon, after a brief, relaxed session with the Executive Committee, he released a statement to the press which was immediately relayed to Russia by the Voice of America.[16]

I welcome Chairman Khrushchev's statesmanlike decision to stop building bases in Cuba, dismantling offensive weapons and returning them to the Soviet Union under United Nations verification. This is an important and constructive contribution to peace.

We shall be in touch with the Secretary General of the United Nations with respect to reciprocal measures to assure peace in the Caribbean area.

It is my earnest hope that the governments of the world can, with a solution of the Cuban crisis, turn their urgent attention to the compelling necessity for ending the arms race and reducing world tensions. This applies to the military confrontation between the Warsaw Pact and NATO countries as well as to other situations in other parts of the world where tensions lead to the wasteful diversion of resources to weapons of war.

The climax had passed, but the crisis dragged on for several more weeks as Fidel Castro did all he could to undermine the bargain struck by Khrushchev and Kennedy. He refused to permit United Nations officials to supervise the destruction of the missile sites, a job carried out by Soviet technicians. U Thant failed to move Castro, despite several trips to Havana, and Khrushchev finally had to send Anastas Mikoyan, the Kremlin's chief troubleshooter, to Cuba to deal with Fidel. Castro snubbed Mikoyan; urged on by the Chinese Communists, he continued to block on-site inspection of the dismantling process. Finally the United States had to rely on visual inspection at sea as Russian captains pulled back tarpaulins to reveal the missiles lashed to the decks of their ships. Eventually the Navy reported that forty-two MRBMs, apparently all the missiles Russia had placed in Cuba, had been withdrawn.

Only the IL-28 bombers remained. Castro claimed these Ilyushins were a gift from Khrushchev that could not be reclaimed. Khrushchev tried to hold out on the bombers, claiming they were not part of the missile deal, but Kennedy remained firm; finally Mikoyan won Castro's reluctant consent to return them to the Soviets. On November 20 a smiling Ambassador

[16] *Public Papers of the Presidents: Kennedy, 1962*, p. 815.

Dobrynin again called on Robert Kennedy to present a letter from Khrushchev to President Kennedy agreeing to remove the bombers. At a press conference later that same day, John Kennedy issued a statement that marked the formal end of the crisis.[17]

. . . I have today been informed by Chairman Khrushchev that all of the IL-28 bombers now in Cuba will be withdrawn in 30 days. He also agrees that these planes can be observed and counted as they leave. Inasmuch as this goes a long way towards reducing the danger which faced this hemisphere 4 weeks ago, I have this afternoon instructed the Secretary of Defense to lift our naval quarantine.

In view of this action, I want to take this opportunity to bring the American people up to date on the Cuban crisis and to review the progress made thus far in fulfilling the understandings between Soviet Chairman Khrushchev and myself as set forth in our letters of October 27 and 28. Chairman Khrushchev, it will be recalled, agreed to remove from Cuba all weapons systems capable of offensive use, to halt the further introduction of such weapons into Cuba, and to permit appropriate United Nations observation and supervision of these commitments. We on our part agreed that once these adequate arrangements for verification had been established we would remove our naval quarantine and give assurances against an invasion of Cuba.

The evidence to date indicates that all known offensive missile sites in Cuba have been dismantled. The missiles and their associated equipment have been loaded on Soviet ships. And our inspection at sea of these departing ships has confirmed that the number of missiles reported by the Soviet Union as having been brought into Cuba, which closely corresponded to our own information, has now been removed. In addition, the Soviet Government has stated that all nuclear weapons have been withdrawn from Cuba and no offensive weapons will be reintroduced.

Nevertheless, important parts of the understanding of October 27th and 28th remain to be carried out. The Cuban Government has not yet permitted the United Nations to verify whether all offensive weapons have been removed, and no lasting safeguards have yet been established against the future introduction of offensive weapons back into Cuba.

Consequently, if the Western Hemisphere is to continue to be protected against offensive weapons, this Government has no choice but to pursue its own means of checking on military activities in Cuba. The importance of our continued vigilance is underlined by

[17] *Public Papers of the Presidents: Kennedy, 1962,* pp. 830–831.

our identification in recent days of a number of Soviet ground combat units in Cuba, although we are informed that these and other Soviet units were associated with the protection of offensive weapons systems, and will also be withdrawn in due course.

I repeat, we would like nothing better than adequate international arrangements for the task of inspection and verification in Cuba, and we are prepared to continue our efforts to achieve such arrangements. Until that is done, difficult problems remain. As for our part, if all offensive weapons systems are removed from Cuba and kept out of the hemisphere in the future, under adequate verification and safeguards, and if Cuba is not used for the export of aggressive Communist purposes, there will be peace in the Caribbean. And as I said in September, "we shall neither initiate nor permit aggression in this hemisphere."

We will not, of course, abandon the political, economic, and other efforts of this hemisphere to halt subversion from Cuba nor our purpose and hope that the Cuban people shall some day be truly free. But these policies are very different from any intent to launch a military invasion of the island.

In short, the record of recent weeks shows real progress and we are hopeful that further progress can be made. The completion of the commitment on both sides and the achievement of a peaceful solution to the Cuban crisis might well open the door to the solution of other outstanding problems.

May I add this final thought in this week of Thanksgiving: there is much for which we can be grateful as we look back to where we stood only 4 weeks ago—the unity of this hemisphere, the support of our allies, and the calm determination of the American people. These qualities may be tested many more times in this decade, but we have increased reason to be confident that those qualities will continue to serve the cause of freedom with distinction in the years to come.

II

Initial Reactions to the Crisis

IN THE FIRST year after the crisis, John F. Kennedy's handling of the Cuban situation won the warm approval of the American people. Journalists were generous in their praise of his conduct, commenting on the nice combination of flexibility and toughness that characterized his response to the Soviet threat. Kennedy's hard-nosed, self-consciously pragmatic style had attracted many Americans at the start of his presidency, but his early actions had proved disappointing. Would-be admirers were dismayed by his inept handling of Congress, by his ruthless tactics in rolling back steel prices, and by his failure of judgment in the Bay of Pigs invasion. In the Cuban missile crisis they finally found the Kennedy they had been looking for, and the result was adulation on a national scale. Public opinion polls showed that nearly 80 per cent of the American people approved of his conduct as President, and journalists added him to the pantheon, comparing him to Wilson and Roosevelt. Yet even amidst this chorus of praise, a few individuals voiced their misgivings about Kennedy's brinksmanship and raised issues that would form the crux of a developing scholarly controversy over the Cuban missile crisis.

STEWART ALSOP AND CHARLES BARTLETT

Eyeball to Eyeball

The most influential of the journalistic accounts of the missile crisis appeared in the Saturday Evening Post *in early December 1962. Stewart Alsop, long a leading advocate of a firm foreign policy toward Russia, and Charles Bartlett, known to be a close personal friend of the President, combined to write an inside account of how the Kennedy administration had formulated its policy. Bartlett's intimacy with the President led most observers to assume that this was a semiofficial version of the crisis; and the editors of the* Post *boasted that the authors had privileged access to State Department and White House files. It is doubtful, however, that the President approved of the authors' slanted portrayal of Stevenson's role in policy-making, which touched off an embarrassing public controversy.*

"WE'RE EYEBALL to eyeball, and I think the other fellow just blinked." Those words, spoken in a casual aside by Secretary of State Dean Rusk at the climactic moment of the Cuban crisis, deserve to rank with such immortal phrases as "Don't fire till you see the whites of their eyes," and "We have met the enemy and they are ours." For Rusk's words epitomize a great moment in American history.

Stewart Alsop and Charles Bartlett, "In Time of Crisis," *Saturday Evening Post,* CCXXXV (December 8, 1962), 16–20. Reprinted by permission of the authors.

President Kennedy, on November 14, said that the Cuban crisis might well mark "an important turning point in the history of relations between East and West." At the moment Rusk spoke, the turning point had come, and the essential nature of the Cold War was changed in a way that will affect all our lives.

For some days a handful of men, operating largely in secret, held our destinies in their hands. The roles these men played—and especially the yet unreported role played by United Nations Ambassador Adlai Stevenson—make a fascinating story. But what follows is not another day-to-day recapitulation of the Cuban crisis, which has not yet completely run its course. It is, instead, an attempt to extract from the high drama of the crisis its inner meaning, as that meaning is understood by the men who steered the course of the United States in the shadow of nuclear war.

The best way to understand the crisis is to concentrate on certain untold episodes of the drama which illuminate its true significance. Let us start with that moment when Dean Rusk made his memorable remark.

The blockade of Cuba which President Kennedy had announced in his historic speech on Monday night, October 22, went into effect at 10 A.M. on Wednesday, October 24. At that hour the members of the Executive Committee of the National Security Council filed into the Cabinet Room of the White House.

NINE MEN AROUND THE TABLE

The Executive Committee had been officially created only a few days before by the President, but it had already achieved the Washington distinction of an abbreviation—ExComm. Nine men sat around the table that Wednesday morning.

The President, his lips compressed and his manner more absorbed than usual, sat at the head of the table. Insistently he asked questions, and when the answers were slow in coming, he tapped his front teeth impatiently with his forefinger, a characteristic gesture. John McCone, chief of the Central Intelligence Agency, started the meeting, as he started all the ExComm meetings, with an intelligence briefing.

Others around the table were Rusk, Defense Secretary Robert McNamara, Treasury Secretary Douglas Dillon, Attorney General Robert Kennedy, General Maxwell Taylor, Chairman of the Joint Chiefs, Presidential Assistant McGeorge Bundy, and the President's speechwriter and sounding board, Theodore Sorensen. These are the nine men who made—and who in the future will make—the live-or-die decisions when the chips are down.

The atmosphere in the Cabinet Room that morning was calm but somber. The President had said that the blockade was only a first step, and that, if the Soviet missiles were not removed, "further action" would be taken. Further action might be a total blockade, air strikes against the missile bases, or even an invasion of Cuba. Given such action, few in that room had any doubt that the Soviets would react violently, in Berlin or elsewhere. Already, the world was on a lower rung of the ladder that might lead to nuclear war.

That morning, about two dozen Soviet ships were steaming toward Cuba. Khrushchev had denounced the blockade as an "act of piracy," and in the UN, Zorin had said that no Russian ship would submit to search. One of the ExComm members recalls: "There wasn't one of us in that room who wasn't pretty sure that in a few hours we'd have to sink one of those Russian ships."

"SEND THAT ORDER IN THE CLEAR"

Before that happened, the President was determined to give his opposite number time to think. He ordered that the Navy screen around Cuba should not intercept a Russian ship until absolutely necessary. "Send that order in the clear," he said, perhaps recalling his own troubles as a junior naval officer with complex code forms. "I want it to go through without delay."

The day wore on. Reports came in which indicated that some of the Soviet ships appeared to have changed course, and that others had gone dead in the ocean. No one recalls a precise and jubilant moment when it became apparent that Khrushchev's ships were not going to challenge the American blockade after all. But at some point that afternoon Dean Rusk expressed the growing conviction of the group when he nudged McGeorge Bundy and made his "eyeball to eyeball" remark.

The blink was then no more than a mere dip of the Soviet eyelash, and for four more days the two great nuclear powers remained "eyeball to eyeball." But that first small Soviet blink was a great moment in history all the same.

Its meaning was later summed up by the President's brother, Attorney General Robert Kennedy: "We all agreed in the end that if the Russians were ready to go to nuclear war over Cuba, they were ready to go to nuclear war, and that was that. So we might as well have the showdown then as six months later." But Khrushchev's final and unmistakable blink did not come until the next Sunday. One of the ExComm members calls that day "Sunny Sunday" and, the day before, "Black Saturday."

On Saturday morning, October 27, the evidence of Soviet intentions pointed both ways. The Soviet ships had indeed turned back. But U-2 reconnaissance planes over Cuba had shown work on the Soviet missile sites proceeding on a crash basis. The night before, the famous, still-secret Friday night letter from Khrushchev to Kennedy had arrived. It was a curious document, which also pointed both ways.

The letter, in four sections, began arriving at the State Department toward eleven o'clock in the evening. The first and third parts came first. The President read them, remarked that he saw nothing new in them, and went to bed, leaving instructions not to be awakened unless there was something really new in the other two parts.

The President was not awakened. The letter was long, rambling, emotional and contradictory. For the first time Khrushchev officially acknowledged the existence of his strategic missile sites in Cuba. But a missile, he said, was like a pistol—

it could be used to defend or attack, depending on the intentions of the user. His intentions, he piously maintained, were purely defensive, the missiles were under his control alone, and they would be used only in defense against aggression.

In a passage which bore the unmistakable Khrushchev imprint, he compared the President and himself to two men tugging on a rope with a knot in the middle. If both went on tugging, the knot could only be cut "with a sword," Khrushchev warned. "Mr. President," he wrote in effect, "if you will stop tugging on your end, I will stop tugging on mine."

This sounded hopeful—but what did it really mean? The letter was purposely Delphic. It could be read as a veiled offer to remove the Cuban missiles in exchange for an American commitment not to invade Cuba. It could also be read as a not-very-veiled threat of nuclear retaliation against any American attack on Cuba.

U-2 PICTURES SHOW RED MISSILES

Thus, when ExComm met at ten on Black Saturday, the evidence was mixed. Khrushchev might be looking for a way out. But he might also have decided to play it rough, by seeking to confront the United States with an accomplished fact. The U-2 pictures showed that the missiles would be fully operational in a few days. If Khrushchev could delay a showdown for those few days, we would be looking down the gun barrel of a fully operational Soviet missile complex 90 miles from our shores.

On the morning of Black Saturday two pieces of evidence came in to suggest that Khrushchev had decided to play it rough. At ten o'clock still another Khrushchev letter was broadcast over Moscow radio. In it Khrushchev upped the ante, demanding the dismantlement of the American-controlled missile bases in Turkey in exchange for the removal of the Cuban missiles. This was bad news. It suggested that Khrushchev was trying to play for time, against the approaching day when his missiles would be in place.

Worse news followed soon. Shortly after 10 A.M. one of our U-2's was shot down over eastern Cuba by one of the newly installed Soviet surface-to-air missiles, known as the SA-2. This was the first time an SA-2 had been fired in Cuba. These sophisticated weapons were certainly under Soviet control. They could be used to blind the eyes of the American intelligence while Khrushchev played for time.

One of those present at the Saturday morning meeting recalls it as "the worst meeting we ever had." For the first time there were signs of short tempers and frayed nerves. The meeting broke up for a late lunch. At 4 P.M. ExComm reconvened, this time in the elegant Oval Room of the White House. The President presided in his rocker, while his advisers sat uncomfortably about on the white-and-gold French furniture.

Again the news was bad. McNamara reported that two low-flying reconnaissance planes had been fired on, seemingly confirming Khrushchev's intention to play it rough. The moment of decision had arrived.

On one point all present agreed. The Soviet missiles had to be removed or destroyed before they were operational. The next Tuesday, only three days away, was fixed as the latest date for destroying Khrushchev's missiles and antiaircraft rockets with an air strike. The strike might have to come even earlier. An air strike against Cuba would clearly be the next rung on the ladder to nuclear war. Russians as well as Cubans would be killed, and a violent reaction from Khrushchev seemed certain. Perhaps there was still time to avoid that next rung on the ladder.

THE ATTORNEY GENERAL'S SUGGESTION

It was Bobby Kennedy who suggested what has since been dubbed "the Trollope ploy." The Victorian novelist Anthony Trollope had a standard scene: A young man with no marital intentions makes some imprudent gesture toward a marriage-hungry maiden—he squeezes her hand, even kisses her. The lady instantly seizes the opportunity by shyly accepting what she chooses to interpret as a proposal of marriage.

Robert Kennedy suggested that the President simply interpret the Friday night letter as a proposal for an acceptable deal, ignoring all the other implications. The President agreed.

"If I understand you correctly, . . ." he wrote, then the deal was on. If Khrushchev would remove his offensive weapons from Cuba, under suitable conditions, the blockade would end, and Cuba would not be invaded.

The letter was sent at 8 P.M. At the same time other means, which are still secret, were used to make abundantly plain to Khrushchev the nature of the choice he faced. "K had not very many hours to make up his mind," says one ExComm member, "and he knew it."

As the meeting broke up near midnight, the President remarked that "now it could go either way." All those present knew if it went the wrong way, we might be close to nuclear war. Not one of them really expected what happened on Sunny Sunday. John McCone heard of Khrushchev's Sunday morning offer—to remove the bases on the terms stated by the President—while he was driving back from nine o'clock Mass. "I could hardly believe my ears," he recalls.

This was, of course, the final, unmistakable blink. It proved once and for all that Khrushchev was *not* "ready to go to nuclear war over Cuba." He is still not ready to do so. It is important to understand what this means—and what it does not mean.

KHRUSHCHEV: ZIGZAGS AND RETREATS

It does not mean that all danger of nuclear war has passed. Nor does it mean that a showdown policy will always force Khrushchev to retreat—on this point the President, in his post-mortems with his advisers, has been insistent. It *does* mean that Khrushchev is a good Leninist—that he has what Lenin called the "ability to make all necessary practical compromises . . . zigzags and retreats." In short, if we respond firmly where our vital interests are threatened, Khrushchev will choose "zigzags and retreats" rather than nuclear war. This we now know and in this way the essential pattern of the cold war has been altered.

What, then, did Khrushchev hope to achieve in Cuba? How did he hope to achieve it, and why did he fail? Two small but significant scenes in the drama throw a useful light on the answers to these questions. Scene One is played in low key, and unless you understand its meaning, it is a rather dull little scene, which any good director would cut out of a play.

McGeorge Bundy is dining quietly in his pleasant house in the northwest section of Washington. The telephone rings, and when Bundy picks it up he recognizes the familiar voice of Ray Cline, chief of intelligence for the CIA. The carefully cryptic conversation that ensues goes about like this:

CLINE: "Those things we've been worrying about—it looks as though we've really got something."

BUNDY: "You're sure?"

CLINE: "Yes. It looks like we're around seven hundred miles, maybe more."

BUNDY: "OK. I'll handle it at my end."

Early the next morning, October 16, Bundy is in the President's bedroom to give him the most disturbing information any President has received since Pearl Harbor.

Scene Two occurs the same day, when Nikita Khrushchev receives the newly arrived American ambassador, Foy Kohler, in his Kremlin office. Khrushchev is genial, and on the subject of Cuba warmly reassuring.

The announcement of the establishment of a Russian fishing port in Cuba, he says, seems to have caused the President some sort of political trouble. He was furious when he heard about the announcement, he insists. He was vacationing in the Crimea at the time—if he had been in Moscow, the announcement would never have been made. Soviet purposes in Cuba are, of course, wholly defensive, and the last thing in the world he wants to do is to embarrass the President on the eve of the elections.

The brilliant, gnomelike Kohler listens impassively, then returns to the embassy to report the substance of the conversation to the President, as Khrushchev knew he would do. Thanks to Bundy's bedroom report, the President already knows that the Soviets are placing missiles in Cuba capable of destroying American cities.

The meaning of these two small scenes can be summarized in two sentences. First, the Soviets tried to lay a trap for the United States in Cuba, using maximum duplicity to that end, in order to achieve maximum surprise. Second, we caught them at it.

The objective of the trap was both political and strategic. If the trap had been successful, our missile warning system would have been by-passed, and the whole strategic balance overturned. But the President and most of his advisers put the main emphasis on the political objective. "If they'd got away with this one," says one member of ExComm, "we'd have been a paper tiger, a second-class power."

COSTLY ATTEMPT TO DUPE U.S.

The laying of the trap represented a huge Soviet investment —175 ships, more than 6,000 men and upward of three quarters of a billion dollars. Planning for the operation started last spring, at the latest. There were two essential elements in the plan. One was a systematic attempt to dupe the American leaders into believing that the Soviets had no intention of doing what they intended to do.

Khrushchev's assurance to Kohler was only one in a series of attempts to deceive. The most elaborate attempt came in early October, when Khrushchev and Mikoyan called in Georgi Bolshakov, a subordinate officer in the Soviet Embassy in Washington, who had arranged for Khrushchev's son-in-law, Aleksei Adzhubei, to interview the President. Khrushchev told Bolshakov that his only intention was to give Cuba defensive weapons. Mikoyan interrupted to say emphatically that it was important for the President to understand that only air-defense missiles, incapable of reaching American targets, were being provided. Bolshakov took all this down in pencil in a little blue notebook. But by the time the contents of Bolshakov's notebook reached the President, the President already knew that Mikoyan's promise was false.

Bolshakov was by no means the only instrument of duplicity.

In early October Soviet Ambassador Dobrynin flatly assured a Cabinet officer that no missiles capable of reaching the U.S. would be placed in Cuba. He gave the same assurance on October 13 to Chester Bowles. Similar assurances were conveyed in an official statement of the Soviet Government, and by Andrei Gromyko to the President on October 18, two days after Bundy's bedroom report.

In short, an essential part of the Soviet plan was to mislead the President of the United States. The attempt failed for two reasons.

First, the Soviet assurances were not wholly believed. In the intelligence community the majority view was that the Soviets would not risk placing strategic missiles in Cuba. The only major dissenter was CIA Director John McCone. In an "in-house" paper for the CIA, written on his honeymoon in September, McCone stated his conviction that the Russians planned to put long-range missiles in Cuba. But even those in the majority had no inclination to trust the Russians' word.

Second, the U-2 flights continued over Cuba, weather permitting, on a biweekly basis, and on October 14 a U-2 took the photographs which caused Cline's cryptic call to Bundy. Here we come to the great mystery of the drama. Why wasn't that U-2 shot down?

One essential element in Khrushchev's plan was to have his antiaircraft rockets ready to shoot down our U-2's *before* his missiles were in place. A U-2 was actually shot down on October 27. But that was two weeks too late—the plot had already been discovered. Why weren't the Russian antiaircraft rockets operational two weeks earlier?

No one really knows. "Somehow the Soviet operation got out of phase," the CIA men say. We Americans can thank God that it did, for otherwise there would have been no reason for Bundy's report to the President, and the outcome might have been unthinkable.

The five harried, secret days which intervened between Bundy's bedroom report and the President's speech to the nation on Monday, October 22, were best summed up by one of the actors in the drama: "At first we divided into hawks and doves, but by the end a rolling consensus had developed, and except for Adlai, we had all ended up as dawks or hoves."

DEBATE: AIR STRIKE OR BLOCKADE?

The hawks favored an air strike to eliminate the Cuban missile bases, either with or without warning. At first the hawks were in a majority. Their number included McCone, Dillon, former Secretary of State Dean Acheson, who was brought in as an elder statesman, General Taylor, all the service chiefs, and eventually Bundy. Secretary Rusk's position does not come through loud and clear—he appears to have been a dawk or a hove from the start. By this the insiders meant that the hawks became less bellicose and the doves became tougher, and they merged as something in between.

The doves opposed the air strike and favored a blockade. Their number included McNamara, Robert Kennedy and Robert Lovett, another elder statesman. Former Ambassador to Russia Llewellyn Thompson must also be counted among the doves, for he warned that Khrushchev must not suddenly be faced with precipitate action to which he might respond on impulse.

Robert Kennedy, surprisingly, was the leading dove. He argued passionately that an air strike against Cuba would be a Pearl Harbor in reverse and contrary to all American traditions. Acheson was the most hawklike of the hawks. He argued that the Pearl Harbor analogy was totally inexact, since the President had repeatedly given warning that the United States would not permit an offensive-weapons buildup in Cuba.

By Saturday, October 20, the rolling consensus had developed. Secretary McNamara, who gave a "brilliant architectural presentation" at the ExComm meeting on Saturday, was the chief instrument of the consensus. The United States, he argued, must "maintain the options"—a favorite McNamara phrase. The blockade would be a first step. The option of destroying the missiles, and even of invading Cuba, would definitely be maintained. If the blockade did not cause Khrushchev to back down, then the missiles could and would be destroyed before they became operational.

STEVENSON'S DISSENTING VIEW

Only Adlai Stevenson, who flew down from New York on Saturday, dissented from the ExComm consensus. There is disagreement in retrospect about what Stevenson really wanted. "Adlai wanted a Munich," says a nonadmiring official who learned of his proposal. "He wanted to trade the Turkish, Italian and British missile bases for the Cuban bases."

The Stevenson camp maintains that Stevenson was only willing to discuss Guantánamo and the European bases with the Communists after a neutralization of the Cuban missiles. But there seems to be no doubt that he preferred political negotiation to the alternative of military action. White House aide Arthur Schlesinger was assigned to write the uncompromising speech which Stevenson delivered at the UN on Tuesday, and tough-minded John McCloy was summoned from a business conference in Germany to work with Stevenson in the UN negotiations.

In any case, the President heard Stevenson out politely, and then gave his semifinal approval to the McNamara plan. He gave his final approval Sunday. That night, while the issue was still being debated, the President made a prediction: "Whatever way the decision goes, those who were against it will be the lucky ones."

Happily the President's prediction was inaccurate. Dean Acheson has generally said that in retrospect the final decision was the right one, and the other ex-hawks agree. By Sunny Sunday, when Khrushchev finally blinked, we were in a far better position to strike at the Cuban bases than we would have been a week before. The Organization of American States and the NATO allies were solidly behind us and, above all, the record of Soviet duplicity was plain for all to see.

The real meaning of that duplicity was summed up this way by one of the members of ExComm: "Now we know where we stand with these people. They're gangsters—and you can't trust a word they say."

As this suggests, none of the men around the President—least of all the President himself—believes that the "important turning point" of which the President spoke means that the Communist tiger is about to change his stripes.

"You've got to remember," one of the wisest Presidential advisers says, "Khrushchev must have been under very heavy pressure, to take the risk he took. He is still under that pressure, and it may become heavier." Yet if you add up all the pluses of the Cuban affair—the unanimous support of the Latin Americans, the stanchness of our European allies, the disillusionment of the neutrals, the exposure of Communist duplicity—they heavily outweigh the minuses.

Some of the pluses are intangible. One is the inner sense of confidence among the handful of men with the next-to-ultimate responsibility. "The Bay of Pigs thing was badly planned and never really thought out," says one of them. "This was different. We knew the facts, knew each other and we thought it through, right to the end."

As always, the ultimate responsibility was the President's. John F. Kennedy is not an outwardly emotional man, and in the bad days there were few signs that he was passing through the loneliest moments of his lonely job. Once he astonished his wife when he called her at midday and asked her to join him for a walk. Another time he insisted, uncharacteristically, that the children be brought back from Virginia to join him in the White House. But he never lost his sense of humor. On the Sunday of Khrushchev's big blink, he made a wry remark to his brother Bobby: "Perhaps this is the night I should go to the theater." No doubt he had Ford's Theater in mind.

"HE NEVER LOST HIS NERVE"

There was something else he never lost. "Once or twice," an ExComm member recalls, "the President lost his temper on minor matters. But he never lost his nerve." This must be counted a huge intangible plus. A President's nerve is the essential factor when the two great nuclear powers are "eyeball to eyeball."

There is one final plus. We now know that Khrushchev is a realist as well as a Communist, that when doctrine conflicts with realities, the realities will govern his conduct. This knowledge holds out hope. The hope is not for a lasting, peaceful world settlement, for that will not happen so long as Communists are Communists. The hope is, instead, that somehow the world will rock along without the kind of war that might destroy us all. That is, after all, a good deal to hope for, and that was the real meaning of Nikita Khrushchev's blink.

ROGER HAGAN

Righteous Realpolitik

Walter Lippmann, in his October 25 column, had first raised the critical question of whether it had been wise or even necessary to take the missile issue to the brink of nuclear war without a resort to traditional diplomacy. As the tension eased, other observers began to question the way Kennedy had dealt with the crisis. The keenest criticism came from a group of scholars in the Northeast led by sociologist David Riesman, who in 1960 had formed Committees of Correspondence (later Councils for Correspondence), modeled after Sam Adam's radical cells in the Revolutionary War era. Roger Hagan, the editor of the group's newsletter, The Correspondent, *wrote a probing critique of American policy for the journal* Dissent *in early 1963.*

THE FAN-MAGAZINE treatment of the handful of men in the President's kitchen cabinet who steered the nation through the crisis of the Cuban blockade has become embarrassing. Washington had already become the Hollywood of the upper middle class, and fashion magazines now have their girls model sweaters playing touch football. Through the slick media, every mannerism of the first family and other administration personalities reverber-

Roger Hagan, "Triumph or Tragedy," *Dissent,* X (Winter 1963), 13–26. Reprinted by permission.

ates through the suburbs of the land. Most accounts of the crisis weeks, therefore, simply carried on in the *Photoplay* tradition. Analysis of the Cuban affair since the crisis has been mostly in terms of operational style and technique, seldom substance—except in the matter of Stevenson. But even there, where a substantive question was raised, it was treated as a case of social obtuseness. Nobody had told Adlai that the hardnosed look was the new style, so the poor fellow came wearing his old attire: nothing a quick trip to the tailor couldn't fix. By and large it has come to be the *manner* of the operators in Washington that is important to most college-educated Americans, so they were pushovers for the Cuban blockade. It was an exciting vicarious experience, and not one to be questioned. Who questions the premises of *Ben Hur?* The result, of course, was that a lot of flimsy arguments were swallowed whole.

There are unquestionably some impressive aspects of the President's performance. If we grant the existence of a crisis demanding immediate and dangerous action, we can celebrate that Kennedy chose the moderate and cautious course of a naval blockade on arms shipments. Given the American, and his, attitude toward the Castro regime, we can admire his attempt to place a defensive, nonprovocative interpretation on the arms buildup which was proceeding all summer long, and feel sorry that his interpretation finally trapped him out on a limb. Given the history of our slow or negative responses to Khrushchev's soft initiatives and our quick belligerence at his hard ones, we can be glad the President took Khrushchev up on his curious, still-secret letter of Friday night even after the tougher one of Saturday had arrived. The diplomatic gamble paid off and brought the crisis to an end. Furthermore, I for one am grateful to Robert Kennedy for saying that his brother would never be responsible for a Pearl Harbor. He is probably the only person in Washington who does not have to wait and see which way the wind blows before he speaks his mind. Maybe he will save us all, depending, of course, on what is on his mind.

But it is disturbing that he had to say it. Where were our academic friends? Where were the great liberals? Where was Fulbright? The closer one looks, the more disturbing it is. In fact, a lot of alarming limitations have to be granted before one can locate what one admires in the conduct of the Cuban blockade affair. The question is, can we afford to grant them?

We often say that "Kennedy's hands were tied," but one must ask, "Tied by what?" One reads with uneasiness that "there was some acceptance [in Washington circles] of the contention that political considerations had played more than a minor part in the blockade decision," that "the President, and many of those closest to him in the White House, are known to have been smarting under Republican jibes at his 'indecisiveness' in dealing with Premier Fidel Castro and his Soviet allies" (*New York Times,* October 23). To the extent that such considerations were pivotal, it appears that the President was confronted with two alternative kinds of risk: he could take a course that would risk war, or a course that would risk his political future and that of his party. Since things turned out well, it seems to be assumed that he chose the right risk. One cannot let this situation go without criticism, regardless of what one can realistically expect. Is this the kind of judgment that the times demanded?

Kennedy's reaction, while moderate, was within the American consensus. His greatness was the kind that sums up America while keeping it from tripping over its own feet. It was American popular thought in a nutshell when he said that the worst thing we could do would be to do nothing. But there is another kind of greatness that might have been evoked: that which not only epitomizes the weaknesses, strengths, and internal conflicts of a society but finds a new resolution for them, to carry the society beyond itself to a higher level of perception. This we have not been granted, and regardless of the urgency of the matter, the quality in question is apparently not to be called forth. One focuses, fascinated, on the figure of Kennedy struggling with great problems and threats, one man in battle with vast forces, and the word "greatness" comes easily. But one turns back to one's fellow countrymen and finds them neither able to perceive the world differently nor urged to do so, unquestioning of the causes and objects of their belligerence, unlikely to behave differently or more humanely in the future. If anything, their most inappropriate habits of response have been confirmed.

They know now that playing "chicken" pays, and the half-hearted disclaimers of the President and his aides and journalists will not deceive them. They were left to believe that the President endorsed the ignorant abuse of the Monroe Doctrine of *Time* and the Congress, and further that such unilateral declarations constitute international law. And the atmosphere of snapping nerves, which *The Economist* reported during the blockade, continues. It alone reaches new levels in each crisis.

REASONS AND REASONS

The official explanations of the situation disclosed the extent to which the entire justification for risking war had come to rest on shoddy and misleading argumentation. It was hardly an elevation of public discourse. The key argument that the missiles in Cuba seriously altered the strategic balance is, as we shall see, a dubious one to those familiar with the logistics of the matter. Yet at the height of the crisis the Pentagon, or by some reports the White House, passed along, through the *New York Times'* trusting John Finney, an explanation for its concern about the missiles so obscure and confused as to give the impression that not only were we worried about losing our first-strike capacity (and one of the headlines said precisely that, which must have given Marshal Malinovsky a new ax to wield over Khrushchev's head) but that we were even concerned that our retaliatory second strike would be reduced below the deterrent level. Joseph Alsop had made the same comment the day before, warning that, if things proceeded as they were, we might be able to get off "only" fifty warheads at the Russians, and assuming that this would not deter them. It may be that the prospect of losing fifty cities would not deter Joseph Alsop, but the Russians are something else. More to the point, however, the figure was patently wrong, as will be seen.

A few weeks later, Stewart Alsop gave what was meant to be the official McNamara view of the matter in the first of his two controversial *Saturday Evening Post* articles. The stir over the second of these (containing the "Adlai wanted a Munich" charge) has led critics to ignore the first, which as an administration apologia was actually the more important. It justified our urgent maneuver by saying that our deterrent still depended upon SAC bombers and the Ballistic Missile Early Warning System, a combination alleged to be easily broken by Cuban missiles, and that our missile strength was still negligible at the time of the crisis. This falsehood was contradicted by official sources shortly thereafter, but the Stevenson affair obscured the contradictions which undermined the argument from military peril.

The whole question of why the missiles were assumed to be offensive simply because they could reach into our heartland, while our soft intermediate range missiles in Turkey should be assumed to be defensive, never surpassed the level of "because *we* know our intentions are not aggressive." This smug answer was made on the Senate floor by Senator Sparkman (to Senator Chavez), in the Pentagon booklet written for the U.S. troops to calm any possible misgivings about their imminent invasion duty, and in Hanson W. Baldwin's retrospective analysis (*New York Times,* November 7) of the "debate on U.S. bases": "The real measure of the overseas base therefore is its purpose. The United States contention, shared by its allies, has always been that its overseas bases were established solely in answer to Communist aggressive expansionism and at the request of the countries concerned." All made the assumption that the Russian missiles were in Cuba against the will of most Cubans, solely as part of the Soviets' strategic network, and symbolized the enslavement of the Cuban people to an alien power. It was the argument of the demagogue, attempting not to explain but to cut off discussion by playing upon prejudice. The entire discussion had roughly the dignity of the use of the word "nigger."

Another major premise of the President's speech was that the Soviet minister had lied to him. The case for claiming deception in the Gromyko interview was far from clear. The worst statements that Kennedy could attribute to Gromyko were that Soviet assistance to Cuba "pursued solely the purpose of contributing to the defense capabilities of Cuba," that "training by Soviet specialists of Cuban nationals in handling defensive armaments was by no means offensive," and that "if it were otherwise, the Soviet Government would never become involved in rendering such assistance." Was this all false in the same way our claim not to have sent a photo-reconnaissance U-2 over Russia had been false? Kennedy could argue that he had already made the distinction between ground-to-air missiles (defensive) and ground-to-ground missiles (offensive), but the distinction breaks down when applied to any other missile-equipped nation and Gromyko may have been rejecting it. For the Russians, the operative terms may have been in the September 11 statement of the Soviet Government that it had such powerful rockets in Russia that there was "no need to search for sites for them beyond the boundaries of the Soviet Union." They could claim not to have put the missiles in for their own purposes but at the request of the Cuban government, and that they were therefore defensive in intent. Senator Sparkman and most of his colleagues could hardly object to that reasoning.

There is a more clear-cut case of deception in the assurances made to Robert Kennedy by the Soviet embassy official which Alsop and Bartlett report in their partly discredited article; but the President did not refer to this, probably because it was more a "leak" than an official statement, the sort of deception that all governments including our own find useful. There is no reason to doubt that the Soviet leadership wanted to avoid a fuss in America about their missiles until after the latter were operational and the elections were over, and might resort to false leaks to keep one from developing. There is nonetheless something questionable about an attempt to discredit a major representative of Soviet leadership with an internally weak charge for the purpose of developing a righteous rage among the American people.

There are reasons and reasons. If the real reason for our being disturbed over putting Soviet missiles in Cuba was that it constituted, as the first meeting of the National Security Council assumed, "a left hook designed to make Khrushchev look tougher when he comes at us in November, presumably on Berlin"—and this would seem to be the best explanation for Khrushchev's part in the Soviet decision—then one would wish we might have argued the case on those grounds rather than cooking up the pretense that "offensive weapons" can be strictly so defined and spicing it with a mock rage about "deception." The first would have been somewhat cynical but at least honest; the way we chose to handle it will prove to be more vicious than an open cynicism. Most Americans were quite ready to support an aggressive action for the sole purpose of not allowing Khrushchev to strengthen his hand for the Berlin negotiations, and it would have been possible for those who opposed the diplomacy of righteousness and unilateral action to have helped the nation measure the gains from this procedure against the gains from designing a response to promote international legality. The legalists might have lost the argument, but the argument would at least have been to the point.

RIGHTEOUS REALPOLITIK

This is the first tragedy of the Cuban affair; the discussion was never to the point, neither during nor after the crisis. If ever an incident demanded that the role of cheap politics in dictating or restricting policy be isolated, it was the Cuban missile showdown. Yet among the men in the top ranks of the administration, none of them cheap politicians, there is probably not one who could separate out the several kinds of motive and say which most moved him or his chief into what history will probably record as a panic reaction. The point is not that the National Security Council consciously contrived a false rationale while pursuing hidden purposes. Politics, toughness, a sense of nakedness and military peril, a sense of being tested, silly rage, all were probably mingled into an unanalyzed conviction of the necessity of our action. The point is rather to remind us that the task of intellect is to dispel fog, to clarify and evaluate the sources of action—hopefully in time to affect it. If the most intellectual administration in our history did not do this, it is fully as disturbing as if it had done it well and acted solely from cynical arguments. Realpolitik is bad enough, but at least retains reason; righteous realpolitik is insufferable.

Were we naked? We argued that the weapons were offensive. This could have been taken either of two ways (excluding the vague way most Americans interpreted it, as reaffirmation of some sort of blood-thirsty communist nihilism): that the Cubans intended offense, or that the Russians did. If the former, it was downright silly, as silly as the photographs of soldiers stringing barbed wire along the beaches of Key West. Castro's own simple-minded hope was probably to threaten American cities if the U.S. threatened to invade, holding out the prospect of at least a mutual Götterdämmerung. Obviously he could not use them for anything less. Since we insist that Cuba has nothing to deter, and furthermore has no right to deter it, this idea has not been seriously entertained. There would be some justification for ignoring Castro's probable purpose in the fact that the Russians showed no intention of turning the missiles over to Castro and laying themselves open to a war started by Cubans. Castro (by *Newsweek*'s report) had never even been allowed to set foot on a missile site, much to his fury, and Khrushchev took pains to tell William Knox, the Westinghouse vice-president he saw during the crisis, that Russia would retain control of the missiles. However, we did not acknowledge this to be the case. Dean Rusk won a large vote in the OAS for our blockade and possible invasion by saying that intermediate range missiles in Cuba could also reach Latin American capitals.* That he could do so, incidentally, illustrated how little the statesmen of most countries know about strategic theory. The idea that Castro might make this type of threat with his island surrounded by Polaris-bearing submarines, or with even one U.S. missile aimed at

* *Newsweek* of November 12 suggested that there was "some evidence that—deliberately or not—the reach of the missile threat was exaggerated. Mr. Kennedy spoke of medium-range missiles with a range of 1,000 nautical miles and of bases for intermediate-range missiles capable of striking as far north as Hudson's Bay and as far South as Lima—2,200 nautical miles, by Defense Secretary Robert McNamara's count. These are far higher than previous military intelligence estimates for Soviet MRBM's (400 to 700 nautical miles) and IRBM's (1,130 to 1,300 nautical miles). The higher figures, obviously, would tend to strengthen the U.S. hand at home and in Latin America." Making a similar observation, *Aviation Week* called the missiles PRBM's—Political Range Ballistic Missiles. (Coming on the heels of our righteous rage over Soviet deception in a diplomatic interview, the government's possible attempt to deceive the press and the Latin Americans at once, in this and other points, on the grounds that "news is a weapon," did not sit well with the media. The White House was "dismayed by the barrage of criticism.")

Havana ready to punish such folly, seemed somehow credible to them. One doubts that it was to Rusk.

The contention that the missiles were offensive as part of Russia's strategic network, however, cannot be totally dispensed with. It may have been part of the equation which produced the decision in Moscow, although probably not the part most important to Khrushchev. (Raúl Castro spent almost all his time with military men in his early summer visit to Moscow.) Fidel himself cannot have believed that the missiles were to be simply part of the Soviet force, unless he sees himself and all his people as a kamikaze pilot for the Soviet Union. If he were host to the kind of force that could clearly play such a role—that is, a force much greater than what he had received—his entire island would certainly become a primary U.S. target, susceptible to complete destruction should Soviet rockets from any source in the world begin striking the U.S. In other words, if Castro thought that his island was being used to serve larger strategic purposes, he would have been a fool to accept the weapons. Furthermore, if one can distinguish between strategists and simpler military minds, it can be argued that a Soviet strategist would not have found the number or type of weapons in Cuba, or even three times that number, a sufficient increment to justify a first strike, nor even to make Russia substantially more secure from a U.S. first strike.* But some military men believe that more is always better, and their kind of thought cannot confidently be ruled out of the decision process that sent missiles to Cuba.

If one looks at the missiles solely in their way, they were worth trying to get out of Cuba. But even assuming that a Soviet first strike or the threat of one was the motive—and this means assuming an irrational motive of a low order of probability—the means were utterly incommensurate with the end. The missiles and bombers did not add to the Soviet strategic force anything so suddenly destabilizing as had been contended. Four of the thirty IL-28 bombers (range 700 miles) had been assembled.

* This argument is spelled out in R. Hagan and B. Bernstein, "The Military Value of Missiles in Cuba," *Bulletin of the Atomic Scientists*, February 1963.

Between 30 and 40 medium-range (said to be 1,000-mile) missiles were installed or near completion. These could reach only Southern SAC bases most of whose planes would have been dispersed to hundreds of airfields at the first sign of tension anyway. Three or four of the intermediate-range (said to be 2,200-mile) missiles were to have been completed by the end of the year. By that time the United States was to have 144 Polaris missiles under the seas, about 200 land-based intercontinental missiles installed within the United States, sixteen attack carriers with more than 400 attack bombers, 700 SAC B-52 and B-58 long-range bombers, and 700 B-47's which can reach Russia with air refueling. The smallest strategic warhead carried by any of these means is a half megaton, and they range up to 20 or 30 megatons. It was a dissimulation to imply that the missiles and bombers in Cuba, even added to Russia's fewer than 100 ICBM's and inferior force of long-range bombers and missile-firing submarines (Russia has no aircraft carriers), posed a *sudden* threat to America's deterrent capability. One could argue that the buildup would continue, but the Alsop-McNamara view was that we could be vulnerable solely for those two or three early months until our missiles came in, after which our defense combination would be unbreakable. In fact, this combination existed at the time the crisis developed.

All this is not to say that it was not desirable to have the missiles removed from Cuba. Regardless of what one makes of them, they would be an added impetus to the arms race and a possible cause of accidental war. As such their removal would have been a proper aim of negotiation. But an understanding of the weapons' significance does affect the choice of means, and their rate of completion even at its worst hardly justified sudden unilateral action with any risk of immediate war, particularly action which to any extent left the choice, the way out, to the other side.

War was possible, one must recall. The situation was not dependably under American control. At the time it seemed a serious risk. The relative weight given this risk is one of the alarming aspects of the Cuban affair. It can be said that the use of a naval blockade left the choice of whether or not to escalate the possible conflict partly to us, but this would have been so only if the Soviets chose to retaliate there. Washington was apparently not confident that they would, fearing action at Berlin or some other sort of escalation. It is sobering to learn that the "Damage Assessment Center," a unit "crammed with computers and civilian experts and scattered through underground sites around Washington" and "designed to keep the President's nuclear balance sheet up to date, listing the targets destroyed and resources remaining for post-attack operations," was put into full operation during the crisis; or that the key men were ordered to have their bags packed for a quick trip to shelters in Maryland and elsewhere; or that we had already decided on an invasion of Cuba for the following week that would involve killing Soviet personnel, and were not sure what the Russian response would be. Furthermore, to have been assured at the time that the President's action was a safe and controllable measure, one must assume that, should the naval battle that could well have ensued have gone badly, the President would have had the freedom Khrushchev had to negotiate a settlement rather than try a bigger weapon. This is far from certain.

WHEN IS A COUNTRY A COUNTRY?

There is another disturbing portent in our decision to treat the missiles solely as part of the Soviet strategic network when the objective case for it was poor. In ignoring the contention of both Russia and Cuba that the missiles were to help deter aggression, in making our case rest solely on assumed Soviet designs, we confirm our treatment of the first social-revolutionary government in Latin America as a non-country. Let us face facts: Cuba has something to deter. Alpha 66 has made raids out of Puerto Rico. Prominent Senators have been calling for invasion. President Kennedy has never taken back his pledge to rid the hemisphere of Castro and Communism. Every meeting of the OAS is used to isolate Castro and deny him the collective security provisions of its charter. It is entirely understandable that he should suppose more aggression to be underway than actually is. We have threatened the Cuban government and pretended that it exists only as a pawn of the Soviet Union. One of the strongest and probably most heartfelt things Castro and Guevara used to say to the peasants was that under the old system they had not been treated as men, sovereign and responsible. This has strong meaning to any socialist in a country where there are large numbers of exploited poor. We appear to be perpetuating the old system on the level of nationhood. It should not be surprising that the Cubans have subsequently refused inspection and may be looking for ways to cheat on an agreement to which they were not a party.

While the cautious moderates and occasionally corrupt reactionaries who now vote with us in the OAS may not be concerned about this, it is probably safe to say that in the Latin America of five years hence, there will be several countries led by men somewhere between moderate democratic socialism and Castroism. An avowed Marxist, Miguel Arrais, has been elected Governor of the state of Pernambuoco in northeastern Brazil. Guatemala may fall to revolutionaries within months. Peasant riots were reported from Peru in November. Emerging leaders in these countries see the United States now treating Cuba as if it were a society not making its own choices, not to be held responsible for its own acts. Although the theater of retaliation was specified to be Cuba in Kennedy's warnings, the decisions were assumed to be solely Russia's. This looks suspiciously like the way the United States always treated Latin Americans. Certainly there is some pretense involved in treating Castro's Cuba as a stable autonomous society with a legitimated power structure. It is not greater and is probably less than the pretense in treating Formosa, South Vietnam, South Korea, or Bulgaria as such.

This contemptuous attitude, so resoundingly reaffirmed in the Cuban crisis, betrays a deadly failure to anticipate even the immediate future, as if the details of the moment are all we can concentrate upon. One possible purpose of addressing Russia, the lawyers tell us, was to put our blockade on slightly firmer legal grounds: if we had addressed ourselves to Cuba, we would have been stopping the ships of a third party. The improvement in our legal position was hardly impressive, however, particularly when weighed against the effects in the most dangerous areas of the future of continuing the country club approach to international affairs. China should be giving us nightmares, yet once again the message from the top is that we can pretend that troublesome societies do not exist, and that governments are legitimated by seeing things our way on crucial matters. Current estimates are that China may test a nuclear weapon in 1963. When one reflects on the ignorance of the most cosmopolitan Latin American leaders and of most of the American Congress on matters of nuclear strategy, one realizes how unlikely it is that China will ever play the cautious and subtle game of deterrence as the United States and Russia have developed it over the years—particularly when China, unlike Russia, is aware of no community of interest with the West. Yet we take steps neither to give her this community of interest nor to involve her in disarmament agreements. Instead we throw other societies out of our community, which we define ever more exclusively as Western "have" nations, strengthening both China's parochial hatreds and her influence.

Would not the Cuba-Turkey deal have made the same mistake of treating these countries as less than sovereign? It might be worth imagining a hypothetical negotiated settlement to see if the Munich analogy need be applied. If Cuba and Turkey were present at the meetings of Soviet and United States negotiators, each would object that it has a right to its own defense. Each of the great powers would say that while this is so, it must be weighed against the destabilizing effects of placing such weapons near the borders of the great nuclear powers; that the problems of nervousness, public pressure, misperception and the like must be given some weight. It could be pointed out that nuclear weapons controlled too clearly by the great powers are dangerous to small host countries if they appear to make sense chiefly as part of the supplier's strategic force, because the host nation then becomes a prime target. (This is the point Bulganin tried to make to NATO countries in 1957, with some effect.) As suppliers and presumably owners of these weapons, Russia and America would have leverage to use, as well as compensations to offer, and non-invasion pledges might be exchanged. (As it was Cuba might have gotten one from us while Turkey got none from Russia.) The subsidiary weaponry, such as our tactical air bases and radar installations in Turkey, which current discussion pretended would somehow necessarily be lost if we gave up the fifteen Jupiter missiles in Turkey, and Soviet MIG's and anti-aircraft missiles in Cuba, might well remain by agreement.

The implication that the Jupiters are essential to our defense commitments to Turkey was another of the little fibs which filled the news during the crisis to make an easy case for our action. It has never been clear what good the missiles might have done to defend Turkey herself, since if Turkey were invaded and they were used in retaliation, the response would probably be against the U.S. and other lands harboring U.S. bases—which means that we probably would not have used them "first" (in retaliation for conventional armed aggression against Turkey alone) but only as part of a large, coordinated strike in response to a much larger act of aggression. They are slow-fueling and unhardened, so they are useless for a second strike. Now that other missiles have superseded them the use of which is more credible, Turkey would actually be safer with them off her soil in order to be removed from Russia's prime target list should nuclear war break out elsewhere.

If our demand to remove the IL-28's from Cuba proved embarrassing when it came to what type of plane we might base in Turkey, we might do either of two things: change the Turkey-based planes, or, if we still saw long-range planes based there as vital to deterring Soviet expansionism in the Middle East, accept the bombers in Cuba. After all, they pose a far lesser problem to our warning mechanism than did the missiles, they are vulnerable to anti-aircraft missilery already perfected as well as to standard jet fighter defense, and they have a shorter range than even the medium-range missiles were said to have.

In short, negotiations need not have weakened our alliances, and they might have served many far-sighted purposes, among which one of the most vital would have been to further the idea, so essential to whatever world order is possible, of the juridical equality of states.

ROLE OF THE UN

What of law? The question of legality was considered *ex post facto*. Once again the UN was seen as useful only as a cover for an invasion or strong action taken unilaterally by the United States, to be bypassed if it could not so serve. Once again the Organization of American States was to be a rubber stamp or else ignored. It was consulted at all only because Ambassador Thompson urged developing a legal grounding. The Russians, it seems, "had a feeling for 'legality.'" The point, as the *Times* reported the meeting in which he said this, was apparently taken to mean not that we should too, but that we could get more play out of the Russians if we considered this idiosyncracy of theirs. Later, U Thant's effort to introduce arbitration techniques as the crisis was reaching its most dangerous point was seen by Washington only as an inhibition to its thrust. Thant asked Kennedy and Khrushchev on October 24 to suspend for two or three weeks both the blockade and the arms shipments while negotiations were held, and Khrushchev agreed. Though it still looked as if the confrontation that might lead to war was immediately ahead of us, the administration was annoyed with Thant's proposal because it was thought it would (again in the words of the *Times*) "surely disarm [our] powerful diplomatic and military initiative." The administration "doubted that it could ever again regain momentum if negotiations failed, as it was expected they would." It has been a long time since a prizefighter thought he could overrule the referee, or a steel-workers' union a government injunction, on the basis of such a consideration.

These, then, are some of the matters of concern that strike one in reviewing the administration's handling of the crisis of the Cuban blockade. These and others linger on as the celebration of our courage and good fortune dies away: the indictment of our political system inherent in the suspicion, despite all one's charity toward the President and his counselors, that had Khrushchev been able to delay disclosure of his missiles until after the elections, we might have been willing to take the matter before the United Nations rather than acting unilaterally; the way the discussion in the National Security Council "executive committee" seemed to have been limited from the start to procedural questions, with no one asking whether unilateral action of any sort was appropriate; the mechanical way in which we applied the lesson of the U-2 incident, in which Khrushchev disclosed what he knew slowly enough to trap us in false excuses, to the October 18 meeting with Gromyko, so as to develop the pretext of deception for an action that had been decided upon before the deception was produced. And there is the reemergence of Dean Acheson as a "hawk" (urging strong interventionist measures), which suggests a sense in which the crisis of the Cuban blockade represents the reassertion of the seaboard aristocrat's claim for leadership on terms set by the arriviste pseudo-conservative who fought him in the fifties and made Acheson's "giveaway" of mainland China one of the rallying cries of the decade. The phoenix has not quite made it through the fire—another American tragedy.

All this clouds one's thoughts of the future, but not so much as the fear, somewhat contradictory to the foregoing, that the administration really believes the case it made for Russian evilness. "President Kennedy and his most intimate advisors . . . have come away from the nightmare of the last two weeks with a bitter recollection of what they regard as Soviet duplicity," wrote Max Frankel in the *New York Times* "News of the Week" for November 4. "They respect and are grateful for Premier Khrushchev's prudence in the face of disaster, but they are not likely again to think him incapable of the lowest punch in the cold war." Again the convinced are reconvinced, and the juggernaut hurtles on. One wonders whether *Pravda* was reporting similar disillusionment among Soviet leaders after Khrushchev had trapped—or been trapped into trapping—President Eisenhower in the U-2 affair. Khrushchev could of course wait until Kennedy replaced Eisenhower and begin again. We, however, have no such sacramental event to count upon to cleanse the Soviet leadership of its sins, before we must begin discussing with it the thousands of matters demanding each its quantum of respect and good faith. In the vast public relations game which is the cold war, in which each elite must manipulate its own public for every inch of leeway, we do our motivational research very badly. We cannot afford many such triumphs.

And how many can Khrushchev afford? His astonishing freedom to withdraw as he did can be explained only by assuming that a core interest was not threatened by doing so—which would be the case if the chief military value of the weapons was to defend Cuba—and that this possible outcome had been programmed in advance and seen as a less desirable but not wholly negative outcome. Some analysts have gone so far as to suggest that he wanted things to happen precisely as they did, that withdrawal would make him look more interested in peace than toughness and would restore negotiability to matters that had arrived at impasse. This is carrying things a bit far. But it may be that, if other purposes had to be abandoned, he could still hold that the net effect would be positive, because withdrawal would give him the right to say "Look how reasonable I was, now at least give me something to take home to my people" when the discussion turned to Berlin or inspection later. Within Russia, Khrushchev has not staked his reputation on military superiority so much as on proving that peaceful coexistence is possible, that Russia will prosper under such conditions, and that the rest of the world would then come its way. It now appears that this has been the position of the ascendent theoretician Mikhail Suslov as well.

The returns are not all in, but chances are they were proved wrong. This would be clear as soon as they reached the conference tables. The right-wing counterattack against Kennedy's moderation began very early to dissipate the liberating feeling of victory, and with it probably any magnanimity. The crisis was passed and Cuba was still there, perhaps safer than ever. The President himself seemed afraid that he might indeed have committed himself not to invade. The signs are that we held to the on-site inspection demand in Cuba less because of the objective needs of the case than as a precedent to use later in inspection negotiations concerning the test ban, and to delay unto oblivion the non-invasion pledge. Still the rightists felt betrayed.

As a result, the liberals concluded that toughness won, and the conservatives concluded that moderation failed. One early test of what hopefulness remained in these inauspicious circumstances would be our ability to respond to the newly expressed interest of the Russians in the "black-box" proposal worked out by the Pugwash group to detect underground tests. The results were depressing. If Berlin and disarmament negotiations show as negative a yield, and the Chinese make their predictable gain among the incipient revolutionaries in the Southern Hemisphere *vis-à-vis* the Russians, we may find Khrushchev forced into adventurist behavior which will make the Cuban blockade not the last but the first of a series of crises on a new level of peril for the world. It can be argued on military grounds that the counter-escalation factors in our developing counterforce capability invite the non-counterforce nuclear power to spread its arms to local areas of tension in order to forestall a series of local defeats and humiliations without risking the destruction of its homeland.* Cuba, it can be argued, was the first place where this was to be tried, and presumably the theory was not disproved by Russia's being forced to withdraw while the weapons were still being shipped and installed. Our tough and localized behavior was precisely what counterforce makes possible for us. If the Soviet military's answer is weapons dispersal to extra-territorial trouble spots, and if the political result of the Cuban affair is now to make Khrushchev put up or shut up, we may find that our demonstration of resolve has precisely the opposite effect from that intended. If that should be the case, we end having served no long-range pacific or legal goals, either externally or internally, and with our short-range victory turning bitter in our mouths. This may be the greatest tragedy of the Cuban blockade.

* *Cf.* Hagan and Bernstein, *op. cit.*

DAVID LOWENTHAL

The Lost Opportunity

The pacifist critics of Kennedy's policy had their counterparts on the right. Those who viewed communism as a menace to the American way of life found little to applaud in a policy which virtually guaranteed the continuation of a Marxist regime in Cuba. David Lowenthal, the chairman of the Department of Political Science at Boston College, developed the conservative case against Kennedy's policy in an article in William Buckley's National Review *in January 1963. For a fuller and more restrained right-wing criticism of Kennedy's handling of the crisis, see James Daniel and John G. Hubbell,* Strike in the West *(New York, 1963), a book dedicated to the lone American casualty of the missile crisis, U-2 pilot Major Rudolf Anderson, Jr.*

THE APPARENT vigor of President Kennedy's quarantine of Cuba, and the rapidity with which he effected the withdrawal of Russian missiles, left Americans with a false impression. Only in contrast to the feebleness of our previous Cuban policy was this a strong and vigorous act. Given the circumstances, it was the weakest response open to us. It eliminated the most immediate and obvious threat, but no more. And in the process it made concessions that will assist the growth of Communist military power and subversion in this hemisphere.

After the Bay of Pigs disaster of April 1961, we reverted to purely diplomatic and economic measures, only recently adding certain trade restrictions to our own embargo. None of these measures decreased the flow of goods from Communist countries appreciably. Over more than two years, in fact, immense armaments of every description (excluding missiles and bombers) were sent to Castro. During last summer, the military

David Lowenthal, "U.S. Cuban Policy: Illusion and Reality," *National Review,* XIV (January 29, 1963), 61–63. Reprinted by permission of *National Review.*

buildup and the influx of Soviet technicians intensified. The President then issued an open warning against offensive arms in Cuba—which by his own testimony, using his own definitions, did not yet exist there; "defensive" was the term he applied to what they had, and "defensive" implies "legitimate."

This policy courted further disaster. It allowed Cuba to develop into the hemisphere's third most formidable military power. The regime became more impregnable to internal revolution. Its weight in hemispheric politics—and the Russian weight behind it—could increase substantially and add to the thrust of Castro-type insurgency. And if ever it were necessary to invade Cuba, the invading forces would now have to reckon on grave losses before they could succeed. Moreover, by failing to interfere with the arming of Cuba at a very early point, we made it clear to the Soviets that they could upset the balance of power wherever local governments (or rebels) were ready to accept their assistance. A pattern already laid down in Egypt, Laos and the Congo was given our final stamp of tolerance ninety miles off Florida.

Because of our non-intervention, Khrushchev and Castro could proceed to contrive a scheme that might have inflicted enormous damage on Western power, influence and prestige. We cannot know for sure what motivated this daring innovation in Russian missile policy. Was it to pressure our withdrawal from bases in Turkey and elsewhere? Was it to prevent our invading Cuba? Was it to give unmistakable proof of Soviet supremacy? Was the threat of these nearby missiles meant to paralyze us during some momentous act of aggrandizement in West Berlin, and protect Cuba from our retaliation at the same time? Considering the nature of the missile move, it is probable that Khrushchev was playing for the highest stakes. This would point to the last-named objective. In any case, by exploiting his "sovereign" right to export, and Castro's "sovereign" right to import, he almost succeeded in his plot.

The only thing our President did to brake Khrushchev was to warn against an offensive arms buildup. Prior to sure evidence of the missile sites and missiles, he did nothing to stop the flow of armaments into Cuba. And by virtue of the distinction between "defensive" and "offensive," he fastened dangerous encumbrances on our present and future power to act. For can we really tolerate a buildup short of only the most extravagant weapons? And is the distinction practical? A Russian submarine base in Cuba could be defensive; planes that are normally defensive could be turned to offensive uses. Furthermore, if a Cuban defensive buildup is legitimate, we must ask, "Defensive against whom?" Cuba's armed forces are many times too large for defense against any other Latin American country. They can only be defensive against a possible attack from us. And are we certain we will not have to mount such an attack, or assist others to mount one, in the future? Will other measures suffice to bring Castro's downfall? If not, our policy has the curious effect of guaranteeing the ability of a tyrannical and expansionist regime to resist our efforts to overthrow it.

WHAT TO DO?

Faced with solid evidence of the missile emplacements, what could the President do? The time for mere words had passed. The Soviets had shown their willingness to press us to the wall, amid patent assurances from Mr. Gromyko that they had no intention of doing what we knew they were in fact doing. The President could not be sure of the specific purpose of the missiles, but he could be sure their probable uses threatened intolerable, and possibly imminent, danger to this country and its interests. Action was therefore absolutely necessary. But expelling the "offensive" missiles and bombers and keeping others out were the least demanding options available to the President—the bare minimum. Did not the gravity of the barely averted missile threat entitle us to something more than a return to the *status quo ante?* It used to be thought that aggressors deserved to be penalized—*had to be* penalized, in fact, to keep them from trying again.

OPPORTUNITY MISSED

Here in our hands was the opportunity—only rarely afforded by a wily and aggressive enemy—to inflict a drastic defeat upon him. The moment of crisis, the magnitude of the threat to world peace, the incredible deceit practiced upon the U.S., the heightened awareness and anger of allies and neutrals—all argued for a comprehensive and decisive solution of the Cuban problem. The avowed aims of our Cuban policy are to eliminate the Russian presence in this hemisphere, to curb the aggressive and subversive influence engendered by Communism, and to give the Cuban people the republic they originally envisaged. We should therefore have demanded the departure of the Russians together with their "offensive" weapons, and the holding of long-overdue free elections in Cuba under UN supervision. And the means actually employed by the President—the blockade—should have been extended to almost all shipping, by air and by sea. This policy had its risks, and there is no assurance that blockade alone, without invasion, would ultimately have sufficed. But there could be little doubt of the outcome, and we would have acted in full justice, and consistently with our ideals.

To see the weakness with which the President has pursued even his own policy, we need only take note of two facts. First, as of this moment—three months since the crisis began—there is no prospect of on-site inspection in Cuba. Once the Russians promised to withdraw their bombers, we responded by immediately lifting our naval quarantine. Since then we have made no real effort to obtain inspection. The second fact, however, raises issues far graver than the first. The President pledged not to invade Cuba if his original demands were complied with. This amounts to a guarantee that Communist penetration into this hemisphere has a right to exist if it shows no sign of military aggressiveness.

Nothing closer to an explicit retraction of the Monroe Doctrine has ever been made by any President. It would be bad enough if the alien intrusions into the hemisphere were not Communist. But Communism always prospers by deception and violence, and spreads itself by subversion if not by arms—a subversion in which Cuba has been actively and extensively engaged for some time. Moreover, the non-invasion pledge was completely gratuitous. The Communists had engineered a dangerous and provocative missile threat. For their withdrawal of this threat we owed them nothing. Nor did they have any means of wringing a non-invasion pledge from us against our will. They would have to remove the missiles or suffer a direct and devastating air attack on the emplacements. In this part of the world, at least, our navy and air force assure our ultimate control, and Soviet power is of little avail except with our acquiescence. Why, then, did we promise to respect the sovereignty of a regime deserving nothing but our implacable hostility?

The events of recent weeks have not been without their ironical touches. Khrushchev kept his ships coming toward our blockade till the last minute, and, till the last minute at the UN, Zorin denied the very existence of the missiles. Seeing that we meant business, Khrushchev then reversed course. Happy to escape with his missiles intact, and in his hands rather than ours, he promised to remove offensive weapons from Cuba and permit on-site inspection. The missiles left rapidly, and American officials were not much slower in crediting his "good faith" and turning their ire on his nasty Cuban henchman who alone now obstructed further progress. Thus, by swift and quiet withdrawal, Khrushchev skillfully lessened the ill repute that should accrue to him.

We even helped him do so. Instead of mercilessly exploiting our advantages as he exploited his in the U-2 incident of 1960 (where the threat to Russia and the direct deception were much smaller), we eased his way out by terminating official criticism once the missiles were under evacuation. And how quickly—almost eagerly—American officials and the press began to blame Castro's recalcitrance for Mikoyan's unusually long visit to Cuba. Some went so far as to suggest that Russia might be having second thoughts about its liaison with Cuba. Finally, Adlai Stevenson at the UN expressed relief that the world organization had intervened between us and the Soviets and thus terminated the direct and potentially explosive confrontation of the two giants. But he obscured the simple fact that the confrontation—to the extent one occurred—was a beneficial thing, not a disaster. It taught the Soviets something no words of ours or of the UN could have taught them, and only *after* our power had driven their missiles out of Cuba could the UN begin to play any role whatsoever. The morbid and doctrinaire fear of confrontation is a sign of our psychological paralysis in the face of modern weaponry, and its effect is to encourage and protect aggression.

Can the narrow scope of the President's demands in the crisis be justified by the imponderables of the Berlin problem? Viewed in this light, his task was to expel the offensive weapons with the smallest possible disturbance. Otherwise Khrushchev might be given the distraction or excuse he wanted for a new Berlin encroachment. This was certainly a very serious consideration, but it should not have been permitted to decide the issue. First, Khrushchev's Cuban scheme seemed to indicate doubts about his ability to move easily on Berlin without this additional missile threat at his disposal. Once the scheme was uncovered it was worse than useless to him, for a Berlin move in the midst of our anger over Cuba would have been exceedingly dangerous. And the greater the anger we showed, the greater would be his reluctance to try us further.

Khrushchev's scheme proves that he had become contemptuous of our coercive ability in situations calling for preventive action, or for running great risks. Under his leadership, Soviet influence has entered almost every corner of the globe in a wholly unprecedented manner. Who would have thought, prior to 1956, that we would see Soviet pressures or actions in such widely distributed places as Egypt, Laos, Algeria, the Congo and Cuba? Riding on the crest of Soviet missiles and space achievements, and backed by superb conventional forces of every type, Khrushchev has advanced Soviet power and prestige under the hanging threat of our atomic superiority. And his accomplishments in Hungary, Laos, Cuba and Berlin must have added successively to his confidence. The Berlin Wall was his single greatest victory, and it went far toward weakening NATO's innermost spirit. West Berlin itself would be the next target, in a strategy aimed at destroying Western unity and ultimately gaining control of the industrial complex of eastern Europe. The fear that Khrushchev would do something before the year-end to change the status of Germany and West

Berlin pervaded all Europe. The Cuban scheme may have recommended itself as the means of guaranteeing a quick and bloodless success.

One basic fact must have made such ambitions seem practicable. This was the West's proven inability to use its power—*i.e.,* its lack of the will and skill to employ the various techniques of coercion available to it. The increase in American conventional forces of which the administration is so proud, the multiplication of Polaris submarines and other missile installations, the improvement of NATO's strategy—none of these seems to have elevated our stature in Khrushchev's eyes. Here is the most alarming implication of his Cuban move, and it bodes ill for our future in the Cold War.

BAD IMPRESSIONS

For President Kennedy's Cuban response has hardly corrected this impression of our ineptness. The only thing he taught the Soviets was to make their daring moves with the caution they had momentarily—in their overconfidence—forgotten. He *had* to force the missiles out. It is what he could have done but did *not* do that will most strongly impress our Communist foes. He forced them to retract the move, and for a brief while aired their malice before the world. But he did nothing to penalize an action aimed at inflicting an almost mortal wound on us, and he even made a non-invasion pledge that had never been given before. To safeguard Berlin we needed a decisive victory in Cuba. We did not even get the *status quo ante*.

What has happened to the concern for the Cuban people that played so impressive a part in the President's first crisis address? It is hard to avoid the conclusion that we lack serious concern for their welfare. The recent degrading ransom of invasion prisoners reflects this unwillingness to adopt measures designed to liberate the entire country—including the much larger number of domestic political prisoners still languishing in Castro's jails. In 1956 we did little to assist the Hungarian revolution or to penalize the Soviets for the violence and deceit with which they suppressed it. Now we have outdone that record, and the one set in the interim at the Berlin Wall. Here, at our very doorstep, we again showed our unwillingness to act for Cuban liberty with anything like the forcefulness with which the Russians acted for Hungarian oppression. From this incapacity to capitalize on the opportunity his rashness gave us, Khrushchev will draw the appropriate conclusions, and they will not differ essentially from those of Mao. The Marxist prediction of the necessary decline of the West will have been further confirmed for both.

The fault lies not with individuals or parties but with our philosophy of international affairs. We no longer know how to coerce for moral ends, and are strapped by false moralisms and legalisms. We still think international affairs can be based on reason and agreement alone. We still cannot believe the Communists will use any expedient to accomplish our ruin. Not only are we still lacking in a positive policy for pushing them back, but we never punish their encroachments. Retaliation—that cold and harsh purgative of evil in the relations among nations, without which nothing good can survive—never enters our minds. We still respect the principle of the sovereignty and self-determination of Communist nations, without seeing the salient fact that they have no right to the advantages it confers. We are dismayed at the prospect of all-out war, but have yet to understand that the vigorous employment of lesser degrees of force is necessary both to protect our interests and to prevent our antagonists, by a miscalculation of our intention, from making moves to which we can only respond by mobilizing our vastest power.

III

The Problem of Soviet Motivation

THE CONTROVERSY over Kennedy's handling of the missile crisis gradually gave way to the even more elusive question of Khrushchev's motives in embarking on his daring Cuban policy. At the time, most Americans saw the Russian move as an attempt to undermine American security, a feeling intensified by Kennedy's claim in his October 22 television speech that the Cuban missiles put such distant points as the nation's capital and the Panama Canal under nuclear threat. In fact, the forty-two MRBM's in Cuba could not have reached either Washington or the Canal Zone, much less the major population centers in the urban Northeast or California. Robert Kennedy's later claim that the Russian rockets could kill eighty million Americans has never been substantiated. The missiles in Cuba did not even alter the world-wide nuclear balance of power, which, contrary to popular understanding at the time, remained overwhelmingly weighted against the Soviet Union.

Once the concept of a Soviet nuclear leap ahead of the United States had been discredited, scholars began to speculate about a wide variety of possible Soviet motives. The early American discovery of the missiles prevented Khrushchev from unfolding his plans, and though he later offered an explanation for his policy, few scholars accepted it at face value. Instead they engaged in the fascinating game of Kremlinology, trying to guess, on the basis of extremely meager evidence, at the true intent of Khrushchev's Cuban adventure.

NIKITA KHRUSHCHEV

In Defense of Cuba

Six weeks after the crisis, Premier Khrushchev explained why he had placed the missiles in Cuba in a speech to the Supreme Soviet. In a television interview several years later, after he had been deposed from power, Khrushchev expressed views strikingly similar to those in this December 12, 1962, speech. Whatever ulterior motives he may have had, his explanation must be accepted as the standard Russian view of the crisis.

CUBA IS TERRIBLE to the imperialists because of her ideas. The imperialists do not want to reconcile themselves to the idea that little Cuba dared to live and develop independently as her people want to and not in the way which would please the American monopolies. But the question of how people are to live, what road they are to take, is an internal matter for each people!

Flouting generally accepted standards of international relations, the United States reactionary forces have been doing everything from the first day of the victory of the Cuban revolution to overthrow Cuba's revolutionary Government and to

The Worker Supplement, December 23, 1962, as quoted in Henry Pachter, *Collision Course: The Cuban Missile Crisis and Coexistence* (New York, 1963), pp. 243–248. Reprinted by permission of Praeger Publishers.

restore their domination there. They broke off diplomatic relations with Cuba, were and are conducting subversive activity, established an economic blockade of Cuba. Threatening to apply sanctions, the United States began pressing its allies not only to stop trading with Cuba but even not to make available ships for carrying food to Cuba from the socialist countries which came to the assistance of their brothers. This is an inhuman policy—a desire to starve a whole nation.

But even this seemed little to them. Assuming the functions of a policeman, they decided to take the road of the military suppression of the Cuban revolution. In other words, they wanted to usurp the right to the export of counterrevolution.

United States policy in relation to Cuba is the most unbridled, reactionary policy. To declare that Cuba allegedly threatens America or any other country and to usurp on this plea a special right to act against Cuba is just monstrous.

Seeking to justify its aggressive actions, American reaction is repeating that the crisis in the Caribbean was created by Cuba herself, adding that blame rests also with the Soviet Union which shipped there rockets and IL-28 bombers.

But is this so? It is true that we carried weapons there at the request of the Cuban government. But what motives guided us in doing that? Exclusively humanitarian motives—Cuba needed weapons as a means of containing the aggressors, and not as a means of attack. For Cuba was under a real threat of invasion. Piratical attacks were repeatedly made on her coasts, Havana was shelled, and airborne groups were dropped from planes to carry out sabotage.

A large-scale military invasion of Cuba by counterrevolutionary mercenaries was launched in Cuba in April of last year. This invasion was prepared and carried out with full support on the part of the United States.

Further events have shown that the failure of the invasion did not discourage the United States imperialists in their desire to strangle Cuba. They began preparing another attack. In the autumn of this year a very alarming situation was created. Everything indicated that the United States was preparing to attack the Cuban Republic with its own armed forces.

Revolutionary Cuba was compelled to take all measures to strengthen her defense. The Soviet Union helped her to build up a strong army standing guard over the achievements of the Cuban people. In view of the mounting threat from the United States, the Government of Cuba in the summer of this year requested the Soviet Government to render further assistance.

Agreement was reached on a number of new measures, including the stationing of several score Soviet IRBM's in Cuba. These weapons were to be in the hands of Soviet military.

What were the aims behind this decision? Naturally, neither we nor our Cuban friends had in mind that this small number of IRBM's, sent to Cuba, would be used for an attack on the United States or any other country.

Our aim was only to defend Cuba. We all saw how the American imperialists were sharpening knives, threatening Cuba with a massed attack. We could not remain impartial observers in face of this bandit-like policy, which is contrary to all standards of relations between states and the United Nations Charter. We decided to extend a helping hand to Cuba. We saw a possibility of protecting the freedom-loving people of Cuba by installing rockets there so that the American imperialists, if they really decided to invade, would realize that the war which they threatened to start stood at their own borders, so that they would realize more realistically the dangers of thermonuclear war.

Such was the step we took because of the serious aggravation of the situation. We were confident that this step would bring the aggressors to their senses and that they—realizing that Cuba was not defenseless and that American imperialism was [not] all powerful—would be compelled to change their plans. Then the need for retaining rockets in Cuba would naturally disappear.

Indeed, had there been no threat of an invasion and had we had assurances that the United States would not invade Cuba, and would restrain its allies from this, had the United States guided itself by this course, there would have been no need for the stationing of our rockets in Cuba.

Some people pretend that the rockets were supplied by us for an attack on the United States. This, of course, is not wise reasoning. Why should we station rockets in Cuba for this purpose when we were and are able to strike from our own territory, possessing as we do the necessary number of intercontinental missiles of the required range and power?

We do not, in general, need military bases on foreign territories. It is known that we have dismantled all our bases abroad. All people who have any understanding of military matters know that in the age of intercontinental and global rockets, Cuba—this small, far-away island, which is only fifty kilometers wide in some places—is of no strategic importance for the defense of the Soviet Union. We stationed rockets in Cuba only for the defense of the Cuban Republic and not for an attack on the United States. Such a small country as Cuba cannot, naturally, build up such forces as could launch an offensive against such a big country as the United States.

Only those who are not "all there" in the head can claim that the Soviet Union chose Cuba as a springboard for an invasion of the American continent—the U.S. or countries of Latin America. If we wanted to start war against the U.S., we would not have agreed to dismantle the rockets installed in Cuba, which were ready for launching, for battle. We would have used them. But we did not because we did not pursue such aims.

Thus, all talk that Cuba was being converted into a base for an attack on the United States of America was a vicious lie. The purpose of this lie was to cover up the plans of aggression against Cuba. We are loyal to Lenin's principles of peaceful coexistence and hold that all disputes among states should be settled by peaceful means, by way of negotiations.

The developments in the Caribbean confirmed that there was a threat of such aggression. By the third week of October, a large-scale buildup of U.S. naval and air forces, paratroopers and marines began in the South of the U.S., on the approaches to Cuba. The U.S. government sent reinforcements to its naval base at Guantánamo lying on Cuban territory. Big military maneuvers were announced in the Caribbean. In the course of these "maneuvers," a landing was to be made on Viéques Island. On October 22, Kennedy's administration announced a quarantine on Cuba. The word "quarantine" by the way, was merely a figleaf in this case. Actually it was a blockade, piracy on the high seas.

The events developed rapidly. The American command alerted all its armed forces, including the troops in Europe, and also the Sixth Fleet in the Mediterranean and the Seventh Fleet based in the area of Taiwan.

Several airborne, infantry, and armored divisions, numbering some 100,000 men, were set aside for an attack on Cuba alone. Moreover, 183 warships with 85,000 naval personnel were moved to the shores of Cuba. The landing on Cuba was to be covered by several thousand military planes. Close to 20 per cent of all planes of the U.S. Strategic Air Command were kept in the air around the clock with atomic and hydrogen bombs on board. Reservists were called up.

On October 23, immediately after the United States proclaimed the blockade of Cuba, the Soviet government, besides taking defensive measures, issued a Statement resolutely warning that the United States Government assumes a grave responsibility for the destinies of the peace and is recklessly playing with fire. We frankly told the United States President that we would not tolerate piratical actions by United States ships on the high seas and that we would take appropriate measures with this object in view.

At the same time, the Soviet government urged all peoples to bar the road to the aggressors. Simultaneously it took certain steps in the United Nations. The peaceful initiative of the Soviet government in settling the Cuban crisis met with full support by the socialist countries and the peoples of most other United Nations member states.

However, the government of the United States of America continued to aggravate the situation. United States militarist forces were pushing developments toward an attack on Cuba. On the morning of October 27, we received information from the Cuban comrades and from other sources which bluntly said that the invasion would be effected within the next two or three days. We assessed the messages received as a signal of utmost alarm. And this was a well-founded alarm.

Immediate actions were needed to prevent an invasion of

Cuba and to maintain peace. A message prompting a mutually acceptable solution was sent to the United States President. At that moment, it was not yet too late to put out the fuse of war which had already been lighted. Forwarding this message we took into consideration that the messages of the President himself expressed anxiety and the desire to find a way out of the obtaining situation. We declared that if the United States undertook not to invade Cuba and also would restrain other states allied with it from aggression against Cuba, the Soviet Union would be willing to remove from Cuba the weapons which the United States call "offensive."

The United States President replied by declaring that if the Soviet government agreed to remove these weapons from Cuba the American government would lift the quarantine, i.e., the blockade, and would give an assurance on renunciation of the invasion of Cuba both by the United States itself and other countries of the Western Hemisphere. The President declared quite definitely, and this is known to the whole world, that the United States will not attack Cuba and will restrain also its allies from such actions.

But we shipped our weapons to Cuba precisely for the prevention of aggression against her! That is why the Soviet government reaffirmed its agreement to the removal of the ballistic rockets from Cuba.

From the above follow some evident results of the beginning of normalization of the situation over Cuba.

First, it has been possible to avert an invasion which threatened the Republic of Cuba from day to day, and, therefore, to avert an armed conflict, to overcome a crisis which was fraught with the danger of universal thermonuclear war.

Second, the United States publicly, before the entire world, pledged not to attack the Republic of Cuba, and to restrain its allies from doing so.

Third, the most rabid imperialists who staked on starting a world thermonuclear war over Cuba have not been able to do so. The Soviet Union, the forces of peace and socialism, proved that they are in a position to impose peace on the exponents of war.

Which side triumphed? Who won? In this respect one may say that it was sanity, the cause of peace and security of peoples, that won. Both sides displayed a sober approach and took into account that unless such steps are taken as could help overcome the dangerous development of events, a World War III might break out.

As a result of mutual concessions and compromise, an understanding was reached which made it possible to remove dangerous tension, to normalize the situation.

It is, of course, true that the nature of imperialism has not changed. But imperialism today is no longer what it used to be when it held undivided sway over the world. If it is now a "paper" tiger, those who say this know that this "paper tiger" has atomic teeth. It can use them and it must not be treated lightly. It is possible in the relations with imperialist countries to make reciprocal compromises, while, on the other hand, having all means in order to smash the aggressors should they unleash war.

Some people confined themselves to cursing when difficult conditions were created for Cuba. Noisy statements do not reduce the strength of the imperialist forces and Cuba will hardly get any relief from this. The Soviet Union acted differently. It not only exposed the U.S. imperialist intrigues against Cuba. It sent its weapons to Cuba, sent people who were ready to lay down their lives in the struggle for defense of Cuba. And when Cuba was threatened, our men were ordered to defend Cuba against invasion, to fight shoulder to shoulder with the Cubans, to stand to death with the Cuban people. These are genuinely fraternal sentiments, fraternal attitudes, fraternal solidarity. . . .

JOHN F. KENNEDY

The Nuclear Balance of Power

On the evening of December 17, 1962, five days after Khrushchev's speech, John F. Kennedy appeared on a nation-wide television program to be interviewed by representatives of the three major networks. The discussion ranged widely over domestic and foreign issues, but near the end of the hour NBC commentator Sander Vanocur brought up the Cuban missile crisis, asking the President to comment on Khrushchev's speech to the Supreme Soviet.

THE PRESIDENT. I think in that speech this week he showed his awareness of the nuclear age. But of course, the Cuban effort has made it more difficult for us to carry out any successful negotiations, because this was an effort to materially change the balance of power, it was done in secret, steps were taken really to deceive us by every means they could, and they were planning in November to open to the world the fact that they had these missiles so close to the United States; not that they were intending to fire them, because if they were going to get into a nuclear struggle, they have their own missiles in the Soviet Union. But it would have politically changed the balance of power. It would have appeared to, and appearances contribute to reality. So it is going to be some time before it is possible for us to come to any real understanding with Mr. Khrushchev. But I do think his speech shows that he realizes how dangerous a world we live in.

The real problem is the Soviet desire to expand their power and influence. If Mr. Khrushchev would concern himself with the real interests of the people of the Soviet Union, that they have a higher standard of living, to protect his own security, there is no real reason why the United States and the Soviet Union, separated by so many thousands of miles of land and water, both rich countries, both with very energetic people, should not be able to live in peace. But it is this constant determination which the Chinese show in the most militant form, and which the Soviets also have shown, that they will not settle for that kind of a peaceful world, but must settle for a Communist world. That is what makes the real danger, the com-

Public Papers of the Presidents: Kennedy, 1962 (Washington, D.C., 1963), pp. 897–898.

bination of these two systems in conflict around the world in a nuclear age is what makes the sixties so dangerous.

Mr. Vanocur: Ambassador Kennan,* who has some knowledge of the Soviet Union, wrote in one of his recent books that what you are dealing with here is a conditioned state of mind, that there is no misunderstanding here, that the only thing the Soviets really understand is when you present them with a set of facts and say to them, "This is what we are going to do." This they understand. Have you found that there is any way to break through to Mr. Khrushchev, to make him really aware that you are quite sincere and determined about what you say, sir, or is this a total . . . ?

The President. Well, it is difficult. I think, looking back on Cuba, what is of concern is the fact that both governments were so far out of contact, really. I don't think that we expected that he would put the missiles in Cuba, because it would have seemed such an imprudent action for him to take, as it was later proved. Now, he obviously must have thought that he could do it in secret and that the United States would accept it. So that he did not judge our intentions accurately.

Well, now, if you look at the history of this century, where World War I really came through a series of misjudgments of the intentions of others, certainly World War II, where Hitler thought that he could seize Poland, that the British might not fight, and if they fought, after the defeat of Poland they might not continue to fight, Korea, where obviously the North Koreans did not think we were going to come in, and Korea, when we did not think the Chinese were going to come in, when you look at all those misjudgments which brought on war, and then you see the Soviet Union and the United States so far separated in their beliefs, we believing in a world of independent sovereign and different diverse nations, they believing in a monolithic Communist world, and you put the nuclear equation into that struggle, that is what makes this, as I said before, such a dangerous time, and that we must proceed with firmness and also with the best information we can get, and also with care. There

* George F. Kennan, U.S. Ambassador to Russia, March 14, 1952–July 29, 1953.

is nothing—one mistake can make this whole thing blow up. So that—one major mistake either by Mr. Khrushchev or by us here—so that is why it is much easier to make speeches about some of the things which we ought to be doing, but I think that anybody who looks at the fatality lists on atomic weapons, and realizes that the Communists have a completely twisted view of the United States, and that we don't comprehend them, that is what makes life in the sixties hazardous.

ROGER HILSMAN

The Missile Gap

The most revealing picture of the Kennedy administration's analysis of Soviet motives in the missile crisis came in 1967 with the publication of Roger Hilsman's book To Move a Nation. *Hilsman, a well-known political scientist who devised the "strategic hamlet" policy in Vietnam, served as director of the Bureau of Intelligence and Research in the State Department at the time of the Cuban crisis. In this key position he had access to secret intelligence data on the Soviet Union, and he played a major role in interpreting Soviet behavior for the President. The following discussion of Soviet intent, taken from Hilsman's book, thus represents the view that prevailed within the administration in 1962.*

WHAT DID THE SOVIETS hope to accomplish by putting nuclear missiles in Cuba? As with the major policy decisions of all governments, whether dictatorial or democratic, different segments of the Soviet leadership undoubtedly saw particular advantages and disadvantages in putting missiles in Cuba according to their own parochial interests and responsibilities. But the

Roger Hilsman, *To Move a Nation: The Politics of Foreign Policy in the Administration of John F. Kennedy* (Garden City, 1967), pp. 161–165. Reprinted by permission of Doubleday & Company, Inc. Copyright © 1964, 1967 by Roger Hilsman.

Soviet government as a whole seems to have hit upon putting missiles in Cuba as a generalized, strategic response to a whole set of problems, military, economic, and political.

Consider the view from Moscow eighteen months before the missiles decision, in January of 1961. In the Soviet Union, the domestic situation seemed good. Work was proceeding on the party program and on the twenty-year plan for increasing domestic production.

The world situation was also good. First and foremost, the Soviets were still basking in the afterglow of the Sputnik success, and the world generally assumed that the military and strategic balance had significantly shifted in the Soviets' favor. In the United States, a new, young, and presumably inexperienced President had just taken over the reins of government after an extremely close election, and he seemed to have few prospects except continued deadlock politically and recession economically. The Atlantic community had made little progress toward unity. The underdeveloped world was in ferment, offering exciting prospects for the Soviets: Africa, Latin America, and Southeast Asia all seemed full of opportunities. Finally, and most importantly, the Sino-Soviet dispute, although still disturbing, appeared to be contained for the moment. The eighty-one Communist parties had just met, and a *modus vivendi* with the Chinese still seemed possible.

Khrushchev expressed his satisfaction with all these favorable prospects in his speech of January 6, 1961. Confidently, he laid out an ambitious and aggressive program to extend Communist influence throughout the world—from Berlin, where he revived threats of an ultimatum, to the underdeveloped world, which he invited to embark on new and better "wars of national liberation."

But by the spring of 1962, things looked quite different from Moscow. President Kennedy and the West had stood firm on Berlin. There had been movement in the Atlantic community toward unity. The difficulties of dealing with the underdeveloped world had begun to sink in—the expense of foreign aid, the political instability of the emerging nations, their touchiness, their extremist nationalism, their inexperience, and also their instinct and skill in playing the great powers off against each other rather than being dominated by one of them.

And the Sino-Soviet dispute had gotten out of hand. In one sense, Communism is a doctrine of acquiring and using power. The trouble was that the Chinese were behaving like Communists, and the dispute had come to have a dynamism of its own.

Domestically, the Soviet leaders found that the demands they had themselves created with "de-Stalinization" and promises of consumers' goods had become a tiger that they were finding difficult to ride. There were just not enough resources to meet the whole long list of demands—a better life for consumers; the needs of the space program, prestigious though it was; the foreign aid required to play an active, worldwide role; and, above all, the effort to achieve military supremacy.

For the situation here, too, had changed—radically. And for the Soviet leaders this change probably caused the deepest anxiety of all. When the Soviets completed their first experiments with rockets and began to lay out their longer run program, they apparently decided on a bold move. They elected to skip the logical next step—rockets of about 350,000 pounds thrust, like our Atlas—and to leap to giants of about 800,000 pounds. The successful result was the behemoth that gave the Soviets the Sputnik and the lift for their many other space achievements. But this rocket was also intended to serve as the work horse of the Soviet ICBM force, and American intelligence was rightly impressed. As the intelligence community looked at their estimates of 1958, 1959, and 1960, and even through the first half of 1961, they saw a missile gap developing that would come to a peak about 1963. Both the intelligence community and the Air Force made a major effort to win approval for a crash program through orthodox channels, but failed to change the Eisenhower administration's policies. Inevitably, the more convinced among the Air Force and intelligence people then tried an end run through leaks to senators and newspaper columnists who were favorably disposed. Reluctantly, the Eisenhower administration upped the American program. When Kennedy came in, he upped it again.

In the meantime, the Soviets began to deploy their giant rocket as an ICBM near Plesetsk in the north. And this was apparently the fatal blow to their hopes of achieving a decisive advantage. For they discovered, one must assume, that this behemoth was just too big, too bulky to serve as a practical weapon. A newer, smaller, more streamlined missile had to be designed instead, and the Soviet ICBM program must have been set back many months.

The Soviets, of course, knew that their hopes of catching up with the United States had been set back, but so long as the Americans did not know the true situation the Soviets still enjoyed the immediate benefits of seeming to be about to catch up with the United States or even of having just surpassed it. When the Kennedy administration took office in 1961, the evidence on the Soviet missile deployment was still inconclusive. The U-2 flights had been discontinued after Gary Powers had been shot down on May 1, 1960, and even before that, there was great difficulty obtaining pictures of the deployment because of the almost constant clouds over the northern areas of the Soviet Union where the big missiles were being emplaced. Secretary McNamara became skeptical of the higher estimates when he saw them and pressed hard for better intelligence. But even as late as June 1961 the evidence was contradictory and the intelligence community continued to be split, with some Air Force estimates still going as high as three hundred Soviet missiles deployed and some Navy estimates as low as ten. It was not until the summer and fall of 1961 that the Americans discovered the true situation—and decided to tell the Soviets that they knew.

The first news of this came to the Soviets in a speech given in November 1961 by Roswell Gilpatric, Deputy Secretary of Defense. And it was confirmed in a variety of other ways in the weeks that followed.

The American decision to let the Soviets know that we knew was deliberate. But it was made only after much agonizing, since everyone involved recognized that telling the Soviets what we knew entailed considerable risk. Forewarned, the Soviets would undoubtedly speed up their ICBM program. They would do so anyway, of course, but this action to let them know what we knew meant the speed-up would be sooner rather than later. On the other hand, Khrushchev's several ultimatums on Berlin indicated that, if he were allowed to continue to assume that we still believed in the missile gap, he would very probably bring the world dangerously close to war. Thus the decision was reached to go ahead with telling the Soviets that we now knew. Gilpatric was chosen as the instrument because a speech by the Deputy Secretary of Defense was high enough to be convincing to the Soviets but not so high as to be threatening—whereas a speech by the President, the Secretary of State, or the Secretary of Defense might well have been. And the Gilpatric speech was followed by a round of briefings for our allies—deliberately including some whom we knew were penetrated, so as to reinforce and confirm through Soviet intelligence channels the message carried openly through the Gilpatric speech.

For the Soviets, the implications of the message were horrendous. It was not so much the fact that the Americans had military superiority—that was not news to the Soviets. What was bound to frighten them most was that the Americans *knew* that they had military superiority. For the Soviets quickly realized that to have reached this conclusion the Americans must have made an intelligence break-through and found a way to pinpoint the location of the Soviet missiles that had been deployed as well as to calculate the total numbers. A "soft" ICBM system with somewhat cumbersome launching techniques, which is what the Soviets had at this time, is an effective weapon for both a first strike, a surprise attack such as at Pearl Harbor, and a second, retaliatory strike so long as the location of the launching pads can be kept secret. However, if the enemy has a map with all the pads plotted, the system will retain some of its utility as a first-strike weapon, but almost none at all as a second-strike weapon. The whole Soviet ICBM system was suddenly obsolescent.

While the Soviet leaders fretted over these intractable problems, Castro clamored more and more insistently for military protection, magnifying the threat of an American invasion, and —in all probability—himself raising the subject of nuclear missiles. In any case, among the Soviet leadership all these problems, fears, and demands somehow converged on the thesis that at least a temporary and expedient solution to their several problems would be to install some of their older, more plentiful medium- and intermediate-range missiles in Cuba. It would give them a cheap and immediate substitute for the newer, more expensive ICBMs and let them stretch out the ICBM program to ease the pressure on resources. And it would meet Castro's demands and protect what had become, since Castro's self-proclaimed membership in the Communist bloc, not just another "war of national liberation" but the first opportunity to project Soviet power into the Western Hemisphere.

Thus the motive for the decision was strategic in the broad sense that a general improvement in the Soviet military position would affect the entire political context, strengthening their hand for dealing with the whole range of problems facing them —and unanticipated problems as well. But even though general rather than specific security and foreign policy goals were the principal motive, once the decision was made it did offer enticing prospects for specific gains in foreign policy as ancillary benefits. If the move in Cuba were successful and the over-all Soviet position strengthened, their leverage on Berlin would indeed be improved. NATO would surely be shaken and the chances of the U.S. successfully creating a multilateral nuclear force reduced. In Latin America, other potential "Castros" would be encouraged. American power would be less impressive and American protection less desirable, and some of the Latin American states would move in the Soviet direction even if their governments were not overthrown.

Then, too, a successful move in Cuba would cut the ground from under the Chinese Communists and go far toward convincing Communists everywhere that Soviet leadership was strong and Soviet methods in dealing with the "imperialists" effective.

ARNOLD HORELICK

The Soviet Gamble

The puzzle of Soviet motives intrigued nearly everyone who wrote about the Cuban missile crisis. The wide divergence in theories prompted Arnold Horelick, a political analyst for the RAND *Corporation, to undertake a systematic study which would provide the government with a better understanding of how the Russians were likely to behave in future crises. Writing exclusively from open, unclassified sources, Horelick originally presented his analysis as a* RAND *Corporation memorandum in September 1963. The following selection is taken from a slightly abridged version of the memorandum published in* World Politics *in 1964.*

IN A TELEVISION interview not long after the Cuban missile crisis of October 1962, President Kennedy observed that both the United States and the Soviet Union had made serious miscalculations in the Cuban affair. "I don't think we expected that he [Khrushchev] would put the missiles in Cuba," he said, "because it would have seemed such an imprudent action for him to take. . . . He obviously thought he could do it in secret and that the United States would accept it." [1]

As it turned out, of course, deploying strategic missiles in Cuba *was* an imprudent thing for Khrushchev to do, and his expectation that the United States would accept it proved to be mistaken. In the first few weeks after the immediate crisis was resolved by Khrushchev's withdrawal of the Soviet missiles,

Arnold Horelick, "The Cuban Missile Crisis: An Analysis of Soviet Calculations and Behavior," *World Politics,* XVI (April 1964), 363–377. Reprinted by permission of Princeton University Press. The article carried the following footnote on the first page: "This . . . is an abridgment of a RAND Corporation memorandum written by the author as part of the research program sponsored by the United States Air Force under Project RAND. However, views or conclusions contained in this article are those of the author and should not be interpreted as representing the official opinion or policy of the United States Air Force."

[1] *Washington Post,* December 18, 1962.

Soviet affairs specialists turned their attention to the puzzling questions raised by his behavior: (1) Why did Khrushchev deploy strategic weapons in Cuba? (2) What led him to believe he could succeed? (3) Why did he withdraw the weapons so precipitately?

In the months that have elapsed since the first post-crisis flurry of speculation and analysis, a great deal of valuable new information has come to light, particularly in testimony before Congressional committees by high administration officials. In mid-December 1962, Khrushchev broke the silence he had maintained for some six weeks and presented before the USSR Supreme Soviet the first in a series of detailed explanations of his actions.[2]

Although the new American and Soviet materials for the most part bear only indirectly on the questions posed above, they provide an improved basis for attempting to answer them. One minor participant in the events of October 1962, Fidel Castro, reportedly told a friendly French correspondent that the answers to these questions are "a mystery" which may perhaps be unraveled by historians "in 20 or 30 years."[3] Yet if we are to derive any useful foreign policy and defense lessons from the Cuban missile crisis, we can hardly wait that long. Though these questions cannot now be resolved definitively, we must at least arrive at some provisional answers that can be tested against Soviet behavior in the coming months and years. If we fail to do this, we reduce the momentous U.S.-Soviet Caribbean confrontation of October 1962 to mere episodic proportions.

SOVIET OBJECTIVES

Unfortunately, much of the early post-crisis discussion of Soviet objectives was strongly conditioned by observers' atti-

[2] *Pravda*, December 13, 1962. The continuing drumfire of Albanian and Chinese criticism obliged Khrushchev to return to the subject repeatedly, particularly in his East German SED Congress speech (*Pravda*, January 17, 1963) and his Supreme Soviet election speech (*Pravda*, February 28, 1963).

[3] Conversation with Claude Julien, *Le Monde*, March 22, 1963.

tudes toward the policy pursued by the U.S. government in dealing with the crisis and by their appraisals of the probable consequences of its outcome. Among those who criticized the administration for acting recklessly as well as among those who regarded its policy as too cautious, the argument was encountered that the Soviet Union, directly or indirectly, had achieved much of what it intended.[4] In part, perhaps, what brought critics of widely divergent political persuasions to similar conclusions was a shared image, born of Sputnik, of the ten-foot tall Russians who rarely do anything wrong, and a complementary, equally erroneous image, fostered by the U-2 and the Bay of Pigs debacles, of U.S. administrations that rarely do anything right. But to regard the outcome of the Cuban missile crisis as coinciding in any substantial way with Soviet intentions or interests is to mistake skillful salvage of a ship-

[4] Professor Leslie Dewart, who argued that the President played into Khrushchev's hands by *over*-reacting, wrote that "yielding was the essence of the [Soviet] scheme." "The conclusion appears reasonable that Russia set up missile bases in Cuba in full knowledge or expectation of the consequences. It is those very consequences [to compel a shift from "rigidity to negotiableness" in U.S. foreign policy] which she can be presumed to have sought." ("Russia's Cuban Policy and the Prospects of Peace," *Council for Correspondence Newsletter,* No. 21 [October 1962], 17, 21.)

Stuart Chase has similarly suggested that "it is not impossible" that the withdrawal of Soviet strategic weapons from Cuba "was part of a plan, more political than military, to secure a pledge against invasion." ("Two Worlds," *Bulletin of the Atomic Scientists,* XIX [June 1963], 20.)

Those who criticized the administration for reacting too cautiously tended to regard the outcome of the crisis as coinciding less with specific Soviet intentions than with general Soviet interests. For example, David Lowenthal wrote: "It is what he [the President] could have done but did *not* do that will most strongly impress our Communist foes. He forced them to retract the move, and for a brief while aired their malice before the world. But he did nothing to penalize an action aimed at inflicting an almost mortal wound on us, and he even made a noninvasion pledge that had never been given before. . . . We did not even get the *status quo ante.*" ("U.S. Cuban Policy: Illusion and Reality," *National Review,* January 29, 1963, 63.)

Along related lines, Robert D. Crane wrote: "The USSR might conclude that the United States was content with a vague promise of the verified removable of an indefensible Communist military gain. The Soviets on the other hand, demanded—and apparently believed they had received—an assurance against an invasion of Cuba by any country in the Western Hemisphere, which under the circumstances could amount to the creation of a new doctrine strongly resembling a Monroe-Doctrine-in-reverse." ("The Cuban Crisis: A Strategic Analysis of American and Soviet Policy," *Orbis,* VI [Winter 1963], 547–48.)

wreck for brilliant navigation. If the success achieved by the United States in October 1962 proved to be more limited in scope than many believed it would be or had to be, the outcome hardly constituted a net gain for the Soviet Union.

Some observers have imputed to the Soviet Union precisely those objectives they believe that Khrushchev achieved: the securing of desired political concessions from the United States, such as a public pledge by the President not to invade Cuba; or more generalized political gains, including credit for having saved the peace. Even if they had been fully achieved, these objectives would have been blatantly disproportionate to the means expended, and to the costs and risks incurred by the Soviet Union in the undertaking. The Chinese and Albanian Communists, and Castro, too, have correctly—from the Communist point of view—drawn attention to the emptiness of mere verbal pledges by the enemy.[5] Moreover, the U.S. government has withheld a formal pledge, since one of the conditions for it set forth in the Kennedy-Khrushchev correspondence, on-site verification, has not been satisfied. Khrushchev has publicly treated the President's conditional pledge as if it were in full force because he has little else to show for his efforts. While Castro has complained formally to UN Secretary-General U Thant that "officials of the U.S. government declare that they do not consider themselves bound by any promise," [6] Khrushchev has prudently chosen to ignore these statements.

As to any credit Khrushchev may have gained for saving the peace, it is doubtful whether his "reasonableness" persuaded many observers of his dedication to peace who were not so persuaded before the crisis. It is more likely that his decision to withdraw the weapons served only to restore the confidence in

[5] "In no circumstances," the Peking *People's Daily* editorialized on October 31, 1962, can the people of the world trust "the empty promises of the U.S. aggressor." Tirana Radio chimed in the following day: "The Cuban people know from their own experience—the experience of the Bay of Pigs and of all that is happening around them—that Kennedy and the imperialist monopolies represented by Kennedy cannot be trusted." And Castro has said: "We do not believe in the words of Kennedy; but, moreover, Kennedy has not given any word. And if he gave it, he has already retracted it." (Havana Radio, January 16, 1963.)

[6] *New York Times,* November 17, 1962.

him of those whose faith was shaken by the disclosure—or rather by Khrushchev's belated acknowledgment—that the Soviet Union had deployed strategic missiles and bombers in Cuba. On the other hand, the ranks of those, both in the Communist camp and outside of it, who regard Khrushchev as an "adventurer" or "capitulator" have certainly been augmented.[7] The growth of such beliefs about Khrushchev is not likely to enhance his future political effectiveness.

Finally, to achieve the limited political objectives imputed to them by those who contend that the outcome of the crisis was the one intended by the USSR, the Soviet leaders need not have invested so heavily or risked so much. At least 42 IL-28 bombers and an equal number of strategic missiles were brought into Cuba by Soviet ships; nine missile sites were established, six of them with four launchers each for the MRBM's and three of them, fixed sites for the IRBM's, each designed to include four launching positions.[8] Yet a token force of a few conspicuously deployed MRBM's would alone doubtless have sufficed to provoke a U.S. demand that the Soviet Union remove them from Cuba.

The magnitude and character of the Soviet strategic weapon deployment in Cuba cast doubt also on a related hypothesis—namely, that the Soviet Union sought merely to compel the United States to withdraw its missiles from Turkey in exchange for the withdrawal of Soviet missiles from Cuba. Since the United States had only one squadron (15 missiles) of Jupiters deployed in Turkey,[9] only a third the number of MRBM's with a 1,100-mile range known to have been shipped to Cuba would have sufficed to make such a trade seem quantitatively plausible. The costly and essentially unsalvageable fixed sites that were being prepared to receive IRBM's with a 2,200-mile range were altogether superfluous to any intended Cuba-Turkey missile-

[7] The Chinese Communists have accused him of being both.

[8] Briefing by John Hughes, Defense Intelligence Agency, *Department of Defense Appropriations for 1964,* Hearings Before a Subcommittee of the Committee on Appropriations, House of Representatives, 88th Congress, 1st Session (Washington 1963), Part I, p. 7; hereinafter cited as *Hearings.*

[9] *Missiles and Rockets,* January 7, 1963, p. 26.

base exchange since the United States had no equivalent missiles in Turkey, or anywhere else for that matter.

Of course, a mutual withdrawal of missiles from Cuba and Turkey was explicitly proposed by Khrushchev in his October 27 letter to President Kennedy. But the mere fact that Khrushchev proposed such an exchange at one point during the crisis, after the United States had demanded the withdrawal of Soviet strategic weapons, no more proves that this was his objective from the start than his subsequent withdrawal of the missiles without such a *quid pro quo* proves that his ultimate objective was simply to get President Kennedy to promise not to invade Cuba. It is true that the withdrawal of U.S. strategic weapons from Turkey, under apparent Soviet duress, would have given Khrushchev a more tangible return for his trouble than a conditional verbal pledge by the United States not to invade Cuba.[10] It is one thing for the United States and an allied host country to decide jointly to substitute for some bases other means of defense, such as Polaris submarines in adjacent waters; it is quite another for the United States, under Soviet duress, to withdraw from its bases, regardless of the wishes of its allies.

It seems questionable, however, that the Soviets would accept the costs and risks of deploying missiles in Cuba merely in order to remove them in return for the withdrawal of U.S. missiles from Turkey. The phasing out of U.S. missiles deployed overseas, without a Soviet *quid pro quo,* was already known to have been under consideration long before the October 1962 crisis,[11] though the Soviet leaders may not have been certain regarding U.S. intentions. Moreover, because of geographic considerations and the large U.S. advantage in intercontinental nuclear delivery capabilities, a strategic missile base in Cuba was a far more valuable military asset to the Soviet Union than a comparable base in Turkey to the United States. Finally, as

[10] Had the United States accepted the Soviet base-exchange proposal of October 27, Khrushchev would also have received such a U.S. pledge since a reciprocal exchange of no-invasion pledges was part of the proposed bargain.

[11] Secretary McNamara has testified that the long-standing program to replace the obsolete Thor and Jupiter missiles dated from early 1961. (*Hearings,* p. 57.)

pointed out earlier, if the Soviet leaders intended no more than to lay the groundwork for an agreement on the mutual withdrawal of U.S. and Soviet strategic missiles from Turkey and Cuba, they need not have deployed more than a token force of MRBM's and need not have constructed installations for IRBM's at all. It is more likely that the base-exchange proposal was an improvised or perhaps even a prepared fall-back position to cover unfavorable contingencies, but not the Soviet-preferred culmination of the Cuban venture.[12]

Khrushchev's official rationale is that Soviet strategic weapons were deployed in Cuba solely to defend the island against U.S. attack; and that once the threat of such an attack was removed (by the President's conditional undertaking not to launch one), the Soviet weapons, having served their purpose, were withdrawn and peace was preserved. Of course, even on its own terms this rationale is deficient, for Khrushchev also acknowledged, presumably to demonstrate that his decision to withdraw the missiles was not a needless concession, that he took that decisive step only when urgent word reached him that a U.S. attack on Cuba appeared imminent.

Far from deterring the "imperialists," by giving them, in Khrushchev's words, "a more realistic idea of the danger of thermonuclear war," the discovery of Soviet strategic missiles in Cuba provoked a U.S. naval quarantine, a rapid build-up of U.S. Army and Tactical Air Forces in the southeastern part of the country and a world-wide alert of the Strategic Air Command. Thus, it would seem, the deployment of Soviet strategic weapons in Cuba did not succeed, as Khrushchev said he had anticipated, "in bringing the aggressors to their senses." In his words: "In the morning of October 27 we received information

[12] If the base-exchange proposal was a *prepared* fall-back position, the Soviet leaders failed to prepare their propagandists for it. On the same day (October 28, 1962) that it front-paged Khrushchev's base-exchange proposal letter to the President, the Soviet government newspaper, *Izvestiia,* printed on an inside page a commentary which stated: "There are those in the U.S.A. who speculate that in exchange for denying Cuba the ability to repel American aggression, one might 'give up' some American base close to Soviet territory. . . . Such 'proposals,' if you can call them that, merely serve to betray the unclean conscience of the authors." The editor of *Izvestiia* is Alexei Adzhubei, Khrushchev's son-in-law.

from our Cuban comrades *and from other sources* which directly stated that this [U.S.] attack would be carried out within the next two or three days. We regarded the telegrams received as a signal for *utmost alarm,* and this alarm was justified. Immediate actions were required in order to prevent an attack against Cuba and preserve peace."[13]

The action, of course, was Khrushchev's proposal to the President to withdraw from Cuba all the weapons "which you regard as offensive" in exchange for cessation of the quarantine and a pledge by the President not to invade Cuba. It must have appeared to Khrushchev, then, that the United States had not only been prepared to attack Cuba *despite* the presence of Soviet weapons, but precisely *because* the weapons had been brought in, since evidently only by agreeing to withdraw them did Khrushchev believe he could secure from the President assurances that the United States would not attack. Presidential statements, made repeatedly in the months preceding the deployment of Soviet missiles in Cuba, that the United States did not intend to invade if offensive weapons were *not* deployed in Cuba, had apparently not been deemed sufficient; only when such an assurance was made conditional on the removal of Soviet strategic weapons from Cuba, with appropriate international verification, did it become acceptable.

The strange logic of Khrushchev's face-saving explanation of Soviet motives and behavior does not in itself disprove his contention that Soviet missiles were deployed in Cuba solely to deter a U.S. attack; it only indicates that if deterrence of a U.S. attack on Cuba was the sole Soviet objective, the plan backfired: the Soviet weapons provoked rather than deterred.[14]

But there are other reasons for doubting Khrushchev's account of Soviet objectives. These have to do with the appro-

[13] *Pravda,* December 13, 1962; emphasis supplied. The "other sources" may have included the U.S. government.

[14] Khrushchev referred obliquely to this miscalculation in his speech at the 6th Congress of the SED (East German Party) in Berlin on January 16, 1963, when he acknowledged that "this enforced measure [stationing Soviet missiles in Cuba] had the effect of a shock *(shok)* on the imperialists," but argued that only such measures were capable of inducing U.S. statesmen "to make a more sober assessment of the objective reality." (*Pravda,* January 17, 1963.)

priateness of the weapons selected to be deployed in Cuba for the ostensible purpose of deterring a U.S. attack on that country. Surely a threat to destroy several southeastern U.S. cities, or even Miami alone, *if credible,* would have been adequate to deter such an attack. For this, tactical missiles with a range of several hundred miles would have sufficed. It could have been claimed that such weapons were designed to strike at airfields and marshaling and embarkation points in the Florida area from which a U.S. invasion might be mounted. Perhaps by employing a high lofting technique, the MRBM's that were deployed and the IRBM's that were being prepared could have been used to strike close-in targets, but such long-range missiles are not designed for that purpose. Whatever marginal incremental value for local deterrence (of an attack on Cuba) might have been obtained by deploying missiles with ranges in excess of several hundred miles was more than outweighed by the added provocation they offered.

Had the Soviet missiles remained in Cuba, declarations regarding the control arrangements established for them would have been important indicators of the objectives the Soviet Union sought to pursue. To maximize the effectiveness of Soviet missiles deployed in Cuba as a deterrent against a U.S. attack on Cuba and to reduce the risk that their employment, in the event of such an attack, would bring down U.S. nuclear retaliation against the USSR, it might have been desirable for Khrushchev to have the U.S. government believe that the Soviet missiles were at Castro's disposal and under his control.

In the United States Castro had gained a reputation for impulsive, irresponsible behavior. Whether authentic or not, the post-crisis remarks attributed to Che Guevara, that the Cubans were prepared, in the event of a U.S. attack, to strike "the very heart of the United States, including New York," [15] conformed to the image of the Cuban leadership that was widely held in the United States. Once an operational missile capability was

[15] According to Theodore Draper, these remarks were reportedly made by Guevara in an interview with a London *Daily Worker* correspondent, but did not appear in the version published on December 4, 1962. ("Castro and Communism," *The Reporter,* January 17, 1963, p. 44.)

established in Cuba, such beliefs on the part of Americans might have lent substantial deterrent value to the missiles deployed in Cuba.

On the other hand, to bring Cuba-based missiles to bear in support of Soviet interests in confrontations with the United States (for example, in Berlin), belief that the missiles were at the disposal of the *Soviet* leaders would have been essential. Until such time as the Soviet Union might wish to bring the missiles so to bear, however, the Soviet leaders probably would have preferred to keep the question of control in an ambiguous state. Vague, generalized statements, such as characterize most Soviet strategic threats, might have been employed.

A consideration of probably lesser importance may have been that a premature explicit announcement on control would have obliged Khrushchev to accept certain political liabilities, regardless of whether he claimed that the Soviet Union retained control over the missiles or not. In either case, Khrushchev would have had to acknowledge that the Soviet Union was engaging in a military practice that he had repeatedly denounced: establishing a strategic base on foreign territory, if he claimed control for the Soviet Union; proliferation of nuclear strategic weapons, if he announced that the missiles had been turned over to Cuba.

On October 22, 1962, President Kennedy impaled Khrushchev on one of the horns of this dilemma by unilaterally resolving the ambiguity: ". . . it shall be the policy of this nation to regard any nuclear missile launched from Cuba against any nation in the Western Hemisphere as an attack by the Soviet Union on the United States requiring a full retaliatory response upon the Soviet Union." [16]

Initially, the Soviet Union attempted to evade the issue by refusing to acknowledge that it had emplaced strategic weapons in Cuba, while affirming in its first official statement on the

[16] *New York Times,* October 23, 1962. The phrase "*full* retaliatory response upon the Soviet Union" may have implied to the Soviet leaders not only that the United States would not treat the Soviet Union as a sanctuary area if the Cuba-based missiles were fired, but that it did not intend to restrict itself to a limited strategic response ("tit for tat" retaliation).

crisis (October 23) that Cuba alone had the right to decide what kinds of weapons were appropriate for the defense of Cuba.[17] But the same statement, without acknowledging that the military equipment provided to Cuba by the USSR included strategic weapons, also reflected Soviet concern that the U.S. government might feel impelled to strike quickly to prevent operational missiles from falling into Castro's hands. Thus, the following oblique reassurance was offered: "Nuclear weapons, which have been *created by the Soviet people and which are in the hands of the people,* will never be used for the purpose of aggression." [18]

On the same day, privately, Khrushchev made this reassurance explicit during a three-hour conversation in Moscow with Westinghouse Electric vice-president William E. Knox, through whom he presumably wished to communicate informally with the U.S. government. According to Knox, Khrushchev acknowledged that Soviet ballistic missiles had been furnished to Cuba, but were completely controlled by Soviet officers. "But the Cubans were very volatile people, Mr. Khrushchev said, and all of the sophisticated hardware furnished for their defense was entirely under the control of Soviet officers; it would be used only in the event that Cuba was attacked, and it would never be fired except on his orders as Commander in Chief of all of the Soviet Union." [19]

Finally, in his October 27 letter to President Kennedy, the first published Khrushchev letter during the crisis, the Soviet premier informed the President that "the weapons in Cuba that you have mentioned and which you say alarm you are in the hands of Soviet officers." "Therefore," he went on, "any accidental use of them whatsoever to the detriment of the United States is excluded." [20]

It thus seems clear that despite the advantages to be gained from ambiguity regarding control of the missiles in Cuba,

[17] *Pravda,* October 24, 1962.
[18] *Ibid.;* emphasis supplied.
[19] *New York Times,* November 18, 1962.
[20] *Pravda,* October 28, 1962. The implication is that if the weapons had been under Cuban control, the possibility that they might be "accidentally used" could *not* be excluded.

Khrushchev felt compelled to reassure the President explicitly that Castro could not order the missiles to be fired and that there was therefore no need for the United States to make an immediate attack before the missiles became operational [21] in order to forestall a possible irrational act by the "volatile" Cubans. Whatever value the Soviet weapons may have been intended to have as a deterrent of a local U.S. attack on Cuba was seriously diminished by this reassurance.

It is questionable, however, whether deterrence of a local U.S. attack on Cuba was ever regarded by the Soviet leaders as more than a subsidiary and derivative effect of a venture intended primarily to serve other ends. Certainly the size and character of the intended deployment indicate that it was meant to achieve some broader purpose.[22] Castro has been quoted by a friendly source, the correspondent for *Le Monde,* Claude Julien, as having said that the Cuban leaders had considered among themselves the possibility of requesting that the USSR furnish Cuba missiles, but had not come to any decision when Moscow proposed to emplace them: "They explained to us that in accepting them we would be reinforcing the socialist camp the world over, and because we had received important aid from the socialist camp we estimated that we could not decline. This is why we accepted them. It was not in order to assure our own defense, but first of all to reinforce socialism on the international scale. Such is the truth even if other explanations are furnished elsewhere." [23]

Although Castro subsequently issued a refutation of an American press agency version of the Julien interview (not of the original *Le Monde* article),[24] this quotation has the ring of

[21] This did not occur for all MRBM systems until October 28; the IRBM's never achieved operational status, nor, apparently, did the IL-28 bombers. (*Hearings,* pp. 12, 16.)

[22] For example, while the threat posed by MRBM's to cities, including Washington, D.C., in the southeastern part of the United States would, if credible, have been adequate to deter a U.S. attack on Cuba, most U.S. strategic bomber and missile bases would have been beyond the range of those weapons. These bases could have been covered by IRBM's.

[23] *Le Monde,* March 22, 1963.

[24] Havana, *Prensa Latina,* March 22, 1963. Specifically, Castro denied only that "I expressed myself in an unfriendly way at any time about Soviet Prime Minister Nikita Khrushchev." Castro's general refutation

truth. Of course, the deployment of Soviet missiles in Cuba, to the extent that it would have strengthened the Soviet position in its "world-wide" confrontation with the United States, would also have added credibility to Soviet strategic threats, including the threat to defend Cuba against U.S. attack. In fact, the implication of the official Soviet rationale for deploying strategic weapons in Cuba—namely, that the threat posed to the United States by Soviet weapons *based in the USSR* lacked sufficient credibility to deter a U.S. attack on "socialist" Cuba—is one of the troublesome embarrassments with which Khrushchev has had to deal since the Cuban missile crisis.[25]

---

pointedly referred only to the UPI version of *Le Monde's* article: "I do not believe that Julien, whom we consider a friend of Cuba, can be guilty of untruths like *some* of the statements the UPI attributes to him." (Emphasis supplied.) The March 22 TASS version of Castro's denial *omitted* both of the statements quoted above.

After this article was written, Castro was questioned by two other journalists regarding the origination of the plan to deploy Soviet missiles in Cuba. According to Herbert L. Matthews (*Return to Cuba,* Stanford University *Hispanic American Report* series [1964], p. 16), Castro stated flatly on October 23, 1963, that "the idea of installing the nuclear weapons was his, not the Russians'." However, three weeks later, according to Jean Daniel's account of his interview with the Cuban premier, Castro appeared to confirm the account given earlier in the Julien interview: "We thought of a proclamation, an alliance, conventional military aid. . . . They [the Russians] reasoned that if conventional military assistance was the extent of their assistance, the United States might not hesitate to instigate an invasion, in which case Russia would retaliate and this would inevitably touch off a world war. . . . Under these circumstances, how could we Cubans refuse to share the risks to save us?" (Jean Daniel, "Unofficial Envoy: An Historic Report from Two Capitals," *New Republic,* December 14, 1963, pp. 18–19.) Matthews writes that he telephoned Castro after Daniel's account was published and was again told: "We were the ones who put forward the idea of the missiles" (*Return to Cuba,* p. 16).

[25] Khrushchev handled this question gingerly in defending his Cuban policy against Chinese and Albanian criticism in his speech at the Congress of the SED in Berlin on January 16, 1963: "One may object that, under the influence of the most unrestrained incitement, the U.S. imperialists will not keep their promise and will again turn their arms against Cuba. But the forces which protected Cuba now exist and are *growing in strength every day*. It does not matter where the rockets are located, in Cuba, or elsewhere. They can be used with equal success against any particular aggression." (*Pravda,* January 17, 1963; emphasis supplied.) The implicit question is: If so, why were Soviet missiles deployed in Cuba in the first place? The implicit answer is: Soviet-based strategic power was not *then* great enough to deter a U.S. attack, but it is "growing in strength every day" and soon will be (or will appear to be).

Before the crisis, Khrushchev's expressions of strategic support for Cuba were framed in notably cautious and equivocal terms: the USSR's capability to defend Cuba with Soviet-based missiles was affirmed, but a commitment to do so was carefully avoided.[26] Cuban leaders, however, consistently interpreted Khrushchev's words as if they represented a firm, though tacit, commitment. For example, according to Guevara, in January 1961 it was already "well known that the Soviet Union and all the socialist states *are ready to go to war* to defend our sovereignty and that *a tacit agreement* has been reached between our peoples." [27]

It may be assumed that the Cuban leaders had pressed Khrushchev for an explicit and unequivocal commitment to defend Cuba with Soviet-based weapons in the event of a U.S. attack. It was presumably to secure such a commitment, which the Soviet Union was evidently reluctant to give, that Castro in effect volunteered Cuba for membership in the "socialist camp" in 1961. As between an explicit and unequivocal Soviet guarantee, on the one hand, and the stationing of Soviet strategic weapons on Cuban soil, on the other, Castro might well have preferred the former under certain circumstances. To the extent that Castro (1) could have had confidence that the Soviet Union would honor such a commitment; or (2) believed that it would be credited to some serious extent in the United States; or (3) believed that a U.S. attack was unlikely in any case, he might not have deemed it necessary to request the Soviet Union to establish strategic missile bases in Cuba and might have been wary of the political consequences of such a move at home, throughout Latin America, and in the United States.

For the *Soviet Union* to propose that its strategic weapons be

[26] In July 1960, Khrushchev said that "figuratively speaking, in case of need, Soviet artillerymen can support the Cuban people with their rocket fire. . . ." (*Pravda*, July 9, 1960.) The conditional form of this threat "can," not "will," support) was retained in the Soviet Government's statement on Cuba on September 11, 1962, which asserted that the USSR *"has the capability* from its own territory to render assistance to any peace-loving state." (*Pravda*, September 11, 1962.)

[27] *Obra Revolucionaria*, January 25, 1961, quoted by Draper, "Castro and Communism," p. 39. (Emphasis supplied.)

deployed in Cuba, however, may have been another matter. Let us assume that, regardless of the real intentions of the U.S. government, Castro believed the probability of a U.S. attack was not negligible. He may have agreed to the Soviet proposal not only because of his dependence on the Soviet Union, but also because, from the Cuban point of view, if the Soviet leaders believed their "world-wide" position vis-à-vis the United States was such that it required reinforcement by drastic means, the reliability of Soviet pledges to defend Cuba with Soviet-based weapons—equivocal pledges to begin with—must have seemed seriously compromised.[28]

What was the "world-wide" position of the Soviet Union that needed to be reinforced by the emplacement of strategic weapons in Cuba? Despite boastful Soviet efforts to conceal it, the fact is that throughout the cold war the Soviet Union's capacity to strike the United States with nuclear weapons has been very much smaller than the U.S. capacity to strike the USSR. From the start, the bulk of the USSR's strategic nuclear capability has been effective only out to ranges of about 2,000–2,500 miles. The Soviet Union acquired a very potent nuclear capability against Western Europe, first with medium bombers and then with medium- and intermediate-range ballistic missiles of the type it tried to emplace in Cuba. But the Soviet heavy bomber and ICBM forces—that is, the long-range weapons required to reach the United States—did not attain the strength levels that Western observers anticipated they would reach in the 1960's. Inflated beliefs in the West, actively promoted by misleading and deceptive Soviet claims, that the Soviet Union was rapidly acquiring a large intercontinental strike force tended, until the fall of 1961, to deprive continued and even growing U.S. strategic superiority of much of its *political* value.

[28] In the immediate aftermath of the crisis, the pre-crisis positions of the Soviet Union and Cuba on the firmness of Soviet pledges to defend Cuba were sharply reversed. Whereas the Soviet leaders, presumably to placate Castro, offered increasingly strong pledges to defend Cuba, Cuban leaders ignored them and vowed to resist any U.S. attack with their own resources. Later, however, as Soviet-Cuban relations recovered from the estrangement of the fall of 1962, Cuban leaders began to welcome Soviet pledges with great public enthusiasm.

But, in the second half of 1961, the "missile gap" was found, in Secretary McNamara's words, to be "a myth." [29] Confidence in U.S. strategic superiority was restored in the West; moreover, it became apparent, both from Soviet behavior and from the modification of Soviet strategic claims, that the Soviet leaders knew that the West had been undeceived about the strategic balance.[30]

The deployment of strategic weapons in Cuba may have recommended itself to the Soviet leaders as a "quick fix" measure to achieve a substantial, though far from optimal, improvement in Soviet strike capabilities against the United States. Of course, a large increase in the programmed Soviet-based ICBM force would have provided the Soviet leaders with a military capability far more effective (certainly for second-strike purposes) than could be achieved by the emplacement of highly vulnerable MRBM's, IRBM's, and light bombers in Cuba. But such an expansion of the ICBM (and missile-launching nuclear submarine) force could be achieved only gradually and at far greater cost. The Cuban deployment may not have been undertaken as a substitute for such a build-up, but as a stopgap measure, pending its completion.

Certainly the deployment of limited numbers of MRBM's and IRBM's in Cuba would not have solved the Soviet Union's strategic problem. The evident deficiencies of such a force have led some observers to conclude that military considerations were of little importance in the Soviet decision to emplace strategic weapons in Cuba. It is true that the missile sites were soft, very close to the United States, and, after detection, under

[29] Quoted in an interview by Stewart Alsop, "Our New Strategy: The Alternatives to Total War," *Saturday Evening Post,* December 1, 1962, p. 18.

[30] Soviet strategic pronouncements after the fall of 1961 shifted from claims of superiority to efforts to deprive American claims to superiority of political value by emphasizing the adequacy of Soviet retaliatory capability. Soviet leaders began explicitly to declare their readiness to accept strategic parity as the basic assumption from which political settlements should proceed (e.g., Marshal Malinovsky's *Pravda* interview, January 25, 1962). The emphasis in claims regarding the USSR's strike capability against the United States shifted from the *high level* of destruction that could be inflicted to the *certainty* that some unspecified level of retaliation would occur.

close and constant surveillance. They would presumably have been highly vulnerable to a U.S. first strike, even with conventional bombs. As a Soviet first-strike force, the Cuba-based force deployed or being readied as of October 1962 was in itself too small to destroy the U.S. strategic nuclear strike force. Even together with the larger long-range strategic force based in the USSR, it seems most unlikely that the force would have been adequate in the fall of 1962; moreover, there would have been a problem, though perhaps not an insurmountable one, of coordinating salvoes from close-in and distant bases so as to avoid a ragged attack. By the same token, however, the installation of Soviet strategic missiles in Cuba would have complicated a U.S. first strike, improved Soviet capabilities to launch a preemptive attack, and hence reduced the credibility of U.S. strategic deterrence of local Soviet aggression, say, in Europe. As to the first-strike potential of Cuba-based Soviet missiles, they could have brought a substantial portion of U.S. nuclear striking power under an attack essentially without warning; moreover, there is no assurance that the build-up would have stopped with the sites already completed or under construction when the Soviets were compelled to abandon the operation.

Whatever their strategic shortcomings, the additional capabilities with which Cuba-based missiles would have provided the Soviet leaders were not insignificant. It is difficult to conceive of any other measure that promised to produce so large an improvement in the Soviet strategic position as quickly or as cheaply. That the Cuban missile deployment would not in itself have provided the Soviet Union with a retaliation-proof first-strike capability against the United States is hardly a reason for dismissing it as of limited strategic importance, as some observers have attempted to do. As the President subsequently said, the Soviet leaders tried materially to change the balance of power. Certainly, the deployment of Soviet missiles in Cuba, in his words, "would have politically changed the balance of power; it would have appeared to [change it] and appearances contribute to reality." [31]

[31] *Washington Post,* December 18, 1962.

The "world-wide" position of the Soviet Union that needed to be reinforced in the fall of 1962 was not only its strategic position vis-à-vis the United States, but also its position in a range of political issues upon which the strategic imbalance in favor of the United States was having some important bearing. It had become evident, since at least the second half of 1961, that the forward momentum of the Soviet Union in international affairs had largely exhausted itself without yielding the gains which the Soviet leaders had anticipated and the West had feared since the mid-1950's.

These expectations had been fed by mounting evidence of the growing military, scientific, technological, and economic power of the Soviet Union vis-à-vis the West. Some of this evidence was real enough, but much of it, particularly in the realm of strategic power, was illusory. In the framework of the cold war, precisely this realm was central. The effects of other striking achievements, as, for example, in space exploration, were amplified, sometimes out of all proportion to their intrinsic political and military worth, by their presumed bearing on the strategic balance. With the discovery that the "missile gap" had failed to materialize, or had actually materialized in reverse, there was a perceptible change in the world political climate. Western self-confidence was restored and Soviet anxieties must have grown.

Moreover, confident Soviet expectations of a few years earlier in regard to dividends from Soviet military and economic aid to the underdeveloped countries failed to materialize. Western European prosperity had reached a new peak, and despite de Gaulle's intransigence the prospects for growing European economic and political unity must (then, at least) have looked distressingly good to Moscow. At the same time, the unity of the Communist camp was being shattered by the escalating conflict between its two most powerful members. Indeed, the Chinese Communist attack on Khrushchev centered precisely on the unfavorable trend in the cold war which the Chinese attributed to Khrushchev's faulty and overcautious leadership.

Finally, there was the long-smoldering, still unresolved problem of Berlin. After almost four years of threats and retreats,

Khrushchev had still not succeeded in compelling the West to accept a Berlin settlement on Soviet terms. Khrushchev may therefore have sought some quick and dramatic means for achieving a breakthrough that would strengthen the USSR's position—militarily, diplomatically, and psychologically—on a whole range of outstanding issues, and particularly on Berlin.[32]

Rarely, if ever, are such fateful ventures as the Soviet strategic deployment in Cuba undertaken to achieve narrow or isolated objectives. Where nuclear weapons are involved, even small risks are acceptable only if important interests can be advanced by assuming them. It is most unlikely that the Soviet leaders drew up a precise blueprint or detailed timetable for exploitation of the improved military-political position they would have attained had the Cuban venture been successful. But they probably anticipated that the emplacement of strategic missiles in Cuba and their acceptance by the United States would contribute in some degree to the solution of a whole range of military-political problems confronting the Soviet Union and would alter the environment of the cold war in such a manner as to promote new opportunities for political gain whose nature could not be precisely foreseen. . . .

ADAM ULAM

Khrushchev's Grand Design

Nearly all the speculation about Russian motives came from scholars versed in American political traditions and

[32] A link between the Cuban missile deployment and Khrushchev's Berlin strategy was suggested by the Soviet government's statement of September 11, 1962, in which the USSR acknowledged that it was providing military assistance—though of a strictly defensive type—to Cuba, and warned that a U.S. attack on Cuba might unleash the beginning of a thermonuclear war, but at the same time declared a moratorium on new moves in Berlin until after the U.S. Congressional elections. (*Pravda,* September 11, 1962.) Khrushchev may have hoped to discourage any new U.S. action in regard to Cuba until after the elections (i.e., until after the MRBM's, at least, became operational), by offering, in return, to desist from fomenting a new crisis in Berlin, and then, after establishing a strategic base in Cuba, to use this new leverage to press for a favorable settlement in Berlin.

writing from a Washington perspective. Adam Ulam, a specialist on Soviet history and politics at Harvard University, provided a new and valuable insight into Kremlin behavior in his 1968 book Expansion and Coexistence, *a comprehensive history of Soviet foreign policy since the Bolshevik Revolution. Unlike most American commentators, Ulam placed Khrushchev's actions in the missile crisis in the broader context of both his German policy and his contest with the Chinese for leadership of the communist bloc.*

As ONE OBSERVES the course of Soviet foreign policy throughout 1962, one cannot but conclude that the priorities in the minds of the Soviet leaders were as follows: (1) to prevent China from acquiring nuclear weapons, or somehow to limit and control Chinese nuclear armament; (2) to prevent West Germany from acquiring such weapons, which in turn led to (3) the signing of a German peace treaty which would perpetuate the division of Germany and secure a limit on West Germany's war potential.

As to Point 1, it would seem fantastic, as we have seen, that at this late date the Soviet leaders were still hopeful of persuading the Chinese or denying them something they were absolutely determined to obtain. Even in 1958, such hopes were probably forlorn. But as against all that had happened since and as against plain logic, there were still some developments that could keep alive the hope of Chinese compliance, especially in the minds of people who desperately wanted to believe in it. In the first place, China was then enduring a severe economic crisis, the backwash of the "great leap forward," with famine sweeping large parts of the country. In addition the Chinese, in contrast to their openly insolent and defiant tone in 1963, were in 1962 (at least until the Cuban missile crisis) clever enough not to dash Soviet hopes completely or to cut off their channels of communication. *Perhaps* a dazzling Soviet success in the international arena, a demonstration of continuing Soviet dynamism in foreign policy,

Adam Ulam, *Expansion and Coexistence: The History of Soviet Foreign Policy, 1917–1967* (New York, 1968), pp. 661–671. Reprinted by permission of Praeger Publishers.

might persuade the Chinese comrades to trust their nuclear defense to the Russians and to abandon their excessively costly and strategically futile efforts to become a nuclear power?

These hopes may appear as the epitome of naïveté, especially in people as hard-boiled as members of the Presidium of the Communist Party of the Soviet Union. Yet the actual arguments they used with the Chinese, as revealed by official documents, are almost embarrassing in their disingenuousness. As late as the summer of 1963 they were to argue plaintively:

> China is as yet unprepared to produce nuclear weapons in quantity. Even if the People's Republic of China were to produce two or three bombs, this would not solve the question for it either, but would bring about a great exhaustion of China's economy. . . . That is why the most reasonable policy for the People's Republic of China in present conditions . . . would be to devote its efforts to the development of the national economy . . . devoting them to improving the well-being of the Chinese people.[1]

The message was plain: Why do you need atomic weapons? We are protecting you anyway, and we will unselfishly go on producing nuclear weapons to thwart the imperialists; you had better concentrate on producing rice and soybeans! Such arguments must have been greeted with a mixture of fury and amusement, but evidently until the fateful days of October 1962 the Chinese, while stoutly resisting the Soviet leaders' cajoling, left them hoping that *something* might make them change their minds.

Public controversy between the Chinese and the Soviets was stilled, then, in the first months of 1962—largely on the initiative of other Communist parties, for whom the dispute was of course a source of embarrassment and danger. But this also suited Chinese needs and Soviet hopes. A new Sino-Soviet trade agreement, of modest dimensions, was signed. Even the polemic between the Soviet Union and Albania grew less acrimonious, although Albania was thrown out of the Warsaw Pact and Comecon; the Soviets were not going to let the Chinese lead them by the nose. And they were not going to let the Chinese

[1] William E. Griffith, *The Sino-Soviet Rift* (Cambridge, Mass., 1964), p. 363.

dictate their policy toward Yugoslavia either. Yugoslavia *per se* was not of an overwhelming importance to them, even though Tito was an important confidential adviser and guide to such neutralist leaders as Nasser and Sukarno. But a *rapprochement* with Yugoslavia was a useful reminder to the Chinese not to press the Russians too much; after all, Yugoslavia could liquidate Albania overnight. In April Gromyko visited Belgrade.

In the West, the Sino-Soviet dispute was needless to say completely overshadowed by the German problem. The Berlin crisis continued with incidents, notes, and harassment, the Soviets never letting the bothersome issue disappear from the front pages for long. Khrushchev, incorrigibly, continued to titillate and terrify the West with his musings. There were several ways to gore the ox, he implied. He might still sign a separate treaty with East Germany; or there might be just enough accidents in the air approaches to Berlin to persuade people that it was not a safe place to travel to, enough difficulties on the land routes to dissuade people from investing in such a vulnerable location; how sad, then, that West Berlin would become impoverished and depopulated.

Had the Russians been solely interested in Berlin *as such,* it is clear that they could have continued such nervewracking tactics indefinitely, and it is far from certain that they would not have succeeded in securing some change of status for West Berlin. There was considerable division of opinion in the Western alliance—ranging from Olympian disdain on the part of General de Gaulle to Britain's noticeable nervousness. In Washington the young President was subjected to conflicting advice and countless position papers trying to establish what the Russians were really after, how one could stand firm on Berlin and yet minimize the chances of a nuclear war, etc. In fact, for the Soviet policy-makers Berlin was but a promising tool for prying out of the West a more fundamental concession on the German question: an iron-bound guarantee against West Germany getting nuclear weapons.

Soviet fears on this count have never been properly understood in the West, and hence no attempt has really been made either to assuage Soviet susceptibilities on this score or to use the possibility of giving nuclear weapons to Bonn as a bargaining asset. This is so partly because of certain inherent trends in American diplomacy and in the nature of the Western alliance, but also partly because of the difficulty of assessing Soviet thinking on the relationship of nuclear weapons to politics. The Soviets cannot *really* be alarmed by the prospect of Bonn having a few tactical nuclear weapons, ran the prevailing view in the West. Given their own vast superiority in such weapons and rockets, and given the smallness of West Germany, the Russians ought to realize that nuclear weapons in the hands of West Germany could only be purely defensive. Hence, if they really make a fuss about this, it must be for other and devious purposes. But to the Soviets, who would not give one atom bomb to the Poles or Hungarians, the problem necessarily appeared in a different light. What if a nuclear-armed Bonn threatened East Germany? Would the USSR have to launch a pre-emptive attack, thus risking American retaliation? Would she have to launch a suicidal attack on the United States? As to the possibility of a "small" nuclear war, the USSR had to think in political terms: against a *small* nuclear power she would undoubtedly emerge victorious; but could a *Communist regime* survive such a war? What would be the consequences of even one nuclear missile falling on Moscow and destroying the top leadership of the Party and state? That the Russians were genuinely afraid of West Germany possessing atomic weapons was acknowledged somewhat contemptuously by the Communist Chinese in their polemic in 1963. The German issue, then, by 1962 had merged with the problem of "nuclear proliferation."

The Soviets had learned to live with the inescapable—if not exactly comfortable—facts that the United States was a nuclear power and so, in a much smaller way, was Britain. They also realized, if never stated, that, short of some "madmen in Washington" getting their hands on the trigger, the United States would not use her nuclear weapons except under extreme provocation. Therefore the Soviet position on nuclear disarmament had long been that in view of the existence of the two hostile systems such disarmament was, to put it succinctly, impractical, and indeed Soviet participation in the endless international talks on the subject was mainly for propaganda purposes. With the acquisition of a nuclear arsenal of their own, the Soviet leaders evidently concluded that since their nerves were stronger than those of the democracies the continuing nuclear race would redound to their advantage—witness Khrushchev's rocket-rattling. Soviet quantitative inferiority in this race was not considered to vitiate this point. The agitation aroused in the United States during the presidential campaign of 1960 by the issue of the alleged missile gap, the alarm caused in 1961 by the civil-defense (shelter) proposals of the new administration, could be adduced as additional proof of the correctness of this analysis: the capitalists are much more frightened of nuclear war than we *seem* to be.

Once nuclear proliferation became imminent, this Soviet equanimity was shaken, and Soviet interest in nuclear disarmament became real. Soviet spokesmen continued to pay lip service to the idea of complete nuclear disarmament, prohibition of nuclear warfare, eventual destruction of existing nuclear weapons, etc., but the practical difficulties were rightly judged insuperable. The more modest steps, such as a test ban, were evidently thought of little consequence: in 1958 it suited the Soviets to initiate a moratorium on atmospheric tests, but in 1961, when political and possibly technical reasons urged them to resume testing, they did so without compunction. Humanly enough, they were undoubtedly concerned about atmospheric pollution, which reached new heights after the massive tests in 1961 and 1962. But the main incentive to explore what they had previously rejected contemptuously was the welcome prospect of preventing other countries, especially China and West Germany, from acquiring the dreaded weapons. In 1963, after the signing of a partial test ban treaty between the USSR, the United States, and Great Britain, the Chinese publicly attacked the Russians and their motives in signing the pact. To be sure, the charges were highly colored and exaggerated—viz., the allegation that the Soviet leaders were betraying the interests of their own people and no longer cared whether Bonn acquired nuclear arms or not—but the main Chinese point was that the Russians' primary objective was to find some means of preventing China from acquiring the weapons. If we add "and West Germany," we are close to the truth.

How could a test ban signed only by the three nuclear powers accomplish this objective? On the face of it, the treaty would just be an agreement not to test nuclear weapons; it would not ban their further manufacture or, if the powers should so decide, their endowing other states with the armaments. But the treaty could be—and was—open to ratification by other states, which in signing it would *practically* forsake their right to produce atom and hydrogen bombs (an *untested* weapon is not a reliable one). Furthermore, it is clear that the Soviets were hopeful that the treaty would and could be expanded into a rigorous nonproliferation agreement banning the nuclear powers from sharing their weapons and know-how with third parties, and imposing upon the latter an obligation not to develop nuclear weapons of their own.

The following Chinese statement contained in the Russo-Chinese exchange of 1963 deserves very careful reading:

On August 25, 1962, two days before the United States and Britain put forward their draft treaty on the partial halting of nuclear tests, the Soviet Government notified China that U.S. Secretary Rusk had proposed an agreement stipulating that, firstly, the nuclear powers should undertake to refrain from transferring nuclear weapons and technical information concerning their manufacture to non-nuclear countries, and that, *secondly, the countries not in possession of nuclear weapons should undertake to refrain from manufacturing them,* from seeking them from nuclear powers or from accepting technical information concerning their manufacture. *The Soviet Government gave an affirmative reply to this proposal of Rusk's.* The Chinese Government sent three memoranda to the Soviet Government on September 3, 1962, *October 20, 1962,* and June 6, 1963, stating that it was a matter for the Soviet Government whether it committed itself to the United States to refrain from transferring nuclear weapons and technical information concerning their manufacture to China; but that *the Chinese Government hoped the Soviet Government would not infringe on China's sovereign rights and act for China* in assuming an obligation to refrain from manufacturing nuclear weapons. We solemnly stated that we would not tolerate the conclusion, in disregard of China's opposition, of any sort of treaty between the Soviet Government and the United States which aimed at depriving the Chinese people of their right to take steps to resist the nuclear threats of U.S. imperialism, and that *we would issue statements to make our position known.*[2]

It is impossible to exaggerate the importance of this statement. Of immediate relevance here is the light it throws on the Cuban missile crisis, which was ripening and then occurred during the very period when the exchange of notes was taking place between Moscow and Peking (August 25, September 3, October 20).

Is the Chinese statement true, or is it a product of their paranoia about the United States and Khrushchev ganging up on them? The *facts* alleged in it have not been denied in the Soviet rejoinders. Yet we know that in 1962 no agreement between Russia and America on a nuclear test ban was reached. Disarmament talks in Geneva dragged out inconclusively throughout the year. The *apparent* issues preventing agreement were those of inspection and of verification—the Americans holding out for several annual inspections of nuclear sites, the Soviets for none or very few, etc. At the *end of August,* the Russians turned down the latest of the Anglo-American proposals: either for a complete test ban or for one on atmospheric tests alone. The vagaries of the Soviet position—at one time close to agreement, at another resolutely opposed to it—were blamed in Washington on the same factors besetting the American side: the opposition of some military and scientific advisers who were unwilling to relinquish the right to test their toys.

The mystery deepens when we consider that there is no record on the American side of Secretary Rusk making proposals of the kind described in the Chinese statement and certainly none of the Soviet government agreeing to them. That the Russians at the time would or could have stopped China from gaining nuclear armaments must have been held in Washington as an unachievable dream; any Soviet hint to that effect would have been trumpeted very loudly. What, then, is the truth?

[2] *Ibid.,* p. 351, my italics.

Secretary Rusk and Gromyko were in Geneva in late July 1962 for the signing of the final agreement on Laos. There they engaged also in talks on nuclear disarmament, with the usual inconclusive results. The disarmament talks recessed on September 7. The wider issues of disarmament and of the test ban were to be discussed at the meeting of the UN General Assembly in late fall. Now, it is quite likely that in an informal discussion Rusk mentioned the subject of nuclear proliferation and that Gromyko responded, confining himself to his usual noncommittal grunts. Hardly a proposal, hardly "an affirmative reply" by the Soviet government!

As we have seen, the evidence is clear that the Soviet government hoped *somehow* in the summer of 1962 to prevail over China's determination to become a nuclear power. It is less certain, but highly probable, that the alleged "Rusk proposal" was in fact manufactured in the Kremlin. Despite China's first (and presumably violent) reaction on September 3 to "Rusk's proposal," Moscow must have persisted with it, for another Chinese protest had to be dispatched on October 20. By this time, the nature of the "somehow" was becoming clearer.

The Soviet Union's decision to install missiles capable of carrying atomic warheads in Cuba must have been taken sometime around the beginning of July 1962. Around the same time Raúl Castro, Fidel's brother and Cuban Minister of Defense, was in Moscow. It is improbable that he was told *exactly* what kind of missiles the Soviets would install and *quite* improbable that he was told for what purpose; the Cuban leaders—notably Fidel—were always running on at the mouth, and they were probably simply told that the Russians would supply some defensive missiles, the details of which they need not worry about. The Cubans' understandable concern as to what was happening in their own country was no doubt responsible for the dispatch of Guevara to Moscow at the end of August; from the *Russian* viewpoint, there was every reason not to draw attention thus to the strange doings in the Caribbean island. On that occasion an official Soviet communiqué acknowledged that to protect Cuba from "aggressive imperialist" threats, the Soviet government would send armaments and technical specialists to train Cuban servicemen.[3] On September 4, in view of the increasing agitation in the United States over the volume of Soviet shipments to Cuba, President Kennedy issued a statement that American intelligence sources had learned that the Russians were setting up in Cuba "anti-aircraft defense missiles with a slant range of twenty-five miles," radar, etc., and that they were sending military technicians to Cuba (3,500, Kennedy estimated, were already there). The President stressed that as far as was known, no Soviet bases or "offensive ground-to-ground missiles" had been or were being installed. "Were it to be otherwise the gravest issues would arise." [4] (The same day, Ambassador Dobrynin conveyed through the Attorney General a most unusual message to the President: Khrushchev pledged that he would not stir up any international incidents before the American congressional elections in early November!) An official Soviet release one week later fell in with Kennedy's statement. All the shipments to Cuba were purely defensive. Why should the USSR need a missile base near the United States? If need be, "the Soviet Union has the capability from its own territory to render assistance to any peace loving state, and not only Cuba." [5]

As an American overflight of October 14 was to reveal and further investigations to confirm, the Soviet Union was in fact constructing twenty-four launching pads for medium-range missiles (500–1,000 miles) and sixteen for intermediate-range ones (1,000–2,000 miles).[6] There has been considerable dispute about the technical details, but not about the indubitable fact that if they had been completed, a large part of the United States would have found itself within the range of atomic attack from Cuba.

Now, the question of timing is important in analyzing the Soviet reasons for all these things. The dispatch of equipment

[3] Henry M. Pachter, *Collision Course* (New York, 1963), p. 175, quoting a *Tass* communiqué of September 2.

[4] *Ibid.*, p. 176.

[5] *Ibid.*, p. 177.

[6] Arthur M. Schlesinger, Jr., *A Thousand Days: John F. Kennedy in the White House* (Boston, 1965), p. 796.

and specialists must have begun months before, possibly before July, but the fateful step of erecting missile sites and emplacing the missiles could not have begun much more than one month before the United States' discovery of them, i.e., in early September (before that time American overflights revealed only anti-aircraft missiles). The CIA had quite reasonably assumed that the Russians would not proceed to build long-range missile sites until "an operational network of SAM's (anti-aircraft missiles) would make their detection from the air difficult." [7] The conclusion must be that the planning and preparations for the installing of the long-range missiles had been going on for some time, but that the actual decision to install them was taken only in the early days of September and then in a great hurry, forsaking the usual precautions of elaborate camouflage and erection of an extensive anti-aircraft missile network.

Two events of early September may be connected with the Soviet decision hurriedly to put into effect the plans prepared for so long but not yet executed (possibly because of last-minute hesitations and realizations of the vast risks involved): (1) the receipt of the Chinese note of September 3; (2) Khrushchev's decision to attend in person the meeting of the United Nations in late November. Not content with his message of September 4, Khrushchev had his ambassador meet with one of the President's closest advisers, Theodore Sorensen, on September 6. Ambassador Dobrynin, seemingly unnecessarily, repeated that the Russians would do nothing "before the American Congressional elections that could complicate the international situation or aggravate the tension in the relations between our two countries." [8] But *after* that, the Soviets insisted, the problems of a German peace treaty and Berlin must be finally solved, and Khrushchev would, most likely, come at that time to the United States to address the United Nations.

There is therefore a very strong presumption that for some time the Soviet leaders had been toying with the idea of in-

[7] Theodore C. Sorensen, *Kennedy* (New York, 1965), p. 673. And the President's Special Assistant adds, "Why the Soviets failed to coordinate their timing is still inexplicable."

[8] *Ibid.*, p. 667.

stalling nuclear missiles in Cuba and, around the beginning of September, were seized with an irresistible desire to solve the most grueling dilemmas of Soviet foreign policy with this one bold stroke. Once in Cuba, the missiles would become negotiable, their removal conditional upon the United States' meeting Soviet conditions on the German peace treaty and other pressing international issues. Appearing in New York in November, Khrushchev would present to the world a dramatic package deal resolving the world's most momentous problems: the German peace treaty, containing an absolute prohibition against nuclear weapons for Bonn; and a similar proposal in reference to the Far East, where the Soviets would demand a nuclear-free zone in the Pacific and, under this guise, extract a pledge from China not to manufacture atomic weapons. This second part was of course the weakest point of the Soviet scheme. It was unlikely that the Chinese Communists would agree to any limitations on their freedom to manufacture and test nuclear weapons, and evidently they at least implied this in their note of September 3. But the Russians could hope that by their dramatic coup they would create an atmosphere in which the Chinese would have to reconsider. In addition, part of the price the Americans would pay for the removal of the Soviet missiles in Cuba could well be the withdrawal of their protection from Formosa. This would add an almost irresistible incentive for the Chinese at least to postpone their atomic ambitions.

No other explanation fits the tangled story of the Cuban missile crisis or accounts for the risks undertaken by the Soviets at that precise moment. Granted the stakes involved, the risks were not too unreasonable. That the whole operation was undertaken just to force the West out of Berlin is clearly unreasonable. What would it avail the USSR to have Berlin become a free city, if the United States equipped West Germany with nuclear weapons? That the operation was undertaken simply to protect Cuba, as Khrushchev was to "explain" later, is as fantastic as it is mendacious, and the best commentary on this explanation is provided by a party not overly friendly to the United States. Said the Chinese Communists in 1963, repeating their taunts of the preceding year: "Before the Soviet Union sent nuclear weapons into Cuba there did not exist a crisis of the United States using nuclear weapons in the Caribbean Sea and of a nuclear war breaking out. If it should be said that such a crisis did arise it was a result of the rash action of the Soviet leaders." [9]

As for the risks involved, the Russians displayed touching faith in the peacefulness of the American government and people. If, as Soviet propaganda has held, there was a hotheaded faction in Washington eager to loose a nuclear war on the world, held in check only by the combined strength and peaceloving policies of the USSR, then it was reasonable to fear that with Washington's first inklings as to what the Russians were doing, there would be an atomic attack not upon Cuba but upon the source of all trouble, the USSR proper (especially since, as both sides knew, the United States enjoyed a considerable edge in intercontinental ballistic missiles). Yet evidently this contingency was not considered likely, for special emergency measures were announced only after the crisis was in the open; perhaps something would have leaked out if special precautions on civil defense, etc., had been taken in September and early October. Of course there was bound to be a wild wave of excitement and indignation in the United States at the revelation that sixty-four atomic missiles were pointed at the United States from Cuba, but since Khrushchev thought that *he* would make this revelation, he also believed its effect would immediately be countered by his simultaneous generous and far-reaching proposals, for accession to which he would remove the deadly weapons. Warming to his task and to his appearance in the United States, Khrushchev must have thought that in the long run the Americans themselves would be grateful: his gambit would resolve the German problem, remove or delay China's acquisition of atomic weapons, and lay the foundations for far-reaching measures of disarmament. If the Russians were guilty of deception, was it not true that the Americans had really started the game by placing nuclear missiles in places like Turkey, closer to the boundaries of Russia than Cuba was to the United States? The Soviet move was a necessary one to

[9] From an official statement of the Chinese government, September 1, 1963, quoted in Griffith, *op. cit.*, p. 383.

dramatize to the American people the dangerous game their own government was playing and to break the impasse in which the obduracy of de Gaulle and Adenauer had placed America, against the best interests of the American people themselves.

It could be argued, against this construction, that if the ultimate Soviet objectives were so reasonable they could have been reached through negotiations. The Soviets could have intimated that a reasonable American stand on a German peace treaty would induce them to pressure the Chinese, etc., etc. But the inherent flaw of Soviet diplomacy is exactly its unwillingness to divulge its own dilemmas and weaknesses. Any revelation of how serious the Chinese problem was could, the Russians thought, make the Americans harden rather than weaken their position on Germany and on disarmament. One year later, at the signing of the partial test ban treaty and with the Sino-Soviet dispute now in full swing, Khrushchev still refused to talk about China to Harriman. "China was another socialist country, Khrushchev said, and he did not propose to discuss it with a capitalist." [10] And by the fall of 1962 it was probably realized that it was useless to try to *persuade* China to change her intentions concerning a nuclear role. The last hope was to stage a dramatic coup—at one blow achieving aims that had eluded Stalin: a German peace treaty and the removal of American protection from Formosa—that would illuminate the power and dynamism of the Soviet Union and create an atmosphere in which no Communist country, not even China, would dare object to her proposals. If the Chinese raised objections, the USSR would stand justified before the whole socialist bloc in maintaining that she had done all she could do to help Peking restore her sovereignty over Formosa; if the Chinese did not like the conditions, they could henceforth deal with the United States by themselves.

[10] Schlesinger, *op. cit.*, p. 908.

IV

The Continuing Debate

ACADEMIC INTEREST in the Cuban missile crisis subsided after the death of John F. Kennedy—until 1965, when the publication of two major books about the late President's career sparked a debate that still goes on. Arthur Schlesinger's *A Thousand Days* and Theodore Sorensen's *Kennedy* both appeared in the fall of 1965, preceded by heavily promoted and widely read excerpts on the Cuban crisis in mass-circulation magazines. Sorensen gave the more authoritative account, one based on his own participation in the Executive Committee deliberations. Schlesinger wrote from a position of less direct involvement, but if anything his account was more laudatory of Kennedy. Both men, despite their different perspectives and emphases, presented the crisis through the eyes of the President, who emerged as a hero of noble proportions.

A few months later Elie Abe, an experienced newspaper and

television reporter, wrote the first comprehensive narrative of the crisis. Abel interviewed nearly all the high officials of the Kennedy administration, including every member of the Executive Committee, and used the information he gained to reconstruct the course of American policy on a day-by-day basis. Although his account seemed straightforward, the nature of his sources led him to tell the story exclusively from the standpoint of President Kennedy and his advisers. The result was to confirm the impression that the Cuban missile crisis was a personal triumph for Kennedy.

In the fall of 1968, a few months after his tragic assassination, Robert F. Kennedy's account of the crisis appeared, first as an article in *McCall's* magazine, then as a book, *Thirteen Days.* Written in a simple, almost intimate style, this book presented an inside view of American policy by a man who had played a key role in its evolution. With admirable restraint, the President's brother avoided the excesses of adulation that characterized the Sorensen and Schlesinger volumes, but the total impact was to reinforce the existing stereotype. The reader was likely to come away convinced that the Kennedy brothers had saved the nation and the world from a nuclear holocaust.

The overdrawn portrait of a heroic John Kennedy outwitting a devious Nikita Khrushchev was bound to be challenged. Starting as early as 1965, and with greater frequency as the decade advanced, articles began to appear that took issue with the Kennedy legend. Some of the criticism, particularly that from the emerging New Left, went to extremes in reversing the responsibility for the crisis; but much of the critical comment was thoughtful and raised crucial questions that were long overdue. As a result, by the end of the decade the once unchallenged view of the missile crisis as a complete American victory no longer held sway in the academic community, although it still prevailed in the popular mind.

I. F. STONE

What Price Prestige?

I. F. Stone, a crusading Washington journalist who specializes in exposing the fallacies of American defense policy, was one of the first to criticize the accepted version of the Cuban missile crisis. In an essay on Elie Abel's book written for the New York Review of Books *in April 1966, Stone raised a number of questions about Kennedy's policy that became the focus of future debate.*

THE ESSENTIAL, the terrifying, question about the missile crisis is what would have happened if Khrushchev had not backed down. It is extraordinary, in the welter of magazine articles and books dealing with the missile crisis, how rarely this question is raised. The story is told and retold as a test and triumph of the Kennedy brothers. But the deeper reaches of the story are avoided, as if we feared to look too closely into the larger implications of this successful first foray into nuclear brinksmanship. We may not be so lucky next time.

The public impression created by the government when the presence of the missiles in Cuba was verified is that they represented a direct threat to America's cities. For those a little more sophisticated it was said that they threatened the balance of power. But Elie Abel's new book on *The Missile Crisis,* like the earlier accounts by Sorensen and Schlesinger, shows that this was not the dominant view in the inner councils of the White House. Abel quotes McNamara as saying, "A missile is a missile. It makes no great difference whether you are killed by a missile fired from the Soviet Union or from Cuba." But in the week of argument, Abel relates, McNamara came to concede that even if the effect on the strategic balance was relatively small, "the political effect in Latin American and elsewhere would be large." As Sorensen wrote in his *Kennedy,* "To be sure, these Cuban missiles alone, in view of all the other mega-

I. F. Stone, "The Brink," ***New York Review of Books,*** **VI (April 14, 1966), 12–16. Reprinted by permission.** **Copyright © 1966 by I. F. Stone.**

tonnage the Soviets were capable of unleashing upon us, did not substantially alter the strategic balance *in fact* . . . But that balance would have been substantially altered *in appearance* [italics in original]; and in matters of national will and world leadership, as the President said later, such appearances contribute to reality." The real stake was prestige.

The question was whether, with the whole world looking on, Kennedy would let Khrushchev get away with it. The world's first thermonuclear confrontation turned out to be a kind of ordeal by combat between two men to see which one would back down first. Schlesinger relates that in the earlier Berlin crisis, he wrote a memorandum to Kennedy protesting the tendency to define the issue as "Are you chicken or not?" But inescapably that's what the issue came around to. Schlesinger recounts an interview Kennedy gave James Wechsler of the New York *Post* in the Berlin crisis in which the President recognized that no one could win a nuclear war, that "the only alternatives were authentic negotiation or mutual annihilation," *but*—

> What worried him [Kennedy] was that Khrushchev might interpret his reluctance to wage nuclear war as a symptom of an American loss of nerve . . . "If Khrushchev wants to rub my nose in the dirt," he told Wechsler, "it's all over."

At a Book and Author lunch on March 14 (see the account in the *New York Herald-Tribune* next day) Abel recounted a story which should have been in his book. He told of a visit to the President in September 1961, after the Bay of Pigs and the Berlin Wall. Abel told Kennedy he wanted to write a book about the administration's first year. "Who," the President asked despondently, "would want to read a book about disasters?" He felt that Khrushchev, after these two debacles, might think him a pushover. James Reston of the *New York Times,* who saw Kennedy emerge "shaken and angry" from his meeting with Khrushchev in Vienna, speculates that Khrushchev had studied the Bay of Pigs. "He would have understood if Kennedy had left Castro alone or destroyed him; but when Kennedy was rash enough to strike at Cuba but not bold enough to finish the job, Khrushchev decided he was dealing with an inexperienced young leader who could be intimidated and blackmailed." There was an intensely personal note in the Kennedy broadcast which announced the quarantine of Cuba. "This secret, swift and extraordinary buildup of Communist missiles . . . is a deliberately provocative and unjustified change in the status quo which cannot be accepted by this country, if *our courage* [my italics] and our commitments are ever to be trusted again by either friend or foe." It was the courage of John F. Kennedy which was in question, the credibility of his readiness to go the whole way if the missiles were not removed. In the eyeball to eyeball confrontation, it was Khrushchev who was forced to blink first.

This was magnificent as drama. It was the best of therapies for Kennedy's nagging inferiority complex. Like any other showdown between the leaders of two contending hordes or tribes, it was also not without wider political significance. Certainly the fright it gave Khrushchev and the new sense of confidence it gave Kennedy were factors in the *détente* which followed. The look into the abyss made both men really feel in their bones the need for coexistence. But one may wonder how many Americans, consulted in a swift electronic plebiscite, would have cared to risk destruction to let John F. Kennedy prove himself.

A curious aspect of all three accounts, Sorensen's, Schlesinger's, and Abel's, is how they slide over Kennedy's immediate political situation. There might have been dispute as to whether those missiles in Cuba really represented any change in the balance of terror, any substantial new threat to the United States. There could have been no dispute that to face the November elections with these missiles intact would have been disastrous for Kennedy and the Democrats. The first alarms about missiles in Cuba, whether justified or not at the time, had been raised by the Republican Senator Keating. President Kennedy had assured the country on September 4 that the only missiles in Cuba were anti-aircraft with a 25-mile range and on September 13 that new Soviet shipments to Cuba were not a "serious threat." The election was only three weeks off when the presence of nuclear missiles on the island were confirmed on October 15 by aerial photographs. There was no time for prolonged negotiations, summit conferences, or UN debates if the damage was to be undone before the election. Kennedy could not afford to wait. This gamble paid off when he was able on October 28 to "welcome" Khrushchev's "statesmanlike decision" to dismantle the missiles, and on November 2, four days before the election, to announce that they were being crated for removal. But what if the gamble had failed? What if Khrushchev, instead of backing down when he did, had engaged in a delaying action, offering to abide by the outcome of a United Nations debate? The Republicans would have accused Kennedy of gullibility and weakness; the nuclear menace from Cuba would certainly have cost the Democrats control of the House of Representatives. After the Bay of Pigs fiasco, the damage to Kennedy's reputation might have been irreparable even if ultimately some peaceful deal to get the missiles out of Cuba were achieved. Kennedy could not wait. But the country and the world could. Negotiations, however prolonged, would have been better than the risk of World War III. This is how the survivors would have felt. Here Kennedy's political interests and the country's safety diverged.

Could these political considerations have been absent from the discussions and the minds of the Kennedy inner circle as the accounts of the two in-house historians, Sorensen and Schlesinger, and that of Abel would lead us to believe? Sorensen touches on the subject ever so tactfully at only one point. He relates that during the White House debates on what to do about the missiles, a Republican participant passed him a note saying:

> Ted—have you considered the very real possibility that if we allow Cuba to complete installation and operational readiness of missile bases, the next House of Representatives is likely to have a Republican majority? This would completely paralyze our ability to react sensibly and coherently to further Soviet advances.

Given the choice between the danger of a Republican majority in the House and the danger of a thermonuclear war, voters might conceivably have thought the former somewhat less frightening and irreversible.

Sorensen paints a sentimental, touching picture of Kennedy on the eve of the confrontation. "He spoke on the back porch on that Saturday before his speech not of his possible death but of all the innocent children of the world who had never had a chance or a voice." If Kennedy was so concerned he might have sacrificed his chances in the election to try and negotiate. It is difficult to reconcile this concern with the "consternation" Schlesinger reports when Radio Moscow broadcast a Khrushchev letter offering removal of its missiles from Cuba and a non-aggression pledge to Turkey if the U.S. would remove its missiles from Turkey and offer a non-aggression pledge to Cuba. This had been widely suggested at home and abroad, by Lippmann and many others, as a mutual face-saver. "But Kennedy," Schlesinger writes, "regarded the idea as unacceptable, and the swap was promptly rejected."

Abel recalls that early in 1961 the Joint Congressional Committee on Atomic Energy had recommended removal of these missiles from both Italy and Turkey as "unreliable, inaccurate, obsolete, and too easily sabotaged." He reveals that Kennedy in the late summer of 1961 gave orders for their removal. "It was therefore with a doubled sense of shock," Abel writes, "that Kennedy heard the news that Saturday morning. Not only were the missiles still in Turkey but they had just become pawns in a deadly chess game." Would it have been so unthinkable a sacrifice to have swapped those obsolete missiles, which Kennedy removed so soon afterward anyway?

Abel's account indicates that the Kennedy brothers were unwilling to be put in the position of paying any but the most minimal price for peace. Khrushchev's surrender had to be all but unconditional. Abel tells us that Adlai Stevenson at the White House conference on October 20 "forecast grave difficulties" at the UN "concerning the Jupiter bases in Turkey. People would certainly ask why it was right for the United States to have bases in Turkey but wrong for the Russians to have bases in Cuba." He also urged the President to consider offering to withdraw from Guantánamo as part of a plan to demilitarize, neutralize, and guarantee the territorial integrity of Cuba. Both ideas were rejected. "The bitter aftertaste of that Saturday afternoon in the Oval Room," Abel writes, "stayed with him until his death. It was after this encounter that Robert Kennedy decided Stevenson lacked the toughness to deal effectively with the Russians at the UN" and suggested to the President "that John McCloy or Herman Phleger, the California Republican who had served as chief legal adviser to John Foster Dulles, be asked to help in the UN negotiations. McCloy got the job."

All these accounts are appallingly ethnocentric. Cuba's fate and interests are simply ignored. Neither Abel nor Schlesinger nor Sorensen mentions that two weeks earlier President Dorticos of Cuba in a speech to the General Assembly on October 8—before the presence of the missiles in Cuba had been verified—said his country was ready for demilitarization if the U.S. gave assurances "by word and by deed, that it would not commit acts of aggression against our country." This speech contained a cryptic reference to "our unavoidable weapons—weapons that we wish we did not need and that we do not want to use." This was ignored by the American press. Though Stevenson, we now learn from Abel, was soon to favor demilitarization of Cuba, his public reply on October 8 was the State Department line, "The maintenance of Communism in the Americas is not negotiable."

All these possibilities for negotiating a way out indicate that the Cuban missile crisis was not one of those thermonuclear crises requiring instant response and leaving no time for negotiation and no time for consultation. The situation fits that described by George Kennan when he came back from Belgrade in August 1961 and said, "There is no presumption more terrifying than that of those who would blow up the world on the basis of their personal judgment of a transient situation. I do not propose to let the future of the world be settled, or ended, by a group of men operating on the basis of limited perspectives and short-run calculations." Schlesinger quotes Kennan's words to show the atmosphere of those "strange, moody days." He does not of course apply them to the missile crisis. Kennan's anguish may seem that of an outsider, without access to what the insiders alone know. But Sorensen says that at one time in the inner debate Kennedy and his circle "seriously considered" either doing nothing about the missiles or limiting our response to diplomatic action only. "As some (but not all) Pentagon advisors pointed out to the President," Sorensen reveals, "we had long lived within range of Soviet missiles, we expected Khrushchev to live with our missiles nearby, and by taking this addition calmly we would prevent him from inflating its importance."

There was fear in the inner circle that our Western allies might share this cool estimate. Perhaps this was one reason we did not consult them before deciding on a showdown. As Sorensen writes, "Most West Europeans cared nothing about Cuba and thought we were over-anxious about it. Would they support our risking a world war, or an attack on NATO member Turkey, or a move on West Berlin, because we now had a few dozen hostile missiles nearby?" Similarly Schlesinger reveals that Macmillan, when informed of Kennedy's plans, was troubled "because Europeans had grown so accustomed to living under the nuclear gun that they might wonder what all the fuss was about."

To consult was to invite advice we did not wish to hear. Abel reveals that when Acheson arrived as the President's special emissary to let De Gaulle know what was afoot, "De Gaulle raised his hand in a delaying gesture that the long departed kings of France might have envied," and asked, "Are you consulting or informing me?" When Acheson confessed that he was there to inform not consult, De Gaulle said dryly, "I am in favor of independent decisions." But three years later De Gaulle was to make an independent decision of his own and ask NATO to remove its bases in France. One reason for this was the Cuban missile crisis. As De Gaulle said at his last press conference February 21:

> . . . while the prospects of a world war breaking out on account of Europe are dissipating, conflicts in which America engages in other

parts of the world—as the day before yesterday in Korea, yesterday in Cuba, today in Vietnam—risk, by virtue of that famous escalation, being extended so that the result would be a general conflagration. In that case Europe—whose strategy is, within NATO, that of America—would be automatically involved in the struggle, even when it would not have so desired . . . France's determination to dispose of herself . . . is incompatible with a defense organization in which she finds herself subordinate.

Had the Cuban missile crisis erupted into a thermonuclear exchange, NATO bases in France would automatically have been involved: They would have joined in the attack and been targets for the Russians. France, like the other NATO countries, might have been destroyed without ever being consulted. It is not difficult to understand De Gaulle's distrust of an alliance in which the strongest member can plunge all the others into war without consulting them.

Kennedy no more consulted NATO before deciding to risk World War over Cuba than Khrushchev consulted his Warsaw Pact satellites before taking the risky step of placing missiles on the island. The objection to Khrushchev's course, as to Kennedy's, was primarily political rather than military. There is general agreement now that the Russians may have been tempted to put missiles in Cuba to redress in some small part the enormous missile gap against them which McNamara disclosed after Kennedy took office; for this view we can cite, among other studies, a Rand Corporation memorandum written for the Air Force by Arnold L. Horelick.* In retrospect the Air Force turned out to be the victim of its own ingenuity in developing the U-2. So long as the U.S. had to depend on surmise and normal intelligence, it was possible to inflate the estimates of Russian missile strength to support the demand for larger Air Force appropriations; hence first a bomber gap and then a missile gap, both of which turned out to be non-existent. But when the U-2s began to bring back precise information, the nightmarish missile computations hawked by such Air Force

* See his "The Cuban Missile Crisis: An Analysis of Soviet Calculations and Behavior," an abridgment of the Rand memo published in the April 1964 issue of *World Politics*.

mouthpieces as Stuart Symington and Joseph Alsop began to be deflated. Despite the sober warnings of Eisenhower and Allen Dulles that there was no missile gap, the Democrats used it in the 1960 campaign only to find on taking office that the gap was the other way. Militarily the missiles on Cuba didn't make too much difference. Even the Horelick study for the Air Force admits that these missiles "would presumably have been highly vulnerable to a U.S. first strike, even with conventional bombs," and their number was too small for a Soviet first strike. "Moreover," Horelick writes, "there would have been a problem, though perhaps not an insurmountable one, of coordinating salvoes from close-in and distant bases so as to avoid a ragged attack." (If missiles were fired at the same time from Cuba and Russia, the ones from nearby Cuba would have landed so far in advance as to give additional warning time.) Their deployment in Cuba bears all the earmarks of one of those febrile improvisations to which the impulsive Khrushchev was given, as in his proposals for a "troika" control of the United Nations.

Khrushchev was guilty of a foolish duplicity. Gromyko gave Kennedy a message from Khrushchev that he would suspend any action about Berlin until after the November election so as not to embarrass Kennedy. This and a TASS communiqué of September 11 made Kennedy and his advisers feel certain that the Russians would not upset the situation by secretly placing nuclear missiles in Cuba. TASS said the Soviet Union's nuclear weapons were so powerful and its rockets so wide-ranging "that there is no need to search for sites for them beyond the boundaries of the Soviet Union." How could Khrushchev hope to negotiate with Kennedy when the President discovered that he had been so grossly gulled? By first installing the missiles and then telling an easily detected lie about so serious a matter, Khrushchev shares responsibility with Kennedy for bringing the world to its first thermonuclear brink.

Because Kennedy succeeded and Khrushchev surrendered, the missile crisis is being held up as a model of how to run a confrontation in the thermonuclear age. In his February 17 statement advocating negotiations with the Vietcong, and offering them a place in a future government, Senator Robert F.

Kennedy said Hanoi "must be given to understand as well that their present public demands are in fact for us to surrender a vital national interest—but that, as a far larger and more powerful nation learned in October of 1962, surrender of a vital interest of the United States is an objective which cannot be achieved." In the missile crisis the Kennedys played their dangerous game skillfully. They kept their means and aims sharply limited, resisting pressures to bomb the island and to demand the removal of Castro as well as the missiles. For this restraint we are indebted to the Kennedys. But all their skill would have been to no avail if in the end he had preferred his prestige, as they preferred theirs, to the danger of a world war. In this respect we are all indebted to Khrushchev.

The missile crisis is a model of what to avoid. This is the lesson John F. Kennedy learned. "His feelings," Schlesinger writes in the finest passage of his *A Thousand Days,* "underwent a qualitative change after Cuba: A world in which nations threatened each other with nuclear weapons now seemed to him not just an irrational but an intolerable and impossible world. Cuba thus made vivid the sense that all humanity had a common interest in the prevention of nuclear war—an interest far above those national and ideological interests which had once seemed ultimate." This, and not the saga of a lucky hairbreadth balancing act on an abyss, is what most needs to be remembered about the missile crisis, if we are to avoid another.

LESLIE DEWART

The Kennedy Trap

Probing as Stone's queries were, they seemed mild compared with the questions raised by New Left writers about Kennedy's conduct in the missile crisis. The escalation of the war in Vietnam in 1965 led to widespread criticism

Leslie Dewart, "The Cuban Crisis Revisited," *Studies on the Left,* V (Spring 1965), 24–40. Reprinted by permission.

of American policy that went beyond the war itself to deal with all aspects of American activity in the world. Leslie Dewart, a Canadian philosopher who was active in the Committees of Correspondence movement, expressed the radical suspicions about American policy in Cuba in an article in Studies on the Left, *a major vehicle for New Left dissent in the 1960s. In the first part of the article he examined the question of Soviet motivation, concluding that the Russian goal was to force the United States into a general settlement of the Cold War. He then turned to the issue of why Khrushchev's plan failed—why it resulted in a nuclear confrontation and ultimate Soviet retreat rather than in a favorable diplomatic settlement.*

. . . THE EVIDENCE SUGGESTS that at a certain point the Soviets were misled by the U.S. government into the belief that it would accept the deployment of the missiles, whereas in reality it did not intend to do so. On the contrary, the U.S. plan was to feign surprise at the later "discovery" of the missiles and, then, with the backing of an aroused, "managed" public opinion, to demand the unconditional withdrawal of the missiles. Kennedy could not afford to argue with Khrushchev about the legality or the propriety of the move: to do so would have meant, in effect, to enter into negotiations on the question whether the Cuban government, though communist, would be permitted to exist. Deception was the only way to nullify the Soviet scheme. Every other solution would have meant negotiations, which in turn would have implied some compromise.

More precisely, the U.S. government's strategy consisted of the following steps: (1) keep the public partly uninformed, partly misinformed, about the nature of the Soviet buildup, including the presence of the missiles, and about the nature of the Soviet objectives, (2) convey to the Soviets at the right time the impression that the U.S. reluctantly accepted the Soviet move, (3) issue equivocal statements which would not undeceive the Soviets, but which could later be made to appear to domestic (and world) opinion as a stern warning to the Soviet Union against deployment of the missiles, (4) wait, then, about six weeks until the missiles were emplaced (with the added bonus that this would bring the U.S. to within two weeks of national elections), (5) feign astonishment at the "discovery" of the weapons, (6) obtain the backing of public opinion with the pretense that the missiles gravely endangered U.S. security and upset the strategic balance, and with the charge that the Soviets mounted this threat through deception and stealth, and finally, (7) demand the unconditional withdrawal of the bombers and missiles.

Soviet military aid to Cuba had begun on a modest scale shortly before the invasion of April 1961. Its pace quickened noticeably later the same year and during early 1962, but it did not become "alarming" until shortly after Raúl Castro's return from Moscow. Early in August, Cuban exile sources began to report the presence of Soviet troops in Cuba. On August 8th a Cuban exile source calculated that there were about 4,000 Soviet troops. The Cuban and Soviet governments had failed to take the most elementary precautions to keep their presence secret. Simultaneously, rumors about missiles began to flow from the same sources.

No conclusive evidence is publicly available on the date of arrival of the missiles. Castro stated to Jean Daniel that they began to arrive at the end of July 1962. I cannot imagine why he should have wished to falsify the date, and the fact that the exile rumors began in early August would tend to confirm it. On the other hand, the U.S. government maintains that the equipment did not arrive "until about September 8th." [1] Instead of asking *cui bono?* I shall argue *a fortiori,* and continue to suppose that the American date is correct.

In either event, the State Department at first ridiculed the reports of troops and missiles. But the reports became insistent and detailed, with ever increasing estimates in the number of troops. Moreover, the exiles began to enlist the willing ears of several American legislators. Before long the government found it impossible to dismiss the reports on the grounds that they were just exile talk. It now had to contend with the opposition,

[1] *New York Times,* December 12, 1963.

whose charges began to be widely credited. On August 20th the State Department finally admitted the presence of Soviet troops, but claimed that they were "technicians," and falsely insisted that their number was much smaller than reported. American opinion, which since the invasion had subsided noticeably, became electrified and indignant at the presence of the troops. There was a fairly common idea that U.S. security was being endangered by Soviet soldiers so close to home. Some politicians actually fostered this notion, though precisely what conceivable aggressive strategy could have been furthered by Soviet ground troops in Cuba was never discussed. The U.S. government did not enlighten the public or manage to disabuse it of this preoccupation. In fact, Kennedy kept his peace until August 22nd, when under considerable pressure to comment he confirmed the presence of "technicians" in Cuba. Other government sources then amplified: the troops had arrived as early as July 21st. Kennedy's personal intervention, however, seemed only to increase the demands for invasion or blockade.

Abstracting from strategic weapons (which, however, we might keep in mind as an additional possibility), it is not difficult to surmise what the Soviet troops in Cuba meant to Kennedy. They made a military adventure in Cuba extremely risky. Militarily, of course, they counted as nothing, nor did they imply a Soviet guarantee of Cuba. But they did put the onus on the U.S. for the international consequences of an attack. Kennedy thus found himself in the paradoxical position of having to counsel against the course he himself had continued to entertain, and to keep alive in the minds of the American people, during the previous year. (I assume here that the earliest attempts to hide the true state of affairs were motivated by indecision alone. It is possible to determine, as we shall see below, that by September 4th Kennedy's counterscheme was in operation, but it is impossible to determine when he first conceived it. If he had early intelligence of the Soviet plan, it is possible that from the outset the spread of misinformation and the counsel of moderation were intended to permit the Soviets unsuspectingly to proceed. If the missiles arrived in late July, this construction, of course, would be almost imperative.)

At any rate, the containment of public opinion was attempted on a variety of fronts. The number of "technicians" was consistently underestimated by a factor of about 5. The presence of ground-to-air missiles was denied even after the end of August, when their presence was known to the U.S.[2] On August 29th Kennedy stated at a press conference that he was not in favor of invading Cuba "at this time." Such a course, he added, would have had "very serious consequences." He hinted strongly that his words did not mean that he planned to invade at a later time. However, he refused to confirm whether his qualification "at this time," meant that he would favor an invasion in the future. These ambiguities served only to whet the already ravenous appetites of his critics.

One must go back to the newspapers of the day to recall the full force of the indignation and the alarm, to regain the stridency and the hostility, to recapture the fury of the inconsidered as well as the malicious demands—malicious, that is, more in relation to Kennedy than to Castro. "Public opinion" would not merely have backed a decision to invade: it was ready for nothing else. But in this context "public opinion" does not mean the mass of the American people: it means the representatives of the public, particularly the politicians and the mass media. The Soviet troops were providing the American people's personators with an occasion to press for "action." According to the Gallup Poll, among the people only one in four favored the use of force.

At this time, the end of August, a crucial juncture was reached. Until then, as we have seen, the Soviet buildup merely foiled Kennedy's hopes. In this respect the Soviet move was meeting with success. But an undesirable side effect was also accruing. The Soviet policy was inflaming political passions in the U.S.—at a time when an election was looming up. Hence, the Soviet maneuver was achieving a double effect: it deterred Kennedy from invasion, but it excited many others to pursue that very end. This, in turn, excited Kennedy, on whom the political

[2] Henry M. Pachter, *Collision Course: The Cuban Missile Crisis and Coexistence* (New York, 1963), p. 8.

pressures ultimately bore. In short, the Soviet policy did in part deter Kennedy, but it also provided him with additional motives, beyond his original one to take action.

The Soviets, apparently, had not anticipated this. The fact that as late as August 29th Kennedy had not altogether ruled out an invasion must have worried them somewhat. Perhaps for this reason, the Soviets began to explain their policy in public and thus to try to elicit a response out of an annoyingly uninformative administration.

On September 2nd, the Soviet Union confirmed that it was supplying weapons and military "technical specialists" to Cuba, explaining that "as long as the [United States] continue threatening Cuba, the Cuban Republic has every justification for taking necessary measures to insure its security and safeguard its sovereignty and independence, while all Cuba's true friends have every right to respond to this legitimate request." [3] Within two days, on September 4th, Kennedy issued a statement replying to the Soviet submission. This was the first of the two alleged "warnings" to the Soviets against deploying the missiles.

The statement was read by Kennedy to a press conference. It was very brief. Its essential part read:

> There is no evidence of any organized combat forces in Cuba from any Soviet bloc country; of military bases provided to Russia; of a violation of the 1934 treaty relating to Guantánamo; of the presence of offensive ground-to-ground missiles; or of other significant offensive capability either in Cuban hands or under Soviet direction and guidance.
>
> Were it to be otherwise the gravest issues would arise.[4]

If we read this statement assuming the truth of Kennedy's October 22nd statement explaining that it "made clear the distinction between any introduction of ground-to-ground missiles and the existence of defensive anti-aircraft missiles," it is not difficult to construe it as Kennedy intended that it be construed by the public. But does that construction correspond to

[3] *G&M,* September 3, 1962 (AP report).
[4] Text of the statement, *New York Times,* September 5, 1962. Subsequent quotations from this statement refer to the same source.

what he actually said? And is that construction the one which the Soviet Union could have placed on the text?

Kennedy's "warning" was, rather, that the presence of "offensive ground-to-ground missiles" would be considered a grave issue. If this meant that *any* ground-to-ground missile would be considered offensive why did he not simply speak of "ground-to-ground missiles," without further qualifications? Why did he resort to redundancy, "offensive ground-to-ground missiles," which rendered the meaning ambiguous? In contrast, on October 22nd he did not resort to it, and claimed he had warned the Soviets against "any introduction of ground-to-ground missiles."

Nor is this a matter of mere words. There is, after all, a valid distinction between "offensive ground-to-ground missiles," and "defensive ground-to-ground missiles," as we shall see below. If the "warning" of September 4th had conveyed that *all* ground-to-ground missiles would be considered intolerable, because they were offensive, the Soviets might have contested the moral and legal validity of the reasoning, but at any rate its meaning would have been clear to anyone. In point of fact the meaning was not clear.

Other parts of the statement were similarly equivocal. The absence of reference to bombers may be significant, since they had long been suspected as a possibility. The reference to "military bases provided to Russia" seems clear enough until we ask exactly what the term means. If, as the statement partly hinted, it meant a base for stationing "organized combat forces," then the statement's provisions did not apply, since no such base was being contemplated by the Soviets. On the other hand, if it applied to such missile bases as were about to be established, then they would have come under the provisions concerning "significant offensive capability either in Cuban hands or under Soviet guidance." If so, the gravity of the issue depended on what should be construed as *significant* offensive capability. Did this qualification not seem to grant that even *some* offensive capability would be tolerated, as long as it did not endanger American security?

This does not mean that Kennedy's statement was deceptive,

only that it was ambiguous—deception entered only with the statement of September 13th. To the Soviets, who were about to unload the weapons, the ambiguity must have been the source of much worry. What did it really "warn" about? Only one thing was certain: it offered no reassurance against attack. Did it mean, therefore, that the U.S. rejected the Soviet submission of September 2nd, which claimed that the U.S. had no right to invade Cuba? Yet, Kennedy's statement had, in the main, a soothing tone. On the other hand, if it was meant to reveal a peaceful intent, why did it not make clear that Cuba would not be invaded? It would have been easy to convey so, instead of implying once more that for the present—whatever that meant—there was no need to invade. Or did Kennedy's words indicate that he was wavering under pressure? The Soviet Union had stated that the buildup was due solely to U.S. threats against Cuba. Did Kennedy's failure to reply to this point mean that the U.S. reaffirmed, or that it withdrew, such threats? In brief, the first overt attempt to ascertain the U.S. position had failed. It was necessary to clarify the situation. Within the week, on September 11th, the Soviet Union issued a lengthy and detailed statement of policy. This was the document which, according to Kennedy's speech of October 22nd, reassured him that the Soviet Union "had no need or desire to station strategic missiles on the territory of any other nation." Let us now examine the Soviet submission in some detail.

The Soviet statement said that "at first," when only Congress and the press were calling for an attack on Cuba, "the Soviet Union did not pay special importance to this propaganda." [5] But "now, however, one cannot ignore this," because *now Kennedy's own intentions were unclear:* in his message to Congress asking for a reserve call-up he had envisaged "the possibility of rapidly and effectively reacting . . . to a danger that might arise . . . and that he was taking such a step in connection with the strengthening of the armed forces of Cuba" by the Soviet Union. And yet, "what could have alarmed the American leaders, what is the reason for this devil's Sabbeth [sic] raised in Congress

[5] Text of the statement, *New York Times,* September 12, 1962. Subsequent quotations from the statement refer to the same source.

and in the American press around Cuba? [Para.] The point is, they say, that armaments and even troops are shipped from the Soviet Union to Cuba." (Such was indeed the heart of the matter.) What did the Soviet Union have to say in reply?

The first point was that the Soviet Union had the *right* to station troops in Cuba at her request, and to supply her with whatever weapons were required. The right to self-defense was given considerable emphasis. Only as an afterthought, and only incidentally to contrasting the amount of military aid provided with the much larger amount of economic aid, the Soviet Union did allow that it had in fact sent to Cuba "up-to-date weapons" and the troops to handle them, ambiguously suggesting that these weapons were under Cuban control:

> We can say to these people that these are our ships, and that what we carry in them is no business of theirs. It is the internal affair of the sides engaged in this commercial transaction. . . . But we do not hide from the world public that we really are supplying Cuba with industrial equipment and goods . . . we also send agronomists, machine-operators, tractor-drivers and livestock experts. . . . It will be recalled that a certain amount of armaments is also being shipped from the Soviet Union to Cuba at the request of the Cuban Government in connection with the threats by aggressive imperialist circles . . . [as well as] Soviet military specialists, technicians who would train the Cubans in handling up-to-date weapons, because up-to-date weapons now call for high skill and much knowledge.

The hint cannot be considered too broad, especially if we recall that it was unnecessary. By this time, if not earlier, the U.S. had more than second-hand rumors in evidence of the presence of the weapons. (U.S. intelligence has admitted that it first photographed the bomber crates, and detected the nature of the missile cargoes, while the ships were still at sea en route to Cuba.) The problem, thus, was not how to inform the U.S. of the nature of the weapons. The real problem, rather, was twofold: (a) to offer such arguments and reassurances as would incline the U.S. to accept the Soviet policy, and (b) to ascertain to what degree, if any, the U.S. actually accepted the Soviet submissions. Note the semantic skill with which the Soviet

Union began its ambiguous argument: "The armaments and military equipment sent to Cuba are designed exclusively for defensive purposes and the President of the United States and the American military . . . know what means of defense are. How can these means threaten the United States?" Did this question mean that the Soviet Union wanted to know what the U.S. thought, or did it mean that the Soviet Union asserted that the U.S. could not but agree that the "up-to-date" weapons did not threaten the U.S.? Actually, it meant both. And in both senses it betrayed uneasiness about the U.S. attitude towards the Soviet buildup.

Of a different nature was the ambiguity of the expression "designed exclusively for defensive purposes." The Soviet phrase could mean either "*intended* for defense only," or "*capable* of being used only for defense." But, evidently, the Soviets did not think they could expect the U.S. to be reassured by the mere assertion of peaceful Soviet *intentions*. Therefore, it was necessary to demonstrate that the weapons were *capable* of being used only for defense.

The Soviet argument was very simple: under the circumstances in which the weapons were being deployed to Cuba they *could not* be used aggressively. But to understand the nature of the Russian submission we must first consider an elementary point of strategy which the layman often ignores.

The essential determinant of whether a weapon is intrinsically aggressive is not the intention of the user. But neither is it the physical design, the lethal power, the destructive capability, nor any other physical characteristic. The primary standard is the objective situation, that is, the relation the weapon has to a potential victim—in short, the actual possibilities of its being used to attack. A rifle or a pistol is an offensive weapon in relation to an unarmed man. But the same weapons in the Cuban militia's hands could hardly be considered offensive in relation to the U.S. of 1962. By the same token, the short-range missiles once placed in Turkey by the U.S. were offensive weapons when they were first installed, in the sense that they *could* have been used aggressively for a first strike against the Soviets. But in time, when these missiles were neutralized by new Soviet equipment, they ceased to have offensive capability. At first, when the Soviet Union lacked missiles of its own, the U.S. missiles in Turkey deterred a Soviet ground attack on Europe by threatening an "overwhelming" first nuclear strike; now they deterred a Soviet missile attack only because they promised an "unacceptable" retaliatory blow. Thus they had become defensive weapons, unless a way could have been devised (which to date has not) in which they could have been used in connection with "hardened" missiles, or other missiles with "second-strike capability" which released them for a "pre-emptive" or for a wanton attack. (Eventually the Turkey missiles lost even their defensive capability in relation to the U.S., though they retained it, of course, in relation to Turkey alone. It was then that they were withdrawn.)

The argument submitted by the Soviets on September 11th was the exact parallel of the foregoing. It stated that there was a distinction between the missiles which the Soviet Union possessed at home (i.e., "hardened" ICBM's, or "soft" ICBM's with secret locations, or Polaris-type missiles), which *were* capable of threatening aggression by virtue of their capacity to carry out successfully a wanton attack, and the missiles actually sent to Cuba, which *could not* have been successfully so used. Reminding the U.S. of its bases "in Turkey, Iran, Greece, Italy, Britain, Holland, Pakistan and other countries," the Soviet Union submitted that:

> . . . there is no need for the Soviet Union to shift its weapons for the repulsion of aggression, for a retaliatory blow, to any other country, for instance Cuba. Our nuclear weapons are so powerful in their explosive force and the Soviet Union has so powerful rockets to carry these nuclear warheads, that there is no need to search for sites for them beyond the boundaries of the Soviet Union. We have said and we do repeat that . . . the Soviet Union has the possibility from its own territory to render assistance to any peace-loving state and not only to Cuba.

The last sentence particularly stipulated that the missiles in question, which the Soviet Union did not intend to deploy beyond its boundaries (a statement that solicited belief on the grounds that this undertaking in no wise lessened Soviet security), were not those which, in the Soviet submission, were required specifically for the defense of Cuba. In every respect this paragraph remains true even today. For it cannot be said that the Soviet Union did deploy such weapons to Cuba, nor could it be seriously argued that the weapons actually sent gave Cuba a credible capability to launch a wanton nuclear attack on the U.S. Indeed, as Kennedy himself would put it on the very next day: "if the United States ever should find it necessary to take military action against communism in Cuba, all of Castro's Communist-supplied weapons and technicians will not change the result or significantly extend the time required to achieve that result," [6] though on October 22nd he was to claim precisely the opposite, namely, that they "upset the status quo." (And again, less than two months later he would reverse himself once more and admit that *strategically* the missiles did not change the status quo: "the Cuba effort . . . was an effort to materially change the balance of power. . . . Not that they were intending to fire them, because if they were going to get into a nuclear struggle they have their own missiles in the Soviet Union. But it would have *politically* changed the balance of power. . . ." [7])

The missiles that were placed in Cuba, however, would have made an American attack possible only at a price too heavy to be readily acceptable. They had, therefore, an appreciable deterrent effect. But they could not be said to have posed the threat of aggression against the U.S.: for that end they were radically insufficient, given the ratio of their power to that of the U.S. They could have been used only in order to defend Cuba from attack.[8]

[6] *New York Times*, September 14, 1962.

[7] CBS Script of *A Conversation with President Kennedy,* broadcast December 17, 1962 [cited below as *CBS Script*], p. 22 (italics mine).

[8] Henry Kissinger, writing shortly after the crisis, made the point that the missiles had neither offensive nor defensive value for the Soviet Union: "the bases were of only marginal use in a defensive war. In an offensive war their effectiveness was reduced by the enormous difficulty—if not the impossibility—of co-ordinating a first strike from the Soviet Union and Cuba," "Reflections on Cuba," *The Reporter,* November 22, 1962. However, Kissinger failed to consider the possibility that they had defensive value *for Cuba.* Therefore, he fell into the "blunder" fallacy: "it is difficult to explain Soviet actions except as a colossal blunder."

Before we proceed to study the American reply to this document we should consider this question: in view of the foregoing analysis of the Soviet statement of September 11th, how was it possible for Kennedy on October 22nd to pretend to construe its contents as a Soviet disclaimer of intent to deploy nuclear delivery systems to Cuba? The reason is that Kennedy quoted from the document out of context. Indeed, in one instance he actually did violence to the Soviet text itself.

For on October 22nd Kennedy's accusation was that:

> . . . the Soviet Government publicly stated on Sept. 11th that "the armaments and military equipment sent to Cuba are designed exclusively for defensive purposes." That "there is no need for the Soviet Union to shift its weapons . . . for a retaliatory blow to any other country, for instance Cuba," and that "the Soviet Union has so powerful rockets to carry these nuclear warheads that there is no need to search for sites for them beyond the boundaries of the Soviet Union." That statement was false.

Now, the first quoted sentence contained, of course, no more than the gist of the Soviet argument. The U.S. might well have claimed that the argument was invalid or otherwise unacceptable, but the Soviet statement hardly constitutes an undertaking not to send missiles to Cuba. The third quoted sentence referred, in the context, to Soviet ICBM's, not to the missiles actually sent. Indeed, it remains true to this day that it would have been absurd for the Soviet Union to deploy ICBM's to Cuba.[9]

The second quoted sentence, "there is no need for the Soviet Union to shift its weapons . . . for a retaliatory blow to any other country, for instance Cuba," similarly referred in the original context to weapons with second-strike capability. But the Soviet words could not have been easily misapplied by

[9] As late as September 12, 1962, the CIA Deputy Director, General Marshall S. Carter, while briefing the House Committee on Armed Services was still expounding the Soviet argument, namely, "that there was no reason why the Soviets should put in any long-range offensive missiles in Cuba because they had the capacity to fire from the homeland and therefore did not need to go into Cuba," *Hearings,* Committee on Armed Services, U.S. House of Representatives (88th Congress, 1st Session), January 30, 1963 (henceforth cited as *House Hearings*), p. 269.

Kennedy had he quoted the sentence in full: "there is no need for the Soviet Union to shift its weapons for the repulsion of aggression, for a retaliatory blow, to any other country, for instance Cuba." This described much too obviously the second-strike weapons of the Soviet Union. But by omitting the words "for the repulsion of aggression" (which, in turn, necessitated omitting the commas before and after "for a retaliatory blow" in order to disguise the fact that the sentence had been tampered with),[10] the Soviet words were made to mean that the Soviet Union disclaimed all intention of sending *any* missiles to Cuba.

Evidently, this misrepresentation of the Soviet policy was intended to obtain domestic, allied and UN support for the blockade. The blockade, in turn, was necessary as a means to force the unconditional withdrawal of the missiles. For had the U.S. privately approached the Soviet government in reply to the Soviet overture of September 11th it could have done little but negotiate on a basis which Kennedy would have considered an utter defeat. To avoid this utter defeat it was necessary to create the Cuban crisis.

But the crisis stage was yet to come. First it was necessary to reply to the Soviet submission. More specifically, it was necessary to answer that the U.S. accepted the doctrine that the weapons sent to Cuba should be construed as having defensive capability only, and to disclaim the intention of attacking Cuba. On the other hand, if at a later stage the U.S. government was to claim that the weapons were offensive in character, it was necessary to convey the foregoing to the Soviet Union in such manner that the American public did not become aware that this was being done—indeed, the reassurance must be so worded that it could be later construed as an additional warning.

It did not take the administration long to compose such a

[10] In most published versions, though the commas were omitted, the elision of the words was indicated by the conventional three dots. However, the official version published in *The Department of State Bulletin* (as reproduced in the Headline Series, Foreign Policy Association, No. 157, Jan.–Feb. 1963), violates the integrity of the Soviet text even more. It quotes the Soviet statement as follows: "There is no need for the Soviet government to shift its weapons for a retaliatory blow to any other country, for instance Cuba."

reply. Two days after the Soviet statement Kennedy held a press conference. It began with a prepared statement explicitly addressed to both the Soviet Union and to American and allied listeners:

> . . . Ever since communism moved into Cuba in 1958 [sic] Soviet technical and military personnel have moved steadily on to the island in increasing numbers at the invitation of the Cuban Government.
>
> Now that movement has been increased. It is under our most careful surveillance.
>
> But I will repeat the conclusion that I reported last week: that these new shipments do not constitute a serious threat to any other part of this hemisphere.
>
> If the United States ever should find it necessary to take military action against communism in Cuba, all of Castro's Communist-supplied weapons and technicians will not change the result or significantly extend the time required to achieve that result.
>
> However, unilateral military intervention on the part of the United States cannot currently be either required or justified, and it is regrettable that loose talk about such action in this country might serve to give a thin color of legitimacy to the Communist pretense that such a threat exists.[11]

Under the circumstances here outlined these words could have had but one meaning for the Soviet Union: that the U.S. was well aware of the nature of the Soviet buildup due to its "most careful surveillance"; that nevertheless *even the most recent shipments* were not considered a threat to U.S. security, because the weapons did not affect appreciably the overwhelming superiority of the U.S. *in relation to Cuba* and, thus, that the U.S. accepted the view that they had only defensive capability. It also meant, therefore, that the U.S. was in a position to reassure the Soviet Union that no invasion would be launched. The Soviets should disregard "loose talk" about such a move: it did not emanate from those in authority. Kennedy was able to give his personal assurance to the Soviet Union that no such threat existed.

[11] Text of the statement and press conference, *New York Times*, September 14, 1962. Subsequent quotations refer to the same source.

The second part of Kennedy's statement outlined anew the conditions under which the U.S. would revise its stand. It abounded in irrelevancies. It omitted all mention of missiles or bombers:

> But let me make this clear once again. If at any time the Communist buildup in Cuba were to endanger or interfere with our security in any way, including our base at Guantánamo, our passage to the Panama Canal, our missile and space activities in Cape Canaveral or the lives of American citizens in this country, or if Cuba should ever attempt to export its aggressive purposes by force or the threat of force against any nation in this hemisphere or become an offensive military base of significant capacity for the Soviet Union, then this country will do whatever must be done to protect its own security and that of its allies.

The only remotely meaningful condition was the last one. In the context, it simply meant that if it ever became not a matter of defending Cuba, but of significantly enhancing the *Soviet* aggressive capabilities, the U.S. would reconsider. This proposition accepted and confirmed the validity of the strategic distinction between Cuba's defensive capability and the Soviet offensive capability. It drove home the proffered clarification of the U.S. position.

On the other hand, in relation to domestic opinion Kennedy's statement was sufficiently unclear to stimulate the first question from the floor of the press conference: "Mr. President, coupling this statement with the one of last week, at what point do you determine that the buildup in Cuba has lost its defensive guise to become offensive?" Kennedy's reply was difficult to follow:

> I think if you read last week's statement and the statement today —I've made it quite clear, particularly in last week's statement when we talked about the presence of offensive military missile capacity or development of military bases, other indications which I gave last week. All these would, of course, indicate a change in the nature of the threat.

This was not very enlightening, and the second questioner persisted. Once again the reply was evasive and added nothing but tautologies to what Kennedy had already said. Kennedy managed not to betray himself in these two replies, but his evasiveness and obscurity tended to lessen slightly the credibility of his reassurance to the Soviets. Hence, when the Soviet Union on the very next day, September 14th, issued a statement of its own professing to accept Kennedy's words as a declaration that an invasion of Cuba was not being contemplated, it also gave evidence of a remnant of a misgiving: it regretted that the possibility of eventual attack had not been ruled out more definitively. Nevertheless, as events proved, Kennedy's word was believed in by Khrushchev.

As earlier with the Soviet scheme, we must now consider briefly the feasibility of the American counterscheme. The plan was the essence of simplicity. It required, to begin with, no more than the semantic skill to mislead both the Soviets and the American people at the same time. We have seen how this was done. Beyond that, it required only the ability to keep secret the photographic and other intelligence obtained between the time of the "warnings" and the time of the "discovery" of the missiles, several weeks later. Thereafter all normal governmental processes could be followed, including the eventual decision of the Executive Committee of the National Security Council concerning the specific measures to be taken against the Soviet Union. The only information that needed to be guarded for all time is that the U.S. government had knowledge of the missiles at the time when the "warnings" were issued.

In this connection we should note three facts. First, though all aerial reconnaissance of Cuba since 1960 and specifically during the months before the crisis had been done by the CIA's U-2's, on October 14, 1962, and thereafter the job was transferred to the U.S. Air Force's SAC. Indeed, it was the very first SAC U-2 flight on that date that "discovered" the missiles. The CIA is, of course, a more secure and compartmentalized organization than SAC, and the precise nature of the photographic information it gathered could remain the exclusive knowledge within the organization of no more than, say, two people, namely Director John A. McCone and one photographic intelligence officer.

Second, the U.S. government has persistently refused to make public any photographic evidence obtained between September 6th and October 13th. All its "before" pictures are dated September 5th or earlier, while all its "after" pictures are dated October 14th or later. This omission is especially important in the case of the so-called IRBM's which, unlike the fully portable, short-range missiles, required permanent installations and not simply a clearing in the woods. Now, the earliest photograph of IRBM bases made public by the U.S. government is dated October 17th: it shows the bases "nearing completion" and "having the final touches accomplished," [12] so that construction must have begun some time before. Whether it had begun as much as six weeks before remains, of course, an estimate, and is not capable of proof. What can be proven, however, is that these bases were in existence for an unspecifiable time before they were "discovered."

Third, the U.S. government has alleged contradictory and, at times, absurd reasons to explain why (a) it was unable to photograph the missiles at an earlier date, (b) it was able to photograph them, but did not manage to do so, (c) may have photographed them, but lacked conclusive proof with which to back up a public accusation against the Soviet Union. For example, the government insinuated to the House Armed Services Committee that it exhibited only "before" pictures dated September 5th or earlier because later pictures did not have good photographic quality: "We have selected our best photographic materials covering these sites prior to October 14th and would like to review them very quickly. [Para.] This is the Remedios IRBM location as it appeared on September 5th. . . ." [13] To the Senate investigating committee, however, one suggestion was that an amazing series of coincidences had prevented adequate photographic coverage during the period—for instance, a scheduled weekly flight having been cancelled (on account of unexplained difficulties), no one thought of ordering another flight until the next scheduled one, which took place one week later.[14]

[12] *House Hearings,* p. 241.

[13] *Ibid.,* p. 239. The same explanation was read by John Hughes, of the Defense Intelligence Agency, at McNamara's "Special Cuba Briefing," February 6, 1963; see the Department of Defense's transcript, p. 4.

[14] *Senate Report,* p. 8.

(Somehow this flight was "not wholly successful" either.) Taking another tack, the government explained that bad weather *continuously* prevented photography of the whole island between September 5th and 25th—and that after the weather lifted somehow it did not think of photographing the whole island, but only those parts which, as it turned out, did not have missile bases on them.[15]

The administration laid much emphasis on proving to a skeptical world opinion the existence of the missiles. But, strangely, it produced no evidence to support its claim about the exact nature or range of the missiles found in Cuba. Several reports[16] have pointed out that the evidence shown demonstrated only the existence of very short-range missiles, certainly not the type which are usually called IRBM's. The authoritative *Aviation Week* has actually suggested that the missiles should have been called PRBM's—Political Range Ballistic Missiles.[17]

In brief, the American counterscheme required essentially nothing else than security, and that security was ensured by two things. First, some physical secrecy was required, but it was not difficult to preserve. It had to do with the photographic intelligence obtained between September 5th and October 14th. Every other document could be placed in the public domain. Secrecy was required concerning their true meaning—which, in turn, could have been appreciated only in the light of the information that had been suppressed. Second, the number of people who had to be privy to the plan could be kept very small. Indeed, we may even make an intelligent guess at exactly who these were: Robert Kennedy, for obvious reasons; John A.

[15] *Ibid.* At the February 6, 1963, press briefing McNamara denied that there had been a "photography gap," explaining that photographs between September 5th and October 14th had not been shown at the briefing "for lack of time" (transcript, p. 40). At another press conference later that month he reverted to the explanation that somehow reconnaissance flights in late September and early October had not photographed the whole island, but only those sections which, as it turned out, were free from missile bases.

[16] *Newsweek,* November 12, 1962; *Bulletin of Atomic Scientists,* February 1963; *The New Republic,* February 23, 1963; *The New Yorker,* March 2, 1963.

[17] Pachter, p. 11.

McCone and one other CIA man, for reasons already given; Robert McNamara and his intelligence assistant, John Hughes, since in their briefings to House, Congress and public they introduced the equivocations, ambiguities and evasions required to avoid clearing up the mystery of the September 5th–October 14th photographic evidence gap. To these we might add McGeorge Bundy, given his relations to Kennedy, and also because the scheme is very much in his style. Possibly he completed the list. But Dean Rusk might be the last one to be admitted, if only because the forthcoming American case at the UN and in the courts of allied opinion would have to be handled by or through him. These eight persons were all who had to know. Kennedy's scheme was feasible, in the last analysis, because apart from security it hinged almost exclusively on two factors that could be fairly easily controlled by him: what he did not say to the American people, and what he did say to Khrushchev.

To say that the U.S. counterscheme was highly feasible is not to say that it was bound to succeed. Kennedy's plan was, evidently, the last resort of a cornered man. Very probably the idea of misleading the Soviets in order later to protest was put together without any final decision as to what form that protest would take or how effective it could be—the most important thing was to secure popular backing. (As already mentioned, the final decision to blockade was hammered out only between October 15th and October 22nd by the Executive Committee of the NSC.) But, as events proved, the diplomatic position of the Soviet Union was stronger than the U.S. counterscheme allowed. If the Soviet scheme failed the reason was not the U.S. blockade.

The weakness of the blockade was twofold. Diplomatically it suffered from glaring illegality; the presence of even truly offensive capability in Cuba would not have violated international law. Since the crisis was settled bilaterally before the UN case reached its completion, we can only speculate as to what would have happened there. It is certain, in view of the Soviet veto, that the U.S. could not have secured the endorsement of the

Security Council. If the case had gone to the General Assembly, it is doubtful that the U.S. would have fared well. The neutral bloc almost certainly would have voted against. Even the NATO allies, which ultimately would have sided with the U.S., did not show much sympathy with Kennedy's brinksmanship. The U.S. had wholehearted support only from its Latin American satellites.

Militarily also, as events showed, the blockade was ineffective. As long as the U.S. did not go beyond mere blockade the Soviet Union could afford to wait—as in fact it did—and either submit its commercial cargoes to search (under protest), or to use non-Soviet bottoms exclusively to carry ordinary supplies. After all, the weapons already were in Cuba. There was no reason to try to run the blockade. The case at the UN could proceed at its own pace. Eventually the blockade would have had to be lifted—or, at very least, the U.S. would have had to negotiate.

Evidently, Kennedy recognized very soon that the policy announced on October 22nd was not enough to defeat Khrushchev. But he held an ace up his sleeve, namely, his knowledge (probably partly reasoned, but surely intelligence-confirmed) that the weapons in Cuba remained under Soviet control.[18] Towards the end of the week of the crisis "through newspapers and allied nations, the information was leaked out [by the U.S. government] that an air strike [against the missile bases] might be executed 'shortly,' "[19] unless the Soviets agreed immediately to withdraw the weapons.

Of course, this put the situation in a new light. If the bases were attacked the Soviet Union would be placed in an impossible dilemma, for the attack would have directly impinged on *its* military force. It would have had, unthinkably, to submit supinely to military attack upon its troops, or it would have

[18] Even this knowledge was not strictly required. It was enough to know that the Soviets were *manning* the sites, a fact which had never been in doubt.

[19] Pachter, p. 55. In his testimony to the House Committee on Armed Services McNamara confirmed, in answer to the question whether "we were prepared for a time to invade," that "we were prepared for whatever eventuality developed," *House Hearings,* p. 273.

had to reply with its home forces—and this surely meant nothing less than a thermonuclear first strike. Khrushchev admitted defeat when he realized that Kennedy was now determined to launch a first, conventional strike upon the Soviet forces present in Cuba, regardless of consequences; that Kennedy was ready to go to war rather than abide the presence of the missiles, or otherwise suffer a diplomatic defeat of the magnitude here involved. Khrushchev was lost, in short, when he realized that his only alternative to withdrawing the missiles was to order a thermonuclear first strike. Kennedy's victory consisted in having maneuvered Khrushchev into that position.

Whatever Khrushchev's shortcomings, the disposition to go to nuclear war rather than suffer the corresponding humiliation and defeat was not one of them. Though it was probably foolish of him to have tempted a U.S. presidential circle renowned for its political pugnacity and for its Spartan self-conceit, proud of its "lean and mean" international image, it was surely fortunate for the world that he had enough wisdom to limit the risk even at the cost of a catastrophic diplomatic defeat.

But it is supremely ironic, in an episode rich in irony, that although Khrushchev suffered a crushing defeat (which very likely figured largely in his later downfall), Kennedy's victory was less than conclusive. The Cuban crisis so changed the world political climate that before many months had passed Kennedy himself had to face the fact that the forcible overthrow of the Cuban government was no longer expedient. (Shortly after he so declared the Soviet Union finally decided the time was ripe to undertake to regard an attack of Cuba as an attack on itself). Part of the reason may be described analogously to why Britain and France's failure in Suez forbade them further future moves of the same sort: in today's incipient world political organization, organized force against a supposedly illegitimate opponent automatically legitimizes that opponent.

The Cuban crisis legitimized the Cuban Revolutionary Government in a variety of ways. The American move granted belligerancy rights to the Cuban revolution against opposition from the U.S. And the U.S. policy logically implied that as long as Cuba did not offer a military threat to the U.S. (that is, as long as the interdicted weapons were withdrawn and kept out of Cuba), the U.S. had no right to apply military force.

By the same token, Kennedy's counterscheme focused the definition of illegitimacy upon nuclear deterrent weapons, on the grounds that every nuclear deterrent confers "offensive" capability. The logical implication was that other weapons (e.g., those of a parrying type, such as anti-aircraft missiles), were necessarily defensive. Therefore, their presence in Cuba did not justify an American attack. Now, in what category did this leave the Soviet-manned anti-aircraft bases? Or possibly even Soviet manned fighter aircraft? Or other defensive concentrations of Soviet troops? Evidently, they could not be classified as offensive. Ironically, the continued presence of Soviet troops in Cuba was, in the climate of the post-crisis, a sufficient deterrent to accomplish efficiently the defensive role in which the missiles had failed—though not enough, of course, to achieve the full original Soviet aim. In sum, the Cuban *military* situation was not radically changed by the withdrawal of the missiles—any more than it had been radically altered by their introduction. Kennedy eventually had to admit this into his calculations and, therefore, found it advisable to rethink his Cuban policy. Whereas in the climate before the crisis he might have dared to bomb Soviet troops in Cuba, after the crisis such a step had become unthinkable.

It seems, therefore, that there was an element of truth in Khrushchev's assertion that the imperialists learned their lesson. But since the Soviet Union withdrew the missiles long before they learned it, his representation was disingenuous. Moreover, it is probably incorrect to suppose that fear was the principal motive in Kennedy's reappraisal. I would like to think that when Kennedy reversed himself early in 1963 and renounced his alleged right to overthrow the Cuban government, the basic reason was the gradual acquisition, over the months since the previous November, of a world-political sobriety—indeed, a wisdom—which he had not previously enjoyed. We might even guess at an element of remorse, if not at the way in which he had dealt with Khrushchev and with the American people, at least at the way in which he had put the world in danger of thermonuclear holocaust. Whatever the reason, there is ample evidence that after the crisis a retrospective awareness of the enormity of the crisis entered Kennedy's calculations; there was even the hint of an admission that he had not been as clear-sighted during the crisis as he was now:

> When that day comes and there's a massive exchange then it's the end . . . you're talking about . . . 150 million fatalities in the first 18 hours . . . nobody wants to go through what we went through in Cuba very often . . . I think Mr. Khrushchev realizes the care with which he must proceed now as do we . . . Cuba was the first time where the Soviet Union and the United States directly faced each other with the prospect of the use of military forces . . . which could possibly have escalated into a nuclear struggle.[20]

The more general restructuring of Kennedy's world political perceptions became evident a little later in another declaration, in which for the first time since the onset of the cold war (and, to date, also for the last), an American President proposed the only American foreign policy which could make possible a stable peace between East and West. I refer to the policy of ending, rather than winning, the cold war:

> What kind of peace do we seek? Not a *Pax Americana* enforced on the world by American weapons of war . . . I am talking about genuine peace . . . —not merely peace for Americans but peace for all men—not merely peace in our time but peace for all time. . . .
>
> Some say that it is useless to speak of world peace or world law or world disarmament . . . until the leaders of the Soviet Union adopt a more enlightened attitude. I hope they do. I believe we can help them to do it. But I also believe that we must re-examine our own attitude . . . toward the possibilities of peace, toward the Soviet Union, toward the course of the cold war and toward freedom and peace here at home. . . .
>
> For, in the final analysis, our most basic common link is the fact that we all inhabit this planet. We all breathe the same air. We all cherish our children's future. And we all are mortal.[21]

[20] *CBS Script*, pp. 21, 31–32.

[21] Speech of June 10, 1963, at American University *(USIS Texts)*.

For the cold war is not a conflict about whose military dominion shall be imposed upon the world. It is a quarrel about whose concept of peace shall be imposed upon the other side. It is, therefore, indeed tragic, if these words truly signified a sincere conversion, that Kennedy's life was extinguished at the very time when his newly acquired maturity, vision and wisdom had just begun to fructify. For there are no signs that these qualities survived him at any of the high levels of U.S. government. The tragedy of Kennedy's death is not simply that he passed away, but that many like, say, McGeorge Bundy, Dean Rusk and Robert McNamara remained behind, to give to a willing ear and a permissive intellect the same sort of advice that President Kennedy had once taken, but which, through the purifying agony of responsibilities faced, he eventually learned to reject.

POSTSCRIPT (DECEMBER 1970)

It is now beyond all doubt (see especially Robert Kennedy's *Thirteen Days,* first published in *McCall's,* November 1968) that the Soviet Union agreed to withdraw the missiles not because of the blockade but because of Kennedy's threat "that if they did not remove those bases, we would remove them" (Kennedy, p. 170), which was conveyed by Robert Kennedy to Soviet Ambassador Dobrynin on Tuesday, October 30, at 7:45 A.M. Robert Kennedy has confirmed that the U.S. knew that the bases were Soviet manned, and that President Kennedy estimated the consequences of an attack on the bases in these terms: "The Russians, he felt, would have to react militarily to such actions on our part" (p. 173). Robert Kennedy maintains, of course, that no real alternative was open, since the Soviets had deceitfully and secretly, and in defiance of U.S. warnings, installed missile bases which seriously compromised the safety of the U.S. He has given, however, no evidence of this which I have not already considered in my paper and found unsatisfactory.

On the other hand, some readers have objected that I ascribe to Kennedy much more pre-planning than is likely to have been actually the case. I would certainly regret it if I had conveyed the view that Kennedy had carefully worked out what is usually called, in quotation marks, a "plot." My use of the word "scheme" in this connection was unfortunately equivocal: it obscured what surely was Kennedy's day-to-day weaving of a network of decisions which, as I have stressed, in the end entrapped him as thoroughly as it did Khrushchev. But I should have made clear that my reconstruction attempted to trace back not so much the logic of Kennedy's consciousness as the dialectic of human events.

There is, however, another part of my paper which I would not simply emphasize differently today but altogether rewrite anew: my remarks concerning Kennedy's probable attitudes after the crisis. At the time I wrote my paper I was still too much influenced by Kennedy's rhetoric. But the fact is that his actions after the crisis did not speak as eloquently as his speechwriter: the partial test-ban agreement exhausts the list of what is to be remembered in this regard. At any rate, it would be a mistake to exaggerate the importance of the individual, even the President, in the conduct of American diplomacy. A genuine and deep conversion on Kennedy's part would have made some, but probably not a decisive, difference to American foreign policy. Moreover, it is now idle to speculate on what would have happened had Kennedy lived: we know what the course of events has in fact been. And in this respect the conclusion is that the "lesson" taught by Khrushchev appears to have been scarcely what the teacher could have intended. The Soviet unwillingness to precipitate a nuclear exchange, even in defense of a socialist revolution, removed some uncertainties from U.S. policy planning: the removal of fears from Soviet retaliation may have been an important factor in the decision to bomb North Vietnam early in August 1964, after the Gulf of Tonkin incident.

Of course, the Chinese go too far when they say that the Soviet Union has become a turncoat which treasonably collaborates with imperialism against socialism. It would be more exact to say, perhaps, that the Soviet Union has to live with the fact that the Cuban crisis taught American diplomacy how to make brinksmanship successful. The willingness to set off an automatic process, as Kennedy did, which will destroy both players of the international chicken game unless one's opponent takes the initiative in disarming the mechanism—for one has ensured that he alone remains in a position to stop the process—is, of course, insane. Nevertheless, under certain conditions it can pose a more effective threat than the mere possession of lethal machines and the willingness to use them for a direct attack. In other words, irrationality may increase credibility; in relation to a rational opponent a degree of madness can be used methodically in order to blackmail. In the textbooks of American diplomacy the Cuban crisis may long remain the classic instance of the successful use of power, even in the nuclear age, in order to avoid war and at the same time to impose upon a comparably powerful nation one's arbitrary will. There is, tragically, no indication to date that any deeper wisdom drawn from the Cuban crisis is actually at work in the fundamental foreign policy of the United States.

DEAN ACHESON

Homage to Plain Dumb Luck

Stewart Alsop and Charles Bartlett first applied the terms "hawks" and "doves"—later to be associated with the war in Vietnam—to the debate within the Executive Committee on how to deal with the Russian missiles in Cuba. The foremost hawk was Dean Acheson, the only member of the group who did not hold an official position within the Kennedy administration. Kennedy had included Acheson, Secretary of State in the Truman years, because he valued his experience and his tough-minded approach to foreign policy issues. Yet in the end John Kennedy chose to ignore

Dean Acheson, "Dean Acheson's Version of Robert Kennedy's Version of the Cuban Missile Affair," *Esquire,* LXXI (February 1969), 76–77, 44, 46. Reprinted by permission of Harold Ober Associates Incorporated.

Acheson's advice and pursue the more moderate course of action advocated by his brother. Acheson, a proud and sensitive man despite his reputation for aloof detachment, never forgave the Kennedys for this slight. When Robert Kennedy revealed in his book that Dean Acheson had been his main antagonist in the Executive Committee debate, Acheson gave his version of the crisis in an article in Esquire *in February 1969.*

On October 28, 1962, when he seemed to be over the hump of the Cuban missile crisis, I wrote a note to President Kennedy congratulating him on his "leadership, firmness, and judgment over the past touchy week." It does not detract from the sincerity of this message to add that I also thought that he had been phenomenally lucky. Senator Kennedy's account of the crisis reinforces both impressions.

As he has written, his and my appraisal of the situation and recommendations to the President differed from the start. What enters into judgment, as distinct from rationalization of it, is difficult to identify or state honestly. Senator Kennedy seemed at the time—a view strengthened by his account—to have been moved by emotional or intuitive responses more than by the trained lawyer's analysis of the dangers threatened and of the relevance to these of the various actions proposed.

Senator Kennedy has described the White House–State Department–Pentagon group that advised the President on this crisis. I was drawn into the group on the second day of its existence, Wednesday, October 17, 1962, by Secretary Rusk, who showed me the U-2 photographs available and described the situation as it was then known. It became fully known only over the next few days as dispersal of hurricane-cloud cover over Cuba permitted more perfect photographs over a broader area. The facts were that the Soviet nuclear-missile installations in Cuba were extensive and formidable. The shorter-range missiles first discovered were soon supplemented by discoveries of longer-range missiles able to cover the continental United States, parts of Canada, and a good part of South America. The missile sites were remote from populated areas and manned and guarded by Russian personnel. When first photographed, only a few missiles were on launching pads—whether operable or not was unknown. Activity around them on all sites was considerable.

THE ISSUE IN THE ADVISORY GROUP

When Secretary Rusk and I joined the discussion, it soon became evident that three views were held by different members of the group: one, that the weapons in Cuba did not change the balance of power and, therefore, no action was required; two, that they were fast becoming an acute danger and should be removed by military action before they became operable; and, three, that a naval blockade against weapons should be established to enforce a demand that the Soviet Union remove the missiles.

As I recall it, the first of these views was put forward with more weight of authority, though not numbers, than Senator Kennedy's account suggests. At any rate, I hit it hard. In the first place, I did not believe for a minute that these weapons, ninety miles from Florida, did not increase our vulnerability above that theretofore existing. They gave shorter-range missiles the same bearing as intercontinental missiles. In the second place, if the United States government should take a passive position, it would forfeit—and rightly so—all confidence and leadership in the Western hemisphere (also under threat of these Soviet missiles) and in Western Europe. This first attitude was soon abandoned by its advocates.

When the discussion turned to a destruction of the missiles by bombing, Senator Kennedy stated the view expressed in his account. I remember clearly his formulation of it. An attack on the installations, he said, would be "a Pearl Harbor in reverse" and would never be acceptable to his brother. This seemed to me to obfuscate rather than clarify thought by a thoroughly false and pejorative analogy. I said so, pointing out that at Pearl Harbor the Japanese without provocation or warning attacked our fleet thousands of miles from their shores. In the present situation the Soviet Union had installed ninety miles from our coast—while denying that they were doing so—offensive weapons that were capable of lethal injury to the United States. This they were doing a hundred and forty years after the warning given in President Monroe's time that the United States government would regard an attempt by any European power to extend its "system to any portion of this hemisphere as dangerous to our peace and safety" and as manifesting "an unfriendly disposition toward the United States." Moreover, within the last few months the Congress, and within the last few weeks the President, had reiterated this warning against the establishment of these very weapons in Cuba. How much warning was necessary to avoid the stigma of "Pearl Harbor in reverse"? Was it necessary to adopt the early nineteenth-century method of having a man with a red flag walk before a steam engine to warn cattle and people to stay out of the way?

This dialectical approach was dropped in the group, though in discussion with the President alone, he repeated the "Pearl Harbor in reverse" phrase. I remarked that I knew where it came from and repeated my answer to it.

The more serious discussion of the alternatives—destroying the weapons or pressure for their removal by a naval blockade of the island—convinced me that the former was the necessary and only effective method of achieving our purpose. Yet the narrow and specific proposal, pressed by some of us, constantly became obscured and complicated by trimmings added by the military. To the proposal of immediate and simultaneous low-level bombing attacks on the nuclear installations, some wished to add bombing of airfields, SAM sites, and fighter aircraft; and others, the landing of ground troops to assure that the missiles were destroyed or removed. The former would indeed do what Senator Kennedy—and I, as well—deplored, "rain bombs on Cuba and kill thousands and thousands of civilians in a surprise attack." Attacks on the installations would involve no Cubans but about forty-five hundred Russian technicians and troops preparing for hostile action against our country. While a drill book might call for preliminary attack on Cuban defenses, this was not necessary for the action we recommended. If our action should fail—or if, in the more likely event, the blockade should fail—further military action might be necessary. But we, no more than our colleagues, were proposing killing "thousands and thousands of civilians." The charge was emotional dialectics.

To be sure, our proposal raised dangers of a Russian response against the United States or against an ally, such as Turkey or Berlin. But the blockade created what to my mind were greater dangers without any assurance of compensating benefit. Its effect would in any normal expectation be slow, if ships did not attempt to run through it; or, if they did, would produce the very military confrontation that Senator Kennedy so earnestly sought to avoid. But—most important of all—it would give the Russians time for their technicians to make some or all of the missiles operational. Once this occurred, Cuba would become a combination of porcupine and cobra. My criticism of Senator Kennedy's narrative is that it does not face this possibility—indeed, probability—frankly. It is merely stated and dropped.

The basic point, which both General de Gaulle and Chancellor Adenauer pointed out to me the following week, was that a blockade was a method of keeping things out, not getting things out, of a beleaguered spot. In this case, moreover, it was directed not at the controller of the weapons, but at the host of the controller. It seemed a blunt instrument, ill-adapted to the purpose. To argue, as Senator Kennedy quotes Secretary McNamara as doing, that its pressure "could be increased as the circumstances warranted . . . would be understood and yet, most importantly, still leave us in control of events," seems unworthy of the Secretary's able, analytical mind. The opposite seemed to me to be true: the blockade left our opponents in control of events.

General de Gaulle believed that the Russians would not attempt to force the blockade and asked what we would do in that event to remove the missiles. If the government had decided upon any course, I had not been informed of it before being sent off to Europe. Improvising, I replied that the government would immediately tighten the blockade and, if necessary, go further to more positive measures. The General understood.

As I saw it at the time, and still believe, the decision to resort to the blockade was a decision to postpone the issue at the expense of time within which the nuclear weapons might be made operable. The Soviet Union did not need to bring any more weapons into Cuba. The Senator's account reports an intelligence estimate that the nuclear weapons already there represented the equivalent of one-half of the Soviet Union's intercontinental-ballistic-missile capacity and were capable of killing eighty million Americans. That was enough.

The consideration that weighed more heavily on the other side with the Senator and the President was that an air attack on the installations alone might drive the Soviet Union to a spasmodic, reflex nuclear attack against the United States or against, say, American nuclear weapons in Turkey. This would be possible, of course; but analysis seemed to show it as unlikely. (Incidentally, General de Gaulle did not believe that the Kremlin would have responded with either action.) One must recall that both the Russian Ambassador and the Foreign Minister were asserting to the President that no offensive nuclear weapons had been installed in Cuba by the Soviet Union. Their representatives at the United Nations continued to repeat this even after Mr. Stevenson had asserted the contrary in the Security Council. So far, then, as the public record was concerned, a sudden air attack by us on nonpopulated areas of Cuba would have been an attack not on the Soviet Union but on something —not people—in Cuba. This would hardly have called for a reflex attack on the United States at the expense of reciprocal destruction of the Soviet Union.

The Russians would have been better advised to stick to their story that no nuclear weapons were in Cuba and charge that we had nervously fired at shadows created by our own fears. This would not have been easy to disprove, for even the evidence of the photographs could be attacked as faked with dummies. The germ-warfare charges against us in 1951 during the Korean war had been widely believed.

BLOCKADE MERELY POSTPONED CONFRONTATION

If one examines the blockade alternative, Senator Kennedy's story makes abundantly clear that it did not offer any greater chance of evading head-on collision with Moscow's prestige, riding like a figurehead on the prows of her ships approaching Cuba. By October 23 Soviet submarines were moving into the Caribbean. Almost as soon as the blockade went into effect, the government tried, the Senator relates, devices—not too resolute in appearance—for putting off the confrontation. First, the place of challenge was drawn closer to Cuba. Then a tanker was allowed to go through. Then a non-Soviet ship was boarded and passed. What should the Navy do if the Russian ships refused to stop? Shoot off the rudders or propellers? And then take them where? "We could anticipate a rough, fierce fight and many casualties," the President is reported as saying. Meanwhile more photographs of launching pads, missiles, and nuclear storage bunkers "made clear that the work on these sites was proceeding and that within a few days several of the launching pads would be ready for war."

At ten o'clock on Wednesday morning, October 24, a small group sat with the President as Secretary McNamara reported from the War Room two Soviet vessels approaching the U.S.S. *Essex*. A submerged Soviet submarine moved in front of them. "I felt," the narrative states, "we were on the edge of a precipice with no way off." At 10:25 A.M. a message came that the Russian ships had stopped dead in the water. Then came another that several ships in the area were turning around. The Russians, testing us to the last minute, had decided, as General de Gaulle had forecast the preceding Monday, not to attempt to run the blockade. The missiles, however, remained in place.

THE DECISION TO BLOCKADE

To move back a week, discussion within the "Ex-Comm" (Executive Committee of the National Security Council, a courtesy title) after a couple of sessions seemed to me repetitive, leaderless, and a waste of time. I was happy, therefore, when the President asked me to meet with him at 3:45 p.m. on Thursday, October 18. He received me alone for about an hour, listening to my views, as he always did, with courtesy and close attention and examining my reasons and premises thoroughly. His questions revealed full knowledge of Attorney General Kennedy's attitude. I could not tell what impression, if any, I had made. When we finished, he walked from his rocking chair in front of the fireplace to the French doors looking out on the rose garden and stood there for a moment. Then, without turning, he said, "I guess I'd better earn my salary this week." I answered, "I'm afraid you have to. I wish I could help more." With that we parted.

The next morning the "Ex-Comm" group, as the Kennedy narrative reports, decided to break up into two groups and each write out the steps, diplomatic and military, that the President would need to take to put the respective recommendations into effect.

Going into a room with those who favored the air strike, I asked to be excused from further attendance, saying that it was no place for a person holding no position in the government. For an outsider to give advice and counsel when asked was one thing; it was quite another to participate in writing the most secret strategic and tactical plans of a vital military operation, which might soon be put into effect.

On Saturday night, October 20, Secretary Rusk telephoned me and in a guarded way said that the President had decided a matter about which he had talked with me, though contrary to my recommendation. He wanted me to go to France to convey his decision and reasons to mutual friends, leaving by an Air Force plane the next morning.

In a way I had brought this request on myself. In the talk with the President the importance of informing our European as well as Latin American allies of our problem and enlisting their support before—even if only a split second before—acting and our lack at the moment of an ambassador in Paris led me to suggest that the Vice-President would be none too important a representative to send. The Secretary's request brought to mind an observation of Mr. Justice Holmes that we all belonged to the least exclusive and most expensive club in the world, the United States of America. I told him of it and undertook the obligation of membership he proposed, adding the hope I was enough of a lawyer to do a good job for my client, even though I thought he was making a mistake.

This is not the place for an account of that mission, interesting as it was with its interviews in Paris with General de Gaulle, the American military command in Europe, and the NATO Council, and in Bonn with Chancellor Adenauer and Defense Minister Strauss. Hastily getting together money, clothes, passports, instructions, photographs of the missiles, intelligence officers to interpret them, and an ambassador or two on the way back to his post, we were off early Sunday and home again on Wednesday, October 24. On our return the crisis had been going on for ten days without any progress toward getting the missiles disposed of.

ONCE MORE INTO THE BREACH

Returning to Washington on Wednesday afternoon, I found that the tension that had temporarily relaxed with the President's decision to impose the blockade was mounting again as realization grew that this was only another road to military confrontation with the Russians. Avoiding group meetings, I reported on my mission to Secretary Rusk on Wednesday afternoon and to the President on Thursday, pointing out again that the missiles remained in Cuba and that a week's collection of photographs showed alarming progress in the work of mounting them. Time was running out. The air strike remained the only method of eliminating them and hourly was becoming more dangerous.

On Friday evening in the State Department we saw the confused, almost maudlin message from Khrushchev, summarized in the Kennedy narrative. It is enough to say here that in its ramblings it admitted the presence of the weapons in Cuba, but denied that they had been put there to attack the United States, which would mean only mutual destruction. They were there only to protect Cuba against American attempts to overthrow its government, as the United States had attempted to do at the Bay of Pigs and earlier to overthrow the Soviet government soon after its establishment. The suggestion was made that if assurances were given that the United States would not attack Cuba and would abandon the blockade, the removal of the missile sites might be "an entirely different question." The letter then rambled off again on the horror and folly of nuclear war.

At breakfast with Secretary McNamara on Saturday I learned of the second, more formal Russian note conditioning the withdrawal of the Cuban missiles upon our withdrawal of our missiles in Turkey (apparently in ignorance of Khrushchev's earlier message), of the shooting down of a U-2 over Cuba on reconnaissance (the SAM sites or some of them were evidently now operational), and the opinion of the Chiefs of Staff that the air strike could no longer in safety be delayed. With this I agreed, but continued to urge that it be restricted to the Soviet nuclear installations only.

Senator Kennedy's paper tells us that on Saturday afternoon, at a meeting I did not attend, "there was almost unanimous agreement that we had to attack early the next morning with bombers and fighters and destroy the SAM sites. But again the President pulled everyone back." And quite rightly, for this proposal would have achieved the worst of both courses. It would have precipitated violence without accomplishing more than the destruction of the surface-to-air missiles, which had shot down the U-2. It would not have touched the source of the trouble, the nuclear missiles. " 'We won't attack tomorrow,' he [the President] said. 'We shall try again.' " So the report tells us.

What the President tried again was another message to Khrushchev, another postponement of action while Soviet work on the missiles drove on. It was a gamble to the point of recklessness, but skillfully executed, with ideas contributed by Robert Kennedy. It answered, not the official Soviet note, but Khrushchev's confused one, and accepted what seemed to be a muddled proposal for Russian withdrawal of the nuclear missiles in return for an American undertaking not to attack Cuba. If there were divided counsels in the Kremlin—as there were in Washington—the new message proposed to exploit them.

Meanwhile preparations for an air attack went forward. The amazing result was that by the very next morning this hundred-to-one shot certainly appeared to be paying off.

REFLECTIONS ON LUCK

It was not enough, Napoleon observed, that he should have good generals; he wanted them to be lucky generals, also. In foreign affairs brains, preparation, judgment, and power are of utmost importance, but luck is essential. It does not detract from President Kennedy's laurels in handling the Cuban crisis that he was helped by the luck of Khrushchev's befuddlement and loss of nerve. The fact was that he succeeded. However, as the Duke of Wellington said of Waterloo, it was "a damned near thing." And one should not play one's luck so far too often.

What, I was asked at the time, was Khrushchev up to? He had, I thought, formed a low opinion of Presidents Eisenhower and Kennedy at the Paris summit meeting and Vienna respectively. His aim in Cuba was threefold: first, to increase his nuclear first-strike capacity against the United States by about 50 per cent; second, to discredit the United States completely in the Western hemisphere; and third, to force the United States to pay so high a price for the removal of the Cuban missiles as to discredit us in Europe and Asia. He could with some reason believe that his own prestige was not likely to be damaged beyond what a diversion like the Berlin Wall of 1961 could repair. He went to pieces when the military confrontation seemed inevitable. But he need not have done so. Senator Kennedy's narrative does not convince me that an attack would have been inevitable if Khrushchev had "played it cool."

REFLECTIONS ON METHOD

"During all these deliberations," Senator Kennedy has written, "we all spoke as equals. There was no rank, and in fact we did not even have a chairman. Dean Rusk, who as Secretary of State might have assumed that position, had other duties and responsibilities during this period of time and frequently could not attend our meetings." One wonders what those "other duties and responsibilities" were to have been half so important as those they displaced. As a result, "the conversations were completely uninhibited and unrestricted. . . . It was a tremendously advantageous procedure that does not frequently occur within the Executive branch of the Government. . . ." One can be devoutly thankful that this is so.

I can testify to the truth of the statement that members of the group did all speak as equals, were uninhibited, and that they had no chairman. But in any sense of constitutional and legal responsibility they were not equal and should have been under the direction of the head of government or his chief Secretary of State for Foreign Affairs and his military advisers. One cannot escape the conclusion from reading the Kennedy narrative that the chief advice reaching the President during this critical period came to him through his brother, the Attorney General, out of a leaderless, uninhibited group, many of whom had little knowledge in either the military or diplomatic field. This is not the way the National Security Council operated at any time during which I was officially connected with it; nor, I submit, the way it should operate.

THEODORE C. SORENSEN

Kennedy Vindicated

Growing criticism from both the left and the right troubled those who cherished the memory of John F. Kennedy. They believed that the Cuban missile crisis had been the late President's greatest triumph, one beyond petty bickering and partisan squabbling. After the assassination of Robert Kennedy, Theodore Sorensen, the man who had been a political intimate of both brothers, wrote The Kennedy Legacy, *a warm and sympathetic appraisal of the contributions of these two remarkable men. When he came to the Cuban missile crisis, Sorensen made a valiant effort to rebut the criticisms and reassert the claims to President Kennedy's greatness as a statesman.*

. . . THE BERLIN CRISIS OF 1961, to be sure, had been a tough test of Kennedy's mettle. Faced with a dangerous deadline

Theodore C. Sorensen, *The Kennedy Legacy* (New York, 1969), pp. 186–192. Reprinted by permission of the Macmillan Company. Copyright © 1969 by Theodore Sorensen.

which would have required him to abandon a commitment vital to our interests, confronted with a threatened squeeze too subtle for nuclear response but too serious to ignore, he found that he had inherited a "Berlin Contingency Plan" and a military capability in that area which gave him a choice of either nuclear holocaust or abject humiliation. He found as well that his allies and advisers were divided. Some said, in effect: Refuse to talk and fight if pressed. Others said, in effect: Refuse to fight and yield if pressed. Still others said, in effect: Refuse to fight or talk or yield, but think of something. Kennedy, making clear what we would and would not talk and fight about, shrewdly engaged Khrushchev in a long correspondence and other diplomatic exchanges on the issue, meanwhile building the deterrent power of our conventional forces (and mistakenly inspiring a national civil defense craze) and permitting the deadline to pass without notice.

Soviet long-range missiles in Cuba, however, represented a sudden, immediate and more dangerous and secretive change in the balance of power, in clear contradiction of all U.S. commitments and Soviet pledges. It was a move which required a response from the United States, not for reasons of prestige or image but for reasons of national security in the broadest sense. JFK's obligation as President in October 1962 was to find some way of effecting a removal of those nuclear weapons without either precipitating mankind's final war or trading away anyone's security. It was in a very real sense the world's first armed confrontation between two nuclear superpowers.

Ever since the successful resolution of that crisis, I have noted among many political and military figures a Cuban-missile-crisis syndrome, which calls for a repetition in some other conflict of "Jack Kennedy's tough stand of October 1962 when he told the Russians with their missiles either to pull out or look out!" Some observers even attributed Lyndon Johnson's decision to escalate in Vietnam to a conviction that America's military superiority could bring him a "victory" comparable to JFK's. That badly misreads what actually happened. Kennedy himself took pains to point out to Adenauer and others that the Cuban outcome was not a "victory," that it was not achieved solely through military might, and that what success we had in this instance—with the Soviets at a geographic and world-opinion disadvantage—could not be counted on in instances, such as Berlin, which more directly affected Soviet security.

It is true that American military force—namely, a barrier of naval vessels around Cuba—before its effectiveness could be rendered less meaningful by the delivery of all missiles to the island, interposed itself against a potential Soviet force on its way to Cuba. It is true that our superiority in deliverable nuclear power, as well as our superiority in naval power, undoubtedly made the Soviets more cautious than they might otherwise have been about physically challenging our naval quarantine or retaliating with a blockade of West Berlin. It is also true that JFK's address sternly warned that any nuclear missile launched from Cuba against any nation in the Western Hemisphere would be regarded as a Soviet attack on the United States "requiring a full retaliatory response upon the Soviet Union." But these facts should not be taken out of context.

Kennedy in fact relied not on force and threats alone but on a carefully balanced and precisely measured combination of defense, diplomacy, and dialogue. He instituted the naval quarantine without waiting for diplomatic efforts, because once such efforts failed (and he was convinced they would fail), it would be too late to prevent completion of the missiles or get them out without more belligerent and dangerous measures. He chose the quarantine in preference to an air attack because it was a measured, limited step, it offered the Russians both room to maneuver and a peaceful way out, and it did not make armed conflict inevitable. He deliberately called it a "quarantine" rather than a "blockade," which is an act of war. He took no action that would risk civilian lives. He authorized no surprise attacks and no needless risk of American lives. He posed the issue as one between two powers restrained by mutual deterrence, instead of making the unpredictable Castro his opposite number.

Despite his anger at being deceived and his awareness that one misstep meant disaster, he remained cool at all times. He refused to issue any ultimatum, to close any doors, or to insist upon any deadlines, noting only that continued work on the missile sites would "justify" (not necessarily insure) further U.S. action. He made clear to the Soviets both in writing and through his brother that the United States was prepared to talk about peace and disarmament generally and about the presence of our missiles in Turkey specifically, once the Soviet provocation to peace had been withdrawn. He placed the dispute before the United Nations and corresponded with Khrushchev about it almost daily. He was careful to obtain sanction for the quarantine under international law, procuring unanimous authorization from the members of a recognized regional defense group, the Organization of American States (OAS), obtaining its members' multilateral participation, and invoking the self-defense provisions of the UN charter.

Even as Soviet ships and work on the missile sites proceeded, he avoided a confrontation that might force the Soviets to attack. Even after an American plane was shot down, he withheld retaliation in the hopes of an early settlement. On the final crucial Saturday night before the missiles were withdrawn, he adjourned our "Ex Comm" meeting as the hawks began to dominate the discussion and to urge an immediate air strike. He achieved a resolution that was in effect negotiated by mail, one that treated both powers as equals and restored the *status quo ante* instead of destroying Castro. Then he refused to crow or claim victory. He was at each step firm but generous to his adversaries and candid with his major allies, with the American public, and with the Congressional leaders, although he gave advance information to no one and sought advance approval from no one.

While oversimplified comparisons of drastically different situations are dangerous, it is interesting to take each of the above standards and apply it to this nation's role in Vietnam. My own view is that we might have avoided the disastrous escalation of that war had Presidents Kennedy and Johnson followed these same standards. I also think it highly possible that, had each of these standards not been followed in the Cuban missile crisis, this planet might now be in ashes. The medium-range missile sites under rapid construction in Cuba would all have been operational within a few days, according to the intelligence estimates, and some may already have been prepared to respond to any American attack by firing their deadly salvos upon the southeastern United States.

Some ask: What if Khrushchev had not backed down? Others say: Why did we settle for so little? The real question is: Where would we be if JFK had not pursued the above course and accepted Khrushchev's offer in a way that avoided the need for anyone to back down? It was indeed eyeball-to-eyeball, and fortunately both men blinked. Dean Acheson is right in crediting Kennedy with considerable good luck on this awesome occasion; but there was considerable good judgment as well as luck involved in the President's rejection of alternative recommendations, including the recommendation for bombing the missile sites which came from Acheson himself. (In short, among the ways in which JFK was lucky was in not taking Dean Acheson's advice!)

While some have since accused him of taking action to influence the Congressional elections, JFK at the time was convinced his course would hurt his party in the elections. It seemed clear on that fateful Saturday afternoon, October 20, when he made his decision for the quarantine, that an air strike would be a swifter and more popular means of removing the missiles before Election Day, and that a quarantine would encourage a prolonged UN debate and Republican charges of weakness in the face of peril. Yet he never contemplated changing that course for political reasons. Others have since accused him of overreacting for reasons of personal or national prestige to a move that did not really alter the strategic balance of power or pose an actual threat to our own security. But Kennedy recognized that appearances and reality often merge in world affairs; and if all Latin America had thought that the U.S. had passively permitted what was apparently a new threat to their existence, and if all our Western allies had thought that we would not respond to a sudden, secret deployment of missiles in our own hemisphere, then a whole wave of reactions contrary to our interests and security might well have followed.

Throughout this period the role of Robert Kennedy was unusually important. The President confided to me his concern that his Secretary of State in particular had been disappointingly irresolute during the few days preceding JFK's final formulation of the quarantine policy and too fatigued after guiding a brilliant execution of that policy during the following few days; that the Joint Chiefs of Staff had been dangerously inflexible in their insistence on an all-out military attack as the only course the Soviets would understand; and that sooner or later everyone involved would reflect what both Macmillan and McNamara termed the period of most intense strain they had ever experienced.

But Brother Bob displayed not the "emotional dialectics" suggested by some but hardheaded and cool judgment. He was a leader without designation when our little "Executive Committee" group—Rusk, McNamara, Dillon, Bundy, Ball, Taylor, McCone, and a half-dozen others, including me—met with the President. He used his full powers of presence and persistence to extract specific suggestions and objections instead of generalities and to produce concrete progress instead of anxieties. He was instrumental in the early days in rejecting the proposal for surprise attack. He was instrumental in the final days in conveying to the Soviet Ambassador the position that finally prevailed. He helped shape, organize, and monitor the entire effort that remains a standard for all time.

Never before had the Soviets and the Americans peered so clearly at each other down the barrels of their nuclear cannons and contemplated the meaning of attack. The effect was to purge their minds, at least temporarily, of cold-war clichés. If nuclear war were suicidal, if nuclear blackmail were futile, if an accidental nuclear war would be disastrous, surely there had to be a more sensible way of competing against each other than building still more exorbitantly expensive nuclear weapons. The chief lesson learned from this first nuclear crisis was not how to conduct the next one—but how to avoid it. . . .

RONALD STEEL

Lessons of the Missile Crisis

Conflicting interpretations and claims tended to confuse rather than clarify the issues involved in the Cuban crisis.

In an effort to bring light rather than heat to the dispute, Ronald Steel used a review of Thirteen Days *in the* New York Review of Books *to write an extended essay on both the crisis itself and on the major points of disagreement. Though Steel, a former foreign service officer and author of* Pax Americana, *tended to be critical of American policy, he wrote the most comprehensive and in many ways the most thoughtful analysis of the whole controversy.*

IT WAS A TIME, in Khrushchev's memorable phrase, "when the smell of burning hung in the air." Robert Kennedy's account of those thirteen days in 1962—from October 16, when he and his brother were presented with proof that the Russians were secretly building long-range missile bases in Cuba, until October 28, when the Kremlin agreed to dismantle them—shows the view from the inside by one of the key participants. Written with economy and directness, *Thirteen Days* is a valuable historical document with all the elements of a thriller.

This short, terse memoir—bloated by the publisher with superfluous introductions, photographs, and documents—does not, of course, tell the whole story of the missile crisis. There is a good deal about the events leading up to the crisis that is gone over too lightly or deliberately clouded over. The clash of personalities and ambivalent motives is muted and the tone rather detached. But behind the measured prose we see the spectacle of rational minds swayed by passions and the euphoria of power, governmental machinery breaking down into the struggle of individual wills, and decisions affecting the future of humanity made by a handful of men—the best of whom were not always sure they were right. A disturbing description of decision-making in the nuclear age, this posthumous work also offers a revealing glimpse of an enigmatic man who might have bridged the gap between the old politics and the new.

We have come to take the balance of terror so much for

Ronald Steel, "Endgame," *New York Review of Books,* XII (March 13, 1969), 15–22. Reprinted by permission. Copyright © 1969 by Ronald Steel.

granted that it is hard to imagine any situation in which the two superpowers would actually use their terrible weapons. Yet more than once during those thirteen days it seemed as though the unthinkable might actually occur. SAC bombers were dispersed to airfields throughout the country and roamed the skies with their nuclear cargoes. At one point President Kennedy, fearful that some trigger-happy colonel might set off the spark, ordered all atomic missiles defused so that the order to fire would have to come directly from the White House.

The first showdown came on the morning of October 24, as Soviet ships approached the 500-mile quarantine line drawn around Cuba. "I felt," Robert Kennedy wrote of those terrible moments, "we were on the edge of a precipice with no way off. . . . President Kennedy had initiated the course of events, but he no longer had control over them." Faced with this blockade, the Russian ships turned back, and the first crisis was surmounted. No more missiles could get into Cuba. But what of the ones already there that Russian technicians were installing with feverish haste? President Kennedy was determined that they had to be removed immediately, and on Saturday, October 27, sent his brother to tell Soviet Ambassador Dobrynin "that if they did not remove those bases, we would remove them." The Pentagon prepared for an air strike against the bases and an invasion of Cuba. "The expectation," Robert Kennedy wrote of that fateful Saturday, "was a military confrontation by Tuesday."

We know, of course, how it turned out. On Sunday morning the message came through that Khrushchev would withdraw the missiles in return for a U.S. pledge not to invade Cuba. Kennedy had pulled off the greatest coup of his career—the first, and one hopes the last, military victory of the nuclear era. Not a shot was fired, although we came a good deal closer to war than most people realized at the time, or have cared to think about since.

It was a victory not only over the Soviets, but over many of Kennedy's own advisers who favored a more militant course from the start. The drama was played out among a hastily assembled group, which later took on the formal title of the Executive Committee of the National Security Council, that met several times a day in the White House. The sessions were frequently stormy, although the lines were loosely drawn at first. Several of the participants, according to Robert Kennedy, shifted their opinion "from one extreme to the other—supporting an air attack at the beginning of the meeting and, by the time we left the White House, supporting no action at all." A few, such as Dean Acheson and Douglas Dillon, were hawks from the start, and argued for what they euphemistically called a "surgical strike" against the air bases. They were eventually joined by John McCone, General Maxwell Taylor, Paul Nitze, and McGeorge Bundy. Favoring a more moderate course, which settled around a naval blockade to be "escalated" to an attack on the bases only if absolutely necessary were the doves, led by Robert Kennedy and Robert McNamara, and including George Ball, Roswell Gilpatric, Llewellyn Thompson, and Robert Lovett.

Dean Rusk, for the most part, avoided taking a stand, or even attending the sessions. The Secretary of State, in Robert Kennedy's caustic words, "had other duties during this period and frequently could not attend our meetings." It would be interesting to know what these duties were. Robert Kennedy does not elaborate, although he does offer the further intriguing aside that "Secretary Rusk missed President Kennedy's extremely important meeting with Prime Minister Macmillan in Nassau because of a diplomatic dinner he felt he should attend." That was the meeting, one will remember, where President Kennedy agreed to help out Harold Macmillan (author of one of the two Introductions to this volume) on the eve of the British elections by turning over Polaris missiles to Britain after the Skybolt fiasco that had embarrassed the Tories. De Gaulle, predictably, was furious, declared that Britain still valued her trans-Atlantic ties above her European ones, and vetoed her entry into the Common Market. The Nassau accord was a colossal error of judgment that an astute Secretary of State should have been able to prevent—had he not been too busy attending diplomatic dinners.

Some of the hawks were, of course, predictable. It is not surprising that the Joint Chiefs of Staff were eager to use their expensive hardware. "They seemed always ready to assume," Robert Kennedy wrote, "that a war was in our national interest. One of the Joint Chiefs of Staff once said to me he believed in a preventive attack against the Soviet Union." Nor is it surprising that Dean Acheson, among the most recalcitrant of the cold warriors, should have come down on the side of the military. "I felt we were too eager to liquidate this thing," Elie Abel reports him as saying in *The Missile Crisis*. "So long as we had the thumbscrew on Khrushchev, we should have given it another turn every day. We were too eager to make an agreement with the Russians. They had no business there in the first place." Ever since his crucifixion by Congress during the Alger Hiss affair, Acheson has become increasingly reactionary and eager to prove his toughness toward the Communists. His bomb-first-and-talk-later argument found receptive ears in such pillars of the Eastern Republican Establishment as Douglas Dillon, John J. McCloy, and McGeorge Bundy.

Many who were not aware of the drama being played out in the White House during those thirteen days, however, will be surprised to find Robert Kennedy as the leader of the doves and the moral conscience of his brother's administration. Although he does not dramatize his own role, we learn from his account and those of others that he argued against a first strike as contrary to American traditions. "My brother," Abel quotes him as saying, "is not going to be the Tojo of the 1960s." This impassioned plea against a Pearl Harbor in reverse moved even Maxwell Taylor. The general, Abel quotes one of the participants as commenting, "showed what a moral man he is by recommending that we give the Cubans twenty-four hours' advance notice—and then strike the missile bases."

The other outstanding dove of the deliberations was the man in charge of the military establishment, Robert McNamara. The Secretary of Defense, in Kennedy's words, "became the blockade's strongest advocate" and argued that "a surgical air strike . . . was militarily impractical." McNamara was not only a consistent dove, fighting off the belligerent advice of his service chiefs, but disputed the prevailing view that the Russians were trying to upset the strategic balance between East and West. "A missile is a missile," Abel and others have quoted him as saying. "It makes no difference whether you are killed by a missile fired from the Soviet Union or from Cuba." Observing that the Russians had ICBMs and that the only effect of the Cuban-based intermediate-range missiles would be to reduce by a few minutes our warning time in case of attack, McNamara's advice, in effect, was to sit tight.

However valid such advice might have been from a military point of view, it was quite unacceptable politically. John F. Kennedy was especially vulnerable on Cuba, having used it as an issue against Nixon during the 1960 campaign, and then having suffered the ignominy of the Bay of Pigs. The Republicans were pressing him hard on his "do-nothing" policy toward Castro, and former Senator Keating of New York was leading a wolf pack in charging that the Russians were turning Cuba into a base for offensive weapons. Kennedy as Democratic Party leader could not tolerate Soviet missiles in Cuba, even if the civilian head of the Pentagon could.

"If the missiles," Roger Hilsman, head of intelligence in the State Department and then Assistant Secretary of State for the Far East, comments in his book, *To Move a Nation,* "were not important enough to justify a confrontation with the Soviet Union, as McNamara initially thought, yet were 'offensive,' then the United States might not be in mortal danger, but the administration most certainly was." And, according to John Kenneth Galbraith, then ambassador to India, "once they [the missiles] were there, the political needs of the Kennedy administration urged it to take almost any risk to get them out."

Did we, then, nearly go up in radioactive dust to shore up the Kennedy administration's fading image before the November 1962 elections? Not necessarily, for if the missiles did not upset the strategic balance, even a President less image-conscious than John F. Kennedy could not easily accept such an abrupt change in the status quo—least of all in the Caribbean. "To be sure," Theodore Sorensen observed in his *Kennedy,* "these Cuban missiles alone, in view of all the other megatonnage the Soviets were capable of unleashing upon us, did not substantially alter the strategic balance *in fact*. . . . But that balance would have been substantially altered *in appearance* [italics in original]; and in matters of national will and world leadership, as the President said later, such appearances contribute to reality." In fact, Kennedy himself leaned heavily on the prestige argument when he announced the blockade to the nation on October 22.

> This sudden, clandestine decision to station strategic weapons for the first time outside of Soviet soil is a deliberately provocative and unjustified change in the status quo which cannot be accepted by this country, if our courage and our commitments are ever to be trusted again by either friend or foe.

Elevating his rhetoric, as usual, above the needs of the occasion, Kennedy set the stage for a direct military confrontation.

He was acutely conscious of any questioning of his courage, and with the ashes of the Vienna encounter with Khrushchev still in his mouth and another Berlin crisis brewing, he had to get the missiles out of Cuba. But did he have to get them out before the end of October? What would have happened had he negotiated with Khrushchev instead of issuing the ultimatum—delivered to Ambassador Dobrynin on Saturday evening, October 27, by Robert Kennedy—that "we had to have a commitment by tomorrow that those bases would be removed." What would have happened had the negotiations dragged on for a few weeks and some kind of quid pro quo were arranged?

The Russians, of course, would have had the already delivered missiles in place by then. But their withdrawal could still be negotiated and, in any case, the continuation of the blockade would have brought Castro to his knees within a few months. Assuming that the missiles had to be removed, was it necessary, in Robert Kennedy's words, "to have a commitment by tomorrow"? At the time a good many people believed Kennedy had politics in mind during the missile crisis. General Eisenhower, when informed by McCone about the discovery of the missiles, "took a skeptical view," according to Abel, "suspecting perhaps that Kennedy might be playing politics with

Cuba on the eve of Congressional elections." The thought also crossed the mind of Kennedy's old chum, David Ormsby-Gore, then British ambassador to Washington, who felt that "British opinion must somehow be persuaded that the missile crisis was the real thing, not something trumped up by the President for vote-getting purposes." Nor did the elections go unnoticed by the participants in the Executive Committee. I. F. Stone has pointed out Sorensen's comment that during one of the meetings a Republican member passed him a note saying:

> Ted—have you considered the very real possibility that if we allow Cuba to complete installation and operational readiness of missile bases, the next House of Representatives is likely to have a Republican majority? This would completely paralyze our ability to react sensibly and coherently to further Soviet advances.

It is not to denigrate John F. Kennedy's patriotism to assume that he was aware of such possibilities. Nor is it to question the motives of those who took part in those exhausting, often stormy, meetings during the thirteen days. It would have been political folly for Kennedy to have broached the subject of the elections before the Executive Committee, where it would have fallen on a good many unsympathetic ears, and it is exceedingly unlikely that the question was ever formally raised. Nor did the participants believe they were behaving by the rules of partisan politics when they decided that the missiles had to be removed immediately. But of the fourteen-odd people who participated in most of the meetings, only a few—Sorensen, Robert Kennedy, and, of course, the President—could be considered politicians. As politicians who had to fight elections, as leaders of the party which was about to be tested at the polls, they could not have been oblivious to what was going to happen in early November—even if they never mentioned it in the meetings, or to one another.

To do nothing about the missiles, as McNamara's position would imply, or to take the issue to the United Nations, or to compromise by trading the Soviet missiles in Cuba for the obsolete American missiles in Turkey, would have been bad politics at that particular time. Obsessed by his image, Kennedy feared that Khrushchev would not take him seriously if he again backed down in Cuba. This questioning of "our courage," he believed, could tempt the Russians to a policy of adventurism, perhaps in Central Europe. Indeed, the first reading of the missile crisis was that Khrushchev was preparing to force a Berlin settlement on his own terms. Thus did considerations of high strategy and party politics reinforce one another and convince Kennedy that the Russian withdrawal had to be complete, unilateral, and secured by the end of October.

The question of a quid pro quo revolved around the American missiles in Turkey and Italy. These had been placed there five years earlier during the Eisenhower administration's panic over the Sputnik. Designed to redress the strategic balance during a time when the U.S. had no reliable ICBMs, these relatively primitive liquid-fuel missiles had become, in Hilsman's words, "obsolete, unreliable, inaccurate, and very vulnerable." Shortly after his inauguration Kennedy asked that they be removed and was discouraged by the State Department. He raised the question again in early 1962, and despite objections that the Turks disapproved, instructed Dean Rusk to negotiate the removal of the missiles. "The President," Robert Kennedy has written, barely concealing his contempt for Dean Rusk, "believed he was President and that, his wishes having been made clear, they would be followed and the missiles removed."

But his instructions were not carried out, and Kennedy discovered that the obsolete Turkish missiles had become a bargaining foil for Khrushchev. "We will remove our missiles from Cuba, you will remove yours from Turkey," read the note received from the Kremlin on the morning of Saturday, October 27. ". . . The Soviet Union will pledge not to invade or interfere with the internal affairs of Turkey; the U.S. to make the same pledge regarding Cuba." This note, with its quid pro quo, added a new condition to the emotional message received the night before, in which the Soviet premier indicated he would pull out the missiles in return for a U.S. promise not to invade Cuba.

Adding Turkey to the bargain filled the White House advisers with consternation—not least of all because it appeared perfectly fair. "The proposal the Russians made," in Robert Kennedy's words, "was not unreasonable and did not amount to a loss to the U.S. or to our NATO allies." Categorically to reject such a trade would make the U.S. seem vindictive and threaten the support of its allies—none of whom had any wish to be dragged into nuclear war over the issue of Cuba. But to accept the trade would be to invite accusations of weakness and dishonor by the Republicans. Kennedy, needless to say, was furious at the State Department for putting him in such a vulnerable position.

The Kremlin was not the first to raise the issue of trading the Cuban bases for the Turkish ones. In his column of Thursday, October 25, Walter Lippmann suggested a diplomatic solution to get the missiles out of Cuba:

> There are three ways to get rid of the missiles already in Cuba. One is to invade and occupy Cuba. The second way is to institute a total blockade, particularly of oil shipments, which would in a few months ruin the Cuban economy. The third way is to try, I repeat, to negotiate a face-saving settlement. . . . I am not talking about and do not believe in a "Cuba-Berlin" horse trade. . . . The only place that is truly comparable with Cuba is Turkey. This is the only place where there are strategic weapons right on the frontier of the Soviet Union. . . . The Soviet military base in Cuba is defenseless, and the base in Turkey is all but obsolete. The two bases could be dismantled without altering the world balance of power.

This position had already been argued by Adlai Stevenson who, according to Robert Kennedy, on October 20 "strongly advocated what he had only tentatively suggested to me a few days before—namely, that we make it clear to the Soviet Union that if it withdrew its missiles from Cuba, we would be willing to withdraw our missiles from Turkey and Italy and give up our naval base at Guantánamo Bay." With this suggestion Stevenson went a good deal further than Lippmann, who never included Guantánamo in the trade. This won Stevenson the wrath of several of the participants, including Robert Kennedy, who prevailed upon his brother to send John J. McCloy to the UN to handle the Russians during the missile crisis. But time healed some of Robert Kennedy's wrath, and in *Thirteen Days* he wrote:

> Stevenson has since been criticized publicly for the position he took at this meeting. I think it should be emphasized that he was presenting a point of view from a different perspective than the others, one which was therefore important for the President to consider. Although I disagreed strongly with his recommendations, I thought he was courageous to make them, and I might add they made as much sense as some others considered during that period.

Stevenson's proposal was not so heretical as it was treated at the time, or in the inside stories that appeared shortly after the missile crisis. Kennedy was prepared to give up the Turkish bases, but for political reasons could not make it a quid pro quo—although there is some reason to think that he might have done so *in extremis.* On Saturday—when the Russians sent their second note calling for the Turkey-Cuba base trade—Kennedy, according to Abel, told Roswell Gilpatric to prepare a scenario for removing the missiles from Turkey and Italy, and have it ready for the meeting that night. That evening he sent his brother to Ambassador Dobrynin with the demand that the Russians had to promise to withdraw the missiles from Cuba by the following day. The Joint Chiefs of Staff were preparing to bomb the missile sites on Tuesday. Dobrynin, according to Abel, "gave it as his personal opinion that the Soviet leaders were so deeply committed they would have to reject the President's terms."

But while he ruled out an explicit deal, Robert Kennedy told the Soviet ambassador that there need be no problem about the Turkish missiles. "President Kennedy," he said to Dobrynin, "had been anxious to remove those missiles from Turkey and Italy for a long period of time . . . and it was our judgment that, within a short time after this crisis was over, those missiles would be gone." Dobrynin sent on the message to Moscow; President Kennedy, at his brother's suggestion, accepted the more moderate first message from Khrushchev and ignored the second Kremlin note: and an apprehensive Washington awaited the Kremlin's response as plans proceeded for an air strike against the Cuban bases. On Sunday morning the word came through that the missiles would be withdrawn in return for a simple U.S. pledge not to invade Cuba. The worst crisis of the Cold War was over. But even at this moment of triumph, some were not satisfied. "On that fateful Sunday morning when the Russians answered they were withdrawing their missiles," Robert Kennedy revealed, "it was suggested by one high military adviser that we attack Monday in any case."

The resolution of the Cuban missile crisis ironically set the stage for a more cooperative policy from Moscow, culminating in the test-ban treaty of 1963. It also contributed to the euphoria of power that led Kennedy's successor, urged on by Kennedy's advisers, to have his little war in Southeast Asia. Had the U.S. been forced to back down in Cuba, or to work out a Cuba-Turkey trade with the Russians, perhaps Washington might have awakened from the dream of American omnipotence before Lyndon Johnson launched his crusade in Vietnam.

Cuba, in Hilsman's words, was "a foreign policy victory of historical proportions," but in the long run the Russians did not come out of it too badly. They lost a certain amount of face, particularly among the Communist parties of Latin America, and they revealed once again that the interests of the Soviet state take precedence over the world revolution. Peking, for its part, lost no time in gloating that it was "sheer adventurism to put missiles into Cuba in the first place, but capitulationism to take them out under American pressure." Perhaps the Cuban setback contributed to Khrushchev's demise, although it is dubious whether that was a net gain for the West. But the blow to Soviet prestige was washed away with passing time, and the Russians, perhaps because they had their fingers burned in Cuba, refrained from exercises in global management of the kind that obsessed President Johnson and ultimately drove him from office.

What was the lesson of the Cuban missile crisis? There were several: first, that diplomacy gave way to military ultimatums;

second, that there was a failure of intelligence interpretation; third, that the Kremlin's motives were never adequately understood; and fourth, that there is something basically wrong with the whole process of decision-making.

1. *The suspension of diplomacy.* Kennedy's mistake was not, as former Secretary of State Dean Acheson would have it, in failing to brandish the big stick more quickly. Rather it was in deliberately rejecting diplomatic contact when it might have made unnecessary precisely the kind of confrontation that occurred. Instead of using traditional diplomatic channels to warn the Russians that he knew what they were up to, and thus give them a chance quietly to pull back, Kennedy chose to inform the Kremlin of his discovery by a nation-wide radio-TV hookup. He put them, in other words, in the position where a sub-rosa withdrawal was impossible, and public dismantlement of the bases meant humiliation. In doing so, Kennedy violated the first rule of diplomacy in the nuclear age, a rule he himself expounded in his famous speech at American University the following June:

> Above all, while defending our own vital interests, nuclear powers must avert those confrontations which bring an adversary to the choice of either a humiliating retreat or a nuclear war.

To be sure, he did not gloat over the Russian withdrawal, and insisted on treating it as a statesmanlike move. But the Kremlin's withdrawal under a public American ultimatum was a humiliation nonetheless.

President Kennedy certainly had ample opportunity to play it otherwise. There were available not only the Soviet ambassador and the famous "hot-line" direct to the Kremlin, recently installed with such fanfare, but also the Soviet foreign minister, Andrei Gromyko, who came to visit the President on Thursday afternoon, October 18—three days after Kennedy learned of the secret missile sites, but four days before he announced the blockade. Gromyko's visit had been scheduled some time before the discovery of the missiles, and the wily Soviet diplomat did not, of course, mention them. Instead he insisted that the Russians were furnishing purely "defensive" arms to the Cubans and wanted to relieve tensions with the U.S. over Cuba.

Robert Kennedy reports that his brother "listened, astonished, but also with some admiration for the boldness of Gromyko's position." Why should he have been astonished? Did he expect the Soviet foreign minister to confess that his government was secretly setting up long-range missile bases in Cuba? Mastering his astonishment, the President read aloud his statement of September 4 which warned the Russians against putting missiles or offensive weapons in Cuba. Gromyko assured him this would never be done and departed, returning to the Soviet Union a few days later.

The unavoidable question is why didn't President Kennedy tell Gromyko that he knew the truth, and give the Russians a chance to pull back? Robert Kennedy says it was because he hadn't yet decided what course of action to follow and was afraid of giving the Russians a tactical advantage—a judgment, Abel reports, supported by Rusk and Thompson. But Robert Kennedy reports that the President decided on the blockade on Saturday, October 20, two days before his speech to the nation. Why didn't he tell Gromyko on Saturday? The question was raised at the time by Walter Lippmann who, in his column of October 25, warned Kennedy against repeating the mistake of suspending diplomacy that plagued both world wars:

> I see danger of this mistake in the fact that when the President saw Mr. Gromyko on Thursday, and had the evidence of the missile build-up in Cuba, he refrained from confronting Mr. Gromyko with this evidence. This was to suspend diplomacy. If it had not been suspended, the President would have shown Mr. Gromyko the pictures and told him privately about the policy which in a few days he intended to announce publicly. This would have made it more likely that Moscow would order the ships not to push on to Cuba. But if such diplomatic action did not change the orders, if Mr. Khrushchev persisted in spite of it, the President's public speech would have been stronger. It would not have been subject to the criticism that a great power had issued an ultimatum to another great power without first attempting to negotiate the issue. By confronting Mr. Gromyko privately, the President would have given Mr. Khrushchev what all wise statesmen give their adversaries—the chance to save face.

Roger Hilsman argues that Gromyko somehow erroneously assumed that the President really knew about the missiles all the time. He gleans this from various warnings given to the Russians about putting offensive weapons into Cuba—warnings by Chester Bowles, U.S. Ambassador to Moscow Foy Kohler, and the President himself. With all these lectures the Russians might, perhaps, have assumed that Kennedy knew what they were up to, but was keeping it under his hat until after the elections. "The best explanation for Gromyko's behavior," he writes, "seemed to be that the Soviets were hedging, trying to avoid a direct confrontation with the United States in the hope of leaving their hand free for negotiations or, if faced with extreme danger of war, for withdrawing the missiles with the least loss of face." Yet if the Russians assumed that Kennedy knew, presumably they were not plotting a surprise attack. In any case, Hilsman's argument, while it might excuse Gromyko of duplicity, does not justify Kennedy's behavior, and is not offered as a hypothesis by Robert Kennedy.

2. *The failure of intelligence.* Why were the missile sites not discovered sooner? Discovery of the missiles was a total surprise to the President, Robert Kennedy affirms. "No official within the government had ever suggested to President Kennedy that the Russian buildup within Cuba would include missiles." The United States Intelligence Board, in its most recent estimate, dated September 19, advised the President "without reservation . . . that the Soviet Union would not make Cuba a strategic base." It based this on the fact that the Russians had never taken such a step in any of their satellites, and that the risk of U.S. retaliation was too great. Although a number of unconfirmed reports had been filtering through the intelligence network, Robert Kennedy maintains "they were not considered substantial enough to pass on to the President or to other high officials within the government."

But the fact is that Washington had been buzzing for weeks with unconfirmed reports that the Russians were secretly introducing long-range missiles into Cuba. According to Abel, as early as August 22 CIA Chief John McCone told President Kennedy that the Russians were putting SAMs (surface-to-air missiles) into Cuba to protect offensive missile sites, and urged reconsideration of the September 19 intelligence estimate. Meanwhile reports kept flowing in from agents inside Cuba that missiles much longer than SAMs were being delivered, and Castro's pilot had reportedly boasted "we have everything, including atomic weapons." According to Arthur Krock's recent book, the French intelligence agent, Thiraud de Vosjoly (the celebrated Topaz) came back with eyewitness evidence for McCone.

Robert Kennedy says "there was no action the U.S. could have taken before the time we actually did act," since no films were available to offer proof to the rest of the world. But why were photographs not made earlier? When McCone returned from his honeymoon in early October, he discovered that the eastern part of Cuba had not been photographed for more than a month. He immediately ordered the entire island photographed, and the U-2s returned from the flight of October 14 with the proof we now know.

What happened was nothing less than a failure of intelligence, "a failure," in Hilsman's words, "not of rationalization, but of imagination—a failure to probe and speculate, to ask perceptive questions of the data, rather than of explaining away the obvious." Suspicious signs were ignored, Republican charges were dismissed as election year propaganda, and there was a disinclination to probe the evidence.

What induced this state of mind? First, the conviction of the analysts that the Russians would never dare do anything so risky. Second, skepticism about charges made by Republican politicians. Third, reluctance to face a new Cuban crisis on the eve of the Congressional elections. Fourth, a personal message from Khrushchev, delivered by Ambassador Dobrynin to Robert Kennedy on September 4, assuring the President that the Soviets would create no trouble for him during the election campaign and would place no offensive weapons in Cuba. Kennedy had every reason to want to believe Khrushchev, and none of his trusted advisers presented him with any proof to the contrary. There was, of course, McCone. But Kennedy had been burned once over Cuba by the CIA and no doubt was doubly skeptical of its surmises. This skepticism, reinforced by his own desire to accept Khrushchev's assurances, at least until after the elections, and the failure of the intelligence community (and his own advisers) to argue differently, led to the failure to draw the proper inferences from the evidence.

3. *The misreading of the Kremlin's motives.* Why did Khrushchev do it? There is little speculation about this in Robert Kennedy's memoir, for he is concerned with what happened in Washington rather than with Russian motivations. To this day we do not know why the Soviets took such a colossal gamble. The rewards, one must assume, could only have been commensurate with the risks. The first reaction—that the Russians would try to force the Western allies out of Berlin in return for their withdrawal from Cuba—was unconvincing at the time, and is even more so in retrospect. It showed the New Frontier's vulnerability on the Berlin issue, particularly after the disastrous Vienna meeting. But it offers no reason why Khrushchev could rationally have believed that the Western allies would give up their rights in the former German capital. Perhaps the main reason why the Kennedy administration was caught so flat-footed was that it could never figure out why the Russians might find it advantageous to put missiles in Cuba.

An intriguing explanation has recently been put forth by Adam Ulam in his study of Soviet foreign policy, *Expansion and Coexistence*. The Russian leaders, he suggests, installed the missiles in Cuba in order to negotiate a package deal to be announced at the UN in November. The deal would include a German peace treaty, with an absolute prohibition on nuclear weapons for Bonn; plus a similar arrangement in the Far East, with a nuclear-free zone in the Pacific and a promise from China not to manufacture atomic weapons. The Chinese, of course, could be expected to balk at such a proposal, but their support might be won by demanding the removal of American protection from

Formosa as the final price of withdrawing the Soviet missiles from Cuba. This, Ulam argues, "would add an almost irresistible incentive for the Chinese at least to postpone their atomic ambitions."

This is highly imaginative, and almost certainly an explanation that never occurred to Kennedy and his advisers. It may never have occurred to Khrushchev either, although anything is possible. But without using quite so much imagination, one might speculate that the Russians installed their missiles in Cuba for the purpose of having them there, not in order to withdraw them as part of some future bargain. The placing of the missiles, in short, can be explained as a desperate attempt to compensate for a "missile gap" that put the Soviet Union dangerously far behind the United States.

The so-called "missile gap," it will be recalled, was one of the issues used by John F. Kennedy to club the Eisenhower-Nixon administration in the 1960 campaign. Uncritically accepting the propaganda of the Air Force and the aerospace industry, he charged that the Republicans had allowed the nation to fall hostage to Soviet missiles. Shortly after assuming the Presidency, however, Kennedy discovered that the "missile gap" did not exist. U-2 flights over the Soviet Union and the revelations of Colonel Oleg Penkovsky confirmed that the gap was quite the other way around, with the U.S. possessing a crushing superiority over the Soviet Union.

After returning from Vienna, where Khrushchev reportedly badgered him about the Bay of Pigs and led him to fear a new Berlin crisis was brewing, Kennedy decided to let the Russians know that the missile gap was actually in our favor. About the same time he engineered the bomb-shelter scare to show that he was willing to face nuclear war if necessary. Deputy Secretary of Defense Roswell Gilpatric was chosen to unveil the news to the Russians. In a speech on October 21, 1961, he deliberately revealed that we had penetrated Soviet security and knew where their missile sites were located. "Their Iron Curtain," he declared, "is not so impenetrable as to force us to accept at face value the Kremlin's boasts." For the Russians, the implications were, in Hilsman's words, "horrendous." What frightened them was not that we had military superiority, for they knew that all along—but that *we* knew it.

The U-2s had pinpointed the Soviet missile sites and Colonel Penkovsky had revealed that they lagged far behind in missile production. Since the Russians at that time had mostly a vulnerable "soft" ICBM system that could be used for retaliation only if the sites were kept secret, the American discovery meant that their entire missile defense system was suddenly obsolete. Had the United States launched a pre-emptive attack, they would have been largely incapable of retaliating. The balance of terror had broken down and the Russians found themselves, for all practical purposes, disarmed.

Naturally this was intolerable to the Soviet leaders (we can imagine the reaction in Washington if the situation were reversed), and perhaps a cheap answer to the problem was installing some of the older missiles in Cuba. This would help redress the strategic imbalance by confronting the U.S. with additional targets to be knocked out. It would also allow the Russians to stretch out the production of the new "hard" ICBMs without putting a further drain on their resources, help satisfy Castro's demands for protection, and strengthen the Soviet position in the Caribbean and Latin America.

Khrushchev made a serious mistake, the folly of "adventurism," as Peking would say. But could he reasonably have assumed that the Kennedy who had been so ineffectual at the Bay of Pigs and unimpressive at Vienna would suddenly become so intransigent? Nothing fails like failure. But in the context of the times, the effort to redress the missile gap seemed like a gamble worth taking. The worst that could have happened, the Russians probably assumed, was that their deception would be discovered and that they would quietly be told to take the missiles out. By immediately escalating the issue to a public confrontation, Kennedy had created a situation that was getting out of hand. In this respect, Khrushchev's message of October 26, when he offered to withdraw the missiles in return for a U.S.

pledge not to invade Cuba, is instructive. "If you have not lost your self-control," he wrote,

> and sensibly conceive what this might lead to, then, Mr. President, we and you ought not to pull on the ends of the rope in which you have tied the knot of war, because the more the two of us pull, the tighter the knot will be tied. And a moment may come when that knot will be tied so tight that even he who tied it will not have the strength to untie it, and then it will be necessary to cut that knot, and what that would mean is not for me to explain to you, because you yourself understand perfectly of what terrible forces our countries dispose. Consequently, if there is no intention to tighten that knot, and thereby doom the world to the catastrophe of thermonuclear war, then let us not only relax the forces pulling on the ends of the rope, let us take measures to untie that knot. We are ready for this.

Whatever his motives, Khrushchev certainly did not intend a nuclear confrontation, nor in retrospect did the situation demand it. It seems clear that Russian policy was basically defensive and, as John Kenneth Galbraith has recently commented, "in the full light of time, it [national safety] doubtless called for a more cautious policy than the one that Kennedy pursued." One of the hallmarks of the New Frontier was a nagging sense of insecurity that manifested itself in inflated rhetoric (the classic being Kennedy's inaugural address) and self-assumed tests of will, such as Cuba and Vietnam. While Kennedy won his victory, he also had Khrushchev to thank, and as Hilsman has observed, "although putting the missiles into Cuba was threatening and irresponsible, the Soviets handled the ensuing crisis with wisdom and restraint." Kennedy showed his skill in throwing down the gauntlet, but it required greater courage for Khrushchev to refuse to pick it up.

4. *The vagaries of decision-making.* The basic decisions of the missile crisis, as we have seen, were reached in the informal group known as the Executive Committee. Most of the members of the Cabinet were excluded from this group, and, indeed, did not even learn about the crisis until a few hours before Kennedy announced it to the nation. Nor were America's NATO allies, who would have been blown up along with us, consulted

at any point along the way about plans or strategy. When Dean Acheson arrived in Paris to tell de Gaulle of the blockade, the General asked, "Are you consulting or informing me?" Informing, Acheson confessed. "I am in favor of independent decisions," de Gaulle replied, and has remained consistent to that policy ever since.

Some of Kennedy's independent decisions were made in the most curious way. For example, on October 20 it was decided that the U.S. Navy would intercept all ships within an 800-mile radius of the Cuban coast. Three days later David Ormsby-Gore happened to be dining at the White House and observed that 800 miles seemed to be a bit far out. Perhaps, he suggested, the quarantine line could be drawn at 500 miles, thus giving the Russians a bit more time to think. A good idea, replied the President, and on the spot redrew the line—no doubt wisely—over the protests of the Navy. One wonders if any other ambassadors, had they been on as close terms with the President as Ormsby-Gore, might also have had some good suggestions.

We have already learned that the Secretary of State was too busy with other matters to act as chairman of the Executive Committee, or even to attend many of its meetings. It is also instructive to learn how Kennedy, while excluding most of his Cabinet from knowledge of the affair, reached outside the government to tap such venerables as Robert Lovett, John J. McCloy, and the redoubtable Dean Acheson. Recently Acheson, having been bested by Robert Kennedy over the issue of the blockade, has reached into the grave to take a swipe at his old adversary by declaring that the successful outcome of the missile crisis was "plain dumb luck."

In a sense he is right, but for the wrong reasons. He means that President Kennedy was lucky that the Russians didn't make the bases operational before they were discovered. Acheson wouldn't have fiddled around with a blockade or negotiations, but would have joined LeMay in bombing them from the start. As it turns out, there was more time than the participants thought, or accepted, at the time, or that Acheson is willing to admit even today. According to Hilsman, who, as former intelligence chief for the State Department, ought to know, "the two-thousand mile IRBM sites, which were not scheduled for completion until mid-November, never did reach a stage where they were ready to receive the missiles themselves." Kennedy, in other words, had at least two more weeks and could have postponed his ultimatum. Also, it appears that Khrushchev was planning to be true to his word and not make trouble for Kennedy until after the election, when he would unveil the missiles for whatever political purposes he had in mind.

Kennedy was lucky, however, in the sense that Khrushchev chose to withdraw rather than make Cuba a test of national or personal virility. Had Acheson and the other hawks had their way probably none of us would be here to conduct these post-mortems. Robert Kennedy had something quite interesting to say about this. In an interview given just two days before his death, he commented on the advice given in the Executive Committee during the crisis:

> The fourteen people involved were very significant—bright, able, dedicated people, all of whom had the greatest affection for the U.S.—probably the brightest kind of group that you could get together under those circumstances. If six of them had been President of the U.S., I think that the world might have been blown up.

None of these six is particularly malicious or fanatical, and none is in the government today. Yet if a similar crisis were to occur, would the response of the President's advisers be very different from that given by these six in 1962? The lesson of the *Thirteen Days* is to show us just how slender is the thread of our survival, how the fate of mankind rests in the hands of a few individuals driven by perfectly ordinary fears, anxieties, and rivalries. The Cuban missile crisis was a very close call, and it could have gone the other way.

Were the stakes worth it? Even Robert Kennedy was no longer sure. He intended to complete this memoir by adding a discussion of the ethical question involved: what, if any, circumstances or justification gives this government or any government the moral right to bring its people and possibly all people under the shadow of nuclear destruction? It is our common loss that this complex man, who in the last years of his life learned to doubt much of what he had taken for granted, was murdered before he could deal with this question.

ROGER HILSMAN AND RONALD STEEL

An Exchange of Views

Steel's critique of American policy infuriated Kennedy partisans. Roger Hilsman, who had returned to academic life in 1965, felt compelled to respond in a letter to the editors of the New York Review of Books. *The editors published his views, together with a rebuttal from Ronald Steel, in the May 8, 1969, issue. This exchange reflects both the depth of emotion involved in the controversy and the wide divergence of views that persists.*

AS ONE WHO ON OCCASION has been an admirer of Ronald Steel's writings, I was dismayed and saddened to read his review of Robert F. Kennedy's *Thirteen Days*. It is ill-informed; there are gross inaccuracies; and several quotations are so wrenched out of context that the result is simply the opposite of truth. And his overall judgments and conclusions are sometimes not only questionable as scholarship, but naive and simple-minded.

On the questions of quotations out of context, consider the following. Steel writes: "What happened was nothing less than a failure of intelligence, 'a failure,' in Hilsman's words, 'not of rationalization, but of imagination—a failure to probe and speculate, to ask perceptive questions of the data, rather than of explaining away the obvious.' "

But turn to my book, to the conclusions of my chapter, "The Intelligence Post-Mortem: Who Erred?", where one would expect to see my final judgment, and what do you find? "Given the inherent difficulties of espionage and the special circumstances . . . it is probably something to be proud of that the missiles

Roger Hilsman and Ronald Steel, "An Exchange of Views," *New York Review of Books,* XII (May 8, 1969), 36–38. Reprinted with permission.
Mr. Hilsman's article copyright © 1969 by The New York Review. Mr. Steel's article copyright © 1969 by Ronald Steel.

were discovered as early as they were. In sum, Cuba in 1962, it seems to me, must be marked down as a victory for American intelligence—and a victory of a very high order."

Now that is just exactly the opposite of what Steel says my views are. Where did he find the quote he cites? He found it in an earlier part of the chapter, in a discussion not of American intelligence in the Cuban crisis, but of a small sub-unit of CIA involved in shipping intelligence, and the "failure" I speak of was the failure of this tiny sub-unit to report to higher authority that two of the ships bringing arms to Cuba had exceptionally large hatches and were riding high in the water, indicating space-consuming cargo. The sub-unit had not reported these facts—which were suggestive, but not decisive—because these ships, one of which had been built in Japan, were designed for the lumbering trade; and since the Soviets were short on ships, the shipping specialists thought it only natural that they should be using these, and so saw no significance in the reports. The part of the quote Steel left out was the crucial part: "The fact that the shipping specialists did not call these facts to the special attention of their intelligence superiors was clearly a failure. But it was a failure not of rationalization . . ." and so on.

Again, Steel quotes my description of a memo, written the next day, about Gromyko's meeting with the President, which argued that the Soviets would assume from what was said in that meeting and in earlier meetings with Dobrynin, that Kennedy knew about the missiles. Steel then says, "Yet if the Russians assumed that Kennedy knew, presumably they were not plotting a surprise attack." The truth is that the conclusion was a major point of the memo, and the President's plans and actions were based on the judgment that the Soviets were *not* planning a surprise attack. To quote again from my book (page 201), "The Soviets did not put missiles in Cuba with the intent of using them in a military sense any more than the United States put Minutemen ICBM's in Montana with the intent of using them."

And there are many more, either misquotations or straight inaccuracies. It was not "shortly after assuming office" that Kennedy learned there was no missile gap, but in late summer, 1961, following an intelligence breakthrough. And it was not from

U-2 flights and Penkovsky that we learned, as Steel asserts. U-2 flights were never made over the Soviet Union after May 1, 1960. And a moment of reflection on what Penkovsky's job was would reveal how unlikely it is that he would have known. Since Kennedy did not know there was no missile gap until late summer—although he may have begun to suspect it—he could not have decided after the Vienna meeting, as Steel would have it, to let the Soviets know by way of Roswell Gilpatric's speech. Gilpatric gave his speech in October, and the facts are that the decision to make the speech was made in the days immediately preceding it.

Another quotation from Steel: "Meanwhile reports kept flowing in from agents inside Cuba that missiles much longer than SAM's were being delivered . . ." There were in fact only two such reports, as is fully described in my book, which hardly justifies the suggestive phrase, "flowing."

Still another quotation from Steel: "There were available [for diplomacy] not only the Soviet ambassador and the famous "hot-line" direct to the Kremlin, recently installed with such fanfare . . ." Yet the truth is that the "hot line" was installed *after* the crisis, and partly as a result of it

There are many more pieces of misinformation or inaccuracies, but one more will suffice. Steel says McCone "immediately ordered the entire island photographed." In fact, however, McCone had no such power. The decision could be made only by the President on the recommendation of a high level committee. McCone attended a meeting of such a committee at which there was discussion of the fact that a rhomboid-shaped area in Western Cuba had not been photographed for a month. The SAM's were most nearly operational in this part of Cuba, and the discussion centered on the risk to the U-2 of making a surveillance flight, and the possible consequences if it were shot down. Nevertheless, the full group decided to recommend to the President that a U-2 be flown, providing great care be taken in planning the exact route it was to fly.

In addition to distorting the meaning of quotations, Steel also uses the technique of the grave question, implying that the answers have been concealed, when in fact they are readily available. "But why were photographs not made earlier?" Steel asks. I have a long analysis of that question in my book and reach some conclusions that Steel should have found interesting. For example (page 186): "It could reasonably be argued that the U-2 flight of October 14 found the missiles at just about the earliest possible date . . ." I do believe that it could be reasonably so argued, but my own conclusion is that they could have been discovered at least two weeks earlier, but probably not much more. "Given the vagaries of the weather (page 190), it would have been a fantastic stroke of luck if convincing photographs could have been obtained before September 21 . . ." The decision to fly the U-2 was made on October 4, and the subsequent delay was at the operational level. Time was consumed in planning because of the SAM's; there was postponement because of weather; and there was a disgraceful squabble between the Air Force and CIA as to who should fly the plane—all of which is fully documented in my book. The point is simply that Steel's misuse of quotes, his inaccuracies, and his rhetorical questions leave the reader with an impression of mystery and possible conspiracy—yet the facts and the answers to Steel's questions are all laid out in a book he has read—or at least quotes from.

It is against this background of misquotation, inaccuracy, and suggestive rhetoric that Steel's major conclusions must be judged.

One of these conclusions is that the Kennedy administration was caught "flat-footed" in the Cuban missile crisis, and that the reason was that the administration "could never figure out why the Russians might find it advantageous to put missiles in Cuba." Yet the evidence on both counts is in the exactly opposite direction. As described above, a study of the data indicates that if the decision to fly the U-2 that discovered the missiles had been made two weeks earlier, it might have discovered nothing at all. This is not being caught "flat-footed." And there is other evidence. In my book, for example, in discussing the failure of the shipping intelligence unit to report the fact that two of the ships had large hatches (mentioned above), I wrote (page 189): "All that these reports could do, no matter how seriously they were taken, would be to increase sensitivity in Washington to the possibility that the Soviets would put missiles in Cuba. But the people in Washington, as even the public statements of the time show, were already sensitive to the point of nervousness. President Kennedy made several public statements warning the Soviets. He instituted special security precautions concerning intelligence on offensive weapons. Questions were asked on the subject in every Congressional hearing that had even the remotest connection with Cuba. And everyone in official Washington talked about the possibility constantly." This is not being caught "flat-footed."

On the second point, Steel's charge that the administration could never figure out why the Russians might find putting missiles in Cuba advantageous is simply not true. The September 19 estimate, which decided on balance that the Soviets would probably *not* put the missiles in, also pointed out that the advantages were so great that the intelligence community should be extraordinarily alert to detect any evidence that they might be doing so after all. The September estimate put particular emphasis on the military advantages, but alluded to others. Then, once the missiles were discovered, the various advantages and motives were fully debated. Again, to quote from my book (page 201): "Judgments about Soviet motives and purposes were inevitably a salient influence on judgments about policy, and even though no one analysis was singled out at the time for formal approval as authoritative, as time went on, knowledgeable opinion tended to converge." The Soviet decision, I go on to say, "seems to have been an expedient, essentially temporary solution to a whole set of problems—the over-all U.S. strategic advantage and the 'missile-gap-in-reverse,' the exigencies of the Sino-Soviet dispute, and the impossible demands on their limited resources, ranging from defense and foreign aid to the newly created appetite in the Soviet citizenry for consumers' goods. The motive was strategic in a broad and general sense, based on the characteristic Soviet expectation that a general improvement in the Soviet military position would affect the entire political context, strengthening their hand for dealing with the whole range of problems facing them and unanticipated problems as well." It was this fundamental, broad judgment that led to a consensus that the Soviet missiles in Cuba must be removed. For such a sudden upsetting of the world's balance would set in train events that were unpredictable and that might well bring about confrontations in other places that might be much worse, more likely to bring on a war than Cuba.

I might add that this judgment on Soviet motivations also looks good in hindsight, after additional evidence has come in, by way of such books, for example, as Michel Tatu's *Power in the Kremlin.* Tatu, to illustrate, points out the military advantages to the Soviets—the missiles altered "the strategic balance of power in its favor," and did so with missiles that escaped the United States early warning system. Tatu points out that such a strategic advantage, achieved with relatively small expenditure, was a great boon for the Soviet economy. He then goes on (page 231): "There is no doubt that the move was a gamble, but it was not necessarily bellicose. At that state of the balance of terror, Khrushchev had no new motives for wanting actually to use the weapons. The missiles, like the rest of his arsenal, were meant to intimidate, not to be fired. They were to serve as a formidable instrument of pressure on the United States in future negotiations and it is conceivable that Khrushchev himself meant to withdraw them some day—in exchange for substantial concessions, of course." Tatu, in other words, writing later and from Soviet sources, reaches essentially the same judgment.

Steel's most important conclusion, however, revolves around whether or not Kennedy should have used diplomacy instead of blockade to get the missiles out. Steel seems to agree that Kennedy did have to get the missiles out, that this sudden upsetting of the world's balance would bring on uncalculable events even though the Soviets did not intend a sudden, surprise attack. Steel argues that instead of resorting to a blockade coupled with a public demand for the removal of the missiles on a tight deadline, Kennedy should have used diplomacy over a longer period of time, and he suggests that it was "party politics" and the upcoming Congressional elections that determined Kennedy's choice of method and timing.

To support his contention that Kennedy's motive was politics, Steel again quotes me—to the effect that if the United States were not in mortal danger (i.e., of a surprise attack), then the administration most certainly was. But I certainly had nothing in mind so simplistic as the congressional elections. The theme of *To Move a Nation* is that policy-making is a political process. "Policy," I write (page 13), "faces inward as much as outward, seeking to reconcile conflicting goals, to adjust aspirations to available means, and to accommodate the different advocates of these competing goals and aspirations to one another. It is here that the essence of policy-making seems to lie, in a process that is in its deepest sense political." I meant that the administration would be faced with a revolt from the military, from the hard-liners in the other departments, both State and CIA, from not only Republicans on Capitol Hill but some Democrats, too; that it would be faced with all this opposition at home just at the time that it would be undergoing deep and very dangerous challenges from the Soviets, brought on by the alteration in the balance of power wrought by their successful introduction of missiles into Cuba, and which might well put the United States in mortal danger. This was why the administration was in trouble. It was political trouble, all right—but the upcoming elections were the least of it—and this was why they had to get the missiles out.

The question of timing, of the tight deadline, was something else again. The reason the deadline had to be tight was the missiles themselves. Steel quotes me as saying that "the two-thousand mile IRBM sites, which were not scheduled for completion until mid-November, never did reach a stage where they were ready to receive the missiles themselves." The quote is correct, but Steel again chooses what serves his purpose, and leaves out the parts that damage it. He neglects to mention what I said about the MRBM's, as opposed to the IRBM's. The MRBM's would have been operational by October 30th—which is why Kennedy and others on Saturday, October 27th, were talking about "two days"—and that would have meant the Soviets could have launched an initial salvo of 24 missiles followed by a second salvo of 24. Even as it was, Kennedy was taking a risk, for the intelligence community believes, as I describe in my book, that on October 28, the day Khrushchev agreed to pull the missiles out, between 12 and 18 of the missiles were already operational. What is more, the intelligence community believes the IRBM's were in the large-hatch ships headed toward Cuba at the time of Kennedy's speech. If the blockade had been delayed, and the missiles reached Cuba, the blockade would no longer be an effective pressure, and it would probably then have taken a much more risky form of pressure to persuade the Soviets to remove the missiles. As I say, it was the missiles themselves that made Kennedy adopt a tight deadline, not the upcoming elections.

The idea of negotiating quietly with the Soviets about the missiles, of using diplomacy as Steel would have it, was discussed in the Kennedy administration, but was rejected for the reason given above. And again, with the benefit of both hindsight and the additional evidence that has come in from Soviet sources, the decision seems to have been a wise one. Pointing out that work on the missiles already in Cuba, the MRBM's, continued at a furious pace right up to October 28, Tatu says, "It is obvious that if this work could be completed under cover of diplomatic negotiations over broader issues, for example the general problems of foreign bases, Khrushchev would have won all he wanted: not only strategic reinforcement as a result of his newly built Cuban base, but also the diplomatic initiative resulting from his greater strength."

As I say, I was dismayed and saddened by Steel's review. These are extraordinarily difficult and dangerous times; and there is much to be learned from the Cuban missile crisis that would be helpful in dealing with them. The event deserves more serious and responsible treatment from someone with Steel's gifts.

Ronald Steel *Replies*

As a high official in the last Kennedy administration, and perhaps an aspirant for an even higher position in the next one, Roger Hilsman makes a spirited defense of the motives and the methods of those handling the Cuban missile crisis. He seems particularly sensitive to the suggestion that domestic politics might have influenced the administration's attitude toward the Soviet missiles—as though such considerations were beneath the dignity of the Kennedy brothers. In his letter, as in his book, he portrays an administration that, while besieged by evil forces from within and without, nearly always seemed to end up doing the right thing. My article was not intended as a critique of his book, which is mentioned half a dozen times at most, but as an analysis of the missile crisis based on Robert Kennedy's memoir. I wanted to raise some questions which have not been answered by Kennedy, Hilsman, or any other administration officials writing on the subject.

Apparently I have touched a sore spot, since Hilsman, instead of dealing with the substance of my criticism, quibbles over allegedly incomplete quotations, how many weeks constitute a "shortly after," and what kind of teletype machine links Washington to Moscow. But he does not address himself to the major point of my argument: (1) that Kennedy refused to use traditional methods of diplomacy that might have permitted the crisis to be resolved quietly, and instead confronted Khrushchev with a public ultimatum, (2) that he did so because he needed a foreign policy "victory" on the eve of the Congressional elections, (3) that the intelligence analysts had been obtuse in interpreting data (even Hilsman calls them "a little lazy") that were flowing into Washington from official and unofficial sources, (4) that the administration did not understand why the Russians might have found it politically advantageous to put the missiles in Cuba (erroneously connecting it with Berlin) and thus was caught flat-footed when the crisis occurred, (5) that the stakes, as Robert Kennedy suggested in his memoir, were not so high as we were led to believe at the time.

Since Hilsman's objections do not touch on these basic questions, I am really not sure what is the purpose of his letter, unless it be to preserve from further tarnish the reputation of the administration he served. If so, he has not addressed himself to the issues. On the peripheral issues he raises, I would still maintain that the "failure . . . of imagination, a failure to probe and speculate, to ask perceptive questions of the data, rather than of explaining away the obvious" describes not only a unit of the CIA, as he would have it, but the whole intelligence apparatus, including the one he headed. As for the meeting with Gromyko, if Hilsman advised Kennedy that the Russians were not planning an attack, then Kennedy's refusal to confront Gromyko with the facts is even more suspect politically, and merely confirms my suspicion that Kennedy wanted a public confrontation with Khrushchev.

I fail to see how Michel Tatu's speculations offer any "additional evidence" that the Soviet missiles altered the strategic balance of power—particularly since Hilsman agrees with Tatu, and myself, that the missiles "were not to intimidate, not to be fired." If the Soviets were not intending to use the missiles, why was the administration so desperate to prevent the medium-range MRBMs from being installed? These would have posed little, if any, threat to the American deterrent—as McNamara himself states. Was it the United States that would be threatened, or the Kennedy administration that would be intimidated in its dealings with political opponents at home?

If the threat was not military, it must have been political: the Russians would have racked up a point on the cold war scorecard, they would have damaged the bruised image of the administration, they would have set up a military foothold in "our" hemisphere, they would have forestalled an invasion of Cuba, they would have helped bridge the "missile gap in reverse," they would have angered the Pentagon and furnished ammunition for the Republicans. They would have done a number of things—except pose a serious offensive threat to the United States. And in retrospect Kennedy's behavior could be justified only if such a threat existed—which nearly everyone agrees it did not.

Hilsman, along with many administration defenders, seems to be arguing that Kennedy had to be tough not because the danger from the Russians was mortal, but because the danger from the Pentagon and the hard-liners might have been. Thus in his own words, ". . . the United States might not be in mortal danger, but the administration most certainly was." The danger, of course, included not only the loss of Congress to the Republicans, but his "image" before his political opponents at home and his adversaries abroad. Obsessed by the fear that Khrushchev did not take him seriously, Kennedy could not suffer another foreign policy defeat, and identified his own ability to be tough with the nation's "credibility"—thus the build-up over Berlin, the bomb-shelter scare, the "advisers" to Vietnam, and the ultimatum to Khrushchev over the missiles. The usual defense of Kennedy's behavior in these cases is that unless he were "tough," the hard-liners would get hysterical—which is a bit like saying, "Don't mind me if I burn down our house, because if I don't that crazy guy next door might do something irrational."

Like many academicians recruited into the government and transformed into administrators of the American empire, Hilsman seems to consider politics as something more base than "policy." It is certain, however, that the Kennedys did not. President Kennedy knew that he was in trouble, not only from hard-liners in the Pentagon and on Capitol Hill, but from his less-than-inspiring record in office. Heavy Republican gains would have killed chances for passing his legislative program. He certainly did not want to face a crisis in Cuba on the eve of the Congressional elections, but when photographic proof of the missiles became available and the Republican charges could no longer be denied, Kennedy needed a "victory." He did not have time to seek a diplomatic solution that would have involved negotiations dragging on for weeks—not because a few MRBMs represented a deadly threat, but because the elections did.

In retrospect it might have been better had Khrushchev completed the Cuban bases, and they were then used as a basis for negotiations over broader issues. Not only would we have been spared the dangers of marching to the nuclear brink, but we would have been denied what Hilsman calls "a foreign policy victory of historical proportions." That "victory" inspired the euphoria of power that led Lyndon Johnson to become obsessed by the imperial adventure launched so "idealistically" by Kennedy and his advisers. But I would not expect this view to be shared by Hilsman, who not only was a high official of the Kennedy administration, but a leading advocate of such Kennedy misadventures as the "strategic hamlet" program in Vietnam. Now that the empire has begun to crumble, some of its intellectual underpinnings are beginning to seem increasingly flimsy.

V

Scholarly Reassessment

IN THE 1970s and 1980s, scholars began to probe into the issues raised by Kennedy partisans and their critics. Although some of the key documents still remain classified, the gradual release of new information about the crisis enabled historians and political scientists to begin assessing some of the most debatable factors, particularly in regard to American policy. Graham Allison, professor of Government at Harvard University, broke new ground in 1971 with his innovative study, *Essence of Decision*. Using the missile crisis as a way of testing three alternative methods of analyzing the way foreign policy is made, Allison offered new insights into the role of bureaucratic politics and organizational structure in shaping Soviet and American behavior. Allison's book marked the end of contemporary debate and the beginning of sustained scholarly reappraisal of the Cuban crisis.

Three issues stand out in the ongoing academic scrutiny. The first is the question of why President Kennedy did not trade the American Jupiter IRBMs in Turkey for the Russian missiles in Cuba. Nearly all authorities agree that the Jupiters were obsolete. The Eisenhower administration made the decision to deploy them in 1959 as a stopgap measure at a time when many believed that Russia was head of the United States in ICBM development. Shortly after Kennedy took office, reconnaisance satellites revealed that in reality the Russians had not been able to install more than a handful of ICBMs and that the United States was opening up a missile gap in reverse. Despite this shift in the nuclear balance, Kennedy went ahead with the deployment of the Jupiters in Turkey. By the summer of 1962, however, he had doubts about the usefulness of these missiles and had ordered the Defense Department to reassess their military value. Why then did the President not offer to remove the Jupiters in return for Soviet withdrawal of the Cuban missiles?

The usual answer—that political rather than strategic considerations were uppermost in Kennedy's mind—raises the second issue debated by scholars. Some contend that Kennedy was more concerned with appearances than reality, particularly only a few weeks before a crucial congressional election. The winner by only a narrow margin of 1960, JFK had been unable to overcome the conservative coalition of northern Republicans and southern Democrats in Congress to enact his New Frontier domestic program. In November 1962, he hoped not only to avoid the usual off-year loss in Congress, but to gain enough additional liberal Democratic members to ensure passage of such measures as medicare and federal aid to education. In light of his earlier humiliation at the Bay of Pigs, the President needed to avoid looking as though he were backing down in the face of a Soviet challenge in Cuba. But did Kennedy really risk nuclear war simply to win an election? Was his concern for the appearance of power purely partisan, or did it reflect a larger interest in protecting American credibility as a great power that could not be intimidated?

Finally, there is third issue, the question of the impact of the Cuban missile crisis on subsequent American foreign policy.

Kennedy partisans saw the crisis as a fulfillment of the hopes they had placed in their young hero. Amid the wave of emotion that fed the myth of Kennedy as a martyred leader after his assassination, the Cuban missile crisis stood out as his finest moment—the time when he had gone to the very threshold of nuclear war and compelled the Soviets to back down. Yet the more his critics examined the crisis, the more convinced they became that Kennedy had in fact magnified the danger and blown a manageable situation into a grave international crisis. They pointed to the subsequent build-up of Soviet nuclear weapons, which eventually eroded the American strategic superiority of the 1960s, as they argued that JFK's overreaction had forced the Russians to match the Americans missiles for missile. In addition to accelerating the nuclear arms race, critics also suggested that Kennedy's victory over Khrushchev created a mood of national arrogance that contributed to the American involvement in Vietnam. Emerging from the Cuban crisis supremely confident of their power in the world, the nation's leaders failed to appreciate the difficulties they would face in the jungles of Southeast Asia.

Was Kennedy's handling of the Cuban missile crisis a good model for future presidents? Did it bring about a pause in superpower rivalry, marked by the establishment of the hot line between Washington and Moscow and the negotiation of the Partial Nuclear Test Ban Treaty of 1963? Did the crisis, by forcing leaders on both sides to face up to the real possibility of nuclear holocuast, help usher in the efforts at detente by the 1970s? Or did Kennedy miss a chance to reach a comprehensive settlement with the Soviet Union that could have meant the beginning of the end of the Cold War? If the President had realized that the aggressive Soviet behavior in Cuba was possibly a reaction to American nuclear superiority, could he have been more conciliatory with Khrushchev, openly agreeing to remove the Jupiters from Turkey and initiating the kind of broad arms control negotiations that would not begin until the end of the decade? Was the Cuban missile crisis Kennedy's finest hour, his best claim to greatness as president, or was it a lost opportunity, a chance for reversing the momentum of the

Cold War that might have spared the world another quarter century of super power rivalry?

BARTON J. BERNSTEIN

A Jupiter Swap?

Stanford historian Barton J. Bernstein has written extensively on the Cuban missile crisis. As early as 1963, he coauthored an assessment of the military significance of the Soviet IRBMs with Roger Hagan in the Bulletin of the Atomic Scientists. *In other scholarly articles, he has questioned many aspects of the way Kennedy responded to the Soviet action in Cuba. In this essay, published in 1980, Professor Bernstein offers new information on the crucial issue of the Jupiter IRBMs in Turkey and the role they played in Kennedy's diplomacy in 1962. His suggestion that the President might have made a public pledge to remove the American missiles from Turkey if Khrushchev had demanded one was later substantiated by Dean Rusk's 1987 assertion that Kennedy had instructed him to offer such a swap by way of the United Nations.*

PRESIDENT JOHN F. KENNEDY has been variously praised and blamed for his handling of the Cuban missile crisis in October 1962. For most, it was his great triumph: seven days of wide-ranging deliberations and careful planning; and six days of the shrewd use of cautious threats, limited force, and wise diplomacy to achieve victory.[1] For critics, however, it was an unnec-

Barton J. Bernstein, "The Cuban Missile Crisis: Trading the Jupiters in Turkey?" *Political Science Quarterly* 95 (Spring 1980): 97–125. Reprinted with permission from *Political Science Quarterly.*

[1] Arthur M. Schlesinger, Jr., *A Thousand Days: John F. Kennedy in the White House* (Boston, Mass.: Houghton Mifflin, 1965), pp. 808–35; Theodore Sorensen, *Kennedy* (New York: Harper & Row, 1965); Roger Hilsman, *To Move A Nation* (Garden City, N.Y.: Doubleday, 1967), pp. 159–229; and Robert Kennedy, *Thirteen Days* (New York: W.W. Norton, 1969).

essary crisis, or dangerously mishandled, or both: Kennedy should either have acceded to the Soviet missiles in Cuba, or at least tried private diplomacy before moving to the quarantine. Removal of the missiles was not worth the risk of nuclear war.[2]

Many assessments focus on Kennedy's response to the Soviet demand on Saturday, October 27, that the United States withdraw its missiles from Turkey. Publicly, he seemed to reject the Soviet proposal.[3] But did he? Some defenders have claimed—on the basis of hints in Robert Kennedy's memoir[4]—that the president actually struck a private bargain and, hence, indirectly acceded to the Soviet terms.[5] Critics, on the other hand, have either denied that there was such an agreement or have stressed that it was dangerously loose.[6] It required that Premier Nikita Khrushchev trust Kennedy's hedged, private promise and accept public defeat in order to avoid an American invasion of Cuba and possibly all-out war. Why, the critics ask, did Kennedy refuse to accept the Turkey-Cuba trade publicly and thus leave Khrushchev a choice between possible holocaust or humiliation? Was not Kennedy guilty of brinkmanship? What would Kennedy have done if Khrushchev had not retreated and accepted public humiliation?

New evidence—recently declassified minutes, some staff reports, key diplomatic cables, and some published parts of

[2] Barton J. Bernstein, "Their Finest Hour?" *Correspondent* 32 (August 1964): 119–21; idem., "The Cuban Missile Crisis," in *Reflections on the Cold War,* eds. Lynn Miller and Ronald Pruessen (Philadelphia, Pa.: Temple University Press, 1974), pp. 111–42; idem., "The Week We Almost Went to War," *Bulletin of the Atomic Scientists* 32 (February 1976): 13–21; I.F. Stone, "The Brink," *New York Review of Books,* 14 April 1966, pp. 12–16; Ronald Steel, "End Game," *New York Review of Books,* 13 March 1969, pp. 15–22; and James Nathan, "The Missile Crisis: His Finest Hour Now," *World Politics* 27 (January 1975): 256–81.

[3] White House statement, 27 October 1962; Kennedy letter to Khrushchev, 27 October 1962, both in *Public Papers of the Presidents: John F. Kennedy, 1962* (Washington, D.C.: Government Printing Office, 1963), pp. 813–14.

[4] Kennedy, *Thirteen Days,* pp. 94–95.

[5] Though not formally a defender, see Graham Allison, *Essence of Decision: Explaining the Cuban Missile Crisis* (Boston, Mass.: Little, Brown, 1971), pp. 228–29.

[6] For the denials of such an agreement, see Nathan, "Missile Crisis," pp. 268–70 and Steel, "End Game," pp. 15–17; those stressing that the agreement was dangerously loose include Bernstein, "Cuban Missile Crisis," pp. 120, 135, and idem. "Week We Almost Went to War," p. 19.

Robert Kennedy's still-closed papers[7]—reopens these issues about the Turkey-Cuba missile trade and its background. This evidence reveals that President Kennedy was partly responsible for installing the missiles in Turkey and that the president and some advisers, from the early days of the crisis, were privately more flexible than memoirists or critics acknowledged. The new evidence establishes that Kennedy privately offered a hedged promise on 27 October 1962 to withdraw the Jupiter missiles from Turkey at a future time. Unfortunately, these documents do not resolve the problem of what Kennedy would have done had Khrushchev insisted on a public pledge. Would Kennedy have yielded and thus risked weakening his credibility? Or would he have invaded Cuba?

WHO PUT JUPITER MISSILES IN TURKEY?

In 1957 the Eisenhower administration decided to arrange to send missiles to Europe, largely to strengthen NATO, both militarily and psychologically. Even before Sputnik, partly to repair the "special relationship" torn by the Suez debacle, the administration promised Britain sixty Thors—intermediate-range ballistic missiles (IRBMs).[8] And shortly after Sputnik, when administration members feared a "confidence" or "deterrence" gap, the Eisenhower administration gained NATO's unanimous approval for the deployment of missiles on the continent. Most NATO allies, however, fearful of antagonizing the Soviet Union and in many cases of inflaming domestic

[7] Arthur M. Schlesinger, Jr., *Robert F. Kennedy and His Times* (Boston, Mass.: Houghton Mifflin, 1978), pp. 499–532, used the Robert F. Kennedy papers, now at the Kennedy Library, with permission of the family. According to the library, the sections on the missile crisis are still classified, and not organized, and access is still barred to independent scholars (William Moss to Barton Bernstein, 23 January 1979, and Martin McGann to Bernstein, 24 August 1979; and conversation with McGann, 21 November 1979). Schlesinger recently shared some of his notes with me.

[8] Harold Macmillan, *Riding the Storm, 1956–1959* (London: Harper & Row, 1971), pp. 245–46; Michael Armacost, *The Politics of Weapons Innovation: The Thor-Jupiter Controversy* (New York: Columbia University Press, 1969), pp. 190–97.

opposition, refused the weapons. Only Italy and Turkey accepted them.[9]

The agreement with Turkey, completed in October 1959, provided for fifteen Jupiter missiles (IRBMs). The arrangements of ownership and custody were cumbersome: The missiles would be owned by Turkey; the nuclear warheads would be owned by the United States and in the custody of its forces; the weapons could be launched only on the order of the Supreme Allied Commander-Europe (an American) on the approval of both the American and Turkish governments; and the sites would be manned by soldiers of both nations. It was, in principle, a dual-veto system.[10]

The legal provisions raised serious problems about actual practices during a crisis. What would happen if only one nation decided to launch the missiles? How would the complex legal and custodial arrangements—with their checks and balances—actually operate? Could American troops stop the Turkish government, or even panicky Turkish troops, from acting unilaterally? What would happen if the Turks seized control of the weapons and warheads during a local crisis with the Soviets and launched the nuclear missiles, despite American objections? Such questions undoubtedly added to the fears of the Soviet Union, for the missiles would be close to the border. Could the Soviets trust the Turks? Should the United States?

The Jupiters were liquid-fuel IRBMs, taking hours to fire, quite inaccurate, very vulnerable, and hence only useful militarily for a first strike, and thus provocative. The skin of the Jupiter was so thin that a sniper's bullet could puncture it and render it inoperative. "In the event of hostilities, assuming that NATO will not strike the first blow," a then-secret congressional report warned, "the USSR with its ballistic missile capability logically could be expected to take out these bases on

[9] Armacost, *Weapons Innovation,* pp. 175–211.

[10] William H. Brubeck, "Jupiters in Italy and Turkey," 22 October 1962, National Security Files (hereafter NSF), Countries: Cuba, Box 36, John F. Kennedy Library, Waltham, Mass. (hereafter JFKL); W.W. Rostow to Bundy, "Turkish IRBM's," 30 October 1962, NSF, Regional Security Files (hereafter RSF): NATO-Weapons, Box 226, JFKL; *New York Times,* 11 October 1959, pp. 1, 11, and 28 October 1962, p. 31.

the first attack, which undoubtedly would be a surprise attack."[11] Put bluntly, the Jupiters would draw, not deter, an attack.

Why then did various Turkish governments, both before and after the coup of 1960, want these weapons? They added prestige, emphasized Turkey's key role in NATO, and exaggerated the warmth of relations with a great power, the United States. The missiles were political assets abroad and possibly at home. Turkey's military leaders believed that the Jupiters added useful military power.[12] Turkish officials probably did not understand the strategic liabilities; perhaps they believed that the missiles, because of their first-strike capacity and the ambiguity of actual control, were sufficiently frightening to deter the Soviets from pressuring Turkey.

Unlike the Eisenhower planners and the Turkish officials, President Kennedy and Secretary of Defense Robert McNamara worried about the provocative nature of these weapons. As a result, according to some memoirists, Kennedy actually ordered the removal of the Jupiters before October 1962, and thus was shocked and dismayed to learn during the Cuban missile crisis that they were still in Turkey.[13]

Such recollections are misleading. Well before the crisis, Kennedy knew the Jupiters were in Turkey. In fact, his administration, not Eisenhower's, had actually installed these weapons in late 1961 to fulfill the 1959 agreement.[14] Key documents reveal that the actual deployment of the Jupiters did not occur

[11] U.S., Congress, House, Committee on Armed Services, *Hearings on the Military Posture,* 88th Cong., 1st sess., 30 January 1963, pp. 277–81.

[12] Ibid., pp. 277–85; Raymond Hare to Secretary of State, no. 587, 26 October 1962, NSF, RSF:NATO-Weapons, Box 226, JFKL; compare Sorensen, *Kennedy,* p. 3.

[13] Kennedy, *Thirteen Days,* pp. 94–95, implies that JFK had been trying to remove them since 1961. Kenneth O'Donnell and David Powers, with Joe McCarthy, *"Johnny, We Hardly Knew Ye"* (Boston: Little, Brown, 1972), p. 337, states that JFK had given the order five times. Also see Hilsman, *To Move A Nation,* pp. 202–203; Elie Abel, *The Missile Crisis* (New York: Bantam Books, 1968), pp. 168–71; and Allison, *Essence of Decision,* pp. 44, 101, 142, 226.

[14] Headquarters, SAC, *The Development of the Strategic Air Command* (n.p., SAC Historian, 1976), p. 104. I am indebted to Dr. Alfred Goldberg, Historian, Department of Defense, for locating this source for me.

until *after* Kennedy had been in the White House for at least six months, and probably not until the autumn, and they did not become operational until about July 1962.[15]

The first document, a partly declassified report by the Joint Congressional Committee on Atomic Energy, makes clear that construction for the Jupiters had not even started when Kennedy entered the White House. On 11 February 1961 the committee urged that "construction . . . should not be permitted to *begin* on the . . . Jupiter sites [which are necessary for] placing 15 obsolete Jupiters in Turkey." Instead, according to the committee, the government should deploy to the area a Polaris submarine, with its sixteen missiles, operated and controlled by American personnel. That assignment, the committee emphasized, could be made before 1962, when the Jupiters would become operational, and the Polaris would be "a much better retaliatory force." It would be mobile, concealed, and thus virtually immune from a Soviet attack. As a result, unlike the Jupiters, the Polaris would add to deterrence and better protect the United States, NATO, and Turkey.[16]

The second document, a National Security Council (NSC) memorandum entitled "Deployment of IRBM's to Turkey," dated 6 April 1961, confirms that there were no Jupiters then in Turkey and that the administration was considering whether it could back away from fulfilling Eisenhower's 1959 agreement. According to this document, at a March 29 meeting of the NSC, President Kennedy directed that a committee, drawn from the Departments of State and Defense and from the Central Intelligence Agency, "should review the question of deployment of IRBMs to Turkey and make recommendations to him." The committee was to be chaired by a representative from the State Deaprtment, which, unlike the Defense Department, was not deeply troubled by the provocative nature of the Jupiters and which was likely to serve as a partisan for Turkish

[15] House Armed Services Committee, *Hearings on Military Posture,* p. 283.

[16] Report quoted in ibid., pp. 279–80 (emphasis added). For evidence that Polaris missile warheads were often unreliable see *New York Times,* 3 December 1978, p. 32.

interests and resist cancellation of the weapons.[17] Was this appointment of the State Department representative as chair accidental? Probably not. Kennedy, a knowledgeable leader who understood bureaucratic politics, probably cared more about not offending the Turks than about withholding the Jupiters. This message was probably clear to the chair and other representatives.

The details of the committee's activities remain classified, but another document, probably a report from the committee's chairman, establishes that the Jupiters were still not in Turkey in early summer. On June 22, George C. McGhee of the State Department reported to McGeorge Bundy, the president's special assistant for national security, "that action should not be taken to cancel *projected* deployment of IRBM's to Turkey." This conclusion was "based primarily," McGhee explained, "on the view that, in the aftermath of Khrushchev's hard posture at Vienna, cancellation . . . might seem a weakness." American credibility and the president's prestige required doing what the Defense Department regarded as militarily dangerous. In addition, McGhee continued, "the Turkish reaction was strongly adverse" and General Lauris Norstad, commander of NATO, "underlined the military importance of sending IRBM's to Turkey. This makes it unlikely that any attempt [would succeed] to persuade the Turkish military that they should abandon this project."[18]

Unfortunately, Norstad's arguments remain unavailable. An analyst cannot determine whether he failed to recognize the provocative nature of the Jupiters in Turkey, or whether he thought that they would make the Soviets uneasy and thus deter some small-scale adventurism, or whether he believed that the missiles were primarily valuable as symbols of (not weapons for) the alliance. What is clear is that Norstad's reasoning helped undercut the analysis of Secretary McNamara

[17] McGeorge Bundy, "Deployment of IRBM's to Turkey," National Security Action Memorandum, 6 April 1961, NSF, RSF:NATO-Weapons (Cables-Turkey), Box 226, JFKL.

[18] George McGhee to Bundy, "Turkish IRBM's," 22 June 1961, NSF, RSF:NATO-Weapons (Cables-Turkey), Box 226, JFKL (emphasis added); and McGhee to Bernstein, 19 February 1979.

and his "whiz kids," who hoped to make deterrence more reasonable and thus chafed at the resistance of allies, the American brass, and the State Department.

Why did Kennedy accede to deploying the missiles? The documents are still classified. The most likely explanation is that McGhee's report summarized Kennedy's own thinking that summer. The president did not want to seem weak after the debacle at Vienna, where he felt Khrushchev had bullied him. Nor did he wish to weaken the NATO alliance politically and deeply offend a key American ally, Turkey, by reneging on Eisenhower's commitment. Perhaps, as McNamara later hinted, the administration might have been tempted to promise a Polaris for the future, when it would be available, instead of deploying Jupiters *then,* in mid-1961. Because there were no extra Polaris subs then, such a promise in mid-1961 would not have met Kennedy's needs or Turkish hopes. "There would have been," McNamara later explained, "a psychological loss to the West of simply cancelling the program and failing to replace them—the missiles—simultaneously with some other more modern system."[19] Presumably, after the pain of Vienna faded, when U.S. credibility was reaffirmed and more Polaris subs became available, the administration, in 1962 or so, could always try to negotiate such an arrangement with Turkish officials. But in 1961, there was no felt need for haste, since the Jupiters were deemed a minor problem in a nuclear edifice that, for the new administration, required major remodeling and expansion.

DID KENNEDY ORDER REMOVAL?

According to some memoirists, President Kennedy raised with the State Department in early 1962 the issue of withdrawing the Jupiters, which would become operational in about July. At the NATO meeting in May, according to Roger Hilsman, Secretary of State Dean Rusk found that the Turks still objected, pri-

[19] House Armed Services Committee, *Hearings on Military Posture,* p. 283.

marily on political grounds.[20] There is no evidence that the administration offered a Polaris as a substitute, and Turkish officials probably would have found the submarine less attractive. They did not seem to share the Defense Department's concern about an invulnerable deterrent, and the Jupiters offered two notable advantages the Polaris lacked: The missiles, because they were visible, added more tangible prestige; and they were subject, in principle, to some Turkish control.

By the summer, Hilsman claims, Kennedy again raised the matter of removing the Jupiters, this time with Undersecretary of State George Ball, and rejected the State Department's "case for further delay."[21] And in late August, Kennedy raised this subject yet again, this time, surprisingly and dramatically, in the context of Cuba. Still, he did *not* order withdrawal, but only implied a study of its feasibility. Bundy's National Security Action Memorandum No. 181, dated 23 August 1962, expresses Kennedy's thoughts and new fears of missiles in Cuba and Soviet efforts to equate them with the Jupiters.

> The President has directed that the following actions and studies be undertaken in the light of new [Soviet] bloc activity in Cuba.
>
> 1. What action can be taken to get Jupiter missiles out of Turkey? (Action: Department of Defense). . . .
>
> 6. A study should be made of the advantages and disadvantages of making a statement that the U.S. would not tolerate the establishment of military forces (missile or air, or both?) which might launch a nuclear attack from Cuba against the U.S. . . .
>
> 7. A study should be made of the various military alternatives which might be adopted in executing a decision to eliminate any installations in Cuba capable of launching nuclear attack on the U.S. What would be the pros and cons, for example, of pinpoint attack, general counterforce attack, and outright invasion?
> (Action: Department of Defense)[22]

[20] Hilsman, *To Move A Nation,* pp. 202–3; Kennedy, *Thirteen Days,* pp. 94–95.

[21] Hilsman, *To Move A Nation,* pp. 202–3; Kennedy, *Thirteen Days,* pp. 94–95. For additional doubts that Kennedy ever ordered withdrawal, see George Ball to Bernstein, 22 February 1979.

[22] Bundy, National Security Action Memorandum, no. 181, 23 August 1962, Cunliffe-NSC Box, Modern Military Records, National Archives, Washington, D.C.

By shifting responsibility for removal of the Jupiters to the Department of Defense, which, unlike the Department of State, was more concerned about nuclear strategy than about maintaining warm relations with a dependent ally, either Kennedy himself or Bundy had decided to minimize the role of the State Department. So far as the available records and recollection indicate, however, the Defense Department accomplished nothing in the next seven weeks to phase out the Jupiters.[23] Obviously, removing the missiles first required a plan and then probably diplomatic negotiations. General Norstad, as well as Turkish officials, could be an impediment. Probably the Defense Department was again flirting with the possibility of substituting deployment of a Polaris (there were nine) near Turkey for the Jupiters.

Did Kennedy believe that this directive of 23 August 1962 would soon remove the Jupiters? Given that his government had installed them, and they had just become operational in about July, he could not have been so foolishly optimistic. Nor did the memorandum *order* the Department of Defense to act. It asked "What action can be taken?" and stated that there would be a meeting with the president in about nine days "to review progress on these items." Thus it is too simple to conclude, as have some analysts, that Kennedy ordered removal of the missiles and that the bureaucracy thwarted his instructions.[24] Indeed, according to Bundy's recent recollection, the

[23] Since many files are still classified, there may have been some action. Bundy does not recall that there was any action (interview with Bundy, 31 July 1979). At the meeting of August 31 or September 1, with JFK, on the points in this memo, there was, as Henry Rowen recalls, no discussion of item 1 (interview with Rowen, 13 February 1979).

[24] See, for example, Allison, *Essence of Decision,* pp. 101, 141–42, 225–26, who uncritically accepted recollections that JFK had given a clear order and then tries to explain, in terms of bureaucratic politics, why it was not carried out. A more subtle approach would acknowledge that a chief executive may often express preferences (not orders) for policies, and that he may sincerely reinterpret them as *orders* when his own inaction leaves him woefully unprepared in a crisis. In this way, a president can place blame on a subordinate, and other aides who listen to his charges tend to believe that the president actually issued an order, and not simply stated a wish or hope. In later memoirs and journalistic accounts, the president's interpretation dominates and becomes "fact." Practitioners of the "bureaucratic politics" model develop a vested interest in uncritically accepting such dubious evidence precisely because their model so nicely "explains" it. Thus, the model *first* helps define the reliability of the evidence and *then* explains it—a dangerous, circular process.

president did not order withdrawal of the Jupiters until *after* the Cuban missile crisis.[25]

Why did Kennedy in August link the missiles in Turkey to the problem of Cuba? Did he foresee that the Soviet Union would install surface-to-surface missiles ninety miles from the United States? The memoirists tell us that neither Kennedy nor his advisers, with the exception of CIA director John McCone, deemed such Soviet action as likely.[26] Thus, their concern probably was more general: that the Soviets might justify a build-up of troops and even bombers in Cuba by pointing to the Jupiters, which had just become operational. There was already evidence that recent Soviet deliveries to Cuba probably included surface-to-air missiles (SAMs) and possibly planes.

The NSC memorandum had suggested the danger of the Soviets equating "offensive" missiles in Turkey with those in Cuba. Even before a U-2 photographed the Soviet "offensive" missile sites on October 14, therefore, a NSC staff member prepared an argument to stress the political differences between U.S. Jupiters in Turkey and Soviet missiles in Cuba: The Soviet weapons were designed for aggression and deployed secretly; the American weapons were defensive and deployed openly. Put simply, the Soviet action was dangerous and dishonorable, the American action peaceful and honorable.[27] It was a strained, self-righteous document, characteristic of the administration's public pronouncements during the crisis.

THE UNITED STATES CONSIDERS A TRADE

On Tuesday, October 16, when learning of the Soviet missiles in Cuba, some administration members feared that the Soviets

For related critiques, see Dan Caldwell, "A Research Note on the Quarantine of Cuba, October 1962," *International Studies Quarterly* 20 (December 1978):625–33; and Donald Hafner, "Bureaucratic Politics and Those Frigging Missiles': JFK, Cuba and U.S. Missiles in Turkey," *Orbis* 21 (Summer 1977):307–33.

[25] Interviews with McGeorge Bundy, 29 and 31 July 1979.

[26] Hilsman, *To Move A Nation*, p. 170.

[27] I.M. Tobin, "Attempts to Equate Soviet Missile Bases in Cuba with NATO Jupiter Bases in Italy and Turkey," 10 October 1962, NSF, Countries: Cuba, Box 36, JFKL. Also see Thomas Sorensen, "Information Policy Guidance on Cuba," 22 October 1962, Classified Subjects Files (hereafter CSF), Box 48, Theodore Sorensen Papers (hereafter Sorensen Papers), JFKL.

would point to the Jupiters for justification. During the six days, from October 16 to October 21, when the Executive Committee of the National Security Council (ExComm) deliberated on how the administration should respond, United Nations ambassador Adlai Stevenson, Secretary of Defense Robert McNamara, and some other advisers occasionally suggested trading missiles (in Turkey for those in Cuba) to settle the crisis. Apparently the president flirted with this notion.

On Wednesday, October 17, Stevenson warned Kennedy that world opinion would equate U.S. missile bases in Turkey with the Soviet bases in Cuba. Stevenson's memorandum was fuzzy, perhaps because he feared that he was giving unwelcome counsel, for he both warned that "we can't negotiate with a gun at our head" and suggested trading the bases in Turkey for those in Cuba. *"I feel you should* [*make*] it clear that the existence of nuclear missile bases anywhere is negotiable before we start anything," he underlined.[28]

In fairness to Stevenson, on Wednesday, when he offered this counsel, the ExComm was leaning toward an attack on Cuba to eliminate the missiles; in that context, he was probably more concerned to head off disaster than to phrase an exact plan for negotiations. His memo was unclear on key matters: Should Kennedy privately demand that the Soviets withdraw their missiles and also mention future negotiations on the Jupiters? Or should he negotiate on them then? The problems of when, how, and under what conditions to offer a trade—whether explicit or informal—would bedevil thinking on this matter throughout the crisis.

Two days later, on Friday, October 19, according to the ExComm minutes quoted by Arthur Schlesinger, Jr., "more

[28] Adlai Stevenson to President, 17 October 1962, Sorensen Papers. The irrationalities of the classification-declassification system are well illustrated by the fact that the typed copy of this item was declassified by the State Department in August 1974, but the handwritten copy (which is trivially different because of some crossing out) was kept classified until summer 1978, despite requests and appeals for declassification in the intervening years. After Stewart Alsop and Charles Bartlett skewered Stevenson in the press for being a "dove," Stevenson argued that he never meant to imply that the Turkey and Italy bases should be traded as part of a settlement (Stevenson to Arthur M. Schlesinger, Jr., [January 1963], Sorensen Papers).

than once during the afternoon Secretary McNamara voiced the opinion that the US . . . would at least have to give up our missile bases in Italy and Turkey and would probably have to pay more besides . . . to get the Soviet missiles out of Cuba." On Saturday, McNamara again offered the same analysis: "We would have to be prepared to accept the withdrawal of US strategic missiles from Turkey and Italy and possibly agreement to [withdraw in the future from] Guantanamo. He added that we could obtain the removal of the missiles . . . only if we were prepared to offer something in return."[29]

On Saturday, after the ExComm had finally agreed on the quarantine, Stevenson attended the meeting and once more recommended a trade, this time to be announced along with the quarantine. His proposed settlement would have included withdrawal of Jupiters from Turkey and abandonment of the U.S. naval base at Guantanamo.[30] According to Schlesinger, who has seen the classified ExComm minutes, "everyone jumped on Stevenson." Why? Schlesinger claims that most feared that this proposed tactic, by *starting* with concessions, would "legitimize Khrushchev's action and give him an easy triumph."[31] Robert Kennedy later added that the timing and the Guantanamo offer, not the Turkish bases, provoked the anger.[32] Probably, in addition, Stevenson himself provoked ire. Because he was an outsider, not respected by either Kennedy brother, his counsel, even when similar to that of the trusted

[29] Leonard Meeker, memorandum, 19 October 1962, meeting of the Executive Committee of the National Security Council, Arthur Schlesinger Papers, JFKL, quoted in Schlesinger, *Robert F. Kennedy,* p. 515. On the State Department's later suppression (classification) of Meeker's memo, see Abram Chayes, *The Cuban Missile Crisis* (London: Oxford University Press, 1974), pp. vii–viii and 14–15.

[30] Notes on minutes of NSC, 20 October 1962, courtesy of Schlesinger.

[31] Schlesinger, *Robert F. Kennedy,* p. 515. Also see, [Adlai Stevenson?], "Political Program to be Announced by the President," 20 October 1962, Sorensen Papers; [Stevenson?], "Speech Insert on Political Program," n.d. (probably October 17 or 20), Box 48, Sorensen Papers; and Stevenson, "Why the Political Program Should Be in the Speech," n.d. (probably October 21), in CSF, Box 49, Sorensen Papers. The first memo called for sending U.N. observation teams to Turkey, Italy, and Cuba to "insure [against] surprise attack," and suggested discussions on NATO bases in Italy and Turkey. The last memo suggested trading Guantanamo but did not offer the bases in Turkey and Italy.

[32] Kennedy, in interview with John B. Martin, 6 December 1966, cited by Schlesinger, *Robert F. Kennedy,* p. 515; Kennedy, *Thirteen Days,* p. 50.

McNamara, easily rankled the tired members of the ExComm. Whereas they viewed themselves as "tough" and decisive, they viewed Stevenson as indecisive and soft.

President Kennedy "sharply rejected the thought of surrendering [Guantanamo]," according to the ExComm minutes. "He felt that such action would convey to the world that we had been frightened into abandoning our position."[33] He "emphatically disagreed," reports Schlesinger, "that the initial presentation to the UN should include our notion of an eventual political settlement." According to the minutes, "he agreed that at an appropriate time we would have to acknowledge that we were willing to take strategic missiles out of Turkey and Italy if this issue was raised by the Russians. But he was firm in saying that we should only make such a proposal in the future." The quoted minutes in Schlesinger's account leave unclear whether the president was willing to countenance an explicit public trade of the Jupiters, or whether he was suggesting something private, hedged, even evasive.[34]

On Sunday morning, October 21, high-level State Department officials flirted with the Cuba-Turkey missile trade. At an evening meeting, convened by Robert Kennedy, a number of senior government officials agreed, in the words of Abram Chayes, the State Department's legal adviser, "that the Turkish missiles would have to be given up in the end, as the price of settlement." Why not have the United States introduce this offer at the United Nations right after the announcement of the quarantine? Offered at the beginning, such a concession would have various liabilities and seem, according to Chayes's summary of attitudes, "rather weak and defensive [and] inconsistent with the sense of resolution and determination that was judged essential to the success of the quarantine."[35]

Suggesting a trade, W. Averell Harriman, assistant secretary of state for Far Eastern Affairs, counseled President Kennedy

[33] Minutes of NSC, 20 October 1962, quoted in Schlesinger, *Robert F. Kennedy*, p. 515.
[34] Ibid.
[35] Chayes, *Cuban Missile Crisis*, pp. 81–82.

on likely Soviet purposes: "There has undoubtedly been great pressure on Khrushchev for a considerable time to do something about our ring of bases, aggravated by our placing Jupiter missiles in Turkey." Harriman hinted that such a trade might rescue Khrushchev, who, he thought, had been pushed to take such bold action by a tough group in the Kremlin.[36]

On Monday morning, the day the president announced the quarantine, Attorney General Robert Kennedy sketched the administration's public line, at least for the next few days.[37] Fearful that Stevenson might be too soft in dealing with the Soviets at the United Nations, Kennedy pulled aside Schlesinger, then serving as Stevenson's aide, to outline the administration's thinking: "We will have to make a deal at the end, but we must stand absolutely firm now. Concessions must come at the end of negotiation, not at the beginning."[38] His implication: the quarantine, if successful, would frighten the Soviets but not compel them to yield unless the United States also offered some quid pro quo. Did the attorney general have the Jupiters in mind? The deliberations of the past week, especially the Sunday evening meeting, certainly suggested them as part of an exchange.

Why did the president not order the dismantling of the Jupiters before they might become a public bargaining card in the crisis? Probably the time was too short, and probably he was also tempted by the prospect of a future trade and therefore unwilling to discard this extra card. Stevenson, among others, warned of a potential liability: that the Jupiters would also make it harder to persuade the world that the Soviet missiles constituted a new kind of threat. But probably Kennedy was willing to take that risk in order to keep open future options, to protect himself from international embarrassment (would not the sudden dismantling suggest U.S. acknowledge-

[36] W. Averell Harriman, "Memorandum on Kremlin Reactions," 22 October 1962, JFKL.

[37] At one point, Sorensen had sketched a loose Turkey-Cuba missile trade for inclusion in Kennedy's message to Khrushchev (Sorensen, draft, 18 October 1962, CSF, Box 48, Sorensen Papers).

[38] Schlesinger, *A Thousand Days,* p. 811.

ment that Turkey-Cuba missile bases were equivalent?), and to avoid domestic charges of weakness and a sellout.

Plans to Trade the Jupiters

After the president's Monday evening speech announcing the quarantine, some American officials vigorously canvassed the possibility of trading the Jupiters in Turkey as part of the ultimate settlement of the crisis. There were basic questions, as they knew: Whether and, if so, how to exchange the Jupiters, ideally without appearing to do so? Would other weapons meet the military and political needs of NATO and Turkey? If so, could the United States withdraw these missiles without offending most NATO nations and Turkey in particular? "The danger in Turkey can be especially acute," one official warned. "If the Alliance or the US seems to be pulling away from [Turkey] it could lead to the fall of the present government."[39] An uneasy new coalition, shored up by the Turkish military and by American economic aid, the Turkish government could not afford to antagonize its powerful generals or risk a crisis.[40]

Working within these constraints, Undersecretary of State George Ball, W. Averell Harriman, Harlan Cleveland (assistant secretary of state for International Organization), Walt Whitman Rostow (director of the Policy Planning Council), and Stevenson, among others, scratched around for some solution involving the Jupiters. At times, this line seemed to capture the fancy of President Kennedy, but hard questions always lingered for him.[41]

Early in the week, President Kennedy apparently directed the State Department to consider withdrawing the missiles, which spurred Ball to consult key ambassadors. On Wednes-

[39] "Scenario," 26 October 1962, NSF. Countries: Cuba, JFKL. This memorandum also dealt with removal of the thirty Jupiters from Italy.

[40] *New York Times*, 30 October 1962, p. 14; see also, George Harris, *Troubled Alliance* (Washington, D.C.: Brookings Institution, 1972), pp. 83–95.

[41] Bromley Smith, "Summary Record of NSC Executive Committee Meeting, No. 7, Oct. 27, 1962, 10:00 A.M.," NSF, NSC: ExComm Meetings, JFKL. (hereafter cited as "Summary Record, ExComm").

day, October 24, he notified Ambassador Raymond Hare that a trade was being considered and requested an assessment of the political situation in Turkey so "that [we will] not harm our relations with this important ally." Would Turkey accede to withdrawal of the Jupiters, Ball asked, if there was some military replacement—possibly deployment of an American-controlled Polaris or establishment of seaborne, multilateral nuclear force (MLF) within NATO?[42] Both notions had been knocking about Washington for more than a year, and the administration, like Eisenhower's, had been flirting with the creation of a MLF, under NATO, in order to restrain the desire of some European nations, especially France, for an independent deterrent.

Removal of the Jupiters as part of an explicit trade would weaken NATO and injure American relations with Turkey, Hare replied. Turkish officials would greatly resent "that their interests were being traded off in order to appease an enemy." They were proud that, unlike the Cubans, they were not the "stooge" of a great power. Both Turkey's political prestige and military power were at stake, he claimed, and the Jupiters fulfilled both needs.[43]

Could these missiles be used to settle the Soviet-American conflict? Hare was not optimistic but dutifully discussed some programs. He reluctantly suggested a secret Soviet-American agreement (without Turkey's knowledge) and then the prompt dismantling of the missiles. That course would prove attractive in Washington.[44]

On receiving Ball's cable, NATO Ambassador Thomas Finletter also replied that Turkish officials would bitterly resent a trade. He lectured the State Department on the dangers of a "horse trade." It could set a "pattern for handling Russian incursions" elsewhere and thus frighten other members of NATO, who "may wonder whether they will be asked to give

[42] Secretary Rusk (drafted by Ball) to Ambassadors Hare and Finletter, 24 October 1962, NSF, RSF:NATO-Weapons, Box 226, JFKL.

[43] Ambassador Hare to Secretary of State, 26 October 1962, NSF, RSF: NATO-Weapons, Box 226, JFKL.

[44] Ibid.

up some military capability" the next time. Unlike Hare, Finletter did not even glance at the possibility of a secret deal with the Soviets.[45] Perhaps he did not conceive of this strategy; more likely, he did not want to risk mentioning what he deemed a disastrous course.

By Thursday, October 25, while one special NSC committee was sketching the scenario for an air strike, another was outlining a "political path"—a summit meeting while the quarantine continued—to settle the crisis. "It would probably involve discussion over Berlin or, as a minimum, our missile bases in Turkey," the committee warned.[46] A linked proposal, probably from the same committee, suggested an offer "to withdraw our missiles from Turkey in return for Soviet withdrawal of . . . missiles from Cuba." To avoid a crisis in NATO and to assuage Turkish officials, such an offer "might be expressed in generalized form, such as withdrawal of missiles from territory [near] the other [great power]."[47]

On Friday, October 26, Harriman was also urging negotiations to get the missiles out of Turkey. He endorsed the "defanging resolution" of Assistant Secretary Harlan Cleveland: Only nuclear powers should possess nuclear weapons and missiles, and thus the United States and the Soviet Union would not place these systems in the territory of nonnuclear powers. Such terms, Harriman explained, would compel the United States to pull missiles out of Turkey and Italy, but not Britain, which was a nuclear power, and Russia would have to withdraw its missiles from Cuba. By raising the terms to a level of generality, Harriman hoped to conceal what some could regard as a naked trade—missiles in Turkey and Italy for missiles in Cuba. *"Agreement should be put forward not as a trade over Cuba,"* he underlined, but *"as a first and important step to-*

[45] Ambassador Finletter to Secretary of State, Polto 506, 25 October 1962, NSF,RSF: NATO-Weapons, Box 226, JFKL.

[46] "Political Path," 25 October 1962, NSF,NSC: ExComm Meetings, Box 316, JFKL.

[47] Neither the author nor the date is given for this untitled document, but the document begins: "The following political actions might be considered" (Vice-Presidential Security File, Nations and Regions, Policy Papers and Background Studies on Cuba Affair, folder III, Lyndon B. Johnson Library, [hereafter LBJL] Austin, Texas). (This series will hereafter be cited as VP Security File: Cuba.)

wards disarmament."[48] And he believed sincerely that the result would be both a way out of the crisis and a course toward more effective arms control. Harriman was seizing on the crisis to address more basic problems and also offering Khrushchev a way of avoiding humiliation. At first glance, his plan seemed appealingly simple: The negotiations *might* be speedy, and the Soviets would recognize that they could take credit for forcing a trade and for promoting disarmament. But what would happen if the negotiations were not speedy? Would not obtaining the endorsement of NATO and Turkey take too much time?

Even though all the middle-range ballistic missile (MRBM) sites *had been operational* since the first day of the quarantine, and therefore the Soviet could have launched a first salvo of about half their forty-two MRBMs, Kennedy and members of ExComm worried about the continued work on missile sites in Cuba. They seemed to fear that the Soviets would reduce the time required for launching an MRBM, and that they also were advancing quickly on twelve or eighteen launchers for IRBMs (twelve to thirty-six missiles), likely to be ready in about five weeks. The CIA was not sure whether nuclear warheads were in Cuba, but the administration assumed the worst.[49]

The ExComm minutes are scattered with demands that work on the missiles must stop soon. And Kennedy seemed to have a self-imposed deadline of roughly between Sunday, October 28,

[48] Harriman to Under Secretary, 26 October 1962, NSF, Countries: Cuba, Box 36, JFKL. Harriman's first choice was a resolution on denuclearization of Latin America, which excluded the problem of Europe. On October 24, he had argued for the "defanging resolution" (Schlesinger to Stevenson, 24 October 1962, Schlesinger Papers, JFKL).

[49] Central Intelligence Agency, "Readiness Status of Soviet Missiles in Cuba," 23 October 1962, had counted twenty-three (of the ultimate twenty-four) launchers and thirty-three (of the ultimate forty-two) MRBMs, and was unsure whether the warheads were in Cuba (NSF, Countries: Cuba, JFKL; see also, CIA, "The Crisis: USSR/Cuba," 26 October 1962, NSF,NSC:ExComm Meetings, JFKL, which is location of CIA, "The Crisis" reports). For an admission that some MRBMs were operational and probably had nuclear warheads, see McNamara's statement, *Washington Post,* 25 October 1962, p. A-10. Generally newspapers, including the *Washington Post,* disregarded this admission. For the implications on reassessing the crisis, see Bernstein, "Week We Almost Went to War," pp. 13–21. For a tendentious argument, which overlooks this essay and cites an abbreviated version, see Schlesinger, *Robert F. Kennedy,* pp. 517–18, who charges of suppression of evidence. His paperback edition struggles to maintain much of the claim while squirming away from an admission that he failed to research his subject adequately and thus simply missed Bernstein's article in the *Bulletin of the Atomic Scientists.*

to about Tuesday, October 30.[50] As a result, plans involving a trade of the Jupiters had to meet his informal timetable. Those plans that seemed to involve lengthy negotiations would be unacceptable, unless they stipulated a way of getting the Soviets promptly to halt work on the sites.

While Harriman's plan *may* have had this liability, two others—one from a special NSC committee and the other from Rostow—certainly did. On Friday, the special committee offered a proposal, forwarded by Rusk without comment to Kennedy, for a "face-saving cover, if [the Soviets] wish, for a withdrawal of their offensive weapons from Cuba."[51] It was an elaborate, guardedly optimistic scheme suggesting a summit conference, to be preceded by the agreement of NATO and Turkey to accept a multilateral nuclear force and to remove missiles from Turkey and Italy.

Walt W. Rostow, sketching a similar plan, believed that he had devised a way out of the crisis while maintaining all of the "Free World assets" and actually strengthening the NATO alliance. His solution: secure NATO's speedy approval for MLF, presumably with an agreement to dismantle the Jupiters. The Soviets, he acknowledged, "could read it [dismantling] as a way of helping them off the hook"; but it would "nail down the missile portion of the Alliance and [thus thwart Soviet efforts] to disrupt the confidence of the Alliance in the U.S." An additional attraction, for Rostow, was that it achieved goals he had long sought—a stronger NATO, establishment of MLF, and removal of dangerous weapons.[52] But how could these negotiations with NATO nations be completed in a few days?

[50] Harold Macmillan, *At the End of the Day, 1961–1963* (New York: Harper & Row, 1973), pp. 209–11; see also, "Summary Record, ExComm, No.5, Oct. 25, 1962, 5:00 P.M."; and "Summary Record, ExComm, No. 6, Oct. 26, 1962, 10:00 A.M."

[51] Rusk to President, "Negotiations," with attached paper, 26 October 1962, NSF, Countries: Cuba, Box 36, JFKL.

[52] Rostow to Secretary et al., "Alliance Missiles," 26 October 1962, with copy to Bundy in NSF, Countries: Cuba, Box 36, JFKL, discussed trading the missiles in Turkey and Italy. Also see Rostow et al. to Secretary, "Cuba," 25 October 1962, NSF, RSF: NATO-Weapons, Box 226, JFKL; Rostow to Secretary et al., "Negotiations about Cuba," NSF, Countries: Cuba, JFKL; and Rostow to Bundy, [25 October 1962], with memorandum, "Summit," 25 October 1962, NSF, JFKL.

Ideally, the analyst would like to know which ExComm members supported which proposals and what kind of informal dialogue ensued. But for the most part, that kind of evidence is not available. The special NSC committee's proposal went to Kennedy, as did Rostow's, and probably all the reports reached Bundy's desk.[53] By Friday, judging from the contents of the various memorandums, there had been substantial informal dialogue. Many advisers were looking for a road to settlement, and the Jupiters constituted a possible one.

On Friday morning, the ExComm considered whether Kennedy should seek U.N. assistance in arranging negotiations with the Soviets while they halted construction on the missile sites and, as Stevenson suggested, the United States suspended its quarantine. Could the crisis be settled this way? Stevenson, who seemed optimistic, "predicted that the Russians would ask for a new guarantee of the territorial integrity of Cuba and the dismantlement of U.S. strategic missiles in Turkey" in return for withdrawal of missiles from Cuba. Stevenson still regarded these terms as reasonable. But John McCone, the CIA director, was outraged. He resented linking the missiles in Turkey with the Soviet missiles in Cuba. He said, according to the minutes, "the Soviet weapons in Cuba were pointed at our heart and put us under great handicap to carry out our committments to the free world."[54]

Kennedy did not bar the trade outlined by Stevenson. According to the minutes, he said, "we will get the . . . missiles out of Cuba only by invading or trading. He doubted that the quarantine alone would produce a withdrawal of the weapons." After Kennedy spoke, the dialogue quickly shifted from the Jupiters to Stevenson's proposal that the quarantine should be suspended during negotiations. Most ExComm members strongly opposed that concession. The pressure must be maintained, they concluded, to help force a settlement. Curiously,

[53] This conclusion is based partly on the fact that the reports are usually available in the NSF—actually the Bundy files—at the JFKL.

[54] "Summary Record, ExComm, No. 6, Oct. 26, 1962, 10:00 A.M." Also see Stevenson to Secretary of State, 25 October 1962, VP Security File: Cuba, folder III, LBJL.

they did not return to the issue of the Jupiters at that meeting.[55]

Later that Friday, the Soviets indicated terms for settling the crisis: withdrawal of their missiles from Cuba and on-site inspection in return for U.S. termination of the quarantine and a pledge not to invade Cuba. There was not even a hint that the United States must dismantle its Jupiters; the Soviets were asking for less than many American officials had anticipated and than some had proposed to grant.[56]

That Friday night, most ExComm members could find reason for satisfaction. The dangerous crisis would end with one American concession—the pledge not to invade Cuba.[57] Only a few advisers, including McCone and at least some of the Joint Chiefs, were deeply unhappy that Castro would be safe from a United States joint attack.[58] For the rest, the pledge was a small price to pay. According to Secretary Rusk, it was simply a reaffirmation of existing obligations: "we are committed not to invade Cuba [because we] signed the UN Charter and the Rio treaty."[59]

[55] "Summary Record, ExComm, No. 6, Oct. 26, 1962, 10:00 A.M."

[56] "Significantly, and contrary to expectations, Khrushchev did not seek to link the Cuba issue with . . . the Jupiters in Turkey and Italy" ("The Immediate Consequences," n.d. [late October 26 or early October 27], CSF, Sorensen Papers). For a similar statement, also see Hilsman to Secretary, "Implications of the Soviet Initiative on Cuba," 27 October 1962, CSF, Box 48, Sorensen Papers. In searching for a settlement, the ExComm and other advisers had usually dwelled more upon the American missiles in Turkey (and less upon those in Italy), possibly because those in Turkey were closer to the Soviet Union and had provoked more Soviet ire in the past.

[57] Later, Edward Martin sent a telegram to "All ARA Diplomatic Posts," 27 October 1962, pointing out that the no-invasion pledge could be waived "if [Cuba's] breaking of accepted norms becomes flagrant, [for] US would feel . . . free to take whatever measures might be required" (CSF, Box 48, Sorensen Papers). This telegram, as well as the memorandums cited in note 56 and ExComm minutes, suggests that the no-invasion pledge raised fewer problems for the president and the ExComm than did a trade involving removal of the Jupiters from Turkey.

[58] "Summary Record, ExComm, No. 6, Oct. 26, 1962, 10:00 A.M."; John McCone to Mac [Bundy]," 22 November 1962, NSF, Countries: Cuba: General File, 11/21–11/30, JFKL; and evidence presented for attitudes of some members of the Joint Chiefs of Staff on Sunday, in Kennedy, *Thirteen Days,* p. 119. Alexander George has argued that a no-invasion pledge was a major concession that could protect Khrushchev from humiliation (George to Bernstein, 18 May 1979).

[59] "Summary Record, ExComm, No. 6, Oct. 26, 1962, 10:00 A.M."

Would Western Allies Have Accepted a Trade?

On Saturday morning, October 27, the heady optimism speedily collapsed: Some Soviet ships were approaching the quarantine line; the FBI reported that the Soviet delegation was destroying intelligence documents in likely preparation for war; and a surface-to-air missile (SAM) shot down a U-2 over Cuba.[60] Worst of all, a new Soviet message arrived, raising the terms of settlement to require removal of the Jupiters from Turkey. "It was the blackest hour of the crisis," later recalled Roger Hilsman.[61]

How would America's NATO allies, other than Turkey, have responded if the administration had met the Soviet terms and agreed publicly to withdraw the Jupiters? Could Kennedy have negotiated a private trade before the Soviets made their public demand? Had there been more flexibility in the NATO alliance than he had chosen to act upon?

The leaders of most of the NATO allies understood the military liabilities of the Jupiters, so the issues were not primarily strategic (the loss of weapons) but psychological and political: the significance of an American concession on weaponry in Europe in order to deal with problems in the Caribbean.[62] Would Kennedy be viewed as a leader who sold out allies for U.S. interests? Or as a leader who sought peace and

[60] Possibly the ExComm did not learn of the shoot-down of the U-2 until later in the day, for no reference to the event appears in the minutes by Bundy and Smith *until* the second Saturday session (4:00 P.M.). See "Summary Record, ExComm, No. 7, Oct. 27, 1962, 10:00 A.M." and "Summary Record, ExComm, No. 8, 4:00 P.M.; and Bundy, "NSC Executive Committee Record of Action, Oct. 27, 1962, 10:00 A.M. Meeting No. 7" and "NSC Executive Committee Record of Action, Oct. 27, 1962, 4:00 P.M., No. 8," NSF: ExComm Meetings, JFKL.

[61] Hilsman, *To Move A Nation,* p. 220. The Soviet message of October 27 mentioned the missiles in Britain and Italy but specified only those in Turkey as a requirement for a trade. So far as the available materials indicate, no one in the ExComm speculated on why the Soviets added the Jupiters in Turkey to the deal and not *also* those in Italy. Could the Soviets have desired both to raise the ante and to keep the "price" within what seemed acceptable limits? Perhaps Walter Lippmann's suggestion of a Turkey-Cuba missile trade (*Washington Post,* 25 October 1962, p. A-25 and 23 October 1962, p. A-10) seemed to the Soviets an oblique administration offer.

[62] Sorensen, memorandum, 17 October 1962, Cuba files, President's Official Files (hereafter POF) 115, JFKL; Sorensen, *Kennedy,* pp. 680–82.

would pay some reasonable price to avoid plunging NATO and the United States into war?

There is considerable evidence on the attitudes of the German, French, British, Italian, and Canadian governments, and scattered evidence for Belgium, the Netherlands, Greece, Denmark, and Norway. A formal trade, especially a public one, would have unnerved some governments, particularly the German and British, and probably the Dutch; it would have confirmed the analysis of President Charles de Gaulle of France, delighted Canada, and probably pleased the Italian, Belgian, Greek, Danish, and Norwegian governments.

Konrad Adenauer, the steadfast chancellor of West Germany, who always feared that American concessions anywhere might betoken abandonment of Berlin, would undoubtedly have opposed even a private trade.[63] But he had no real leverage and could not threaten to leave NATO or even acknowledge its weaknesses. Unwilling to move toward rapprochement with the Soviet Union, Adenauer and his party depended upon the United States and NATO for both military protection and political prestige. Any trade would have eroded his trust in Kennedy, but it would not have altered Adenauer's policies on the larger issues—Berlin, East Germany, the Warsaw Pact, and the Soviet Union. True, at home, he could have been compelled to defend himself and his party against charges that the United States would also sell out Berlin and thus against demands that an approach to the East was essential. But Adenauer would have succeeded, partly for his reasons. Like Kennedy, Adenauer could have distinguished between Berlin and the Jupiters, for he could have defined the missiles in Turkey as marginal but Berlin as essential to West Germany and the United States.

Charles de Gaulle's position was different. Already moving toward French withdrawal from NATO on the grounds that the alliance meant American domination and blocked France from an independent foreign policy, de Gaulle could use the missile

[63] *New York Times*, 28 October 1962, p. 31; CIA, "The Crisis: USSR/Cuba," 27 October 1962.

crisis—whatever the outcome—to support his analysis. America had acted independently without consultation with allies, he noted. The implication, which he would later exploit, was familiar: "annihilation without representation." In turn, had Kennedy publicly traded the missiles in Turkey, that act also would have confirmed de Gaulle's analysis: the United States would act on its own interests and abandon allies whenever convenient. Probably no likely action by Kennedy in the missile crisis—whether he traded or not—could have blocked de Gaulle's ambitions for establishing France as an independent force. That conception, so intimately related to his quest for national and personal grandeur, would not be punctured by U.S. decisions during the missile crisis.[64] While he technically supported the president in the crisis, the aged French leader hinted that immaturity had led Kennedy and the United States to overreact. President de Gaulle's chiding words, as summarized by the American ambassador, were these: "The French for centuries had lived with threats and menaces, first from the Germans and from the Russians, but he understood the US had not had a comparable experience."[65]

Britain's Prime Minister Harold Macmillan had been a strong supporter of the quarantine and worried, especially in the early days, that Khrushchev would wring concessions that would weaken the alliance. He feared that Khrushchev might have installed the missiles "to trade Cuba for Berlin." Fretting that the quarantine might be inadequate, Macmillan wrote in his diary, Kennedy may " 'miss the bus'—he may *never* get rid of Cuban rockets except by trading them for Turkish, Italian, or other bases. Thus Khrushchev will have won his point." But by Friday, October 26, when the Soviets seemed to be seeking a way out of the crisis, Macmillan was conciliatory. "If we want to help the Russians save face," he asked Kennedy, "would it be worthwhile our [temporarily demobilizing the Thor missiles]

[64] Cyrus Sulzberger, *The Last of the Giants* (New York: Macmillan Co., 1970), pp. 20–22, 1004–06; Charles E. Bohlen, *Witness to History, 1929–1969* (New York: W.W. Norton, 1973), pp. 504–09.

[65] Ambassador Bohlen to Secretary of State, No. 1970, 27 October 1962, VP Security File: Cuba, folder VI, LBJL.

in England during the . . . conference [proposed by the Soviets]?" Kennedy found the suggestion attractive, wanted to mull it over, but feared that it might provoke the Soviets to insist on dismantlings in Turkey and Italy. Though Macmillan had proposed a temporary demobilization of his Thor missiles, he later claimed that, despite the obsolescence of the Jupiters, he would not have agreed to the Soviet proposal on October 27 for their removal. Was this bravado created after the settlement? Probably not. "All America's allies would feel," wrote Macmillan in 1973, "that to avoid the Cuban threat the U.S. . . . had bargained away their protection."[66] Nonetheless, as much as Macmillan would have opposed a public trade, as the dependent ally in the "special relationship" with the United States, he and his party would have probably defended such a trade. Loyalty to the United States would have shaped the Conservative government's public statements.

During that week in late October, American analysis concluded that Norway and Denmark would welcome a trade of the Jupiters to end the crisis.[67] They were probably correct about these two Scandinavian allies, who had steadfastly resisted the emplacement of any nuclear weapons on their soil. When the Soviets made their public demand for including the Jupiters in a settlement, Norwegian government officials endorsed removal of the weapons.[68]

Italy's center-left coalition government reluctantly supported the quarantine, tried to improve relations with the Soviets during the crisis, and anxiously urged Kennedy to negotiate with Khrushchev. On October 27, when an American attack on

[66] Macmillan, *End of the Day,* pp. 187, 210, 212–13. Some British officials did flirt with a Cuba-Turkey missile deal during the early days of the crisis (Bohlen to Secretary of State, No. 2082, 11 November 1962, NSF, RSF: NATO-Weapons, JFKL). For Labour and Liberal party responses, see Manchester *Guardian,* 25 October 1962, p. 2; *Times* (London), 25 October 1962, p. 8, For editorials suggesting a trade, see *Times* (London), 24, 26, and 28 October (accepting the Soviet offer) and Manchester *Guardian,* 23, 24, and 25 October 1962. On British press opinion, also see *Washington Post,* 30 October 1962, p. A-8.

[67] Roger Hilsman, "Trading US Missile Bases in Turkey for Soviet Bases in Cuba," 27 October 1962, NSF, Box 36, JFKL.

[68] *New York Times,* 28 October 1962, p. 31. The Norwegian officials approved the Soviet-proposed deal only if removal of the Jupiters would not strategically impair NATO's defenses. Probably they knew that this criterion was clearly met, for the issue was psychological and political, not strategic.

Cuba seemed imminent, Premier Amintore Fanfani of the Christian Democrats wanted Kennedy to extend his deadline and probably favored the trade of Turkey's Jupiters. The Italian Socialist party, upon which the uneasy government coalition depended, had condemned the quarantine and probably welcomed the trade to end the crisis.[69]

In Canada, Prime Minister John Diefenbaker, long unhappy about U.S. dominance, was publicly tactful but privately critical of the president's actions. So troubled was Diefenbaker by Kennedy's unilateral decisions during the crisis and so fearful that Canada might be dragged into war that he barred U.S. Strategic Air Command bombers from the use of Canadian airfields during the crisis.[70] His devout hope was that war could be avoided, and he did not seem to fear that concessions—and certainly not on the Jupiters—would seriously weaken the NATO alliance.

On Thursday, October 25, Andrew de Staercke, the Belgian ambassador to NATO, privately proposed the deal that the Soviets demanded two days later. He thought, wrote Cyrus Sulzberger, "we [U.S.] should take the initiative in making such an offer." The bases were obsolete, the ambassador argued and he did not see how the Russians would withdraw their weapons unless the United States reciprocated.[71] He apparently was not worried about the loss of prestige to the United States or the impact on NATO and seemed to believe that these matters were less important than a settlement. Unlike de Staercke, and presumably the Belgian government, Dutch governments privately opposed a trade on the grounds that it would undermine NATO's morale.[72] But Greek officials, while publicly discreet, seemed to lean toward de Staercke's analysis. When the Soviets

[69] William Brubeck [through Bundy] to Schlesinger, Jr., "Italy's Center-Left Government and the Cuban Crisis," 20 November 1962, with attachment of same title, 26 November 1962, NSF, Countries: Cuba, JFKL; compare Hilsman, "Trading US Missile Bases in Turkey."

[70] Robert Redford, *Canada and Three Crises* (Lindsay, Ontario: John Deyell, 1968), pp. 184–85; Peyton V. Lyon, *Canada in World Affairs* (Toronto: Oxford University Press, 1968), pp. 43, 53–55.

[71] Sulzberger, *Last of the Giants*, pp. 921–92.

[72] *New York Times*, 28 October 1962, p. 31. The Dutch, because of their role as a sea power, were very troubled by the blockade (Manchester *Guardian*, 24 October 1962, p. 15).

demanded removal of the Jupiters, Greek officials privately indicated that this was an acceptable solution. "Compromise can be the only way out," one government official explained.[73]

In some important Latin American nations, despite their public statements supporting Kennedy, there was probably strong sentiments for a compromise involving the Jupiters, in either a public or private deal. The U.S. government did win unanimous support for the quarantine from the Organization of American States (OAS), but that unanimity was secured, in at least a few cases, by some deft coercion. The main item on the OAS agenda was U.S. economic aid, and Washington first moved for a vote of support for the quarantine. The American message was clear: Aid could depend upon an affirmative vote.[74] Even then, some governments—including Brazil, Mexico, Bolivia, and Uruguay—feared providing full support for Kennedy's actions, as the State Department knew at the time.[75] Hostile to U.S. military intervention in Latin America, many governments there also worried about the backlash in their own countries from radical groups if the United States attacked Cuba. A trade, even a public one, for the Jupiters was attractive if an invasion was the alternative.

The United States' complex alliance systems did rest partly upon faith in its credibility, but many governments also feared

[73] *New York Times,* 28 October 1962, p. 31. Significantly, the NATO Council never *officially* broke ranks to support the trade of the Jupiters over American objections, and the council actually endorsed JFK's *public* position (Finletter to Secretary of State, Polto 512, 28 October 1962, NSF,RSF:NATO-Weapons, JFKL).

[74] Ronald Hilton, "A Note on Latin America," *Council for Correspondence Newsletter,* no. 21, October 1962, pp. 42–44. Also see Manchester *Guardian,* 24 October 1962, p. 15, and *Times* (London), 27 October 1962, p. 8.

[75] These four nations did not support an OAS resolution to allow the use of force to remove the missiles (*Washington Post,* 24 October 1962, p. A-1). For other evidence on negative Latin American attitudes, see, Rusk to Embassy, Rio De Janeiro, 30 October 1962, VP Security File: Cuba, folder III, LBJL; CIA, "The Crisis: USSR/Cuba," 24, 27, and 28 October 1962; and *Hispanic American Report* (Stanford, Calif.) 15 (October 1962), pp. 943–44, 957, 964, 1064. Obviously, an analysis of the likely impact of an American deal might also consider the Central Treaty Organization (CENTO) (which included Turkey but not the United States) and the South East Asia Treaty Organization (SEATO), but the declassified documents reveal almost no specific attention to these two alliances. CIA, "The Crisis: USSR/Cuba," 27 October 1962, noted that two CENTO members—Iran and Pakistan—"have been slow to come out with solid public support of United States action."

that efforts to affirm credibility could be rash and dangerous. They did not usually expect the United States to maintain blind allegiance, and, as the history of recent American foreign relations demonstrated, discretion, tempered force, and the willingness to compromise were also essential to operating the far-flung alliances.

The Saturday Crisis

Saturday was the most painful day of the crisis. For the Ex-Comm and the president, there were no easy answers. Should America bomb the SAM site in Cuba, as the ExComm had previously planned, if a U-2 was shot down? Should the administration yield to the additional demand of exchanging the Jupiters to settle the crisis? The minutes for Saturday's three sessions reveal that the Ex-Comm easily disposed of the first question and devoted agonizing attention to the second.

Some advisers wanted to arrange a way of pulling out the Jupiters without making a clear trade. A trade would injure Turkey, NATO, and the United States, according to their analysis. Was there some way of inducing Turkey to suggest withdrawal of the weapons? Or of placing their withdrawal in some broad context of disarmament? At various points, President Kennedy indicated that he did not want to yield to Soviet pressure but that he would favor some cosmetic arrangement to get rid of the Jupiters in order to settle the crisis. At a few points, he seemed desperate and prepared to countenance a trade. Work on the Soviet missile sites in Cuba must soon stop, Kennedy periodically emphasized, and his lingering implication was that an American attack on Cuba might otherwise become necessary in the next few days.

At times in the Saturday meetings, some ExComm members urged an attack—possibly first on the SAM sites and then on the MRBM and IRBM sites, to be followed by an invasion. Such counsel raised profound questions: Would the Soviet Union then respond against Berlin or elsewhere? Would not NATO and especially Turkey become Soviet targets? Could all-out war then be avoided? An anxious group of men, hardly more than a dozen, assessed actions that might lead to war or peace. And the president, listening to their counsel and trying out his own notions, ultimately had the constitutional and actual power of decision. The vigorous disputes over strategy left him *reasonably* free to choose. In the ExComm, he never faced a monolith, only shifting majorities. He could move toward peace or war. But if he chose the route of concessions, he would risk antagonizing the military chiefs, who were not his natural allies.[76]

At first, according to the minutes of the morning meeting, the opponents of a trade of the missiles came to the fore. Assistant Secretary of Defense Paul Nitze, an ardent cold warrior dating back to the Truman years, forcefully objected to the Soviet proposal: "It would be anathema to the Turks to pull the missiles out. . . . the next Soviet step would be a demand for denuclearization of the entire NATO area." Concessions would only beget demands for more concessions. Where would the United States draw the line? Why should allies trust American promises? Both Rusk and Bundy also resisted the trade, with Bundy stressing, according to the minutes, "we cannot get into the position of appearing to sell out an ally . . . to serve our own interests, i.e., getting the Soviet missiles out of Cuba."[77]

President Kennedy regretted, as the minutes put it, that "the Russians had made the Turkish proposal in the most difficult possible way." Now, he said, because their demand is public "we would have no chance to talk privately to the Turks about the missiles." He favored removing the weapons but did not want to appear to be yielding to a Soviet demand, lest he lose prestige and credibility, injure Turkey and NATO, and give the Soviets a public victory.[78] Could the crisis be settled without risking some American, and presidential, credibility and prestige?

The suggested trade of forty-two Soviet MRBMs (represent-

[76] For JFK's fears of the military, see Paul Fay, *The Pleasure of His Company* (New York: Harper & Row, 1966), pp. 189–190.

[77] "Summary Record, ExComm, No. 7, Oct. 27, 1962, 10:00 A.M."

[78] Ibid.

ing one-third of the entire Soviet strategic arsenal) for fifteen obsolete Jupiters was attractive on military grounds, Kennedy acknowledged. How, he worried, could he "justify risking nuclear war in Cuba and Berlin over missiles in Turkey which are of little military value?" It would even be hard to get political support for such a position, he acknowledged. Yet, he thought, there might be a way out: "We cannot propose to withdraw the missiles, . . . but the Turks could offer to do so. [They] must be informed of the great danger . . . and we have to face up to the possibility of some kind of a trade over the missiles."[79]

The minutes of the morning meeting, like those for later in the day, reveal a sense of desperation, a fear that events were hurtling beyond control, that action was restricted to unpalatable alternatives, and that an attack on the missile sites in Cuba might soon be necessary. Even though the forty-two MRBMs (and even with the addition of twelve or thirty-six IRBMs) did not alter the strategic balance or militarily imperil the United States, no ExComm member (so far as the minutes disclose) challenged the dominating assumption: the United States could not dally more than a few days.[80] But if the work on the sites ceased, Kennedy noted, "we could talk to the Russians."[81]

The two-hour morning meeting ended with agreement on a brief public reply to Khrushchev's demand. The White House statement, widely interpreted in the press as an outright rejection, was actually more subtle and elusive.[82] It left the door open for some future agreement on the Jupiters but never specifically mentioned them. It sidestepped the Soviet demand, asserted that negotiations were impossible until work stopped on the missile sites and they were rendered inoperative, declared that the current crisis in Cuba and European security could not be linked, but mentioned the possibility of postsettlement discussions on arms limitation in Europe, and thus hinted

[79] Ibid.

[80] Sorensen, memorandum, 17 October 1962, POF 115, JFKL; Bernstein, "Week We Almost Went to War," pp. 16–20.

[81] "Summary Record, ExComm, No. 7, Oct. 27, 1962, 10:00 A.M."

[82] White House press release, 27 October 1962. The statement was similar to Stevenson's proposal. (MVF [Forrestal] to President, 27 October 1962, NSF, Countries: Cuba, JFKL).

at a willingness to consider removal of the Jupiters after the resolution of the crisis.[83]

That afternoon, a small, weary group met at the State Department to prepare the president's formal reply to Khrushchev. The strategy was to disregard the most recent Soviet message (dismantling the missiles in Turkey) and accept the Friday suggestion: withdrawal of the Soviet missiles and on-site inspection in return for termination of the quarantine and a pledge not to attack Cuba.[84]

When the ExComm reconvened at 4 P.M., the president revised the draft to stress his offer to discuss, after the resolution of the crisis, the reduction of general tensions, a halt to the arms race, and a détente between NATO and the Warsaw Pact countries. As the minutes indicate, this section was designed as an oblique way of offering to discuss withdrawal of the Jupiters later without specifying them and thus avoiding angering the Turks and appearing weak. According to the minutes, Kennedy "felt that we would not be in a position to offer any trade for several days . . . if we could succeed in freezing the situation in Cuba and rendering the strategic missiles inoperable, then we would be in a position to negotiate with the Russians." When Bundy, who still opposed the trade, warned of a backlash in NATO countries, "the president responded that if we refuse to discuss such a trade and then take military action in Cuba, we would also be in a difficult position."[85]

It was a tortuous, three-hour meeting. The discussion rambled. Like broken shuttlecocks, the proposals ranged widely. Often mixing proposals, ExComm members considered attacking Cuba, or convening a special NATO meeting, or outrightly rejecting the Turkey-Cuba missile trade, and even disarming the Jupiters and then attacking Cuba. In calling for a NATO meeting on Sunday, President Kennedy wavered between supporting a bid for peace and opting for a course toward

[83] "Summary Record, ExComm, No. 7, Oct. 27, 1962, 10:00 A.M." and Bundy, "NSC Executive Committee Record of Action, Oct. 27, 1962, 10:00 A.M." both reveal that the statement was approved at the morning session.

[84] "Summary Record, ExComm, No. 8, Oct. 27, 1962, 4:00 P.M."

[85] Ibid.

war. "If the Russians do attack the NATO countries," Kennedy explained on one occasion, "we do not want them to say that they had not been consulted about the actions we were taking." Toward the end of the session, he returned to his earlier theme: persuading the Turks "to suggest to us that we withdraw our missiles."[86] That would not be easy, he acknowledged, since they had just issued a statement sharply rejecting the Soviet demand for an explicit trade.

Probably in the last thirty minutes of the meeting, the Joint Chiefs of Staff, presumably McNamara, and some others offered a zany solution: defuse the Jupiters in Turkey, inform the Soviets, and then attack Cuba.[87] That plot is outlined in part of a chilling draft message to NATO: "Wishing to minimize the possibility of . . . an attack upon Turkey, and possibly upon other NATO countries, the United States is willing, if the other members of NATO so desire, to render the Jupiter missiles . . . inoperative . . . and [thus] to notify the Soviet Government before moving against the Soviet missiles in Cuba."[88] The theory seemed to be that dismantling the Jupiters would meet part of the Soviet demand for a trade, emphasize that Kennedy was trying to restrict military activities to this hemisphere, reduce Soviet anger and fear, and probably protect Turkey and NATO from reprisals. The attack would remove the Soviet missiles and pay a bonus: elimination of Castro ("the bone in our throat"). The obvious liability was that the attack might kill 15,000–20,000 Soviets and thus compel the Soviets to retaliate—probably in Europe. As a majority in the ExComm

[86] Ibid.

[87] Robert McElroy interview with Donald Wilson, 18 December 1974 (copy of transcript in my possession); Wilson to Bernstein, 20 February 1979. Both Sorensen and Bundy denied any knowledge of the plan, and Sorensen implied that ExComm had never considered it (McElroy interviews with Sorensen, 18 December 1974, and Bundy, 27 February 1975; Bernstein interview with Bundy, 31 July 1979; compare Sorensen, *The Kennedy Legacy* [New York: Macmillan Co., 1969] p. 190.) Because the minutes have been "sanitized," one cannot be sure of McNamara's position ("Summary Record, ExComm, No. 8, Oct. 27, 1962, 4:00 P.M."). Because of his presidency of the World Bank, he will not discuss American policy in which he participated (McNamara to Bernstein, 6 August 1979).

[88] "Message to the North Atlantic Council and the Governments of all NATO Countries," [27 October 1962], NSF, Countries: Cuba, Box 36, JFKL.

seemed to be shifting to this plot, the president adjourned the meeting.[89]

At least a few lingered in the room to discuss the bizarre course of the meeting. According to the minutes, Vice-President Lyndon B. Johnson asked, "Why were [we] not prepared to [accept the Soviet trade] if we were prepared to give up the use of U.S. missiles in Turkey?" The arguments of maintaining credibility, of keeping faith with NATO, of meeting obligations to Turkey did not seem to impress him. His chief aim was peace. Undersecretary Ball agreed, noting "that last week we thought it might be acceptable to trade the withdrawal of the missiles in Turkey if such action would save Cuba." Why not now? he asked. Accept the Soviet terms, he suggested, and replace the Jupiters with a Polaris sub.[90]

When the ExComm met for an hour that evening at 9 P.M., the advisers talked of an invasion of Cuba, planned ways of adding pressure on the Soviets, prepared for a NATO meeting on Sunday, and again discussed the Turkey-Cuba missile trade. Kennedy decided to activate twenty-four air reserve squadrons (14,000 men) in preparation for the invasion and to frighten the Soviets. If any more surveillance planes were fired on over Cuba, Kennedy decided that "we should take out the SAM sites by [bombing them]."[91]

The group agreed not to raise with Turkish officials the question of withdrawing the Jupiters and instructed Ambassador Finletter to inform NATO that an American attack on Cuba was near but that the president still hoped that the crisis could be settled "within the framework of the Western Hemisphere." Finletter was directed to warn NATO delegates that an American attack might unleash a Soviet attack against their nations, but to encourage free expression, while reminding

[89] Sorensen, *The Kennedy Legacy*, p. 190; McElroy interview with Wilson, 18 December 1974. Robert Kennedy states that the president ordered the Jupiters defused "so that he personally would have to give permission before they were used" (Kennedy, *Thirteen Days*, p. 98).

[90] "Summary Record, ExComm, No. 8, Oct. 27, 1962, 4:00 P.M." On Johnson, also see handwritten notes, item 143A [probably Oct. 27], VP Security File: Cuba, folder V, LBJL.

[91] "Summary Record, ExComm, No. 9, Oct. 27, 1962, 9:00 P.M."

them that elimination of the missiles in Cuba was essential to maintaining NATO's strategic strength (not just the United States's). Finletter was instructed not to "hint of any readiness to meet [the] Soviet Jupiter proposal."[92]

Given the fears of some NATO allies, did not these instructions encourage them to push for a compromise? Had the ExComm devised tactics to lead NATO to suggest acceptance of the Turkey-Cuba missile exchange? Or was the ExComm sincerely willing to be further limited if NATO made a different recommendation and even opposed the trade? Perhaps the answer is that approval of a public trade would have enabled the administration to yield with dignity ("for the sake of allies upon their request") but opposition would not have blocked a secret deal.[93]

War seemed near. Shortly after midnight, Kennedy sent special messages to Adenauer and de Gaulle: "The situation is clearly growing more tense and if satisfactory responses are not received from the other side in forty-eight hours, the situation is likely to enter a progressively military phase."[94] The hedged implication: invasion of Cuba on Tuesday. Adenauer loyally supported Kennedy, but de Gaulle, having retreated into privacy until the French voters cast their ballots, refused to see the American ambassador. Even with war near, the French leader, ever disdainful, would not modify his ways and thus reinforced, at least for himself, his sense of olympian superiority.[95]

What neither the NATO delegates nor the United States's chief European allies could know was that Kennedy was still mulling over a trade. Toward the close of the Saturday night meeting, according to the minutes, the attorney general summarized the strategy: "We would . . . hold off one more day a decision on accepting the Turkish/Cuban missile trade offer of

[92] Rusk (drafted by Bundy and U.A. Johnson) to Finletter (with copies to U.S. ambassadors to all NATO nations), 28 October 1962, NSF, JFKL.

[93] Finletter to Secretary of State, Polto 512, 28 October 1962, NSF, JFKL.

[94] President to Bohlen, 28 October 1962, and President to Dowling, 28 October 1962, VP Security File: Cuba, folder VI, LBJL.

[95] Bohlen to Secretary of State, Nos. 1975 and 1976, 28 October 1962, VP Security File: Cuba, folder VI, LBJL.

the Soviets."[96] Then what? Was there any significance that the taker of minutes had not cast the matter in the negative: We will delay on *rejecting* the offer?

So far, this discussion has omitted one important set of events that evening: Robert Kennedy's secret meeting with Soviet ambassador Anatoly Dobrynin, at 7:45 P.M., before the evening session of the ExComm. Acting on the instructions of the president and Secretary Rusk, the attorney general invited Dobrynin to a private meeting at the Justice Department. Two points seem reasonably clear: the attorney general delivered both a virtual ultimatum and a loose private promise. According to his memoir, the ultimatum was: "if the [Soviets] did not remove those [missiles], we would remove them."[97] And in response to Dobrynin's question about America's withdrawing the Jupiters from Turkey, according to Robert Kennedy's secret memorandum and confirmed by his memoir: "there could be no quid pro quo—no deal of this kind could be made [on removal of the Jupiters]. It was up to NATO to make the decision. I said it was completely impossible for NATO to take such a step under the present threatening position. . . . If some time elapsed—and per . . . instructions—I said I was sure that these matters could be resolved satisfactorily."[98]

To frighten the Soviets, the attorney general may have dramatized the pressures on the president to invade Cuba. According to Khrushchev's first memoir in 1970, the meeting with Dobrynin, based on the ambassador's report, went, in Khrushchev's own words, "something like this: Robert Kennedy looked exhausted [and said], 'The President is in a grave situation, and he does not know how to get out of it. We are under very severe stress. In fact we are under pressure from our military to use force against Cuba. . . . an irreversible chain of events could occur against his will.' " And, still according to

[96] "Summary Record, ExComm, No. 9, Oct. 27, 1962, 9:00 P.M."
[97] Kennedy, *Thirteen Days*, pp. 107–08.
[98] Robert Kennedy to Dean Rusk, 30 October 1962, quoted in Schlesinger, *Robert F. Kennedy*, p. 522; and Kennedy, *Thirteen Days*, 108–09; compare, O'Donnell and Powers, *"Johnny, We Hardly Knew Ye,"* pp. 337–39. Robert Kennedy actually implied removal also of the thirty missiles from Italy (Kennedy, *Thirteen Days*, p. 109).

Khrushchev, the attorney general also warned: "If the situation continues much longer, the President is not sure that the military will not overthrow him and seize power."[99]

Probably this last theme (fear of military overthrow) was Khrushchev's or Dobrynin's embroidery, or perhaps one or the other misunderstood why Kennedy felt under pressure from the military to act.[100] This theme, published well after the end of the crisis, also had another advantage: It allowed Khrushchev to present himself as a man of peace—a leader who had rescued Kennedy from his bellicose generals and admirals—and thus to obscure his acquiescence in response to a virtual ultimatum.

WHAT IF THE SOVIETS HAD NOT YIELDED?

After Robert Kennedy delivered his virtual ultimatum and loose pledge, painful questions lingered for the Kennedy brothers that Saturday night and through the dawn of Sunday: Would Khrushchev and his associates accept this hedged, private offer (of future withdrawal of Jupiters) when the Soviets had demanded a firm public pledge?

For the Soviets, as the Kennedys understood, there were difficult questions: Why should the Soviets rely upon Kennedy's and NATO's future approval? Turkey had opposed withdrawal in the past. Why not again? Would the United States

[99] Nikita Khrushchev, *Khrushchev Remembers,* trans. Strobe Talbott (Boston, Mass.: Little, Brown, 1970), pp. 497–98; compare, idem., *Khrushchev Remembers: The Last Testament,* trans. Strobe Talbott (Boston, Mass.: Little, Brown, 1974), pp. 509–14. Also see Anatoly Gromyko, "U.S. Manipulations Leading to Cuban Missile Crisis," in *USSR International Affairs* (FBIS) (7 September 1971): G6–7. Gromyko's article, which originally appeared in *Voprosy Istorii* [Problems of history] 8 (August 1971), cites *Thirteen Days* as the source but calls Kennedy's agreement to remove the Jupiters from Turkey and Italy "a specific promise." Khrushchev makes the same claim (*The Last Testament,* p. 512), as does Anatoly Gromyko. "The Caribbean Crisis," in *Mezhdunarodnye konflikty* [International conflicts], eds. V.V. Zhurkin and Ye.M. Primakov (Moscow: Institute of World Economics and International Relations and the Institute of USA Studies, 1972), pp. 70–95. (This is available in translation from the Joint Publications Research which is published by the U.S. Department of Commerce. Office of Technical Services, Washington, D.C.)

[100] For disconcerting evidence suggesting that the president *might* have had fears, see Fay, *Pleasure of His Company,* pp. 189–90.

coerce Turkish officials if they were recalcitrant? Moreover, since the main value of the removal of the Jupiters for the Soviets was symbolic, what would be the value of this private, hedged promise? Would it give Khrushchev even a small victory in the Soviet hierarchy? Certainly, it could not help him save face internationally, since no one would know of the deal. Publicly, he was still confronting a clear American demand: back down and face public humiliation; or delay, have Cuba attacked and Soviet soldiers killed, and then back down or escalate. Ultimately, the choices were retreat or escalation.

What would Kennedy have done in Khrushchev's place? Critics of the missile crisis have stressed JFK's fears of an electoral and bureaucratic backlash and also his own lust for combat and victory.[101] In view of these needs and pressures, would he have backed down on Sunday, October 28, or at any time, if their roles had been reversed? Probably not. Did he expect Khrushchev to do so? In his memoir, Robert Kennedy states: "The President was not optimistic nor was I. [We had] a hope, not an expectation [that Khrushchev would retreat]."[102]

If Khrushchev had not retreated, what would the president have done? A few of the memoirists, Robert Kennedy included, have asserted that the United States would soon have attacked Cuba.[103] Can the memoirists be trusted on such a matter? Or were they reaffirming credibility after the fact to prove the president's (and possibly their own) toughness? After all, Robert Kennedy, after his meeting with Dobrynin, had summarized the administration's position late Saturday night: Delay a decision one more day *on accepting* the Turkish-Cuba missile deal. Does that frail evidence indicate that President Kennedy would have offered a *public* pledge in order to avoid the attack?

101 Bernstein, "The Cuban Missile Crisis"; and Steel, "End Game."

102 Kennedy, *Thirteen Days,* p. 109.

103 Ibid. Schlesinger, *A Thousand Days,* p. 830; compare, Sorensen, *Kennedy,* pp. 715–16. Alexander George, "The Cuban Missile Crisis," in *The Limits of Coercive Diplomacy,* Alexander George et al. (Boston, Mass.: Little, Brown, 1971), pp. 126–31, doubts that the president would have attacked Cuba without first trying other tactics. Chayes, *Cuban Missile Crisis,* p. 100, leans in this direction.

Such a pledge would have been painful for him. It might have denied him the appearance of victory and even confirmed that the Soviet deployment was analagous to the installation of the missiles in Turkey. Would that have made the quarantine of Cuba appear reckless? Perhaps. Certainly the hawks, especially in the Pentagon and CIA, would have been embittered.[104] They would have tried to thwart his future policy. The Republican party would have condemned him for "selling out" United States and NATO interests.[105] His party might have suffered a sharp setback in the November congressional elections. That electoral defeat would have imperiled his foreign policy and further emboldened the hawks in the bureaucracy.

The United State's—and Kennedy's—international prestige and credibility would have been somewhat weakened, at least briefly, even though some NATO governments would have endorsed the settlement. Kennedy could have blunted some of the criticism at home and abroad by encouraging European allies to support the trade publicly. He might have called upon Latin American powers for similar assistance. There were also other ways of shoring up that prestige and credibility: for example, a public announcement a few days or weeks later that a Polaris submarine would replace the Jupiters. That act would not have violated the agreement with Khrushchev, but it might have punctured charges that Kennedy had made a great concession. In fact, in April 1963, when the administration quietly withdrew the Jupiters from Turkey,[106] it did send a Polaris submarine to the area.

[104] See Hilsman, letter, *New York Review of Books,* 9 May 1979, pp. 36–37.

[105] *New York Times,* 28 October 1962, p. 24; Sorensen, "G.O.P. Charges that," 28 October 1962, Box 41, Sorensen Papers. On later Soviet-American difficulties, see Bernstein, "Kennedy and Ending the Missile Crisis: Bombers, Inspection, and the No Invasion Pledge," *Foreign Service Journal* 56 (July 1979):8–12.

[106] McNamara to President, 25 April 1963, POF 115, JFKL, informed Kennedy that "the last Jupiter missile came down yesterday" and that it would be flown out at the end of the week. On the administration's earlier (October 29) commitment to removal, see Chayes, *Cuban Missile Crisis,* p. 98, n. 52.

On October 29, the State Department informed Ambassadors Hare and Finletter that they could assure embassies that "no 'deal' of any kind was made involving Turkey" (Rusk to Embassy, Ankara and Paris, 29 October 1962, NSF, RSF: NATO-Weapons, JFKL). In 1963, McNamara told the House Appropriations Committee, "without any qualifications whatsoever there was absolutely

Still, the unanswerable questions linger: What would Kennedy have done? Would he have risked appearing weak? Was he strong and brave enough? Could he have escaped the "credibility trap"? Or would he have succumbed to the expectations of voters, to the needs of his party and the foreign policy he hoped to pursue, and to the demands of hawks in the bureaucracy? How free did he feel to choose the path of public concession?*

THOMAS G. PATERSON AND WILLIAM J. BROPHY

The Political Dimension

Two scholars have offered the fullest analysis of the role of domestic politics in influencing Kennedy's handling of the Cuban missile crisis. Thomas G. Paterson, an historian at the University of Connecticut best known for his studies of the origins of the Cold War, and William G. Brophy, an historian at Stephen F. Austin State University in Texas, deal with two central issues. The first is the degree to which partisan political considerations entered into the deliberations of the Kennedy administration and influenced the final choice of policy. Their other major concern is with the political consequences of the crisis, especially the question of whether or not Kennedy's diplomatic victory affected the outcome of the congressional elections.

---

no deal, as it might be called, between the Soviet Union and the United States regarding the removal of the Jupiter weapons from either Italy or Turkey" (U.S., Department of Defense, *Appropriations for 1964,* 88th Cong., 1st sess., 1963, pt. I, 57).

*The author expresses his gratitude to Alexander George for his criticism and counsel and to the Stanford University Arms Control and Disarmament Program for assistance.

Paterson, Thomas G. and Brophy, William J., "October Missiles and November Elections: The Cuban Missile Crisis and American Politics, 1962," *Journal of American History,* 73 (June 1986), 87–119. Copyright Organization of American Historians, 1986. Reprinted by permission.

"I TOLD YOU that the President would move on Cuba before [the] election," Sen. Norris Cotton of New Hampshire reminded his constituents a week after President John F. Kennedy had dramatically announced that the United States was imposing a quarantine against Cuba to force Soviet missiles from the Caribbean island. Another Republican standing for reelection in 1962, Rep. Thomas B. Curtis of Missouri, told voters in his district that the Cuban missile crisis was "phony and contrived for election purposes." Republican Sen. Barry Goldwater of Arizona, like many others, suspected that the Kennedy administration had played politics with foreign policy to help Democrats in the congressional elections of November 6.[1]

The claim—and fear—that presidents play politics with foreign policy, especially in electoral seasons, is familiar and often well founded. Throughout American history, suspicions have flourished that presidents take unusual and sometimes extreme diplomatic or military steps, utter hyperboles, practice deceit, or manufacture foreign crises to improve their own and their party's chances at the polls. Like political leaders before him Kennedy had invited imputations that he exploited foreign-policy issues for political gain or that he made diplomatic decisions in response to domestic political pressure. Indeed, about a month before the missile crisis, Kennedy had made a conspicuous political decision in foreign affairs: to sell Hawk missiles to Israel. American Jews had lobbied intensely for the sale; some of them had even withheld contributions from congressional candidates until they saw Kennedy act on the deal. The sale of those short-range missiles, the administration ex-

[1] Press Release, Oct. 30, 1962, Norris Cotton Papers (University of New Hampshire Library, Durham); Thomas B. Curtis to Thomas G. Paterson, Jan. 6, 1984 (in Paterson's possession); *New York Times*, Oct. 23, 1962, pp. 1, 8; *ibid.*, Oct. 24, 1962, p. 16; *ibid.*, Oct. 27, 1962, p. 7; *ibid.*, Sept. 10, 1964, p. 17. See also F. Clifton White, *Suite 3505: The Story of the Draft Goldwater Movement* (New Rochelle, 1967), 82; and Frank S. Meyer, "The 1962 Elections: The Turning of the Tide," *National Review*, Dec. 4, 1962, p. 434. Many congressional manuscript collections contain letters from constituents who charged John F. Kennedy with political gamesmanship in his handling of the missile crisis. See, for example, the letters in box 145, Milton R. Young Papers (University of North Dakota Library, Grand Forks).

plained at the time, was designed to balance Communist weapons shipments to Egypt, Iraq, and Syria. But "the reason it was done was politics," the United States ambassador to Egypt, John S. Badeau, later concluded.[2]

Politics certainly preoccupied Kennedy in the fall of 1962. The president and his aides eagerly looked to the forthcoming elections to produce a more sympathetic Congress. To be sure, the Democrats controlled the Senate 65–35 and the House of Representatives 263–174. Yet the Democratic administration could never count on a working majority for its domestic proposals. House committees were chaired by conservative southerners; and in the Senate, Republicans and southern Democrats often teamed up to thwart Kennedy's requests. Medicare failed by a 52 to 48 vote; the farm bill lost by five votes in the House. In 1961 only 48.4 percent of Kennedy's legislative initiatives gained approval; in 1962, 44.6 percent. Democratic gains or the prevention of losses in the 1962 elections, then, promised to ease or at least not to aggravate Kennedy's struggle with Congress. Even more, as Sen. J. William Fulbright (Democrat from Arkansas) privately remarked: "If he doesn't get them [Congress] in hand and cooperating, his regime will be a failure."[3]

Some historians and political scientists have also thought that the president was driven in the Cuban missile crisis as much by political motives as by considerations of national

[2] John S. Badeau, *The Middle East Remembered* (Washington, 1983), 176; *New York Times,* Sept. 27, 1962, pp. 1, 3. For other arguments that Kennedy made key decisions in part to avoid or deflect Republican criticism, see Stephen Pelz, "John F. Kennedy's 1961 Vietnam War Decisions," *Journal of Strategic Studies,* 4 (Dec. 1981), 356–85; and Lucien S. Vandenbroucke, "Anatomy of a Failure: The Decision to Land at the Bay of Pigs," *Political Science Quarterly,* 99 (Fall 1984), 484–85. For Richard M. Nixon's charge that Kennedy exploited the Cuban issue for political gain in 1960, see Richard M. Nixon, *Six Crises* (New York, 1968), 379–84; and Kent M. Beck, "Necessary Lies, Hidden Truths: Cuba in the 1960 Campaign," *Diplomatic History,* 8 (Winter 1984), 37–59.

[3] Lewis J. Paper, *John F. Kennedy: The Promise and the Performance* (New York, 1979), 275; Theodore C. Sorensen, *Kennedy* (New York, 1965), 339–49; Arthur M. Schlesinger, Jr., *A Thousand Days: John F. Kennedy in the White House* (Boston, 1965), 708–709; Herbert Matthews, Memorandum of Conversation with J. William Fulbright, July 3, 1962, box 27, Herbert Matthews Papers (Butler Library, Columbia University, New York, N.Y.).

security or prestige. James A. Nathan, Barton J. Bernstein, and others have suggested that Kennedy boldly confronted the Soviets and initially eschewed quiet diplomacy to resolve the conflict because a forthright, public display of toughness would disarm Republicans who had been lambasting the administration over Cuba and would improve Democratic chances in the congressional elections and because private talks could not be kept secret—leaks would be inevitable and politically damaging to the administration. Kennedy partisans such as Theodore C. Sorensen and Arthur M. Schlesinger, Jr., in contrast, have downplayed or discounted politics in their accounts of presidential decision making during the crisis. But even they have noted a linkage between the election results and the crisis. Another Kennedy appointee, Roger Hilsman of the Department of State, has been frank in recalling that "behind the policy choices loomed domestic politics." Indeed, "the United States might not [have been] in mortal danger but the administration most certainly was." But Hilsman's memoir nonetheless stressed questions of strategy and international prestige over domestic politics, and he later explained that by "domestic politics" he meant, not the forthcoming elections specifically, but general bureaucratic politics within the administration and relations with Congress. Other writers have found a coincidence between the crisis and the congressional elections, but they have not investigated the relationship. Soviet works on the subject have found Kennedy's behavior rooted in United States intentions to crush the Cuban Revolution, not in American politics.[4]

[4]James A. Nathan, "The Missile Crisis: His Finest Hour Now," *World Politics,* 27 (Jan. 1975), 262–65; Barton J. Bernstein, "The Cuban Missile Crisis," in *Reflections on the Cold War: A Quarter Century of American Foreign Policy,* ed. Lynn H. Miller and Ronald Pruessen (Philadelphia, 1974), 131–33; Barton J. Bernstein, "Was the Cuban Missile Crisis Necessary?" *Washington Post,* Oct. 26, 1975, p. D1; Barton J. Bernstein, "The Week We Almost Went to War," *Bulletin of the Atomic Scientists,* 32 (Feb. 1976), 17; Barton J. Bernstein, "The Cuban Missile Crisis: Trading the Jupiters in Turkey?" *Political Science Quarterly,* 95 (Spring 1980), 124; Ronald Steel, "Endgame," *New York Review of Books,* March 13, 1969, p. 15; I.F. Stone, "The Brink," *ibid.,* April 14, 1966, pp. 13–14; Richard J. Walton, *Cold War and Counterrevolution: The Foreign Policy of John F. Kennedy* (New York, 1972), 103–104, 130; Louise FitzSimons, *The Kennedy Doctrine* (New York, 1972),

Scholars cannot now be definitive about the relationship between politics and the Cuban missile crisis. Some documents remain unavailable to researchers, and participants kept no records of some conversations during the crisis.[5] Presidents, moreover, necessarily make decisions that derive from a complex mix of private thoughts and public pressures that the historian cannot easily untangle. And American voters are usually influenced by many issues—some personal, some local,

---

169–72; Fen Osler Hampson, "The Divided Decision-Maker: American Domestic Politics and the Cuban Crisis," *International Security,* 9 (Winter 1984–85), 130–65. Arthur M. Schlesinger, Jr., wrote that "it is hard to estimate the impact of the Cuba week on the election, though foreign crisis usually strengthens the administration in office." Schlesinger, *Thousand Days,* 794–833, esp. 832–33. Theodore C. Sorensen commented that the Democrats did well in 1962 through hard work "aided to an undeterminable extent by [Kennedy's] handling of the crisis." Sorensen, *Kennedy,* 354, 667–722. See also Theodore C. Sorensen, *The Kennedy Legacy* (New York, 1969), 187–91; Arthur M. Schlesinger, Jr., *Robert Kennedy and His Times* (Boston, 1978), 512–13, 517, 530; Kenneth P. O'Donnell and David F. Powers with Joe McCarthy. *"Johnny We Hardly Knew Ye": Memories of John Fitzgerald Kennedy* (Boston, 1972), 307–43; and Henry M. Pachter, *Collision Course: The Cuban Missile Crisis and Coexistence* (New York, 1963), 18–20. For Roger Hilsman's perspective see Roger Hilsman, *To Move a Nation: The Politics of Foreign Policy in the Administration of John F. Kennedy* (Garden City, 1967), 176, 196–97; and Roger Hilsman and Ronald Steel, "An Exchange of Views," *New York Review of Books,* May 8, 1969, pp. 36–38. Other writers' accounts include, for example, Herbert S. Dinerstein, *The Making of a Missile Crisis: October 1962* (Baltimore, 1976), 185–90; Graham T. Allison, *Essence of Decision: Explaining the Cuban Missile Crisis* (Boston, 1971), 187–89; David Detzer, *The Brink: The Story of the Cuban Missile Crisis, 1962* (New York, 1979); Herbert S. Parmet, *JFK: The Presidency of John F. Kennedy* (New York, 1983), 277–300; Richard N. Lebow, "The Cuban Missile Crisis: Reading the Lessons Correctly," *Political Science Quarterly,* 98 (Fall 1983), 443–45; Elie Abel, *The Missile Crisis* (Philadelphia, 1966), 56–57, 78; and Marc Trachtenberg, "The Influence of Nuclear Weapons in the Cuban Missile Crisis," *International Security,* 10 (Summer 1985), 162. For Soviet views, see Anatolii A. Gromyko, "The Caribbean Crisis," *Soviet Law and Government,* 11 (1972), 3–53; Anatolii A. Gromyko, *Through Russian Eyes: President Kennedy's 1036 Days* (Washington, 1973), 168–81; and Ronald R. Pope, ed., *Soviet Views on the Cuban Missile Crisis: Myth and Reality in Foreign Policy Analysis* (Washington, 1982).

[5] For example, there seem to be no records of several conversations Robert F. Kennedy and the president held between meetings as they walked, stood on the balcony, or swam together in the White House swimming pool. President Kennedy's National Security Council Executive Committee (ExCom) also held "informal meetings" for which there appear to be no records. W.W. Rostow, "Participation in Cuban Missile Crisis Meetings, October 1962," Memorandum for the President, Oct. 5, 1968, Office Files of the President, Lyndon B. Johnson Papers (Lyndon B. Johnson Library, Austin, Texas). As well, at this writing, many documents remain security classified, closed by donor's request, or unprocessed: Robert F. Kennedy's Security Classified File; some summaries of National Security Council and ExCom meetings; transcripts of tapes for meetings of October 18 and 22.

some national, some international. Still, by posing precise questions and by applying extensive and heretofore largely unexplored research materials, scholars can refine the problem. We address it here with five sets of questions, organized chronologically.

First, how important was the Cuban issue to Republicans, Democrats, and the Kennedy administration in the fall of 1962 *before October 16,* the day the president was informed about the presence of the missiles? Before that date, just how troubled was Kennedy by Republican charges that he was ignoring evidence of "offensive" Soviet weapons in Cuba? Because the Cuban issue was becoming the noisiest one and the president preferred to make Medicare the dominant issue, did Kennedy welcome or seek a crisis over Cuba that would enable him to fend off his critics before the elections?[6] Put another way, was the political threat to the Democrats sufficient to cause the president to manufacture or dangerously manipulate a confrontation with the Soviet Union?

Second, *from October 16 to October 22,* the day the president stirred the world with a major television address, did Kennedy and his advisors think about the political consequences of their policy choices or make diplomatic and military decisions based on their anxiety over the forthcoming November elections? Did the decision to announce the discovery of the missiles and United States countermeasures via public television rather than through private negotiations stem from political motives?

Third, *from October 22 to October 28,* when the crisis abated after Soviet agreement to withdraw the missiles in exchange for a pledge by the United States not to intervene in Cuba again, did Kennedy and the Democrats play politics with the crisis?

Fourth, *from October 28 to election day November 6,* did the president and the Democrats attempt to exploit for political advantage the American "victory" over the Soviets?

Finally, *on November 6,* was the outcome of the congres-

[6]The 1962 "campaign kit" of the Democratic National Committee, for example, was devoted almost entirely to the Medicare issue. The *Democratic Fact Book,* part of the kit, devoted only a paragraph to Cuba. Democratic Fact Book (Aug. 1962), box 23-G-4-2F, Senatorial Files, Hubert H. Humphrey Papers (Minnesota Historical Society, St. Paul).

sional elections determined by people's perceptions that the president—and his party—had handled the Cuban crisis so well that they should be rewarded with votes? Did the missile crisis measurably shape the behavior of the American voter in 1962? In the elections the Republicans lost four seats in the Senate and gained only two seats in the House—an unusually poor performance in midterm elections for a party out of power. Without the missile crisis would the Republicans have made the traditional comeback of the party out of power?

Prospects for 1962

The political climate appeared favorable to the Republicans in 1962. Only once in the twentieth century, in 1934, had the party of an incumbent president improved at midterm its position in the House of Representatives; and not since that year had the party in power in the White House enhanced its strength in the Senate. In fact, in midterm elections from 1938 through 1958 the party out of power had gained 75, 46, 55, 28, 21, and 50 House seats and 7, 9, 13, 5, 1, and 15 Senate seats. In 1962 Republican leaders privately projected gains of 10 to 20 House seats for their party; publicly they expressed the hope of electing the additional 44 members needed to become the majority in the House.[7] "History is so much against us," President Kennedy lamented at a press conference. The historian and presidential assistant Schlesinger urged Kennedy to distance himself from the elections so as to avoid being personally blamed for the expected defeats. With his legislative program under attack and fearing the loss of 15 to 20 House seats, the president decided instead to campaign actively.[8]

Month after month and analysis after analysis, it became evident to the White House that 1962 promised to be an unusual political year. The Democrats were going to do well. The nature of the Kennedy victory in 1960, for example, suggested

[7] U.S. Bureau of the Census, Department of Commerce, *Historical Statistics of the United States*, pt. 2 (Washington, 1975), 1083; *Congressional Quarterly Almanac, 1962* (Washington, 1962), 1034.

[8] Schlesinger, *Thousand Days*, 756, 757; Sorensen, *Kennedy*, 353–54.

that midterm election tradition was likely to be broken. In 1960, for the first time in the twentieth century, the party that regained the presidency after being out of the White House failed to increase its congressional representation. Kennedy ran further behind the congressional candidates of his ticket than any other president elected since the beginning of the two-party system. As a rule he did not help Democratic candidates. Democratic Rep. John Blatnik of Minnesota believed that in his state the congressional candidates actually helped Kennedy more than he helped them. On a national basis in 1960, Democratic House candidates ran five percentage points ahead of Kennedy. Normally the successful presidential candidate attracts the votes of both party loyalists and independents and carries into office marginal nominees of his own party. Then, in the midterm contests, the marginal candidates must run without the benefit of the presidential coattails, and many lose. In 1960, however, Kennedy did not help to elect such vulnerable representatives. Thus the type of person most likely to be defeated by Republicans in 1962 was not holding office. From that perspective the probable outcome of the midterm elections was a new Congress that would resemble the old one.[9]

American voting behavior, especially that of the independent voter, also suggested that the Democrats would score gains in 1962. One-fifth of the electorate that year considered itself independent of party affiliation. Independents of that time were less prone to vote in off-year elections than were people who identified themselves as Republicans or Democrats. One analyst for the Democratic National Committee read this to mean that the Democratic party, as the more popular party by a four-to-three margin in registrations, would actually pick up seats in both houses. And, he advised, given the fading of the religious issue, Democratic gains would be made among voters who had

[9] Angus Campbell, "Prospects for November: Why We Can Expect More of the Same," *New Republic,* Oct. 8, 1962, pp. 13, 14–15; John Blatnik interview by Joseph E. O'Connor, Feb. 4, 1966, Oral History Interview, transcript, p. 32 (John F. Kennedy Library, Boston, Mass.). Arthur M. Schlesinger, Jr., Memorandum for the President, Aug. 27, 1962, box 18, Arthur M. Schlesinger, Jr., Papers, *ibid.; Newsweek,* Oct. 1, 1962, p. 24.

cast ballots against Kennedy in 1960 because he was a Roman Catholic.[10]

Polling data also revealed the improbability of a Republican victory in 1962. Throughout the year George H. Gallup's organization measured party preference. Polling results indicated a slight slippage for the Democrats but revealed no discernable trend toward the Republican party, even during the critical months of September and October (see table 1). The polls released by Gallup on October 24 and November 5 were particularly telling. The interviews for the October 24 release were conducted between October 1 and 7; polling data for the November 5 release were obtained between October 29 and November 2. Thus Gallup completed one set of interviews after Cuba had become a serious campaign issue but before the missile crisis and another set after both Kennedy's public confrontation with the Soviets and the Soviet decision to remove the missiles. No appreciable difference in results existed between the polls. Gallup also asked Americans which political party they thought "could do a better job of handling" the

Table 1

Preferences for Congressional Candidates, 1962
(By Party)

Month	*Percentage Preferring the Democratic Party*	*Percentage Preferring the Republican Party*
January	60	40
March	61	39
May	58	42
July	55	45
September	57	43
October	56	44
November	55.5	44.5

SOURCE: *Los Angeles Times,* Nov. 5, 1962.

[10] George Belknap to Hubert H. Humphrey, memorandum, n.d., box 23-G-4-2F, Senatorial Files, Humphrey Papers; Campbell, "Prospects for November," 13–15.

Table 2

Preferences for Parties to Handle National Problems, 1962

Month	*Percentage Preferring the Democratic Party*	*Percentage Preferring the Republican Party*	*No Difference*
August[a]	34	17	35
September[b]	38	20	30
October[c]	35	20	33

SOURCE: Gallup Organization polling data (Roper Center, Institute for Social Inquiry, University of Connecticut, Storrs).
NOTE: Numbers do not add up to 100 because some respondents had no opinion or gave answers that did not fit the three categories.
[a]Poll conducted August 23–28.
[b]Poll conducted September 20–25.
[c]Poll conducted October 19–24.

country's problems. On that question, too, the Democrats consistently outscored the Republicans (see table 2).[11]

Another polling organization, Louis Harris and Associates, Inc., directly supplied the president with data and recommendations based on its findings. In an October 4, 1962, memorandum Louis Harris told Kennedy that he was "more in control of this election than ever before," provided that he continued to stress the Republicans' dangerous partisanship on foreign and domestic issues. By early October, Harris reported, civil rights, war and peace, and medical care had emerged as dominant issues. Harris's analysis revealed that Kennedy's handling of the Mississippi crisis (the tension and violence surrounding the enrollment of a black student, James Meredith, at the University of Mississippi in September) had won favor in key northern industrial states by as much as a three-to-one margin. Democrats could therefore emphasize the need for the type of strong leadership Kennedy had demonstrated by his sending of federal troops to Mississippi, as well as hit Republican obstructionism on other domestic issues, such as aid to the unemployed, depressed areas, the ill, and college students.

[11]George H. Gallup, *The Gallup Poll: Public Opinion, 1935–1971* (3 vols., New York, 1972), III, 1788.

Harris also advised that Mississippi had taken "some of the edge off the Cuban issue," although most interviewees disapproved Kennedy's record on the latter (62 to 38). Still, a majority (68 to 32) opposed going to war in Cuba, and majorities ranging from 70 to 80 percent applauded Kennedy's toughness in holding the line in Berlin. On Cuba, Harris counseled, the Democrats should say that the Republicans were reckless, that they "would deliberately shoot craps with the destiny of this nation, would play petty politics with the national security." By reiterating such themes in domestic and foreign affairs, Harris prophesied, "you can alter the outcome in at least half the major Senate and Gubernatorial campaigns and can affect the results in 20 swing House Districts." Overall, then, the pollster Harris sketched for the president a rosy election picture just a couple of weeks before the missile crisis. Nowhere in the document was there the slightest hint that another foreign crisis, well managed by the White House, would improve already good Democratic chances in November.[12] The precrisis information from analysts thus pointed to an impressive Democratic performance in the midterm elections.

The Cuban Issue before October 16

Soon after Fidel Castro's triumph in January 1959, Cuba became a political issue in the United States. When the Republicans were making foreign policy under President Dwight D. Eisenhower, Democrats had asked why Castro and the increasingly radical Cuban Revolution were permitted to rise and flourish. When the Democrats under Kennedy were formulating foreign policy, Republicans charged that the administration was doing too little to unseat Castro and was allowing the Soviets to convert the Caribbean island into a Communist outpost. After Cuba and the Soviet Union signed a trade and

[12] Lou Harris, "The New Shape of this Campaign," Memorandum to the President, Oct. 4, 1962, box 105, President's Office Files, John F. Kennedy Presidential Papers (Kennedy Library) (by permission of Louis Harris and Associates, Inc.).

aid agreement in February 1960, critics of the Castro regime who had been arguing that the Cuban Revolution had earlier turned "red" felt vindicated. The next month President Eisenhower ordered the Central Intelligence Agency (CIA) to train anti-Castro Cuban exiles for an invasion of their homeland. In July, in an attempt to cripple the Cuban economy and thus to weaken Castro, the administration cut Cuba's sugar quota, virtually stopping imports from the island; in October most American exports to Cuba were prohibited.[13]

Those events in the deterioration of Cuban-American relations sparked debate in the United States, particularly in the campaign of 1960. Kennedy repeatedly upbraided the Republicans, charging that they had let Cuba become a Communist satellite. Just before leaving office, Eisenhower broke diplomatic relations with Cuba. In April 1961 came the bungled CIA operation at the Bay of Pigs and swirling debate over its failure. As Kennedy lamented after the debacle, he had "handed his critics a stick with which they would forever beat him." The Bay of Pigs, Sorensen later said, was the administration's "heaviest political cross."[14] With strident rhetoric echoing between Washington and Havana, the Kennedy administration set about to destroy the Castro government. The clandestine Operation Mongoose, begun in late 1961, included sabotage, paramilitary raids, disruption of the sugar trade, circulation of counterfeit money, and other so-called dirty tricks. As well, the CIA plotted to assassinate Castro. The secret war against Cuba did not weaken Castro's hold on the island, and it probably stimulated Cuban requests for Soviet protection. Nor

[13] For the basic issues in United States–Cuba relations, see Cole Blasier, *The Hovering Giant: U.S. Response to Revolutionary Change in Latin America* (Pittsburgh, 1976); Lester D. Langley, *The United States and the Caribbean in the Twentieth Century* (Athens, Ga., 1982); Maurice Halperin, *The Rise and Decline of Fidel Castro: An Essay in Contemporary History* (Berkeley, 1972); Richard E. Welch, Jr., *Response to Revolution: The United States and the Cuban Revolution, 1959–1961* (Chapel Hill, 1985); Morris H. Morley, "Toward a Theory of Imperial Politics: United States Policy and the Processes of State Formation, Disintegration and Consolidation in Cuba, 1898–1978" (Ph.D. diss., State University of New York, Binghamton, 1980).

[14] Peter Wyden, *Bay of Pigs: The Untold Story* (New York, 1979), 310; Sorensen, *Kennedy,* 669.

did the covert operations disarm the Republicans, because the Kennedy administration, of course, could not take public credit for such activities. Then came the United States–engineering expulsion of Cuba from the Organization of American States in January 1962 and the imposition of a complete United States embargo on trade with Cuba the next month. As Cuba inched toward a closer relationship with the Soviet Union, the State Department, in March, complained about "Sino-Soviet bloc" military aid to Cuba.[15]

The question of a Soviet arms buildup in Cuba took on serious political dimensions in the summer of 1962 when Republican leaders began to mount an unrelenting attack against the Kennedy administration. The growing Soviet military presence in Cuba, of course, held significance in itself as a challenge to United States hegemony in Latin America. But it also provided an effective campaign issue that probed one of the administration's most vulnerable spots. And it served to divert attention from Republican vulnerabilities stemming from their opposition to popular New Frontier programs. Republicans thus strove to make Cuba, not Medicare, the leading topic of the congressional campaigns.

The Republican indictment held that the administration was willfully withholding from the American people damning information about the enlargement of the Soviet military presence in Cuba and was underestimating the Soviet threat in the Caribbean. Whereas Kennedy argued that Soviet technicians had been stationed on the island, Republicans called them troops. Whereas Kennedy had insisted that Soviet missiles in Cuba were "defensive" (short-range surface-to-air), Republicans labeled them "offensive" (surface-to-air *and* surface-to-surface). Decrying a Soviet besmirching of the Monroe Doctrine, Republicans demanded immediate action—either a blockade or an invasion of Cuba. Uneasy Democrats dismissed such pleas as election-year high jinks but could not shed the charge that

[15] Schlesinger, *Robert Kennedy and His Times*, 468–98, 533–58; U.S. Department of State, "Sino-Soviet Bloc Military Aid to Cuba," Press Release No. 195, March 27, 1962, Kenneth Keating Papers (University of Rochester Library, Rochester, N.Y.).

Kennedy was timid in curbing the flow of Soviet arms and personnel to Cuba. Kennedy himself admitted at a press conference on August 22 that supplies "in large quantities" had reached Cuba. Seven days later, in answer to charges made by Republican Sen. Homer E. Capehart, who was seeking reelection in Indiana, the president insisted that technicians, not troops, were accompanying the arms.[16]

Kennedy's statements hardly satisfied Kenneth B. Keating. The Republican senator from New York, who was not standing for reelection, became his party's chief protagonist on Cuba, making some twenty-five public statements prior to the missile crisis. In speech after speech Keating presented details that made him appear authoritative. In his first major assault, on August 31, he said, for example, "On August 13 five Soviet torpedo boats unloaded from Soviet ships, and are now moored at La Base." On September 4 in the Senate, Keating added more details on the Soviet military buildup and claimed there were missiles in Cuba, although as was common for him at first, he made little distinction between short-range, "defensive," surface-to-air missiles (SAMS) and longer-range, "offensive," surface-to-surface missiles (medium-range—MRBMS—and intermediate-range—IRBMS) that could reach the United States. That day the president tried to quiet the clamor by meeting with congressional leaders of both parties and by stating that neither Soviet combat troops nor ground-to-ground missiles existed in Cuba. But, he assured all, if "offensive" Soviet weapons ever appeared in Cuba, the "gravest issues would arise." The next day Keating dismissed the president's explanation: "Who is to say whether a weapon is offensive or defensive? It depends on the direction in which it is aimed." With others, such as Senator Goldwater, adding their voices of criticism, Senate Minority Leader Everett Dirksen of Illinois declared that "we Republicans are not dragging Cuba into the campaign, but the people are."[17]

[16] *Public Papers of the Presidents of the United States, John F. Kennedy: Containing the Public Messages, Speeches, and Statements of the President, January 1 to December 31, 1962* (Washington, 1963), 638, 652.

[17] *Congressional Record*, 87 Cong., 2 sess., vol. 108, pt. 14, Aug. 31, 1962,

The president temporarily took the initiative on September 7. Without specifically mentioning Cuba or Berlin, he asked Congress for standby authority to call up 150,000 military reservists to meet challenges "in any part of the free world."[18] Just hours before, Senator Dirksen and Rep. Charles A. Halleck (Republican of Indiana) had urged a more specific focus: a joint congressional resolution authorizing the president to use troops if necessary to "meet the Cuban problem." Although former President Eisenhower warned against making Cuba "an object of partisan fighting," many Republicans were determined to do just that in the congressional campaigns. Sen. Hubert H. Humphrey of Minnesota counterattacked for the Democrats. On September 11 he chastised "swaggering irresponsibles" in Congress who were trying "to make political capital." Even if there were threatening missiles in Cuba—and he denied that there were—the United States could destroy them in one day. One should not "lose a night's sleep worrying about the might of Cuba," Humphrey remarked. Unmoved, on the next day three Republican senators proposed amendments to the reserve mobilization bill; they would empower the president to "take such action as is necessary" to prevent the violation of the Monroe Doctrine in Cuba.[19]

"The Congressional head of steam on this is the most serious that we have had," National Security Affairs adviser

---

pp. 18359–18361; *ibid.,* Sept. 4, 1962, pp. 18438–18439; *New York Times,* Sept. 5, 1962, pp. 1, 2; press release, Sept. 5, 1962, Speech File, Keating Papers; *Congressional Quarterly Almanac, 1962,* 333. For a chronology of relations between Cuba and the United States and the politics related thereto, see Republican Congressional Committee, "The Cuban Issue: A Chronology," May 1963, box 551, John Sherman Cooper Papers (University of Kentucky Library, Lexington); and U.S. Congress, Senate, Committee of Foreign Relations, *Events in United States–Cuba Relations: A Chronology 1957–1963* (Washington, 1963).

[18] *Public Papers . . . Kennedy,* 665. The Senate approved the measure on September 13. The House passed it on September 24. Kennedy signed the bill into law on October 3.

[19] *Congressional Quarterly Almanac, 1962,* 333; *Congressional Record,* 87 Cong., 2 sess., vol. 108, pt. 14, Sept. 11, 1962, pp. 19073–19075; Humphrey to James Reston, Sept. 17, 1962, box 23-J6-3B, Senatorial Files, Humphrey Papers; Republican Congressional Committee, "Cuban Issue," 9. For examples of Republican charges of Democratic appeasement over Cuba, see *ibid.,* 8–9; and *Congressional Record,* 87 Cong., 2 sess., vol. 108, pt. 14, Sept. 11, 1962, p. 19003.

McGeorge Bundy told the president. Bundy feared that the administration "may appear to be weak and indecisive." The president must speak out with "a very clear and aggressive explanation" of United States policy to establish that the Cuban problem was "within our control." Bundy opposed any congressional authorization to use American power unless it was stated in general terms like those in the Formosa Resolution (1955) or the Eisenhower Doctrine (1957). At his press conference on September 13, the president took Bundy's advice and opened with a formal statement: "If at any time the Communist buildup in Cuba were to endanger or interfere with our security in any way . . . or if Cuba should . . . become an offensive military base of significant capacity for the Soviet Union, then this country will do whatever must be done to protect its own security and that of its allies." Still, the Republicans pressed the attack, with Keating claiming that the short-range missile facilities in Cuba could be transformed into intermediate-range sites.[20]

On September 29 the Senate adopted the Cuba Resolution expressing United States determination to use arms if necessary to prevent Cuban subversion or aggression in the hemisphere and the island's conversion into an externally supported military base endangering United States security. Backed by Democrats as consistent with the president's statement of September 13, the measure also passed the House by a wide margin. Keating dismissed the resolution as "worthless" unless the United States followed it up with a "more decisive policy." Although Kentucky Sen. John Sherman Cooper voted for the resolution, he cautioned his Republican colleagues not to use Cuba as "a political gambit."[21]

[20] McGeorge Bundy, "Memorandum on Cuba for the press conference," Sept. 13, 1962, box 48, Theodore C. Sorensen Papers (Kennedy Library); *Public Papers . . . Kennedy,* 674; "Selected Cuba Chronology—1962," Political Files, Keating Papers; *Congressional Quarterly Almanac, 1962,* 334; Newsletter, Sept. 13, 1962, Cotton Papers; Republican Congressional Committee, "Cuban Issue," 9.

[21] *Congressional Record,* 87 Cong., 2 sess., vol 108, pt. 15, Sept. 20, 1962, p. 20058; *Congressional Quarterly Almanac, 1962,* 334–35; Press Release, Sept. 20, 1962, Speech Files, Keating Papers; Remarks, Sept. 20, 1962, box 551, Cooper Papers.

Senator Kenneth B. Keating using a Minuteman missile model as a pointer, January 13, 1963. *Kenneth B. Keating Papers. Courtesy University of Rochester Library, Rochester, New York.*

Political gambit it was, and the Republicans were successful in making Cuba a troublesome political issue for the Democrats, who were put in the unenviable position of seeming to be hiding something. Mail poured into politicians' offices demanding forthright action against Cuba.[22] In the Times Square subway station in New York City, a "Directomat" machine that gave Republican Sen. Jacob Javits' views was punched most

[22] See, for example, Lee Metcalf Papers (Montana Historical Society, Helena).

often during the last week of September for "What is the Javits Record on Cuba and Castro?" Professional polls showed that Cuba had grown into a prominent issue for the American electorate. Kennedy tried instead to stress domestic issues. In a campaign swing through the Midwest on October 5–7, the president barely mentioned foreign policy.[23]

But Kennedy could not easily ignore Keating's major Senate speech of October 10. In that speech Keating boldly claimed that intermediate-range missiles, capable of striking targets in "the American heartland," had been installed in Cuba. Six launching pads were being prepared, he said. Did Keating know for sure? He could not have. He possessed no conclusive evidence about Soviet "offensive" missiles in Cuba. As Republican Sen. Bourke B. Hickenlooper of Iowa recalled: "I had the same information that Ken Keating had, but basically it came from Cuban refugees, and I couldn't depend upon its reliability or separate fact from wishful thinking."[24] Nor, of course, did anyone in the administration have such information—not even Keating's alleged informant or informants in the government. Although government officials had received in late September and early October reports from observers in Cuba, they reasonably concluded that such reportage was questionable and "soft."[25]

[23] Press Release, Javits Campaign Headquarters, Sept. 30, 1962, ser. 1, box 28, Jacob Javits Papers (State University of New York, Stony Brook). Gallup polls asked: "What do you think is the most important problem facing this country today?" In August only 2% mentioned Cuba. In late September 25% cited Cuba. In the poll conducted October 19–24, 26% mentioned Cuba. Gallup Organization polling data (Roper Center, Institute for Social Inquiry, University of Connecticut, Storrs). A September *Des Moines Register and Tribune* poll asked whether Cuba was a "serious threat" to American security; 81% answered "yes." IOWA 62–168, *ibid. A Minneapolis Tribune* poll of late September found that 78% thought Cuba a "serious threat" to the United States. Minn. 215, *ibid.* Once during his campaign swing, Kennedy criticized the Republicans for having "ignored" Latin America in the 1950s. *Public Papers . . . Kennedy,* 737.

[24] *Congressional Record,* 87 Cong., 2 sess., vol. 108, pt. 17, Oct. 10, 1962, p. 22957; *ibid.,* Oct. 9, 1962, p. 22889; Bourke B. Hickenlooper to William P. Knowland, Jan. 2, 1963, box 29, Bourke P. Hickenlooper Papers (Herbert Hoover Presidential Library, West Branch, Iowa).

[25] Mystery surrounds Kenneth B. Keating's sources, for the senator, who died in 1975, repeatedly refused to divulge them. He may have received information from Florida-based Cuban exiles and their organizations or from officers in the Department of Defense. Keating's papers at the University of

Actually, Keating and administration officials learned about Soviet surface-to-surface missiles in Cuba at just about the same time. On October 14 intelligence officials learned from photographs taken during a U-2 surveillance flight that such missiles were in Cuba. Had bad weather on October 11, 12, and 13 not prevented the U-2 aircraft from flying over Cuba, intellegence officials could have had hard, confirming evidence at just about the same time Keating was making his public case about intermediate-range missiles. United States officials had all along been monitoring (U-2 planes made runs over parts of Cuba on August 29, September 5, 17, 26, and 29, and October 5 and 7) the flow and positioning of Soviet weapons. When they discovered the "offensive" missile sites in western Cuba, they acted vigorously against them, as they said they would if and when they received proof. Keating's "soft" data ultimately proved to be correct. But the president, recalled Secretary of State Dean Rusk, needed more than "speculation, guesswork, fears"; he had to have "very clear and precise and hard information" that "offensive" weapons were in Cuba before he could confront the Soviets and rally other nations behind United States action. The president, it should be noted, never ordered specific U-2 flights to counter specific Republican criticisms; apparently he did not participate in selecting dates for flights before October 16 but, rather, approved decisions made by officials in the CIA and the Department of Defense.[26]

Rochester provide very few clues, and former members of his staff, who communicated with Paterson by telephone or letter, have been unable or unwilling to provide details. See *U.S. News & World Report,* Nov. 19, 1962, p. 86; Kenneth B. Keating, "My Advance View of the Cuban Crisis," *Look,* Nov. 3, 1964, pp. 96, 99, 100, 102, 104, 106; Hilsman, *To Move a Nation,* 177–80; United Press International, release, Oct. 19, 1964, Keating Papers; *Congressional Record,* 87 Cong., 2 sess., vol. 108, pt. 14, Aug. 31, 1962, pp. 18359–18361; and Robert R. McMillan, "A Look Back at Cuban Missile Crisis," *Newsday,* Oct. 14, 1983, p. 72.

[26]Only the Sept. 5 and Oct. 14 flights covered the western portion of the island (where the Soviets were deploying the missiles), because United States officials feared a plane would be shot down by a surface-to-air missile. For a discussion of intelligence gathering from four sources—ships docking in Cuba, refugees, CIA agents in Cuba, U-2 flights—see Hilsman, *To Move a Nation,* 159–92. The U-2 flights were the most swift, accurate, and reliable. Intelligence data from a variety of sources, including U-2 flights, reached top-level officials such as Vice Pres. Lyndon B. Johnson. Col. Howard Burris, memoranda, box 6, Vice Presidential Security File, Johnson Papers; John A. McCone interview

On October 16, the very day Kennedy was being shown the shocking U-2 photographs of sites for medium-range (1,100 miles) and intermediate range (2,200 miles) missiles, the chairman of the Republican National Committee tagged Cuba the dominant issue of the fall campaign—a "symbol of the tragic irresolution of the Administration." On the eve of the missile crisis, then, the Republicans seemed to have outmaneuvered the Democrats over Cuba, but not so much so, analysts and pollsters reported, to deny the Democrats an impressive showing in the forthcoming midterm elections. By mid-October, in fact, monotonously repeated Republican accusations had lost some of their punch, press coverage of Cuba had decreased, and other events—Mississippi, Berlin, and an Organization of American States meeting—had diverted attention. Still, the new information discovered by the U-2 might boost the Republicans by demonstrating that they had been right all along. Kennedy saw political trouble ahead. "We've just elected Capehart in Indiana, and Ken Keating will probably be the next President of the United States," remarked Kennedy when he first saw the U-2 pictures.[27]

October 16–October 22

From the presentation of the aerial photographs of missile sites in Cuba to the president on the morning of October 16 to Kennedy's nationally televised speech in the evening of October 22, a specially constituted group of advisers, later called the Executive Committee (ExCom) of the National Security Council, met frequently to debate courses of action. The options of invasion, bombing, blockade, and diplomacy were explored in exhausting sessions often marked by frank disagree-

---

by Joe B. Frantz, Aug. 19, 1970, John A. McCone Oral History Interview, *ibid.;* Hilsman to Paterson, Dec. 12, 1984 (in Paterson's possession); "The Cuban Missile Crisis," cond. by Alfred P. Sloan Foundation (New York, N.Y.), Jan. 27, 1983, transcript of videotape (in Sloan Foundation's possession).

[27] *New York Times,* Oct. 17, 1962, pp. 1, 24; Montague Kern, Patricia W. Levering, and Ralph B. Levering, *The Kennedy Crisis: The Press, the Presidency and Foreign Policy* (Chapel Hill, 1983), 117–22; O'Donnell and Powers with McCarthy, *"Johnny We Hardly Knew Ye,"* 310.

ment and changing minds. To what extent did the president and his top advisers think or talk politics during that tense week? Did "the political needs" of the administration compel it "to take almost any risk to get them [the missiles] out," as Kennedy's ambassador to India, John Kenneth Galbraith, later suggested?[28] Did political considerations shape the two key decisions? The chief decision was to quarantine Cuba to prevent further military shipments to the island and to impress the Soviets with the serious American intention of forcing the missiles out. The second major decision was tactical: to inform the Soviets of United States policy through a television address rather than through private negotiations or traditional diplomatic channels.

The several sources for October 16–22 available to the scholar reveal some discussion of politics within the small circle of presidential advisers. Yet the transcripts of the two meetings of October 16, Sorensen's private papers, National Security Council documents, a postcrisis internal report, Defense Department briefings, former President Eisenhower's memoranda of conversation with Kennedy and CIA officials, notes or recollections of such legislative leaders as Sen. Richard B. Russell of Georgia, oral histories, memoirs, the president's appointment books and "doodles," and other materials suggest that politics was very seldom discussed and did not determine the choice of the naval blockade.[29] Nor do the

[28] Steel, "Endgame," 15.

[29] The October 16 transcripts ("Kennedy tapes"), National Security Council minutes, Sorensen's papers, various oral histories, Frank A. Sieverts' report, "The Cuban Crisis, 1962," and the president's appointment books and "doodles" are in the Kennedy Library. Eisenhower's memoranda are in Post-Presidential Papers (Dwight D. Eisenhower Library, Abilene, Kans.). Richard B. Russell's notes of an October 22 meeting with Kennedy are in his papers at the University of Georgia. Briefings such as that of October 22 have been released to researchers by the Defense Department. Among the memoirs by participants are Richard F. Kennedy, *Thirteen Days: A Memoir of the Cuban Missile Crisis* (New York, 1969); Sorensen, *Kennedy;* Hilsman, *To Move a Nation;* Dean Acheson, "Dean Acheson's Version of Robert Kennedy's Version of the Cuban Missile Affair," *Esquire,* 71 (Feb. 1969), 76–77, 44, 46; George W. Ball, *The Past Has Another Pattern: Memoirs* (New York, 1982); O'Donnell and Powers with McCarthy, *"Johnny We Hardly Knew Ye";* Charles E. Bohlen, *Witness to History, 1929–1969* (New York, 1973); Maxwell D. Taylor, *Swords and Plowshares* (New York, 1972); and U. Alexis Johnson and Jef Olivarius McAllister, *The Right Hand of Power* (Englewood Cliffs, 1984).

historical records indicate that the tactic of a surprise television address rather than a private advance warning was shaped by politics, although questions cloud this issue.

For many reasons Kennedy felt compelled to act decisively against the Soviet emplacement of missiles in Cuba. First, he felt tricked, for the Soviets had told the United States on more than one occasion that they would not put into Cuba missiles that could reach the United States and that they would refrain from actions that might aggravate international tensions before the fall elections.[30] Second, Kennedy's long-standing Cold War posture and ardent desire to discipline or to remove Castro urged upon him a confrontationist policy, as did his tendency to personalize international contests and his need to prove his toughness and to win—evident in his October 16 comment on learning about the missiles that "he can't do that to *me!*"[31] He was moved to act, too, by the appearance of a shift in the strategic balance of power and of a diminution of United States standing in Latin America, a traditional sphere of influence.[32] Kennedy was, of course, also cognizant of his Republican-induced public pledges to take resolute action against offensive weapons in Cuba. To the extent that presidents must always act

[30] Sorensen, *Kennedy,* 667; Kennedy, *Thirteen Days,* 26; Stewart Alsop and Charles Bartlett, "In Time of Crisis," *Saturday Evening Post,* Dec. 8, 1962, p. 18; Chester Bowles, *Promises to Keep: My Years in Public Life, 1941–1969* (New York, 1971), 418; Dinerstein, *Making of a Missile Crisis,* 181; Hilsman, *To Move a Nation,* 166; Thomas G. Paterson, "Bearing the Burden: A Critical Look at JFK's Foreign Policy," *Virginia Quarterly Review,* 54 (Spring 1978), 193–212.

[31] Quoted in Allison, *Essence of Decision,* 193. See also Paterson, "Bearing the Burden," 193–212; Garry Wills, *The Kennedy Imprisonment: A Meditation on Power* (Boston, 1983); James D. Barber, *The Presidential Character: Predicting Performance in the White House* (Englewood Cliffs, 1972), 293–343; Graham Allison, "Cuban Missiles and Kennedy Macho: New Evidence to Dispel the Myth," *Washington Monthly,* 4 (Oct. 1972), 14–19; Thomas M. Mongar, "Personality and Decision-Making: John F. Kennedy in Four Crisis Decision," *Canadian Journal of Political Science,* 2 (June 1969), 200–225.

[32] Ball, *Past,* 289. Sorensen has noted that the strategic balance "would have been substantially altered in *appearance;* and in matters of national will and world leadership, as the President said later, such appearances contribute to reality." Sorensen, *Kennedy,* 678. Kennedy said to his advisers on October 16: "It makes them look like they're coequal with us. . . . After all this is a political struggle as much as military." Treasury Secretary C. Douglas Dillon added it would appear "We're scared of the Cubans." "Off-the-Record Meeting on Cuba," 6:30–7:55 P.M., Oct. 16, 1962, Presidential Recordings transcript, pp. 14–15, 46 (Kennedy Library).

in a political arena and to the extent that politics refers to the politician's desire to fulfill promises, politics demanded that Kennedy remove the missiles. But presidents have always enjoyed considerable freedom of action in the making of foreign policy, and, in this case, politics or anxiety over the congressional elections did not decide specific courses of action. On October 16 Secretary of Defense Robert McNamara appreciated the distinction between acting in general and acting in particular when he recognized that the administration had "a domestic political problem" on its hands because of previous presidential statements. Yet "we didn't say we'd go in . . . and kill them, we said we'd *act*. Well, how will we act?" McNamara, for one, preferred a blockade of Cuba instead of military options.[33]

At the two ExCom meetings of October 16, there was scant political discussion. In the first meeting the advisers worried about keeping the news secret until they had decided on policy. Keating's name came up, prompting speculation about his sources of information. Should the Senator be interviewed to check out his data? The president thought Keating would prove unhelpful, and Attorney General Robert F. Kennedy feared the senator would say "afterwards that we tried to . . . dun him." The participants in the meeting largely discussed the operational status of the missiles, alternatives for removing them, and Soviet motives.[34] Nowhere in the transcripts of the two October 16 meetings are there comments to the effect that the administration or the Democratic party would suffer in November or after if a certain decision, such as one for an air strike, was not made.

Politics was not adjourned, of course. While his advisers puzzled over policy, the president went on the campaign trail. Campaign plans had called for Kennedy to travel across the nation, especially on weekends in late September and October. Until October 20 Kennedy kept his political schedule; on that day, feigning a head cold, he canceled his politicking and re-

[33] "Off-the-Record Meeting on Cuba," 6:30–7:55 P.M., Oct. 16, 1962, Presidential Recordings, transcript, p. 46 (Kennedy Library).

[34] "Off-the-Record Meeting on Cuba," 11:50 A.M.–12:57 P.M., Oct. 16, 1962, Presidential Recordings, transcript, p. 19, 26, *ibid*.

turned to Washington. His speeches before then, as Harris had advised, recommended the election of Democrats to insure the passage of critical domestic legislation. Kennedy gave little attention to foreign policy and gave no hint of an impending crisis. He did not sound an international "time of peril" theme. He did not try to entice Republicans into statements they would find embarrassing after the missile crisis became public. In short, the president did not play politics with Cuba at three stops in Connecticut on October 17, or in Springfield, Illinois, Cleveland, and Chicago on October 19.[35]

On October 18, during a crisis meeting, Secretary of the Treasury C. Douglas Dillon passed a handwritten note to Sorensen. "Have you considered the very real possibility," Dillon asked, "that if we allow Cuba to complete installation & operational readiness of missile bases, the next House of Representatives is likely to have a Republican majority? This would completely paralyze our ability to react sensibly & coherently to further Soviet advances." This curious document is one of the few time-of-crisis records that speak directly to the relationship between politics and decisions. It came from a *Republican* serving in Democratic administration—a Republican who seemed strangely to favor a Republican defeat in November. Actually, Dillon was using the political argument only to move the advisors toward his hardline position that decisive military action must be taken against Cuba—a position that was losing ground to the option of a blockade. Dillon apparently concluded that the president was *not* thinking politically and that a political case would persuade him to accept the use of substantial military force. The president and his other aides, of course, may have pondered the impact of their decisions on the congressional elections, but neither their records nor their

[35] Arthur M. Schlesinger, Jr., Memorandum to the President, Aug. 13, 1962, box 18, Subject File: Politicking, Schlesinger Papers; boxes 40–41, Speech Files, President's Office Files, *ibid.;* O'Donnell and Powers with McCarthy, *"Johnny We Hardly Knew Ye,"* 307; *Public Papers . . . Kennedy,* 695–804. Vice President Johnson, touring several western states, did speak about ridding Cuba of Castro and the Soviets. But his speeches were probably prepared before October 16 and were not coordinated with missile crisis officials in Washington. Memorandum, n.d., Johnson Papers; Democratic National Committee News Release, "Honolulu Remarks of Lyndon B. Johnson," Oct. 21, 1962, Statements of Lyndon B. Johnson, Johnson Papers.

decisions demonstrate such. And they did not accept Dillon's recommendation for an air strike, which would have conceivably proved more attractive to voters than a quarantine, which held the potential of a drawn-out crisis, and which in itself could not prevent the continuing assembly of missile components already in Cuba. As Dillon knew, moreover, Kennedy had no intention of ever accepting operational missiles.[36] The question was never whether to act but, rather, when to take which action.

Meanwhile, politicians not privy to the secret deliberations of the president's advisors continued to spar over Cuba. The Cuban issue, Kennedy remarked to Sorensen on October 20, was "very harmful to the Democrats," because it proved that the Republicans had been right. And whereas some critics would condemn the Democrats for having been "soft" on Communism and Castro, others would soon denounce them as a war party. Kennedy believed "that whichever way he turned it was politically damaging at home," Sorensen recalled. But on the next day, Eisenhower, having not yet been consulted or briefed by Kennedy officials but, like the press, perhaps sensing forthcoming momentous decisions regarding Cuba, quarreled with his party chairman's designation of Cuba as the dominant issue of the campaign. "I think that probably we have heard the last of it. At least I hope so."[37]

[36] C. Douglas Dillon to Sorensen, Oct. 18, 1962, box 48, Sorensen Papers; Dillon to Paterson, March 13, 1985 (in Paterson's possession). For Kennedy's vow on October 18 that operational medium-range ballistic missiles in Cuba would not be permitted, see Frank A. Sieverts, "The Cuban Crisis, 1962," [1963], p. 48, box 49, National Security File (Kennedy Library).

[37] Officials of the Democratic National Committee (DNC) were working to counter the Republicans on the Cuban issue. They drafted a hard-hitting presidential speech on Cuba that proclaimed that Republican "fire-eaters" themselves had "helped Castro to power and floundered in a morass of indecision while Castro and his Red advisors won firm control of the island." Cuba was "a false issue in this campaign to divert attention from the real issues." On October 22, the day Kennedy was scheduled to deliver his televised address, Press Secretary Pierre Salinger called DNC headquarters to "kill" the paper. "Kill," handwritten word on draft speech, n.d., box 681, White House Central Files (Kennedy Library). According to Sorensen, Kennedy said little about the political ramifications of the crisis during the crisis. Theodore Sorensen interview by Carl Kaysen, March 26, 1964. Theodore Sorensen Oral History Interview, transcript, pp. 64–66 (Kennedy Library). Eisenhower quoted in *New York Times,* Oct. 22, 1962, pp. 1, 21.

President John F. Kennedy addressing the nation by television, October 22, 1962. *Courtesy John F. Kennedy Library, Boston, Massachusetts.*

On October 22 Washington throbbed with anticipation. At noon the White House had announced an important 7:00 P.M. presidential speech, and journalists had already determined that Cuba was the topic. Some twenty congressional leaders—Congress was not in session, and the members were campaigning or vacationing—were summoned to the nation's capital for a special meeting with the president. First, at 3:00 P.M., Kennedy convened the full National Security Council. Mentioning the "domestic aspects of the crisis," he told its members that he wanted "one song" sung "to make it clear that there was now no difference among his advisers as to the proper course to follow." Secretary Rusk stated that "if anyone thought our response was weak, they were wrong," for he expected a "flaming crisis." Rusk's comments suggest that some administration officials worried that critics would say that the quarantine was inadequate and that the Democrats were still too timid on Cuba. The president may have thought similarly when he entered the 5:00 P.M. legislative leaders' meeting to explain his ultimatum to the Soviets and the imposition of a naval blockade. The Republicans in the group proved conciliatory, but some Democrats, in a tense exchange with the president, urged military action. Senator Russell, chairman of the Armed Services Committee, and Senator Fulbright, chairman of the Foreign Relations Committee, advocated an invasion of Cuba. Russell went further. He favored "knocking out" the missiles with "bombs and rockets." An annoyed Kennedy departed the meeting to get ready for his television address, muttering to Sorensen that "if they want this job, they can have it—it's no great joy to me."[38]

The president's advisers and most scholars have explained the choice of a television speech—a surprise public statement—to inform the Soviets as necessary to the success of United States policy. From the beginning Kennedy's aides discussed the usefulness of a public ultimatum—"a statement to the world." The question was timing: Should it be delivered without prior notice to the Soviet Union and Cuba, or should it follow diplomatic approaches to the two governments? ExCom

[38] "Minutes of the 507th Meeting of the National Security Council on Monday, October 22, 1962, 3:00 P.M., Cabinet Room," box 313, National Security File (Kennedy Library); Neil MacNeil, *Dirksen: Portrait of a Public Man* (New York, 1970), 205–207; Kennedy, *Thirteen Days,* 53–54; Sorensen, *Kennedy,* 702–703. Russell and J. William Fulbright believed that an invasion would be less likely to lead to nuclear war with the Soviet Union because it would pit American soldiers against Cubans rather than against Russians, who might stand aside. "RBR Cuba Notes," Special Presidential File, ser. 15, Oct. 1962, Richard B. Russell Papers (University of Georgia Library, Athens); *Congressional Record,* 93 Cong., 1 sess., pt. 31, vol. 119, Dec. 10, 1973, pp. 40353–40354.

on October 17 discussed the option of a diplomatic overture. One scenario included approaches to Nikita S. Khrushchev and Castro; they would be told of American plans to force the missiles out of Cuba, and if no satisfactory reply was received within forty-eight hours, Kennedy would go on television to announce the installation of the blockade. But in the end the president and his advisers decided to surprise the Soviets with a public address. They thought that Americans had to be told early because "no responsible President would have tried to mobilize the Navy for a quarantine without telling the American people exactly what he was doing." It was believed, too, that a dramatic media speech exposing Soviet perfidy would rally world opinion to United States policy. As well, ExCom members feared that Khrushchev himself might issue a "blustering ultimatum" and delay negotiations until all the missiles became operational. In other words, the "initiative" would shift to the Soviets.[39]

One time when Kennedy conceivably could have issued the private warning was October 18, when the president met in the White House with Soviet Foreign Minister Andrei Gromyko. The journalist Water Lippmann published a widely read column of October 25 criticizing the president for suspending diplomacy—for not showing Gromyko the photographs and informing him that the United States would soon announce a policy to force the dismantling of the missiles. If Kennedy had discussed the issue with Gromyko, "the President would have given Mr. Khrushchev what all wise statesmen give their adver-

[39] "Off-the-Record Meeting on Cuba," 6:30–7:55 P.M., Oct. 16, 1962, p. 46 (Kennedy Library); Sorensen to Paterson, Dec. 13, 1984 (in Paterson's possession); Edwin M. Martin to Paterson, Jan. 14, 1985, *ibid.;* Ball to Paterson, Dec. 17, 1984, *ibid.;* U. Alexis Johnson to Paterson, Dec. 3, 1984, *ibid.;* Roswell L. Gilpatric to Paterson, Nov. 28, 1984, *ibid.;* Dean Rusk to Paterson, March 30, 1984, *ibid.;* Allison, *Essence of Decision,* 201–202. It is difficult to understand the importance of "initiative" in this crisis. ExCom member Charles Bohlen, former ambassador to the Soviet Union, recommended on October 18 that "diplomatic action" be taken—that Kennedy communicate with Khrushchev "privately." Bohlen added, "I don't quite see the urgency of military action—if it leaks and we have already initiated diplomatic action we should be able to handle it." Bohlen, *Witness to History,* 491–92. Indeed, United States military superiority in the region was never doubted, and any shift in initiative would have been short-lived. Adlai Stevenson also urged negotiations before taking public action. John Bartlow Martin, *Adlai Stevenson and the World: The Life of Adlai E. Stevenson* (Garden City, 1978), 721–23.

saries—the chance to save face." Kennedy later rebutted that by October 18 he had not yet settled on a policy, he did not have complete information from reconnaissance, and he "did not want to give him [Gromyko] the satisfaction of announcing what he was doing." Kennedy added: "This way we held the initiative." Moreover, Gromyko's prevarication in that meeting—that the Soviets would not place offensive missiles in Cuba—convinced some Kennedy officials that private diplomacy would not work.[40]

Although little evidence is now available to sustain such an argument, it is plausible that the vehicle of a surprise, public television speech was selected for its anticipated domestic political impact.[41] First, a dramatic speech announcing bold action would surely rally Americans around the Democratic administration. Second, a tough-minded speech would take the campaign issue away from the Republicans and possibly disarm critics who thought Kennedy pusillanimous toward Communism. Third, Kennedy might have reasoned that quiet, private negotiations could not have been conducted in secret for very long. The inevitable leaks would perpetuate charges that the administration was concealing information and underplaying the military threat. And even if the negotiations proved successful, Republicans would sneer that unsavory deals with the archenemy had been struck in secret or that opportunities for purging the Western Hemisphere of Castro and the Soviets had been squandered. Whatever the case, the speech's effect warmed Democrats, for the public reponse to the president's stand was positive.

October 23–October 28

After his televised statement Kennedy and his aides waited anxiously for the Soviet response. The quarantine was put in place. Khrushchev and Kennedy exchanged letters, and Soviet

[40] Ronald Steel, *Walter Lippmann and the American Century* (Boston, 1980), 535; *Public Papers . . . Kennedy,* 899; U. Alexis Johnson to Paterson, Dec. 3, 1984.

[41] ExCom discussed the "political content" of the address. Tentative Agenda for Off-the-Record NSC Meeting, October 21, 1962, 2:30 P.M.," box 313, National Security File (Kennedy Library).

officials met secretly with Americans in Washington. On October 28 the Soviet Union agreed to withdraw the missiles, and the United States promised not to invade Cuba in the future. That promise did not spring from domestic political calculations but from a desire to end a dangerous crisis. A pledge not to invade Cuba, after all, would hardly satisfy Republicans, who could be expected to argue in the 1964 presidential campaign that Kennedy had permitted the "Red menace" to remain in the Western Hemisphere. Still, during those hair-trigger days, did Kennedy and the Democrats play politics with the crisis? Preoccupied with the danger of nuclear war, exhausted from the ordeal of decision making, fearful that some naval officer on patrol in the Caribbean might make a military mistake, wondering whether Castro might escalate tensions by seizing control of the missiles, and pressed by some advisers to act militarily because they believed the Russians were stalling, the president, not surprisingly, spent little time on political considerations. But he did work to reduce the partisanship over Cuba, hoping to create a national consensus. Not only would such unity at home signal Khrushchev that he could not count on exploiting divisions within the United States; it also would take the issue out of the congressional campaign.

For the most part, Republicans quickly endorsed the president's policy. As one Republican put it, Cuba was "dead for the duration." Keating allowed that the president "has taken Cuba out of politics." As much as they backed Kennedy's policy, however, Republicans also grumbled that the crisis was politically motivated. Some crowed that the president would not have acted had it not been for the opposition party's pressure, and others criticized the administration for not going all the way—getting rid of the Castro regime. Sorensen prepared a memorandum answering each of those complaints. On that which held that Kennedy was driven to act by politics, Sorensen's note answered with an emphatic "NO!"[42]

In this period the administration sought to mold a popular,

[42]*New York Times,* Oct. 23, 1962, p. 18; *ibid.,* Oct. 24, 1962, p. 16; "Statement of Senator Cotton on President Kennedy's Speech on Cuba," Oct. 22, 1962, Cotton Papers; *Chicago Tribune,* Oct. 27, 1962, pt. 1, p. 5; TCS [Sorensen], "GOP Charges That," memorandum, Oct. 28, 1962, box 48, Sorensen Papers.

bipartisan consensus. The ExCom meeting of October 23 discussed the need for "unity on the home front." The release of low-level photographs of the missile sites "to prove to laymen [the] existence of missiles" might help, thought the Kennedy advisers. The president ordered his cabinet to cancel all campaign appearances. He called Eisenhower and urged Republicans not to make the Cuban crisis partisan. "I replied I was sure they wouldn't," recalled the former president. In another effort at bipartisanship, Kennedy sent the respected Repubican public servant John J. McCloy to join Ambassador Adlai Stevenson at the United Nations. Republicans were brought into the foreign-policy discussions, Sorensen said, because "Republicans in and out of Congress would be much less likely to attack a McCloy or a [CIA Director John] McCone, McNamara or Dillon." The administration also provided regional State Department briefings for public officials of both parties in New York, Chicago, Atlanta, Fort Worth, and San Francisco.[43]

Nearly every account of the crisis quotes a discussion of October 24 between the president and his brother Robert, which the latter related in his memoir, *Thirteen Days.* At the time Soviet ships were heading toward the naval blockade; violent confrontation seemed possible. "It looks really mean, doesn't it," the president said. "But, then, really there was no other choice. If they get this mean on this one in our part of the world, what will they do on the next?" The attorney general replied: "I just don't think there was any choice, and not only that, if you hadn't acted, you would have been impeached." The president agreed: "That's what I think—I would have been impeached."[44] Does that exchange demonstrated that the Kennedys acted to save themselves politically? Actually it demon-

[43] McGeorge Bundy, "Executive Committee Minutes, October 23, 1962, 10:00 A.M.," box 8, Vice Presidential Security File, Johnson Papers; Lyndon B. Johnson, handwritten notes for ExCom meeting, 10:00 A.M., Oct. 23, 1962, *ibid.;* Malcolm Moos, "Interview with President Dwight D. Eisenhower, Gettysburg, Pa., Nov. 8, 1966," box 11, Post-Presidential Papers: Augusta, Ga., Eisenhower Papers; Sorensen interview, 69; *New York Times,* Oct. 25, 1962, pp. 1, 21.

[44] Kennedy, *Thirteen Days,* 67.

strates little, because President Kennedy intended to act, to force the missiles from Cuba, from the moment he learned about them. He never hesitated in that intention; thus impeachment for inaction was a farfetched notion. Assuming that the conversation occurred exactly as reported, it was an exaggeration perhaps induced by the tensions of the moment.

If the president engaged in political partisanship during this period, it was understated. On October 25, for example, he wrote a letter intended for public release to Gov. Gaylord A. Nelson of Wisconsin, who was running for the Senate against incumbent Republican Alexander I. Wiley. Kennedy apologized for having had to cancel his campaign trip to the Badger State, "because your election is important to the nation." Without specifically mentioning the missile crisis, he went on: "More than ever before, we need men in the United States Senate who have the judgment, imagination, courage and leadership to meet the critical tests confronting our country." Since there could have been no doubt about the nation's "critical test" at that moment, the letter amounted to a campaign document exploiting the Cuban crisis to help a Democrat. Yet this appears to be the only instance of presidential politicking during the tense days of October 23–38. Even Lyndon B. Johnson, the most political of politicians, jotted down nothing of a political nature during high-level meetings in that period.[45]

October 29 to Election Day, November 6

From the time of the American–Soviet agreement to the day of the midterm elections, the politics of the Cuban question heated up again. Kennedy's actions had not removed the issue from the campaign, for Republicans once again tried to win favor at the polls by charging that Kennedy's Cuba policy had failed: Cuba remained a Soviet military ally; the Monroe Doctrine stood repudiated; Castro still sat atop a Communist re-

[45] John F. Kennedy to Gaylord A. Nelson, Oct. 25, 1962, box 691, White House Central Files (Kennedy Library); Johnson, handwritten notes, Oct. 23–26, box 8, Vice Presidential Security File, Johnson Papers.

gime, bent on subversion in Latin America; and one way of ousting both the Castroites and the Soviets from the island in the future—invasion—had been denied by presidential pledge. Furthermore, with Castro's obstruction of onsite inspection by United Nations officials, suspicions grew that the missiles were not being removed. Unsubstantiated stories circulated by Cuban exiles suggested that the missiles were being hidden in caves.[46] As of election day Kennedy could not unequivocally demonstrate that all the missiles had been shipped back to the Soviet Union. And to gather evidence of dismantling, American surveillance planes crossed Cuba, always with the risk of being shot down, as had happened once already, on October 27. Kennedy now approved such intelligence flights on a one-by-one basis, apprehensive of an attack that would inflame Cuban-Soviet-American relations, force him to retaliate, and spark war. The political damage at home would also be great, for it would seem to confirm Republican complaints that Kennedy had not really solved the Cuban problem. In this period the administration and Democratic leaders continued efforts to build a popular consensus, worked to reassure the public that the missiles were in fact departing, and sought to counter Republican "sniping."[47] As before October 16, American politics and Cuba became conspicuously intertwined.

President Kennedy must have grimaced when he read what Eisenhower said at a campaign rally in Syracuse, New York, on October 29. The former president had not long before urged that Cuba be taken out of the campaign, but now he turned partisan. Only Republican prodding, evident in the Cuba Resolution, he argued, had enabled Kennedy to act forcefully in the crisis. The next day several right-wing Americans organized the

[46] Wallace F. Bennett to Kennedy, Nov. 1, 1962, box 47, White House Central Files (Kennedy Library). At the November 6, 1962 ExCom meeting, Kennedy called attention to such stories, which, he was told, were never substantiated. The president "asked that this fact be brought to the attention of appropriate news editors." "NSC Executive Committee Record of Action, November 6, 1962, 6:15 P.M., Meeting No. 21," box 8, Vice Presidential Security File, Johnson Papers.

[47] Samuel C. Brightman to Pierre Salinger, Oct. 31, 1962, box 47, White House Central Files (Kennedy Library).

San Cristobal missile site shown in reconnaissance photograph of October 23, 1962, released on November 2, 1962. *Still Media Depository, United States Department of Defense, Washington, D.C.*

Committee for the Monroe Doctrine. Backed by some Republican congressmen, by pundits such as William F. Buckley, Jr., and by former military officers such as Adm. Arthur W. Radford, the committee protested that Kennedy had guaranteed a "Communist colony" in violation of the Monroe Doctrine's invocation against the extension of a foreign "system" into the Western Hemisphere. Other Republicans pressed the question. For example, Goldwater joined Rep. Bob Wilson, chairman of the House Republican campaign committee, to ask the president to abrogate the agreement with the Soviet Union. The no-invasion pledge, they complained, had "locked Castro and Communism into Latin America and thrown away the key to their removal." The *Chicago Tribune,* a staunchly Republican newspaper, ran a front-page cartoon showing a Democratic donkey holding a placard lettered "Read All about Cuba." A forlorn elephant remarks: "But only a couple of weeks ago, you were begging me not to mention the Cuban issue." The cartoon was titled "Last Minute Drive for Votes."[48]

Did Kennedy and the Democrats use Cuba in a drive for votes during the last week of the campaign? They did, but they were puzzled about how to go about it without appearing to be crass. The Democratic National Committee prepared drafts of some "fairly rough speeches" on Cuba for candidates, but whether they were used is not clear. Kennedy sent letters meant for publication to candidates, playing on the theme of the need for "men of strength" in "this hour of national crisis." From the beginning of the crisis, the White House had managed the news. The president restricted his advisers, telling those present at the ExCom meeting of October 30, for example, that all discussions with the press had to have his autho-

[48] *New York Times,* Oct. 30, 1962, pp. 1, 16; *ibid.,* Oct. 31, 1962, p. 19; Edward V. Rickenbacker to Sen. Jack Miller, Dec. 10, 1962, with attachments, box 145, Young Papers; Marvin Liebman to Rickenbacker, "Committee for the Monroe Doctrine: *Report #1,*" memorandum, Nov. 5, 1962, box 65, Liebman Associates Papers (Hoover Institution Archives, Stanford, Calif.); *Congressional Quarterly Almanac, 1962,* 338; Republican Congressional Committee, "Cuban Issue," 14; Press Release, Nov. 1, 1962, Cotton Papers; *Chicago Tribune,* Nov. 2, 1962, p. 1.

rization. He wanted a consistent story to come out of the State and the Defense departments, and he also sought to prevent Cuban exiles from buying radio time to attack United States policy. As well, the president released aerial photographs just three days before the election in order to prove the dismantling of the Soviet missile bases.[49]

Kennedy's aides thought that a large voter turnout on November 6 would help the Democrats. But how could the administration induce voters to the polls without appearing to be crassly exploiting the missile crisis? Secretary of Agriculture Orville Freeman proposed that friendly commentators be encouraged to urge citizens to vote Democratic in "this hour of crisis" to demonstrate to the world national backing for the president's policy toward Cuba. A few days later Schlesinger advised the president to capitalize on the Cuban crisis by issuing a statement himself, "calling on the nation to show its gratitude for its democratic opportunities by voting in unprecedented numbers next Tuesday."[50]

Advisers to the president discovered in the Advertising Council a way to arouse voter participation without their suffering the stigma of playing politics with foreign policy. Assistant to the President Timothy J. Reardon, Jr., suggested to the president of the Advertising Council, a business-funded nonprofit organization that produced advertisements deemed "in the public interest," that a heavy vote in November would indicate to the Soviets that Americans "in times of crisis" value "our free system of government." Reardon recommended a

[49] "NSC Executive Committee Record of Action . . . Meeting No. 21," Johnson Papers; Kennedy to Edmund G. Brown, Oct. 31, 1962, box 47, White House Central Files (Kennedy Library); "NSC Executive Committee Record of Action, October 30, 1962, 10:00 A.M., Meeting No. 13," box 8, Vice Presidential Security File, Johnson Papers; Kern, Levering, and Levering, *Kennedy Crises,* 123–40; Press Release, Nov. 2, 1962, box 5, Schlesinger Papers; *Public Papers . . . Kennedy,* 821. Kennedy decided on November 5 not to release pictures or information gathered from aerial reconnaissance missions on November 4. "NSC/Executive Record of Action, November 5, 1962, 10:00 A.M., Meeting No. 20," box 8, Vice Presidential Security File, Johnson Papers.

[50] Orville Freeman to Robert F. Kennedy, Oct. 29, 1962, box 12, Attorney General's Personal Correspondence, Robert F. Kennedy Papers (Kennedy Library); Arthur Schlesinger, Jr., Memorandum for the President, Nov. 1, 1962, box 5, Schlesinger Papers.

mass-media campaign. In response the council prepared several announcements and on October 29 sent them to every television and radio station in the United States. One of the sixty-second announcements read: "It is well to remind ourselves that these weeks of crisis do not mean the end of Communist threats to our security. *They will threaten us again.* . . . Let's show the Communists. Let's pile up the biggest vote in history." Two days later a similar advertisement was airmailed to 105 metropolitan daily newspapers. Pleased with the project, Press Secretary Pierre Salinger then asked the council to produce a one-minute film of former President Eisenhower's appealing for a large vote, to go along with a similar film, provided by the White House, of Kennedy's saying much the same. During the evening of November 2, the council air-expressed prints of both films to the major networks and 335 television stations; and it sent audiotapes of the messages to radio networks.[51]

Through that supposedly nonpartisan effort, the administration effectively linked the president's successful handling of the crisis with the elections. Yet analysts remained uncertain how the Cuban crisis would affect voters. Some speculated that apathetic voters would be stimulated to go to the polls; others predicted a low turnout; some concluded that the crisis would help incumbents of both parties; still others wrote that the Democrats would benefit. Surely the Republican and the Democratic manipulations of the Cuban issue just before the elections aroused voter interest. November 6, 1962, marked the largest turnout of eligible voters (47 percent) in any midterm election since 1922.[52]

[51] The Advertising Council estimated that about 35,000 television and radio messages were aired; at least 50 newspapers published the advertisement. T. S. Repplier to Broadcaster, Oct. 29, 1962, with attachments, box 693, White House Central Files (Kennedy Library); Arthur M. Wilson to Timothy J. Reardon, Jr., Oct. 29, 1962, *ibid.;* T. J. Reardon, Jr., Memorandum for the President, Nov. 13, 1962, *ibid.;* Repplier to the President, Dec. 4, 1962, *ibid.;* Salinger to Repplier, Dec. 17, 1962, *ibid.*

[52] *New York Times,* Oct. 26, Oct. 28, Oct. 30, 1962; Violet M. Gunther to Morris H. Rubin, Oct. 29, 1962, box 19, American for Democratic Action Papers (State Historical Society of Wisconsin, Madison); Matty Matthews, "1962 Senatorial Campaign Prospects," Nov. 2, 1962, box 23-G-4-2F, Senatorial Files, Humphrey Papers; *Congressional Quarterly Almanac, 1962,* 1047.

Election Day, November 6: The Outcome of House and Senate Races

The elections of 1962 barely changed party alignment in the House. On the whole incumbents did well, and because most incumbents were Democrats, Democrats did well by the measurements of previous midterm elections. The Eighty-eighth Congress, elected on November 6, numbered 259 Democrats and 176 Republicans. The previous Congress was controlled by the Democrats, 263 to 174. Thus the Democrats lost only four seats, and the Republicans gained only two. Republican gains came in the South (5 seats); Democrats won 9 new seats in the West; in the Midwest the Democrats lost, but the Republicans made no gains, and in the East, both parties lost seats (see table 3).[53]

Because so many incumbents were victorious, can the defeat of those Republican incumbents who lost be explained by Kennedy's handling of the missile crisis? Did the election results stem from voter reaction to the crisis? Domestic-policy issues, local political peculiarities, the nature of the 1960 election, the strength of the Democratic party in voter registration, reapportionment, and the ancient practice of gerrymandering—

Table 3

Party Division in the 87th and 88th Congresses (By Geographic Section)

	East		*South*		*Midwest*		*West*		*Nation*	
87th Congress	129		120		129		59		437	
88th Congress	122		119		125		69		435	
87th Congress	D	R	D	R	D	R	D	R	D	R
(by party)	68	61	111	9	51	78	33	26	263	174
88th Congress	D	R	D	R	D	R	D	R	D	R
(by party)	65	57	105	14	47	78	42	27	259	176
Net Change	D	R	D	R	D	R	D	R	D	R
by Party	−3	−4	−6	+5	−4	—	+9	+1	−4	+2

SOURCE: *Congressional Quarterly Almanac, 1962* (Washington, 1962), 1034.

[53]*Congressional Quarterly Almanac, 1962,* 1034.

not the Cuban missile crisis—best explain the Republican party's failure to make significant gains in the House. In the nation as a whole, 206 representatives had to run in new or substantially altered districts. Reapportionment had allocated ten additional congressional districts to the West, and the Democrats won all but one of those new districts. Eight of the new districts were in California; Democrats won seven of them in large part because of a radical gerrymander.[54]

In California, redistricting victimized three incumbent Republicans: John H. Rousselot, Edgar W. Hiestand, and Gordon L. McDonough. Rousselot, a first-term congressman and member of the John Birch Society, represented Richard M. Nixon's old district. After gerrymandering, this conservative Republican district was transformed, with the Democrats enjoying a 62 to 38 percent advantage in registered voters. Democratic State Assemblyman Ronald B. Cameron defeated Rousselot by earning 53.1 percent of the popular vote. Hiestand, another John Birch Society member, was a sixth-term congressman who lost to Everett G. Burkhalter of the Los Angeles City Commission. After the state legislature altered Hiestand's district, it had 37,000 more registered Democrats than Republicans. Burkhalter won with 52.1 percent of the vote. McDonough, an eighteen-year House veteran, suffered as well from the gerrymandering of his district. He found himself with a new district in downtown Los Angeles, politically inhospitable for a conservative Republican. The state assembly had given his opponent, Edward R. Roybal, a liberal on the Los Angeles City Commission, a Democratic lead of 47,000 registered voters. Roybal took 56.5 percent of the popular vote on November 6. Two other California districts were also tailored to meet the needs of the Democratic Assemblymen Charles H. Wilson and Richard T. Hanna, both of whom won House seats by comfortable margins.[55]

Certainly the missile crisis affected voters in California and

[54] *Ibid.*, 1034, 1062; Victor C. Ferkiss, "Our '4-Party' System," *Nation,* Dec. 1, 1962, p. 368.

[55] *New York Times,* Sept. 2, 1962, p. 26; *Time,* Nov. 16, 1962, pp. 23–25; *Congressional Quarterly Almanac, 1962,* 1034, 1046; *Congressional Quarterly's Guide to U.S. Elections* (Washington, 1975), 846.

elsewhere in the West, but the intrusion of the crisis into the campaign season may not necessarily have helped Democrats. In the West both successful Republicans and successful Democrats had favored a strong stand against Cuba. In California's Eleventh District, for example, Democratic candidate William J. Keller lost badly to Rep. J. Arthur Younger. When he analyzed the outcome, Keller concluded that voters on the whole preferred incumbents, regardless of party. He also thought insufficient funds had hindered his campaign. But he fingered the Cuban missile crisis as a culprit in two ways. First, the briefing the administration gave to incumbents such as Younger "hurt," because it marked them as leaders. Second, the crisis caused the president to cancel his campaign visit to the Golden State. "We felt the campaign was hitting its stride until Cuba, then fell off and never recovered." On the other hand, the missile crisis may have set back Nixon's California gubernatorial candidacy. Elsewhere in the West, the Cuban crisis does not appear to have decided election results.[56]

In the Midwest, where the Democrats lost four seats and the Republicans gained none, redistricting and nonforeign-policy issues best explain electoral outcomes. Rep. Walter H. Judd of Minnesota, a prominent, conservative Republican spokesman on foreign policy and a twenty-year veteran of the House, had to seek reelection in an altered district. His district was changed to include all of Minneapolis, including the Demo-

[56]Frank H. Jonas, "The 1962 Elections in the West," *Western Political Quarterly,* 16 (June 1963), 384; Totton J. Anderson and Eugene C. Lee, "The 1962 Election in California," *ibid.,* 409; Royce D. Dalmatier, Clarence F. McIntosh, and Earl G. Waters, eds., *The Rumble of California Politics, 1848–1970* (New York, 1970), 347; William J. Keller to Charles Daley, Nov. 9, 1962, box 683, White House Central Files (Kennedy Library); Hal Cruzan to Charles Daley, Nov. 9, 1962, *ibid.;* Alice Franklin Bryant to Kennedy, Oct. 11, Oct. 14, 1962, box 980, *ibid.* In Washington, for example, Democratic candidate Alice Franklin Bryant lost very badly to Republican Congressman Thomas M. Pelly. Probably her image as a "peace candidate" lost her many votes. *Ibid.* In Montana, both incumbent Congressmen won—one a Democrat and the other a Republican, and Cuba was only one of many issues. In the First District, successful liberal Arnold Olsen ran on a platform of support for Kennedy's domestic legislation. In the Second District, conservative Republican James Battin targeted Kennedy's farm program. A post-election report on Battin's victory did not mention Cuba. Thomas Payne, "The 1962 Election in Montana," *Western Political Quarterly,* 16 (June 1963), 441–42; "Memorandum on Second Congressional District of Montana," n.d., box 686, White House Central Files (Kennedy Library).

cratic Farmer-Labor (DFL) party stronghold of North Minneapolis. On election day Judd carried his old precincts by 10,860 votes; but he lost the new precincts by 16,997 votes, and DFL candidate Donald M. Fraser defeated the incumbent.[57]

In Michigan, too, the Cuban issue seems to have counted minimally. In an at-large election, Democrat Neil Staebler beat his Republican opponent largely on domestic issues. Kennedy's handling of the Cuban issue before and after the crisis produced mixed results, according to Staebler's postelection analysis. Before October 22 Staebler had opposed a naval blockade of Cuba, scolding his Republican rival for advocating one. Then, when Kennedy imposed a blockade, Staebler had to struggle to "minimize the damage" to his campaign. He believed that the Cuban crisis was "a very helpful emotional stimulant, arousing many more people to vote"; it meant "a net change in our favor" but not enough to have decided the election. In Michigan's Sixth District, the incumbent Republican candidate won, and domestic issues were preeminent; "the Cuban triumph" yielded very few votes for the Democrat.[58]

Support for Kennedy's farm program proved lethal in 1962. In Kansas incumbents Robert Dole (Republican) and J. Floyd Breeding (Democrat) were pitted against one another in a new district. Breeding campaigned in support of the farm program; he not only lost to Dole—he also failed to carry twenty-one rural counties from his old district. In a new Illinois district, seven-term Rep. Peter F. Mack, Jr. (Democrat) was upended by Republican Paul Findley, another incumbent. Findley's active opposition to the farm bill apparently secured his victory. Overall in the nation every Republican incumbent from a farm district who sought reelection was victorious.[59]

[57] *Minneapolis Tribune,* Oct. 16, 1962, p. 4; *ibid.,* Oct. 28, 1962. Upper Midwest Sec., pp. 1, 5; *Congressional Quarterly Guide to U.S. Elections,* 847.

[58] Neil Staebler earned 52% of the popular vote to Alvin Bentley's 47.9%. *Congressional Quarterly Guide to U.S. Elections,* 847; Neil Staebler to John F. Kennedy, Nov. 17, 1962, box 686, White House Central File (Kennedy Library). In the Sixth District Republican Charles E. Chamberlain beat Democrat Don Hayworth. "Report on the Sixth District of Michigan Congressional Campaign," n.d., box 686, *ibid.*

[59] *Congressional Quarterly Almanac, 1962,* 1046; *Time,* Nov. 16, 1962, p. 23; "Whose Victory Was It?" *New Republic,* Nov. 17, 1962, pp. 5–6.

The Republican gain of five seats in the South might be attributed to southern opposition to Kennedy's civil rights advocacy and to the Meredith episode in Mississippi. Votes for Republican candidates surpassed previous levels throughout the region. Reapportionment may also explain the results. Seven southern states suffered an attrition of eight seats in the national redistribution, and all those seats were Democratic; but Florida gained four seats, Maryland one, and Texas one. Republicans won three of the six new seats. They also gained one seat each in West Virginia and North Carolina, where reapportionment matched incumbents in redrawn districts. In both cases Democratic-controlled gerrymanders backfired.[60] Finally, in the East, as elsewhere, the Cuban crisis was but one of several influences on voters choosing members of the House.

As for the Senate races, five incumbent senators were defeated in 1962—three Republicans and two Democrats. Republicans Capehart of Indiana and Alexander Wiley of Wisconsin lost for reasons not directly related to the Cuban issue. If anything, the missile crisis may have helped both to better showings. The defeat of the third Republican, Joe H. Bottum of South Dakota, was due to a combination of factors, only one of which was the Soviet-American confrontation over Cuba. The incumbent Democrat who lost in Wyoming—J. J. Hickey—was victimized by his own hand. He was actually an interim senator who had resigned the governorship to be appointed to the national position. The public resented his self-serving tactic. A heart attack, moreover, trimmed Hickey's campaign schedule. His opponent, former Gov. Milward L. Simpson, was a popular figure who campaigned on a states' rights, anti-Communist, be-tough-with-Cuba platform that also included rejection of Medicare. Personalities rather than issues probably decided the election.[61] The other incumbent Democrat to lose was Sen.

[60] *Congressional Quarterly Almanac, 1962,* 1031–1034, 1062.

[61] *Ibid.,* 1038; Charles Beall, "The 1962 Election in Wyoming," *Western Political Quarterly,* 16 (June 1963), 478; *New York Times,* Oct. 30, 1962, p. 13; Sen. Maurine B. Neuberger of Oregon campaigned for J. J. Hickey but knew he was "unsalvageable." Maurine B. Neuberger to Wayne Morse, Nov. 20, 1962, box 120, ser. B, Wayne Morse Papers (University of Oregon Library, Eugene).

John A. Carroll of Colorado. The Republicans swept the state in 1962, pushing Rep. Peter H. Dominick past Carroll. Although Dominick had hammered Carroll for not having earlier taken a hard stand against the Soviet military buildup in Cuba and although Carroll had tagged his opponent a "junior warhawk," public dissatisfaction with long-term Democratic control of state politics and perhaps anti-Catholic bias decided the election.[62]

A closer look at the losses of the Republican incumbents reveals that while Cuba was an issue other issues counted as much or more. Bottum's loss in South Dakota owed a great deal to state politics. When Republican Sen. Francis Case died in June 1962, the governor turned the choice of a successor over to the central committee of the Republican party. Many candidates vied for the position, and after a rancorous meeting lasting ten hours, Bottum won the interim seat and was duly appointed. The Republican party was rife with squabbling factions, and Bottum, who had a reputation as a "hatchet man" for his party, proved a weak and vulnerable candidate. Further complicating Bottum's chances was an allegation that he and his wife were alcoholics—a change Bottum seemed to substantiate through a tear-filled public denial. George McGovern also ran an effective campaign, which included a Charles Guggenheim film, *The Dakota Story.* This masterful piece of propaganda depicted McGovern as courageous (World War II battle scenes), God-fearing (old family church footage), educated (student and professor) and patriotic (Food for Peace director who combatted Communism). With a substantial lead at the beginning, Bottum slipped in the polls before the Cuban missile crisis. By election day McGovern had taken the lead, helped in part by Kennedy's handling of the crisis. "His people," Schlesinger reported to the president before the election, "feel that Cuba has played a big role in this shift."[63]

[62] Democrats had held the governorship since 1954, and John A. Carroll's wife was Catholic. The religious issue had also been apparent in Colorado in 1960. *Denver Post,* Nov. 5, 1962, p. 3; Curtis Martin, "The 1962 Election in Colorado," *Western Political Quarterly,* 16 (June 1963), 421–25; Jonas, "The 1962 Elections in the West," 377.

[63] Arthur Schlesinger, Jr., "Good News from South Dakota," Memorandum

The most conspicuous incumbent to lose in 1962 was Republican Senator Capehart. He, more than anyone else seeking reelection had spoken to the Cuban issue. The president campaigned in the Hoosier State for the Democratic candidate Birch E. Bayh, Jr., a state representative. The White House also asked Louis Harris to conduct an intensive survey of Indiana voters. Harris discovered that Capehart's lead over Bayh was modest in the early stages of the campaign, despite the fact that Capehart was a three-term incumbent with name recognition. Harris learned too that Capehart evoked little enthusiasm among the electorate. Many voters found Capehart weak and indecisive, "a wind-bag, and playing politics too much." Capehart, moreover, had a negative rating on taxes, Medicare, unemployment, and inflation. Some complained about the senator's "intemperate views on going to war with Cuba," but in the Harris poll only 1 percent of his constituents saw Cuba as the paramount issue of the campaign even though Capehart tried to make it such. Bayh won just 50.3 percent of the vote. It does not appear that voters turned Capehart out because of his stand on Cuba or because of the president's stewardship of the crisis, but because Capehart failed to establish a positive image on the issues and as a personality against a young, energetic candidate who ran a high-exposure campaign. The Cuban missile crisis may have actually helped Capehart because it permitted him to use the "I was right all along" refrain.[64]

Age, asperity, and the issue of Medicare best explain the defeat of the dean of Republican senators, Wiley of Wisconsin. Wiley was seventy-eight years old and seeking a fifth term. His Democratic challenger, Gov. Gaylord A. Nelson, who was

---

for the President, Nov. 2, 1962, box 652, Staff Memoranda—Schlesinger, President's Office File (Kennedy Library); Robert S. Anson, *McGovern: A Biography* (New York, 1972), 121–26; George S. McGovern, *Grassroots* (New York, 1977), 89–91; *Minneapolis Tribune,* Oct. 25, 1962, p. 5.

[64] Louis Harris and Associates, Inc., "The Race for United States Senator—Indiana," n.d., box 105, Subjects, President's Office File (Kennedy Library); Schlesinger, *Thousand Days,* 18; *New York Times,* Sept. 1, 1962, p. 18; *ibid.,* Oct. 14, 1962, pp. 1, 43; *ibid.,* Oct. 29, 1962, p. 20; *Time,* Nov. 16, 1962, p. 26; *Los Angeles Times,* Nov. 4, 1962, sec. G, p. 2.

forty-six, made age an issue. Throughout the campaign Wiley displayed a grumpy explosiveness and carelessness. Medicare and drug control, he said, were "pipsqueak issues." In early October a reporter asked him whether he had changed his opposition to Medicare. The senator shot back: "Keep your damn nose out of my business and I'll keep my nose out of yours." When the reporter rose later to ask another question, Wiley boomed: "Keep your mouth shut." About two weeks later Wiley told reporters before a press conference that he wanted questions "without any nigger in the woodpile," and he shouted down still another reporter. Wiley apologized, but his style antagonized many. The *Burlington Standard Press,* a conservative Republican newspaper, abandoned Wiley and endorsed Nelson.[65] Without doubt Nelson's greatest asset was his opponent.

Before the missile crisis Nelson believed he had Wiley "on the run," in part because Congress had recessed and Wiley had come home to display his offensive style. But then the Cuban missile crisis intruded. Nelson feared it set back his campaign. First, the president canceled a scheduled trip to Wisconsin. Second, as Nelson noted at the time, "it has removed Wiley from the state just when his true character was becoming apparent to the voters." And, third, because Wiley was called to Washington to meet with Kennedy on October 22, the crisis "portrayed him as one of sixteen Congressional leaders upon whom the President counts." One of Nelson's close associates remarked: "This [Cuba] was no break for us." Nelson quickly applauded the quarantine and tried to contrast the president's (and Nelson's) "statesmanship" with Wiley's "slogans without meaning." But Wiley claimed headlines, making much of his supposed importance during the crisis. One press release read: "Re-called to Washington by the President for consultation on the Cuban situation, Senator Wiley also has been conferring with top defense and intelligence officials." The Cuban missile

[65] *Milwaukee Journal,* Oct. 16, Oct. 9, Oct. 21, 1962; *Chicago Tribune,* Oct. 28, 1962, pt. 1, p. 6. For criticisms of Alexander Wiley, see also *Sheboygan Press,* Oct. 16, 1962; and *Janesville* [Wisconsin] *Daily Gazette,* Oct. 11, 1962.

crisis may have reinvigorated Wiley's campaign, but Democrat Nelson won nonetheless with 52.6 percent of the vote.[66] The president's handling of the crisis, then, actually boosted a Republican—just as Kennedy had feared might happen.

In other senatorial contests the influence of the Cuban issue varied. In New Hampshire a fractured Republican party permitted Thomas J. McIntyre to become his state's first Democratic senator since 1932. In Idaho the two incumbents, Democrat Frank Church and Republican Leonard B. Jordan won. Jordan beat Rep. Gracie Pfost even though her record on foreign and domestic issues was similar to Church's. The Cuban issue was not decisive in the results. In Utah it was only one of several issues, but Republican incumbent Wallace F. Bennett, who had urged a blockade and war against Cuba before the missile crisis, exploited his initiative on the Cuban issue, and it may have helped him. In South Carolina local Democrats believed that the missile crisis augmented Sen. Olin D. Johnson's vote count by diverting attention from the Mississippi controversy. As Johnston told the president by telephone in the midst of the missile crisis, "Your stand . . . meant a lot to our party down there—brought the people together." Johnston's drawing of 57.2 percent of the vote, however, suggests that he had the election well in hand before the Cuban crisis. Finally, to cite another senatorial contest, incumbent Republican Dirksen, Senate minority leader, defeated Democratic Rep. Sidney R. Yates in Illinois. Dirksen was one of the leaders the president had called to Washington. But by then the senator's reelection seemed certain, and Kennedy had given only lukewarm support to Yates. The state's other senator, Democrat Paul H. Douglas, concluded that Dirksen and Kennedy had essentially struck a bargain wherein the president would not work to

[66] Gaylord A. Nelson to Humphrey, Oct. 23, 1962, box 691, White House Central Files (Kennedy Library); *LaCross Tribune,* Oct. 28, 1962; campaign tape recording, 1962, box 208, Gaylord A. Nelson Papers (State Historical Society of Wisconsin); Press Release, Oct. 27, 1962, box 18, Alexander I. Wiley Papers, *ibid.* For the Nelson-Wiley contest, see also *Milwaukee Tribune,* Oct. 26, Oct. 28, 1962; *Chicago Tribune,* Oct. 28, 1962, pt. 1, p. 6; *Milwaukee Journal,* Oct. 28, 1962; *Time,* Nov. 16, 1962, p. 26; and *Minneapolis Tribune,* Oct. 28, 1962, p. 4B.

unseat the senator. At one point during the missile crisis, Kennedy had remarked personally to Dirksen that he did not need to campaign. "You're just as good as in." The press had picked up this bit of news, speculating that Kennedy had written off a member of his own party.[67]

A familiar theory holds that voters tend not to favor newcomers in times of crisis. To the extent that this is true, the Cuban missile crisis benefited Senate and House incumbents—and 1962 was a good year for incumbents. As Republican Rep. Thomas B. Curtis of Missouri later explained, the missile showdown "gave all the incumbents running for reelection a great build-up. We were important. . . . This is what saved the Democrat controlled Congress, the great plus given to incumbents. Of course, Republican incumbents got the same benefit, but we were in the minority and we stayed in the minority."[68] But the proposition that voters prefer not to change leaders in moments of crisis does not adequately explain the complexity of the 1962 election. Many of the losers of both parties were Washington veterans (Judd, Capehart, Wiley, Yates, Pfost, Rousselot, Hiestand, McDonough, and Carroll, among others). And some of the winners were newcomers to national office (Bayh, McIntyre, Nelson, and Simpson, among others). In some cases, moreover, such as in North Carolina and Kansas, congressional reapportionment had paired incumbents against one another, ensuring the defeat of some.

The effects of the Cuban missile crisis seem indiscriminate. The crisis helped some Democrats and hurt some Democrats; it buoyed some Republicans and weakened some Republicans. In many instances Cuba was not even a conspicuous campaign issue. The historian cannot identify one election in 1962 de-

[67] *Congressional Quarterly Almanac, 1962,* 1032; William O. Lewis, "The 1962 Election in Idaho," *Western Political Quarterly,* 16 (June 1963), 433–34; Stewart L. Grow, "The 1962 Election in Utah," *ibid.,* 465; Robert L. Stoddard to Kennedy, Nov. 13, 1962, box 47, White House Central Files (Kennedy Library); Olin D. Johnston telephone call to Kennedy, memorandum, Oct. 26, 1962, box 155, President's Office File (Kennedy Library); Paul H. Douglas, *In the Fullness of Time: The Memoirs of Paul H. Douglas* (New York, 1972), 573–75; MacNeil, *Dirksen,* 205–206.

[68] Thomas B. Curtis to Paterson, Feb. 13, 1984 (in Paterson's possession).

cided by voter reaction to the missile crisis—not a single outcome where the Cuban issue made the difference between victory and defeat. The results of the House and the Senate races, in other words, are best explained by the mix of other factors discussed in this article: personalities and their public images; local politics; domestic issues; reapportionment and gerrymandering; superior Democratic party registration; and the nature of the 1960 election.

Kennedy did not engage Cuba and the Soviet Union in the missile crisis in October in order to silence his noisy Republican critics or to attract votes for Democrats in November. As Kennedy knew before October 16, the Democrats already enjoyed a formidable position in the elections. Republicans had taken the initiative on Cuba through their constant scolding of the administration, but they had not persuaded voters to dump Democrats. The Democrats had no political need to manufacture a war scare, and Kennedy did not welcome a new Cuban crisis. From October 16 to October 22, Kennedy's choice of the quarantine was not dictated by politics, although the tactic of the television address may have been. From the alarmist speech to the fading of the crisis on October 28, Kennedy ruminated about the political effects of the imbroglio, but, again, his decisions did not reflect a partisan stance; he did not, for example, shift from the potentially unworkable and slow-paced quarantine to immediate and decisive military action. From October 28, when Khrushchev capitulated to Kennedy's ultimatum, to the election on November 6, both Republicans and Democrats exploited Cuba for political advantage. Neither party, it seems, particularly profited from the Cuban missile crisis on election day. The politics of the Cuban issue in the fall of 1962 was spirited and acrimonious but had limited impact on either the president's momentous decisions after the secret debate in Washington or the voter's decisions after entering polling places in every district in the United States.

As for what did shape President Kennedy's decisions in the Cuban missile crisis, scholars will find the answers, as they have already begun to do, in the study of his personality traits, calculations of national security and hemispheric hegemony, and perceptions of international power, prestige, and credibility.

JAMES A. NATHAN

Cold War Model

Both historians and political scientists have examined the missile crisis to see what lessons it offers for the conduct of foreign policy. Some have seen it as a classic case of brinksmanship, drawing the conclusion that the best way to preserve peace is for the United States to remain strong and not shrink from military confrontations. Others have found the crisis very disturbing as a model for Cold War diplomacy; they point out that Khrushchev and Kennedy came very close to touching off a nuclear exchange. In this selection, political scientist James A. Nathan of the University of Delaware offers a sober assessment of the crisis, suggesting that Kennedy's hawkish policy may well have had an unfortunate impact on the subsequent conduct of American foreign policy.

INTRODUCTION

Historians know there is a rhythm to their craft. Events are examined and orthodoxies are established. Then comes a chipping away of previously held convictions. New understandings emerge and stand, at least for a while; and then comes another

James A. Nathan, "The Missile Crisis: His Finest Hour Now," *World Politics* 27, no. 2 (January 1975). Copyright © 1975 by Princeton University Press. Reprinted with permission of Princeton University Press.

*Most of the arguments contained in this article appeared in a paper delivered at the 1974 Annual Meeting of the American Political Science Association, Chicago, August 29–September 2, 1974.

tide of re-evaluation. The Kennedy Administration's shimmering hour—the Cuban missile crisis—has just begun to have its luster tarnished by critics. Yet few have subjected the event to a complex review of its meaning in terms of the assumptions, policy processes, and relationships of the cold war.[1]

My contention is that the crisis became something of a misleading "model" of the foreign policy process. There are seven central tenets of this model, each of which was "confirmed" by the "lessons" of the Cuban crisis:

(I) Crises are typical of international relations. The international environment is a constant collision of wills that is a surrogate of war and, at the same time, takes place at the doorstep of war. Crises are objective elements of the international system—but they also have a profoundly psychological element of "will" and "resolve."

(2) Crises are assumed to be manageable. The skills of personality, training, and organizational expertise that have been developed in the national security machinery during the past twenty-five years can be orchestrated by a vast bureaucracy in controlled and responsive movements.

(3) Although crises are a chracteristic of the international system, the domestic system is one of order and consensus, and is insulated from the necessities of international politics. Public opinion can be controlled to lend support for a particular foreign policy; but rarely do appurtenances of the domestic sector have their own imperatives.

[1] "Revisionist" critiques of the Cuban crisis are becoming more frequent. But most are rather polemical and thin. For a sample of some of the better ones, see Richard J. Walton, "The Cuban Missile Crisis" in *Cold War and Counter Revolution* (Baltimore 1972), 103–43; Leslie Dewart, "The Cuban Crisis Revisited," *Studies on the Left,* v (Spring 1965), 15–40; John Kenneth Galbraith, "Storm Over Havana: Who Were The Real Heroes?" (review of *Thirteen Days* by Robert F. Kennedy), *Book World,* January 19, 1969, 16; I. F. Stone, "The Brink" (review of *The Missile Crisis* by Elie Abel), *New York Review of Books,* April 1966, 13; Ronald Steel, "End Game," *New York Review of Books,* March 13, 1969, reprinted in Steel, *Imperialists and Other Heroes* (New York 1971), 115; Louise FitzSimmons, *The Kennedy Doctrine* (New York 1972), 126–73.

(4) Diplomacy is a mixture of the instrumentation of force and bargaining. An essential element of crisis management is the ability to reconcile the inherent forward dynamic of violence, threats of violence, and the instruments of violence with negotiation.
(5) The United States can control the process of crisis negotiation to "win." "Winning" results in the conclusion of the events themselves. Political crises therefore terminate by definition, almost like medical crises.
(6) The Soviets seldom negotiate serious matters except under extreme duress.
(7) Military questions are too critical to be left in the hands of strictly military men and organizations that are not in step with the needs of crisis management. Crisis management can and must be a civilian enterprise.

After the Cuban missile crisis, there were the beginnings of détente with the Soviet Union. The test-ban treaty, the hot line, and a more civil exchange between the two powers are widely believed to stem from the favorable resolution of the missile crisis. Yet the model and the usual inherent assumptions on the meaning of Cuba can be challenged. Nevertheless, the Cuban missile crisis stands as a watershed of the cold war and in the history of the contemporary international system.

I. MASTERY OR LUCK?

By far the most intense experience in East-West relations occurred in October 1962, when the Russians were discovered to have placed forty-two medium-range missiles in Cuba. In Khrushchev's apt description, it was a time when "a smell of burning hung heavy" in the air.[2] Kennedy's apparently controlled and masterful way of forcing Khrushchev to withdraw the missiles in the thirteen-day crisis has become a paradigmatic example of the way force can be harnessed to a policy by

[2] Roger Hilsman, *To Move A Nation* (New York 1967), 48, 157; also cited in Steel, *Imperialists and Other Heroes*, 115.

an elaborate manipulation of threats and gambits, negotiation and intimidation. Academic and government analysts have viewed Kennedy's response as a highly calibrated dissection of alternatives instead of seeing his actions as largely an intuitive response to a threat to his administration's electoral future, pride, and strategic posture. As Hans J. Morgenthau, the eminent scholar and a critic of the Kennedy Administration, concluded: "The Cuban Crisis of 1962 . . . was the distillation of a collective intellectual effort of a high order, the like of which must be rare in history."[3] Much of this analysis—so drenched in the cool light of hindsight—bears a suspicious resemblance to the logical and psychological fallacy of reasoning, *post hoc, ergo proper hoc*.[4] Nevertheless, the dominant lesson Americans have drawn from the Cuban experience has been a joyous sense of the United States regaining mastery over history.

For many years Americans had felt threatened by the Soviet challenge to world order—especially since that challenge had been reinforced by growing Russian strategic capability. But after Cuba, the fears of precipitate expansion of a Soviet–American dispute into a final paroxysm of nuclear dust were dissipated. After Cuba, "escalation" became the *idée fixe* of academics and policy-makers—a vision of a ladder of force with rungs separated by equivalent spaces of destruction, each with its own "value," running out toward darkness. Escalation became the dominant metaphor of American offcialdom. Each rung could be ascended or descended with the proper increment of will and control. Events and military machines could be mastered for diplomatic ends. As Robert McNamara exalted after the exciting and frightening Cuban climax: "There is no longer any such thing as strategy, only crisis management."[5] Dennis Healy, the British Labor Party "shadow" Defense Minister called the Kennedy Administration's performance a

[3] Morgenthau, *Truth and Power, Essays of a Decade, 1960–1970* (New York 1970), 158.

[4] A current review of this enormous literature is contained in Charles F. Hermann, ed., *International Crisis: Insights from Behavioral Research* (New York 1972).

[5] Cited by Coral Bell, *The Conventions of Crisis: A Study in Diplomatic Management* (London 1971), 2.

"model in any textbook on diplomacy."[6] Journalist Henry Pachter described Kennedy's execution of crisis management as "a feat whose technical elegance compelled the professionals' admiration."[7] Similarly, the Wohlstetters made Cuba into a general historical principle about the use of force in times of great stress: "where the alternative is to be ruled by events with such enormous consequences, the head of a great state is likely to examine his acts of choice in crisis and during it to subdivide these possible acts in ways that make it feasible to continue exercising choice."[8]

The decisions as to what steps should be taken to deal with the implantation of the missiles were hammered out in the ExCom meetings. Although court chroniclers of the Kennedy Administration have pored over each detail, the impression now is not one of all choices having been carefully weighed and considered. Rather, in retrospect, there appears to have been a gripping feeling of uncertainty and pressure. Robert Kennedy, for instance, at the height of the crisis, looked across at his brother and almost fainted at the horror of what they were contemplating: "Inexplicably, I thought of when he was ill and amost died; when he lost his child, when we learned that our oldest brother had been killed; of personal times of strain and hurt. The voices droned on, but I didn't seem to hear anything. . . ."[9]

There were reports that one Assistant Secretary was so disconcerted and fatigued that he drove into a tree at 4 a.m. Robert Kennedy recalled, "The strain and the hours without sleep were beginning to take their toll. . . . That kind of pressure does strange things to a human being, even to brilliant, self-confident, mature, experienced men."[10] And President Ken-

[6] Alexander George and others, *The Limits of Coercive Diplomacy* (Boston 1971), 132.

[7] Pachter, "J.F.K. as an Equestrian Statue: On Myths and Myth Makers," *Salmagundi* (Spring 1966), cited in George, *ibid*.

[8] Albert and Roberta Wohlstetter, "Controlling the Risks in Cuba," *Adelphi Paper No. 17* (London, Institute for Strategic Studies, April 1965), 19.

[9] Kennedy, *Thirteen Days: A Memoir of the Cuban Missile Crisis* (with "Afterword" by Richard Neustadt and Graham T. Allison) (New York 1971), 48.

[10] Kennedy (fn. 9), 22; Sorensen, *Kennedy* (New York 1969), 705; Hermann (fn. 4), 33.

nedy, although deliberately pacing himself, wondered if some of his principal advisors had not suffered mental collapse from the long hours and pressure. Tense, fearful, and exhausted men planned and held together the American policy response to the Russian missiles.

The consensus of most behavioral research is that men operating under such acute stress are scarcely capable of considered judgment. Strain and fatigue commonly produce actions which are "caricatures of day-to-day behavior."[11] Although the stress of crisis decision-making concentrates and focuses the collective mind, it does not allow for the kind of elegant dissection of events that is now read into the Cuban affair. Events can take charge of decision-makers; on October 25, 1962, Robert Kennedy reported that he felt, as Soviet ships drew near the edge of the American quarantine, that "[W]e were on the edge of a precipice with no way off. . . . President Kennedy had initiated the course of events, but he no longer had control over them."[12] John F. Kennedy's calm public face, discipline, and cool control gave a sense of intellectual engagement in the crisis which yielded no hint of the mute wasteland he was contemplating. But his private anxiety is well recorded, and a case can be made that dispassionate analysis of problem-solving was all but precluded by the psychology of the situation.

It was very close. The military and the "hawks"—a term coined by journalistic descriptions of the ExCom deliberations—were pushing for actions ranging from a "surgical strike" to an all-out invasion of Cuba. Such options would have demanded the stark choice of an even greater Soviet humiliation or a Soviet response in kind. Ironically, a "surgical strike" was not really practical, for there was no guarantee that more than 90 percent of the missiles could be extirpated. Even after an American air attack, some of the missiles could have survived and been launched. And "surgical" always was a misnomer to describe an estimated 25,000 Cuban fatalities, not to speak of the 500 sorties which American planes would have had to run in order to "take out" the Soviet missiles and

[11] See Thomas W. Milburn, "The Management of Crisis," in Hermann (fn. 4), esp. pp. 263–66.

[12] Kennedy (fn. 9), 48–49.

bombers. Nevertheless, if six out of fourteen members of the ExCom group had had their way, the blockade of Cuba would have been an attack, which Bobby Kennedy called a "Pearl Harbor in reverse." It is no wonder that President Kennedy estimated the world's chance of avoiding war between one out of three and even.[13]

The illusion of control derived from the crisis was perniciously misleading. Although many Americans shared the belief of historian Schlesinger that the Cuban crisis displayed to the "whole world . . . the ripening of an American leadership unsurpassed in the responsible management of power . . . [a] combination of toughness . . . nerve and wisdom, so brilliantly controlled, so matchlessly calibrated that [it] dazzled the world,"[14] President Kennedy's control was in fact far from complete. For example, the main instrument of pressure was the blockade run by the Navy. Following the suggestion of British Ambassador Ormsby-Gore, Kennedy decided to move the blockade closer to Cuba, from 800 miles to 500 miles, in order to give the Russian ships heading toward Cuba more time. The order was given but never carried out. The blockade remained at 800 miles.

McNamara had sensed the Navy's lack of responsiveness to civilian commands and had gone to the "Flag Plot," or Naval Operations Center, where he could talk to ship commanders directly by voice-scrambled radio. McNamara pointed to a map symbol indicating that a ship was in a spot where he had not wanted it. "What's that ship doing there?" he asked. Anderson confessed, "I don't know, but I have faith in my officers."[15] McNamara's unease with the apparent lack of responsiveness of the Navy to civilian command prompted him to inquire what would happen if a Soviet captain refused to divulge his cargo to a boarding American officer. Chief of Naval Operations Anderson picked up a Manual of Naval Regulations and rose to defend the Navy against any implied slight about Navy pro-

[13] Sorensen (fn. 10), 705.
[14] Arthur M. Schlesinger, Jr., *A Thousand Days* (Boston 1965), 840–41.
[15] Jack Raymond, *Power at the Pentagon* (New York 1964), 285–86.

cedure. "It's all in there," Anderson asserted. McNamara retorted, "I don't give a damn what John Paul Jones would have done. I want to know what you are going to do, now!" The last word—again, however—was the Navy's: Admiral Anderson patronizingly soothed the fuming Defense Secretary, "Now, Mr. Secretary, if you and your deputy will go to your offices, the Navy will run the blockade."[16] As McNamara and his entourage turned to leave, Anderson called to him, "Don't worry, Mr. Secretary, we know what we are doing here."[17]

Just when the first Soviet-American encounter at sea seemed imminent, William Knox, the president of Westinghouse International, who happened to be in Moscow, was surprised by an abrupt summons from Premier Khrushchev. The voluble Soviet leader, perhaps half-convinced that Wall Street really manipulated American policy, gave a frightening summary of the strategic situation in the Caribbean. He warned that if the U.S. Navy began stopping Soviet ships, the Soviet subs would start sinking American ships. That, Khrushchev explained, would lead to World War III.[18]

Only a little later, the Navy began to force Soviet subs to the surface in order to defend its blockade—well before Kennedy had authorized contact with surface vessels. Kennedy was appalled when he learned that military imperatives are distinct from diplomatic necessities and can, all too often, conflict. When he found out that the Navy was intent on surfacing ships, he was horrified: "Isn't there some way we can avoid having our first exchange with a Russian submarine—almost anything but that?" McNamara replied, "No, there's too much danger to our ships. There is no alternative." The President's brother wrote that "all six Russian submarines then in the area or moving toward Cuba from the Atlantic were followed and harassed and,

[16] Elie Abel, *The Missile Crisis* (Philadelphia 1969), 155–56. Abel interviewed the witnesses to this episode, some of whom did not agree as to Anderson's exact words. Anderson, Abel reports, could not recall ever having said this.

[17] William A. Hamilton, III, "The Decline and Fall of the Joint Chiefs of Staff," *The Naval War College Review*, XXIV (April 1972), 47.

[18] Abel (fn. 16), 151–52; Hilsman (fn. 2), 214; W. E. Knox, "Close-up of Khrushchev During a Crisis," *New York Times Magazine*, November 18, 1962, p. 128.

at one time or another, forced to surface in the presence of U.S. military ships."[19] One can only wonder what would have happened if one of the Russian subs had refused to surface and had instead turned on its pursuers.

Events were only barely under control when at the height of the crisis, on October 26, an American U-2 plane fixed on the wrong star and headed back from the North Pole to Alaska via Sibera. To compound matters the Alaskan Air Command sent fighter-bombers to escort the plane home, and the U.S. fighters and the spy plane met over Soviet territory before proceeding back.[20] To survive a Strangelove series of incidents like these, even given the assumptions of the day, can hardly be characterized as more than luck. It would not seem to be the mastery that Schlesinger and other court scribes delight in recalling and extolling.

II. THE DOMESTIC FACTOR

Why was there a crisis in the first place? The answer is found, in part, in one of the unacknowledged necessities in the conduct of American international affairs—domestic political considerations.[21] The Kennedy Administration's sense of its own precarious electoral position, the coming of the November midterm elections, and the place Cuba had occupied in public debate, all augured for an immediate and forceful response, no matter what the strategic reality was of having Russian missiles near American borders. The imperatives of American domestic politics during an election year had been building for some time. On August 27, 1962, for example, Republican Senator Homer E. Capehart of Indiana declared, "It is high time that the American people demand that President Kennedy quit

[19] Kennedy (fn. 9), 55.

[20] Irving Janis, *Victims of Group Think* (Boston 1972), 163; Henry Pachter, *Collision Course* (New York 1963), 58.

[21] Leslie Gelb and Morton Halperin, "The Ten Commandments of the Foreign Affairs Bureaucracy," *Harpers*, Vol. 244 (June 1972), 28–37; Leslie Gelb, "The Essential Domino: American Politics and Vietnam," *Foreign Affairs*, L (April 1972), 459–76.

'examining the situation' and start protecting the interests of the United States."[22] Former Vice President Nixon, on the gubernatorial campaign stump in California, proposed that Cuban communism be "quarantined" by the naval blockade.[23] Republicans in both Houses had warned the administration that Cuba would be "the dominant issue of the 1962 campaign."[24] The chairman of the Republican National Committee jabbed at Kennedy's most sensitive spot—his concern for foreign policy "resolve": "If we are asked to state the issue in one word, that word would be Cuba—symbol of the tragic irresolution of the administration."[25]

The pressure mounted. As the political campaign began, one observer spotted a sign at a Kennedy rally in Chicago which read, "Less Profile—More Courage."[26] The widely respected and conservative *London Economist* reported that America had become "obsessed" by the "problem" of Cuba;[27] and I. F. Stone despaired in his *Weekly* that Cuba was a bogey which shook Americans, in the autumn of 1962, even more than the thought of war.[28] The domestic pressure on the American President was so intense that one member of Camelot, former Ambassador John Kenneth Galbraith, wrote: "once they [the missiles] were there, the political needs of the Kennedy administration urged it to take almost any risk to get them out."[29] This skeptical view was shared by none other than former President Eisenhower, who suspected "that Kennedy might be playing politics with Cuba on the eve of Congressional elections."[30]

[22] "Capehart: U.S. Should Act, Stop 'Examining Cuba,'" *U.S. News and World Report,* September 10, 1962, p. 45.
[23] *New York Times,* September 19, 1962.
[24] "Cuban Crisis," *Data Digest* (New York 1963), 35, cited by Thomas Halper, *Foreign Policy Crisis: Appearance and Reality in Decision Making* (Columbus, Ohio 1971), 132.
[25] "Notes of the Month: Cuba: A U.S. Election Issue," *World Today,* XVIII (November 1962), 543; Halper (fn. 24), 132.
[26] Quincy Wright, "The Cuban Quarantine of 1962," in John G. Stoessinger and Alan Westin, ed., *Power and Order* (New York 1964), 186.
[27] *Economist,* October 6, 1962, p. 15.
[28] "Afraid of Everything but War," *I. F. Stone's Weekly,* September 17, 1962, p. 1.
[29] Quoted in Steel (fn. 1), 119.
[30] Abel (fn. 16), 78.

Nor, as Ronald Steel pointed out, were the "principals"—the ExCom—insulated from domestic considerations in their deliberations.[31] One Republican member of the crisis planners sent Theodore Sorensen—Kennedy's alter ego—a note that read: "Ted—have you considered the very real possibility that if we allow Cuba to complete installation and operational readiness of missile bases, the next House of Representatives is likely to have a Republican majority?"[32] Similarly, McGeorge Bundy, chief advisor to two presidents, wondered, when the missiles were first reported, whether action could be deferred until after the election.[33] If the missile installations were completed earlier, there would be, arguably, both a strategic and an electoral problem facing the administration.

What was the worrisome substance of change in the strategic balance represented by the placement of forty-two missiles? To Robert McNamara, the Secretary of Defense, it seemed that "A missile is a missile. It makes no great difference whether you are killed by a missile from the Soviet Union or from Cuba."[34] About two weeks later, on television, Deputy Secretary of Defense Roswell Gilpatrick confirmed the debatable meaning of the missiles: "I don't believe that we were under any greater threat from the Soviet Union's power, taken in totality, after this than before."[35] Indeed, Theodore Sorensen wrote in a memorandum to the President on October 17, 1962—five days before the blockade was ordered—that the presence of missiles in Cuba did not "significantly alter the balance of power." Sorensen explained, "They do not significantly increase the potential megatonnage capable of being unleashed on American soil, even after a surprise American nuclear strike." Sorensen confessed, in conclusion, that "Soviet motives were not understood."[36]

[31] Steel (fn. 1), 121.
[32] Sorensen (fn. 10), 688.
[33] George (fn. 6), 89.
[34] Hilsman (fn. 2), 195.
[35] *New York Times*, November 12, 1962.
[36] *Wilmington Morning News*, January 25, 1974.

III. JUST A DIRTY TRICK?

To Khrushchev, the missiles offered the appearance of what former State Department analyst Roger Hilsman called a "quick fix" to the Soviet problem of strategic inferiority. Khrushchev was under enormous pressure from the Russian military who rejected his "goulash communism" and were pushing for a vast increase in the Soviet arms budget.[37] The Cuban missile ploy was probably Khrushchev's response to the prospect of Russian strategic inferiority which was reported by the Kennedy Administration as it admitted that the Democratic pre-election charge of a "missile gap" had not been based on fact. The American announcement that the "gap" had been closed was accompanied by a Defense Department plan, dated October 19, 1961, for production of over one thousand missiles by 1964.

One purpose of the Soviet moves in Cuba was, therefore, to gain the *appearance* of parity with the Americans. The employment of twenty-four MRBM's and eighteen IRBM's *seemed* to be a dramatic movement in that direction. But such an increase posed no real threat to American retaliatory strength, or to increasing American superiority. As Henry Kissinger noted at the time, "The bases were of only marginal use in a defensive war. In an offensive war their effectiveness was reduced by the enormous difficulty—if not impossibility—of coordinating a first strike from the Soviet Union and Cuba."[38]

The U.S. Administration knew that the Soviets were not striving for more than an appearance of strategic equality. As Kennedy later reflected, they were not "intending to fire them, because if they were going to get into a nuclear struggle, they have their own missiles in the Soviet Union. But it would have

[37] Walter W. Layson, "The Political and Strategic Aspects of the 1962 Cuban Missile Crisis," unpub. Ph.D. diss. (University of Virginia 1969), 18–87; Thomas W. Wolfe, *Soviet Power and Europe, 1945–1970* (Baltimore 1970), 73–99, 100–194.

[38] Henry Kissinger, "Reflections on Cuba," *The Reporter,* XXVII, November 22, 1962, p. 22.

politically changed the balance of power. It would have appeared to, and appearances contribute to reality."[39] In the 1970's, by contrast, "appearances" were less important while the Americans were arranging a complex international order which verged on duopoly. Indeed, beginning in 1970, Soviet submarines and tenders began to visit Cuban ports.[40] And by 1973, Soviet submarines with Polaris-type missiles were regularly stopping in Cuba. What protest there was by the Nixon Administration seemed so muted as to be almost inaudible.[41]

Why was Kennedy so concerned about "appearances"? Perhaps he felt that the American people demanded an energetic response, given their purported frustration over Cuba. The administration's evaluation of the public mood supported the notion that firmness was a requisite of policy. Although repeated Gallup polls before the crisis showed 90 per cent of Americans opposing actual armed intervention in Cuba,[42] Kennedy's own sense was, as his brother pointed out, that if he did not act, he would have been impeached.[43]

Another explanation for Kennedy's concern that he would not "appear credible" to Khrushchev dates from the time, less than two years earlier, when he decided not to use air support for the Bay of Pigs invasion. According to James Reston's impression upon seeing Kennedy ten minutes after the two leaders had met in Vienna, "Khrushchev had studied the events of the Bay of Pigs; he would have understood if Kennedy had left Castro alone or destroyed him; but when Ken-

[39] Interview, December 17, 1962, *Public Papers of the Presidents,* John F. Kennedy (Washington, D.C. 1963), 898.

[40] *New York Times,* December 6, 1970. According to the authoritative *Aviation Week,* the Russians also began to schedule regular stops of long-range aircraft at about the same time. December 21, 1970, pp. 16–17.

[41] For a description of the forceful but private insistence that the building of a Soviet base at Cienfuegos be halted, see Marvin and Bernard Kalb, *Kissinger* (Boston 1974), 209–12. Nevertheless, sporadic press reports indicate that Soviet nuclear submarines are putting into Cuba up to this day. See Barry Blechman and Stephanie Levinson, "U.S. Policy and Soviet Subs," *New York Times,* October 22, 1974; *Washington Post,* October 26, 1974.

[42] "How U.S. Voters Feel About Cuba," *Newsweek,* October 13, 1962, p. 138, Halper (fn. 24), 133.

[43] Kennedy (fn. 9), 45, and "Afterword," 114.

nedy was rash enough to strike at Cuba but not bold enough to finish the job, Khrushchev decided he was dealing with an inexperienced young leader who could be intimidated and blackmailed."[44] Similarly, George F. Kennan, then the United States Ambassador to Yugoslavia, met the President after the Vienna summit session and reported that he found Kennedy "strangely tongue-tied" during these talks. Later, he recalled for a Harvard oral history interviewer:

> I felt that he had not acquitted himself well on this occasion and that he had permitted Khrushchev to say many things which should have been challenged right there on the spot.
>
> I think this was definitely a mistake. I think it definitely misled Khrushchev; I think Khrushchev failed to realize on that occasion what a man he was up against and also that he'd gotten away with many of these talking points; that he had placed President Kennedy in a state of confusion where he had nothing to say in return.[45]

Kennedy expressed concern to Reston and others that Khrushchev considered him but a callow, inexperienced youth and that he soon expected a "test." "It will be a cold winter," he was heard to mutter as he left the Vienna meeting. Khrushchev may indeed have been surprised at the forceful reaction of Kennedy, particularly after the young President had accepted the Berlin Wall in August 1961 with no military response and had temporized in Laos in 1961 and 1962.

Perhaps, as Hilsman has argued, the Soviets assumed that the fine American distinctions between "offensive and defensive" missiles were really a *de facto* acknowledgment of the Soviet effort in Cuba. One could conjecture that this was what led Khrushchev to promise, and to believe that Kennedy understood, that no initiatives would be taken before the elections. In any case, Kennedy's concern about his "appearance" and the national appearance of strength kept him from searching very far for Soviet motivation. His interpretation was that it was a personal injury to him and his credibility, as well as to Amer-

[44] Reston, "What Was Killed Was Not Only the President But the Promise," *New York Times Magazine,* November 15, 1964, p. 126.

[45] *New York Times,* September 1, 1970; *New York Daily News,* August 31, 1970.

ican power. He explained this sentiment to *New York Post* reporter James Wechsler:

> What worried him was that Khrushchev might interpret his reluctance to wage nuclear war as a symptom of an American loss of nerve. Some day, he said, the time might come when he would have to run the supreme risk to convince Khrushchev that conciliation did not mean humiliation. "If Khrushchev wants to rub my nose in the dirt," he told Wechsler, "it's all over." But how to convince Khrushchev short of a showdown? "That son of a bitch won't pay any attention to words," the President said bitterly on another occasion. "He has to see you move."[46]

IV. TRUE GRIT AND CRISIS DIPLOMACY

The missile crisis illuminates a feature of the American character that came to be considered a requisite personality trait of the cold war: being "tough." Gritty American determination had become the respected and expected stance of American statesmen under stress in confrontations with the Soviets from the earliest days of the cold war. When Truman, for example, dispatched an aircraft carrier, four cruisers, a destroyer flotilla, and the battleship Missouri to counter Soviet pressure on the Turkish Straits, he told Acheson, "We might as well find out whether the Russians [are] bent on world conquest now as in five or ten years."[47] Clark Clifford gave more formal expression to this sentiment when he advised Harry Truman, in a memo, in late 1946: "The language of military power is the only language which disciples of power politics understand. The United States must use that language in order that Soviet leaders will realize that our government is determined to uphold the interest of its citizens and the rights of small nations. Compromise and concessions are considered, by the Soviets, to be evidence of weakness and they are encouraged by our 'retreats' to make new and greater demands."[48]

[46] Schlesinger (fn. 14), 391.
[47] Walter Millis, ed., *The Forrestal Diaries* (New York 1951), 192.
[48] Arthur Krock, *Memoirs* (London 1968), 228–29.

The American concern with its appearance of strength was a mark of the Kennedy Administration. One White House aide recalled that, especially after the failure of the Bay of Pigs, "Nobody in the White House wanted to be soft. . . . Everybody wanted to show they were just as daring and bold as everybody else."[49]

In the Cuban crisis, the cold-war ethic of being "tough" exacerbated the discrepancies between the necessities of force and the necessities of diplomacy and negotiation. As a result, diplomacy was almost entirely eclipsed. In fact, it was hardly tried. According to Adam Yarmolinsky, an inside observer of the Executive Committee of the National Security Council, "90 per cent of its time" was spent "studying alternative uses of troops, bombers and warships. Although the possibility of seeking withdrawal of the missiles by straightforward diplomatic negotiation received some attention within the State Department, it seems hardly to have been aired in the Ex-Com." Yarmolinsky confesses that it is curious that no negotiations were considered. Nor were economic pressures ever suggested by the foreign affairs bureaucracy. Only a series of military plans emerged, and they varied from a blockade to a preemptive strike.[50]

Kennedy knew the Russians had deployed missiles on October 16. But, instead of facing Soviet Foreign Secretary Gromyko with the evidence while the Russian was giving the President false assurances that missiles were not being installed, the President blandly listened without comment. Whether or not the Russians believed that Kennedy must have known, the effect of the charade was an absence of serious negotiations. Instead of using private channels to warn the Russians that he knew and intended to act, Kennedy chose to give notice to the Russians in a nationwide TV address. After that, a Soviet withdrawal had to be in public and it almost had to be a humiliation. When the Soviets attempted nonetheless to bargain for a graceful retreat, their path was blocked. Kennedy

[49] Hugh Sidey, *John F. Kennedy, President* (New York 1964), 127.
[50] Yarmolinsky, *The Military Establishment* (New York 1971), 127.

refused Khrushchev's offer of a summit meeting "until Khrushchev first accepted, as a result of *our deeds* as well as our statements, the U.S. determination in the matter."[51] A summit meeting, Kennedy concluded, had to be rejected; for he was intent on offering the Russians "nothing that would tie our hands." We would only negotiate with that which would "strengthen our stand."[52] If there were to be any deals, Kennedy wanted them to seem a part of American munificence. He did not want a compromise to be tied to the central issue of what he conceived to be a test of American will and resolve."[W]e must stand absolutely firm now. Concessions must come at the end of negotiation, not at the beginning," Robert Kennedy cautioned.[58]

In other words, the Soviets had to submit to American strength before any real concessions could take place. When Khrushchev offered to exchange the Cuban missiles for the Jupiter missiles stationed in Turkey, Kennedy refused, even though he had ordered the missiles out months earlier; in fact, he had thought they were out when Khrushchev brought them to his attention. (The Jupiters were all but worthless. A marksman with a high-powered rifle could knock them out.[54] They took a day to ready for firing and the Turks did not want them.) Kennedy, however, did not want to appear to yield to Soviet pressure even when he might give little and receive a great deal. An agreement would have confounded the issue of "will." As Kennedy's Boswell put it, the President wanted to "concentrate on a single issue—the enormity of the introduction of the missiles and the absolute necessity of their removal."[55]

In the final act of the crisis, Kennedy accepted one of two letters sent almost simultaneously by Khrushchev. One contained the demand for removal of the Turkish missiles; the other did not. Kennedy accepted the latter. Khrushchev's second letter began with a long, heartfelt, personal communication

[51] Kennedy (fn. 9), 44–45; (emphasis added).
[52] Sorensen (fn. 10), 699.
[53] Schlesinger (fn. 14), 811.
[54] Hilsman (fn. 2), 202.
[55] Schlesinger (fn. 14), 810.

and made no mention of a *quid pro quo.* Kennedy's response was a public letter to Khrushchev, temperate in tone, in which he accepted the more favorable terms he preferred and further detailed American conditions. It is said that Kennedy published his response "in the interests of both speed and psychology."[56] But this procedure of publishing the private terms of an interchange with another head of state was a considerable departure from diplomacy. It was not negotiation; it was, in this context, a public demand. Public statements during a crisis lack flexibility. Compromise is almost foreclosed by such a device, because any bargaining after the terms have been stated seems to be a retreat which would diminish a statesman's reputation. Since reputation was the stake in Cuba as much as anything else, Kennedy's response was hardly more than a polite ultimatum. In private, Kennedy was even more forceful. Robert Kennedy told Soviet Ambassador Dobrynin, "We had to have a commitment by tomorrow that those bases would be removed. . . . If they did not remove those bases, we would remove them. . . . Time was running out. We had only a few more hours—we needed an answer immediately from the Soviet Union. . . . We must have it the next day."[57]

As a result of the crisis, force and toughness became enshrined as instruments of policy. George Kennan observed, as he left forty years of diplomatic service: "There is no presumption more terrifying than that of those who would blow up the world on the basis of their personal judgment of a transient situation. I do not propose to let the future of mankind be settled, or ended, by a group of men operating on the basis of limited perspectives and short-run calculations."[58]

In spite of occasional epistles from the older diplomatists, the new managers who proliferated after Cuba routed those who most favored negotiations. In an article in the *Saturday Evening Post,* one of the last "moderates" of the Kennedy Administration, Adlai Stevenson, was attacked for advocating

[56] Sorensen (fn. 10), 714.
[57] Kennedy (fn. 9), 87.
[58] Schlesinger (fn. 14), 397; also cited by I. F. Stone, *In a Time of Torment* (New York 1968), 23.

"a Munich." The source of the story, it was widely rumored, was President Kennedy himself.[59]

The policy of toughness became dogma to such an extent that nonmilitary solutions to political problems were excluded. A "moderate" in this circumstance was restricted to suggesting limited violence. Former Under Secretary of State Ball explained his "devil advocacy" in Vietnam, in which he suggested that there be a troop ceiling of 70,000 men and bombing be restricted to the South: "What I was proposing was something which I thought had a fair chance of being persuasive . . . if I had said let's pull out overnight or do something of this kind, I obviously wouldn't have been persuasive at all. They'd have said 'the man's mad.' "[60]

This peculiar search for the middle ground of a policy defined in terms of force was abetted by the sudden sense on the part of Kennedy's national security managers that the military was filled with Dr. Strangeloves. There was some warrant for this fear. Time and time again, during the crisis, the military seemed obsessed by the opportunity to demonstrate its potential. When asked what the Soviet reaction would be to a surgical raid on their missiles and men, General Lemay snapped, "There will be no reaction." When the crisis ended on Sunday, October 25th, one of the Joint Chiefs suggested that they go ahead with a massive bombing the following Monday in any case. "[T]he military are mad," concluded President Kennedy.[61] Robert Kennedy recalled acidly that "many times . . . I heard the military take positions which, if wrong, had the advantage that no one would be around at the end to know."[62]

In part, it was as a result of the Cuban crisis that the civilians of the American defense and foreign policy bureaucracy grew to despise the military. Hilsman reports that later in the Kennedy Administration, an official prepared a mock account of a high-level meeting on Vietnam in which Averell Harriman

[59] Walton (fn. 1), 119. The article was by Stewart Alsop and Charles Bartlett, "In Time of Crisis," *Saturday Evening Post,* December 8, 1962.

[60] Gelb and Halperin (fn. 21), 36.

[61] Schlesinger (fn. 14), 831; Neustadt and Allison, in "Afterword," in Kennedy (fn. 9), 126.

[62] *Ibid.*, 26.

"stated that he had disagreed for twenty years with General [Brute] Krulak [Commandant of the Marines] and disagreed today, reluctantly, more than ever; he was sorry to say that he felt General Krulak was a fool and had always thought so." It is reported that President Kennedy roared with laughter upon reading this fictitious account.[63] Hilsman also delighted in telling a story about General Lemnitzer, Chairman of the Joint Chiefs of Staff, who once briefed President Kennedy on Vietnam: "This is the Mekong Valley. Pointer tip hit the map. Hilsman, watching, noticed something, the point tip was not on the Mekong Valley, it was on the Yangtze Valley."[64] Hilsman's recollection of the general's error became a common office story.

Ironically, while the military was increasingly thought to be rather loutish and ill-prepared, civilians were starting to rely more and more on military instrumentalities in the application of which, with few exceptions, they were not trained, and whose command structure they despised as being second-rate at best. Civilian "crisis managers" felt, after Cuba, that they should have control and that the military could not be trusted and had to be made more responsive to the political and civilian considerations of policy. To many observers, as well as to these managers, the "failures" of the Cuban missile crisis were not failures of civilian judgment but of organizational responsiveness. The intelligence establishment, for instance, had not discovered the missiles until the last minute. McNamara never really secured control over the Navy. U-2 flights were sent near the Soviet Union to "excite" Soviet radar at the height of the crisis; until Kennedy ordered their dispersal, American fighters and bombers were wing to wing on the ground, almost inviting a preemptive Soviet blow. Moreover, American tactical nuclear weapons and nuclear-tipped IRBM's in Turkey and Italy were discovered to be unlocked and lightly guarded.[65] All this led

[63] Hilsman (fn. 2), 512–13; John McDermott, "Crisis Manager," *New York Review of Books,* IX, September 14, 1967, 4–10. The fictitious paper, written by James Thompson, also took on the whole Vietnam decision-making team.
[64] David Halberstam, *The Best and the Brightest* (New York 1972), 255.
[65] *Washington Post,* May 26, 1974.

observers and policy-makers to believe that crisis management demanded the President's organizational dominance and control, because the military and intelligence organizations were inept and their judgment was not reliable or at times even sane.

V. CUBA AND THE AMERICAN CENTURY

After Cuba, confidence in the ability of U.S. armed superiority to command solutions to "crises" in a way that would favor American interests expanded in such a way that Americans again began to speak of the American century. For a period before the crisis there had been a national reexamination. There were fears of national decline in the face of startling Soviet economic growth. Advances in Russian rocketry had led Americans to believe that not only were they in a mortal competition with the Soviets, but that the outcome was uncertain. Now, however, most of these doubts seemed to have dissipated.

The Cuban missile crisis revived the sense of the American mission. Henry R. Luce once rhapsodized in a widely circulated *Life* editorial that Americans must "accept wholeheartedly our duty and opportunity as the most powerful and vital nation in the world and in consequence to exert upon the world the full impact of our influence for such purposes as we see fit, and by such means as we see fit."[66] After the crisis, Arthur Schlesinger could lyrically resurrect this tradition: "But the ultimate impact of the missile crisis was wider than Cuba, wider than even the western hemisphere. . . . Before the missile crisis people might have feared that we would use our power extravagantly or not use it at all. But the thirteen days gave the world—even the Soviet Union—a sense of American determination and responsibility in the use of power which, if sustained, might indeed become a turning point in the history of the relations between east and west."[67]

[66] Luce, *The American Century* (New York 1941), 23, and *Life,* February 17, 1941, p. 63. Actually, Luce had been on record with this message from the age of twenty. See W. A. Swanberg, *Luce and his Empire* (New York 1972).

[67] Schlesinger (fn. 14), 840, 841.

Similarly, Professor Zbigniew Brzezinski, then a member of the Planning Council of the Department of State, proclaimed that American paramountcy was the lesson of Cuba. Brzezinski explained, "The U.S. is today the only effective global military power in the world."[68]

In contrast to the United States, Brzezinski declared, the Soviets were not a global power. Although Khrushchev may at one time have believed otherwise, the Cuban crisis demonstrated the limits of Soviet capabilities. "The Soviet leaders were forced, because of the energetic response by the United States, to the conclusion that their apocalyptic power [nuclear deterrent power] was insufficient to make the Soviet Union a global power. Faced with a showdown, the Soviet Union didn't dare to respond even in an area of its regional predominance—in Berlin. . . . It had no military capacity to fight in Cuba, or in Vietnam, or to protect its interests in the Congo." No doubt the historic American sense of divine purpose and the almost Jungian need to be the guarantor of global order received a strong fillip from the Cuban crisis. Brzezinski concluded: "What should be the role of the United States in this period? To use our power responsibly and constructively so that when the American paramountcy ends, the world will have been launched on a constructive pattern of development towards international stability. . . . The ultimate objective ought to be the shaping of a world of cooperative communities."[69]

The overwhelming belief of policy-makers in American superiority seriously eroded deterrence. The Soviet Union reached the same conclusion as the United States—that a preponderance of military power, ranging across the spectrum of force from PT craft to advanced nuclear delivery systems, was the *sine qua non* of the successful exercise of political will. Before fall of 1962, Khrushchev's strategic policy, in the words of a Rand Kremlinologist, "amounted to settling for a second-best

[68] "Background" remarks to a conference for editors and broadcasters May 22, 1967, cited in Hans J. Morgenthau, *A New Foreign Policy for the United States* (New York 1969), 19. For Brzezinski's edited remarks, see "The Implications of Change for United States Foreign Policy," *Department of State Bulletin,* LVII, July 3, 1967, pp. 19–23.

[69] *Ibid.*

strategic posture."[70] The missile crisis, however, manifestly demonstrated Soviet strategic weakness and exposed every Soviet debility that Khrushchev's verbal proclamation of superiority had previously covered.

VI. CUBA AND DETERRENCE

After Cuba, the Soviet military, responding to the humiliating American stimulus, demanded a higher priority to strategic arms and a cutback on the agricultural and consumer sectors of the Soviet economy. Although Khrushchev and Kennedy were by then moving toward a détente—best symbolized by the signing of the test-ban accords of mid-1963—many in the Kremlin saw this as but a breathing spell in which the Chinese might be isolated and Soviet arms could catch up. Naval preparations, especially the building of Polaris-type submarines, were intensified.[71] Soviet amphibian landing capability—something in which the Soviets had shown little interest before—was revitalized and expanded. As Wolfe noted, "From the time of the first test-launching . . . of 1957 to mid-1961 only a handful of ICBM's had been deployed. . . . After Cuba, the pace of deployment picked up, bringing the total number of operational ICBM launchers to around 200 by the time of Khruschev's ouster."[72] Although the West still outnumbered the Russians by four to one in numbers of launchers at the time, the Russians worked furiously, and by September 1968, they commanded a larger force than the United States.[73] Worldwide "blue water" Soviet submarine patrols were initiated; and a decision was taken under Brezhnev and Kosygin to extend the Soviet navy to "remote areas of the world's oceans previously considered a zone of supremacy of the fleets of the imperialist powers."[74]

70 Wolfe (fn. 37), 134.

71 David Woodward, *The Russians at Sea: A History of the Russian Navy* (New York 1964), 229–30.

72 Wolfe (fn. 37), 182–83.

73 Statement by Secretary of Defense Clark M. Clifford, *The Fiscal Year 1970–1974 Defense Program and Defense Budget,* Department of Defense, January 15, 1969, p. 35.

74 Fleet Admiral V. Kasatonov, "On Battle Watch," *Krasnaia zvezda,* July 30, 1967; cited in Wolfe (fn. 37), 446.

After the missile crisis, the cold-war establishmentarian John McCloy, representing President Kennedy, was host to Soviet Deputy Foreign Minister V. V. Kuznetzov. McCloy secured an affirmation from Kuznetzov that the Soviets would indeed observe their part of the agreement to remove the missiles and bombers from Cuba. But the Soviet leader warned, "Never will we be caught like this again."[75]

The Soviets were to yield again to U.S. strength in Vietnam and the Middle-East. But each time, the usable strategic leverage of the United States grew weaker. Thus, the structure of the international system and international stability was shaken in three ways.

First, the United States became confident that its power would prevail because global politics had become "unifocal."[76] But American military primacy began to erode as soon as it was proclaimed, when the Soviets fought to gain at least a rough strategic parity.

Second, nations, once cowed, are likely to be less timid in the next confrontation. As Kennedy admitted some time later, referring to the Cuban missile crisis, "You can't have too many of those."[77] Just as Kennedy feared he had appeared callow and faint-hearted in successive Berlin crises, and thus had to be tough over Cuba, the Soviets were likely to calculate that they must appear as the more rigid party in future confrontations or risk a reputation of "capitulationism." For weeks after the missile crisis, the Chinese broadcast their charges of Russian stupidity and weakness to the four corners of the globe. The Chinese labeled Khrushchev an "adventurist" as well as a "capitulationist," and therefore not fit for world Communist leadership. The Russian answer was to accuse the Chinese of being even "softer" than they for tolerating the Western enclaves of Macao and Hong Kong.[78] The charge of who was the most capitulationist, the Chinese or the Russians, grew almost

[75] John Newhouse, *Cold Dawn: The Story of SALT* (New York 1973), 68.
[76] George Liska, *Imperial America: The International Politics of Primacy* (Baltimore 1967), 36 ff.
[77] K. J. Holsti, *International Politics* 2d ed., Englewood Cliffs, 1972), 325.
[78] Michel Tatu, *Power in the Kremlin: From Khrushchev to Kosygin* (New York 1968), 319–20.

silly; but these puerile exchanges had their own dangers in terms of deterrence.

Third, once a threat is not carried out—even after an appearance of a willingness to carry it out has been demonstrated—the ante is upped just a bit more. Morgenthau described a two-step process in nuclear gamesmanship, "diminishing credibility of the threat and ever bolder challenges to make good on it. . . . [T]he psychological capital of deterrence has been nearly expended and the policy of deterrence will be close to bankruptcy. When they reach that point, the nations concerned can choose one of three alternatives: resort to nuclear war, retreat, or resort to conventional war."[79]

Morgenthau's observation captured the dilemma of American policymakers after Cuba. The problem was that nuclear superiority had been useful, but each succeeding threat (since no nuclear threat has ever been carried out) would necessarily be weaker than the last. Yet, how could security managers translate military power into political objectives without such threats? Daniel Ellsberg recalled the quandary of U.S. security managers:

> McNamara's tireless and shrewd efforts in the early sixties, largely hidden from the public to this day, [were to] gradually control the forces within the military bureaucracy that pressed for the threat and use of nuclear weapons. [He had] a creditable motive for proposing alternatives to nuclear threats. . . . [I]n this hidden debate, there was strong incentive—indeed it seemed necessary—for the civilian leaders to demonstrate that success was possible in Indochina without the need either to compromise Cold War objectives or to threaten or use nuclear weapons.
>
> Such concerns remained semi-covert: (for it was seen as dangerous to lend substance to the active suspicions of military staffs and their Congressional allies that there were high Administration officials who didn't love the Bomb). . . ."[80]

But after the Cuban crisis, the option of "low-level violence" became more and more attractive. Conventional and limited deployments of force became increasingly necessary as con-

[79] Hans J. Morgenthau, *A New Foreign Policy for the United States* (New York 1969), 212–13.

[80] Daniel Ellsberg, *Papers on the War* (New York 1972), 292–93.

ventional force was considered less forbidding than the nuclear abyss. After all, the symbolic or "psychological capital" of deterrence rested on the notion of resolve. And one way to demonstrate political will was through the resurrection of conventional force as an instrument of demonstrating "commitment"—a commitment whose alternative form was a threat of nuclear holocaust. The latter was bound to deteriorate with the advent of a viable Soviet retaliatory capability and the knowledge that the Soviets had collapsed once under a nuclear threat and might not be willing to be quite so passive again. Many national security managers found they could navigate between the Scylla of nuclear war and the Charybdis of surrender with the serendipitous discovery of the "lifeboat" of the 1960's—limited war. It would not prove to be a sturdy craft.

Of course, the assumptions of the planners of limited war—as they emerged victorious from the Cuban crisis—were as old as the cold war. They dated from the Truman Doctrine's Manichean presentation of a bipolar global confrontation where a gain to one party necessarily would be a loss to the other. A world order of diverse centers of power, with elements of superpower cooperation, where gains and losses would be less easily demonstrable, was not so demanding of military remedy. A multipolar world would be less congenial to the belief that the only options available to policy-makers were either military force or retreat. Maneuver and negotiation, in such a world, would again become part of diplomacy. But such a development was to come about only after the tragic failure of the military remedy had been demonstrated in Vietnam.

VII. THE BY-PRODUCTS OF SUCCESS

There were other effects related to the exuberant reaction to the Cuban crisis. As the United States began to feel that power and force were successful solvents to the more sticky problems of the cold war, the role of international law declined precipitously.[81]

[81] Dean Rusk reflected earlier, obligatory American statements about international legal order and American foreign policy when he declared:

Moral pontifications appeared increasingly hypocritical after Cuba. But after all, hypocrisy, in the words of H. L. Mencken, "runs, like a hair in a hot dog, through the otherwise beautiful fabric of American life."[82] The participants in the crisis knew the blockade was an act of war that had little basis in international law. After the crisis was over, even lawyers began to see law as but another instrumentality of American policy. The conclusion reached by American academics was that "International law is . . . a tool, not a guide to action. . . . It does not have a valid life of its own; it is a mere instrument, available to political leaders for their own ends, be they good or evil, peaceful or aggressive. . . . [The Cuban missile crisis] merely reconfirms the irrelevance of international law in major political disputes."[83]

Dean Acheson summarized the code of the cold war as it was confirmed by the Cuban experience: "The power, prestige and position of the United States had been challenged. . . . Law simply does not deal with such questions of ultimate power. . . . The survival of states is not a matter of law."[84]

George Ball, former Under Secretary of State, wrote: "No one can seriously contend that we now live under a universal system or, in any realistic sense, under the 'rule of law.' We

---

Our foreign policy has been reflected in our willingness to submit atomic weapons to international law, in feeding and clothing those stricken by war, in supporting free elections and government by consent, in building factories and dams, power plants and railways, schools and hospitals, in improving seed and stock and fertilizer, in stimulating markets and improving the skills and techniques of others in a hundred different ways. Let these things stand in contrast to a foreign policy directed towards the extension of tyranny and using the big lie, sabotage, suspicion, riot and assassination as its tools. The great strength of the United States is devoted to the peaceful pursuits of our people and to the decent opinions of mankind. But it is not healthy for any regime or group of regimes to incur, by their lawless and aggressive conduct, the implacable opposition of the American people. The lawbreaker, unfortunately in the nature of things, always has the initiative, but the peacemaking peoples of the world can and will make themselves strong enough to insist upon peace.

Cited in Halberstam (fn. 66), 327.

[82] H. L. Mencken, "Editorial," *American Mercury,* IX, November 1926, 287. cited in Halper (fn. 24), 157.

[83] William P. Gerberding, "International Law and the Cuban Crisis," in Lawrence Scheinman and David Wilkinson, eds., *International Law and Political Crisis: An Analytic Casebook* (Boston 1968), 209–10.

[84] Richard J. Barnet and Marcus Raskin, *After Twenty Years* (New York 1965), 229n.

maintain the peace by preserving a precarious balance of power between ourselves and the Soviet Union—a process we used to call 'containment' before the word went out of style. It is the preservation of that balance which, regardless of how we express it, is the central guiding principle of American foreign policy."[85]

The UN was used in the Cuban Crisis, not as Kennedy had told the General Assembly the year before, as "the only true alternative to war,"[86] but as a platform where Adlai Stevenson, the eloquent American representative, could deal "a final blow to the Soviet case before world opinion."[87]

Epitomized by Cuba, crisis after crisis pointed out the stark irony: Americans, who had so long stoked the talisman of international law, now seemed to do so only when their interests were not jeopardized. Otherwise, law became merely a rhetorical flourish of United States policy. International law was still a part of the admonition that "armed aggression" and "breaches of the peace" cease and desist. But, in back of these legalistic and moralistic injunctions, the armed cop became more and more apparent. As General de Gaulle had observed earlier, the conclusion that American idealism was but a reflection of the American will to power became almost inescapable after the Cuban crisis.[88] Few obeisances about the need for law in international society disguised the sense that America had abandoned her ancient, liberal inheritance in the zesty pursuit of world order.

Another effect of the crisis was to differentiate the "great powers"—the United States and the Soviet Union—from other states which were literally frozen out of a major role in structuring global politics. After all, the major "chips" of big-power poker were simply not accessible to other governments—even

[85] George Ball, "Slogans and Realities," *Foreign Affairs*, XLVII (July 1969), 624.

[86] John F. Kennedy, "Let Us Call a Truce to Terror," address to the General Assembly of the United Nations, September 23, 1961, *Department of State Bulletin*, October 16, 1961, p. 619.

[87] Schlesinger (fn. 14), 824.

[88] For General de Gaulle's analysis, see his *Mémoires de Guerre*, Vol. II, *L'Unité* (Paris 1956), 97–98.

those with modest and nominally independent nuclear forces. For no other nations had the capability of making even plausible calculations of either preemptive or second-strike blows against a greater power, much less basing national strategies on such possibilities. As a result, Europeans were offered the appearance of some control in their nuclear lot with the ill-fated MLF. But the nuclear trigger was still in the hands of the United States, and so was the final squeeze. Not only were the weapons of great-power diplomacy increasingly inaccessible to other states, but the other tools of statecraft also receded from the grasp of those with modest resources. The spy, for instance, was largely replaced by satellite reconnaissance. Intellectual musings on great-power conflict became differentiated from other strategic thinking. Gradually, the Soviets and the Americans created a shared private idiom of force; and a curious dialogue began between the congressional budget messages of the Secretary of Defense and the periodic revisions of *Strategy* by Marshal Sokolovsky.[89] Allies became mere appurtenances of power whose purpose, in the duopolistic structure of international society, was increasingly symbolic. Thus, for example, the OAS was asked to validate the U.S. blockade at the same time the American quarantine was announced.

Similarly, Dean Acheson flew to Paris and other European capitals to confer with American allies about the coming confrontation over Cuba.

> "Your President does me great honor," de Gaulle said, "to send me so distinguished an emissary. I assume the occasion to be of appropriate importance." Acheson delivered President Kennedy's letter, with the text of the speech to be delivered at P-hour, 7 P.M. Washington time. He offered to summarize it. De Gaulle raised his hand in a delaying gesture that the long-departed Kings of France might have envied. "May we be clear before you start," he said. "Are you consulting or informing me?" Acheson confessed that he was there to inform, not to consult. "I am in favor of independent decisions," de Gaulle acknowledged."[90]

[89] Marshal Z. D. Sokolovsky (introduction by Raymond Garthoff), *Military Strategy: Soviet Doctrine and Concepts* (New York 1963). (Subsequent editions were translated by RAND for internal use by government officials.)
[90] Abel (fn. 16), 112.

For the Europeans, Gaullists and Leftists alike, it appeared that there was a high likelihood of nuclear annihilation without representation.[91] In spite of European gestures of support, the alliance received a shock from which it did not recover. The British, in the midst of a vicious internal debate about whether or not to abandon nuclear weapons, decided they were necessary to buy even minimum consideration from their American allies. The French did not debate; they accelerated their nuclear programs while withdrawing from a military role in the alliance.

On the Soviet side, it was equally apparent that Russian interests would not be sacrificed to sister socialist states. Castro was plainly sold out. The weak promise tendered by the Kennedy Administration not to invade the island was probably cold comfort as Castro saw his military benefactors beat a hasty retreat from American power. Embarrassingly, Castro began to echo the "capitulationist" theme of Chinese broadcasts. Privately Castro said that if he could, he would have beaten Khrushchev to within an inch of his life for what he did. Soviet Foreign Minister Mikoyan was dispatched to Cuba and stayed there for weeks, not even returning to the bedside of his dying wife, but Castro's fury was unabated. Whatever the motive for Khrushchev's moves in Cuba, the Chinese were also enraged.[92] Any attempts the Soviets had made prior to October 1962 to dissuade the Chinese from assuming a nuclear role lost their validity when it became obvious that the Russians would not risk their own destruction for an associate.

By 1963, a new era of East-West relations was unfolding. The United States still cultivated the asymmetrical assumptions of the cold war, but the Soviet Union was at least admitted as a junior partner in a duopolistic international system which began to be characterized as détente. The relaxation was favorable to Kennedy, who wanted to begin to deal with the Soviets without the ideological rancor that had poisoned previous rela-

[91] Amitai Etzioni, *Winning Without War* (Garden City, N.Y. 1965), 46.
[92] Adam Ulam, *Expansion and Coexistence* (New York 1968), 675. Ulam (pp. 668–70), suggested that Krushchev aimed at precluding both Chinese and German acquisition of nuclear weapons.

tions, and who had a vision of Soviet "responsibility" which was to be enlarged upon by succeeding administrations. The Soviets, too, sought a détente. Given their acknowledged strategic inferiority, they could hardly expect to be successful in another series of confrontations. Moreover, the Chinese began to present formidable ideological and political difficulties for the Russians, whose new interest in improved relations with the United States caused intense fears in China of American-Soviet collusion. At the same time, the Soviets began to fear a Sino-American agreement that would be detrimental to their interests. As Michael Suslov, chief ideologue of the Soviet Union, explained in early 1964, "With a stubbornness worthy of a better cause the Chinese leaders attempt to prevent the improvement of Soviet-American relations, representing this as 'plotting with the imperialists.' At the same time the Chinese government makes feverish attempts to improve relations with Britain, France, Japan, West Germany, and Italy. It is quite clear that they would not refuse to improve relations with the United States, but as yet they do not see favorable circumstances for such an endeavor."[93]

CONCLUSION

Thus, by 1964, the crisis had precipitated a change in the global structure of power. American paramountcy had been self-proclaimed; the seeds of détente had been sown by a shared vision of nuclear oblivion; and the ingredients for a great-power condominium were becoming clear. If it had not been for the war in Vietnam, the present framework of international affairs might have been with us ten years earlier. Tragically and ironically, the "lessons" of the Cuban missile crisis—that success in international crisis was largely a matter of national guts; that the opponent would yield to superior force; that presidential control of force can be "suitable," "selective," "swift," "effective," and "responsive" to civilian authority; and that crisis management and execution are too dangerous and events move

[93] *Ibid.*, 691.

too rapidly for anything but the tightest secrecy—all these inferences contributed to President Johnson's decision to use American air power against Hanoi in 1965. The Cuban crisis changed the international environment but riveted American expectations to the necessities of the diplomacy of violence. Even the language of the Gulf of Tonkin Resolution was almost identical to that which Kennedy's legal advisors had drawn up for the OAS in October of 1962.[94] Although the Cuban crisis created substantial changes in distinguishing superpowers from other states, the realization of the equality of the superpowers and of the indications that they could join in a relationship which had some elements of condominium and some elements of the classic balance of power was suppressed until the American agony in Vietnam drew to a close.

[94] Remarks by William P. Bundy, University of Delaware, October 16, 1973.

BIBLIOGRAPHY

The list below is composed of the standard books on the Cuban missile crisis. In addition, there is an extensive body of scholarly literature in article form. Those interested in seeking further information should consult the footnotes in the selections in this volume, particularly the three by Barton J. Bernstein, by Thomas G. Paterson and William J. Brophy and by James A. Nathan.

Ellie Abel, *The Missile Crisis* (Philadelphia, 1966).

Graham Allison, *Essence of Decision: Explaining the Cuban Missile Crisis* (Boston, 1971).

Abram Chayes, *The Cuban Missile Crisis: International Crises and the Role of Law* (New York, 1974).

David Detzer, *The Brink: Cuban Missile Crisis, 1962* (New York, 1979).

Herbert S. Dinerstein, *The Making of a Missile Crisis, October 1962* (Baltimore, 1976).

Raymond L. Garthoff, *Reflections on the Cuban Missile Crisis* (Washington, 1987).

Roger Hilsman, *To Move a Nation: The Politics of Foreign Policy in the Administration of John F. Kennedy* (Garden City, 1967).

Robert F. Kennedy, *Thirteen Days: A Memoir of the Cuban Missile Crisis* (New York, 1969).

Nikita S. Khrushchev, *Khrushchev Remembers* (Boston, 1970).

Nikita S. Khrushchev, *Khrushchev Remembers: The Last Testament* (Boston, 1974).

David L. Larson, ed., *The "Cuban Crisis" of 1962: Selected Docu-*

ments, Chronology and Bibliography, 2nd ed. (Lanham, MD., 1986).

Mario Lazo, *Dagger in the Heart: American Policy Failures in Cuba,* 2nd ed. (New York, 1970).

Henry Pachter, *Collision Course: The Cuban Missile Crisis and Coexistence* (New York, 1963).

Arthur M. Schlesinger, Jr., *A Thousand Days: John F. Kennedy in the White House* (Boston, 1965).

Arthur M. Schlesinger, Jr., *Robert Kennedy and His Times* (Boston, 1978).

Theodore C. Sorenson, *Kennedy* (New York, 1965).

Theodore C. Sorenson, *The Kennedy Legacy* (New York, 1969).

Adam Ulam, *Expansion and Coexistence: The History of Soviet Foreign Policy, 1917–1967* (New York, 1968).

Edwin Weinthal and Charles Bartlett, *Facing the Brink: An Intimate Study of Crisis Diplomacy* (New York, 1967).

A NOTE ON THE EDITOR

Robert A. Divine has taught at the University of Texas at Austin since 1954. Widely regarded as one of the leading authorities on 20th century U.S. foreign policy, he has also received major awards for both graduate and undergraduate teaching. Author or editor of 20 books, he was educated at Yale University and is married and the father of four.

DATE DUE

MAY 2 4 1999			
APR 2 5 2002			

GAYLORD PRINTED IN U.S.A.

E841 .C84 1988 c.1
100105 000
The Cuban missile crisis / edi
3 9310 00085705 0
GOSHEN COLLEGE-GOOD LIBRARY